IMMORTAL HOUNDS

HOUNDS

5

Ryo Yasohachi

VERTICAL
COMICS

Table of Contents

Chapter **28**   **No Escape** ———————————— 005

Chapter **29**   **But We Were Drinking Buddies** ——— 037

Chapter **30**   **Mama** ——————————————— 061

Chapter **31**   **I'll Take Her** ————————————— 093

Chapter **32**   **The Raid's True Aim** ——————— 125

Chapter **33**   **Task Force** ———————————— 153

Previous Volume Summary

In another world, "death" does not exist. The criminals known as Vectors spread the disease RDS across the land. There is but one method of transmission: "to love a Vector." However, Shigematsu's daughter, Marie, died of RDS with no clear route of infection. The Anti-Vector Unit led by Lieutenant Kenzaki must contend with this new threat of death that has descended upon their world...

Characters

Escape Artists
A dark organization that hides Vectors from the law.

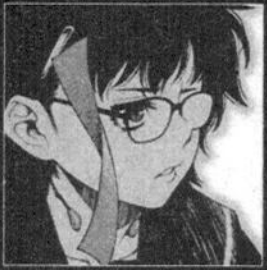

Rin Kazama
A girl who has infiltrated the MPD; essentially a hound. Called "Rin" by the MPD and "Fuurin" by the organization.

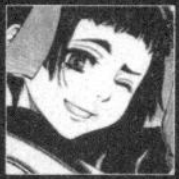

Kiriko
Helps Vectors escape alongside Rin. Competent but treated like a novice.

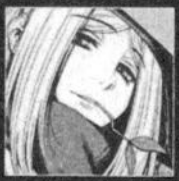

Karigane
Formerly an instructor. Very strong in combat.

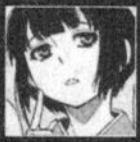

Karatachi
Mama's handmaiden.

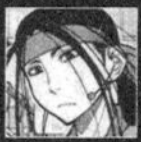

Sayori
Part of Kiriko's graduating class. Nicknamed "Miss Chin."

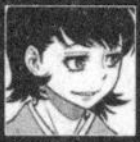

Hiiragi
Serves Mama along with Karatachi.

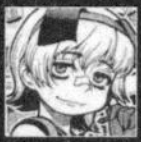

Misago
Another of Kiriko's graduating class. In charge of obtaining weapons.

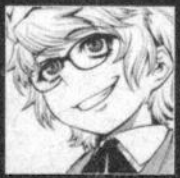

Mama
A mysterious woman who manages the Escape Artists. She and Rin share similar facial features.

Tousai Precinct
A group of three led by Kenzaki comprises the Anti-Vector Unit.

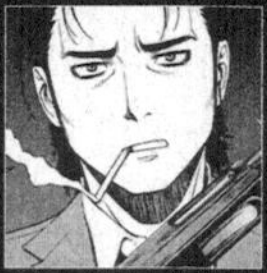

Shin'ichi Kenzaki
Chief. His sister, Ikumi, was killed by a Vector. An "immortal hound" who corners culprits.

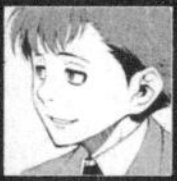

Masaki Wakabayashi
Kenzaki's subordinate. Easygoing but has a devious side.

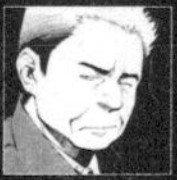

Kouzou Shigematsu
Kenzaki's subordinate despite being his elder. His daughter Marie may have been killed by a Vector.

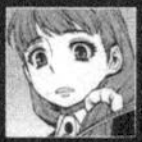

Kyoko Ikegami
Administrative officer. Wakabayashi's drinking buddy.

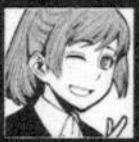

Naomi Tamaru
Married mother of one. Her husband works in a different precinct.

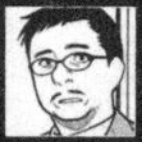

Takurou Kusunoki
Chief of the detective division. Classmate of Shigematsu.

UNDO
Short for the United Nations Disease-control Office

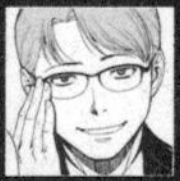

Kanai
Director. The UNDO has no right to carry out investigations or make arrests. Carries out executions of Vectors captured by the police.

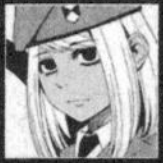

Camellia Kuribayashi
Kanai's aide-de-camp. A UN Military First Lieutenant.

Rescue

Remove

Vectors
A group of murderers who spread Resurrection Deficiency Syndrome (RDS). Those who love them become incapable of revival.

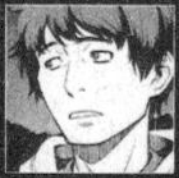

Teruyoshi Kouda
The Vector who killed Ikumi, Kenzaki's sister. Currently active as an Escape Artist.

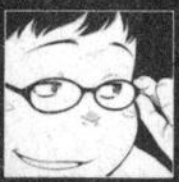

Tsutomu Takamiya
A Vector who has killed three women working night jobs. Called "Fatass" by Kenzaki.

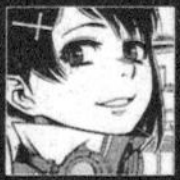

"Snow White"
A Vector who has killed 39 men. Is constantly on the move, quickly changing location.

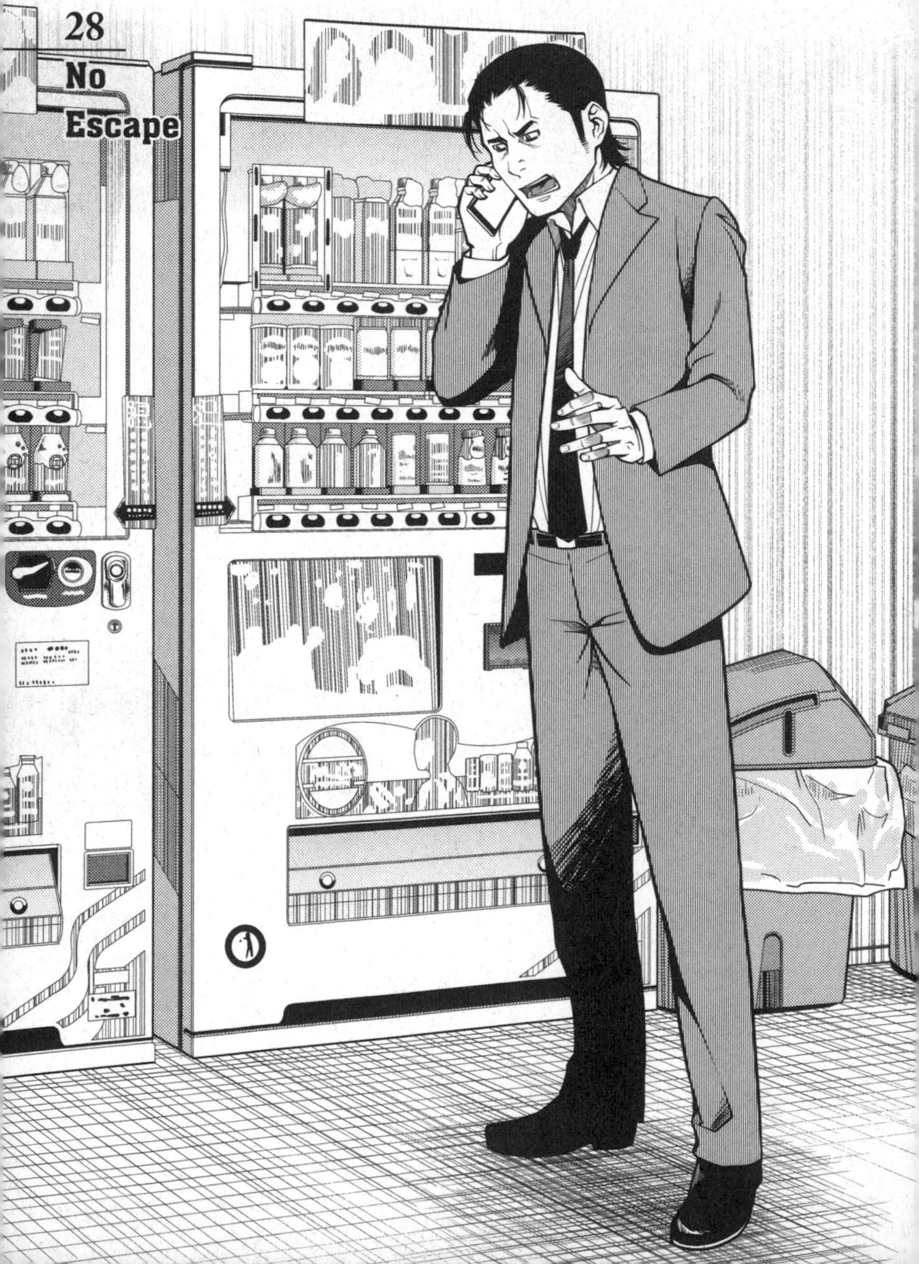
28
No
Escape

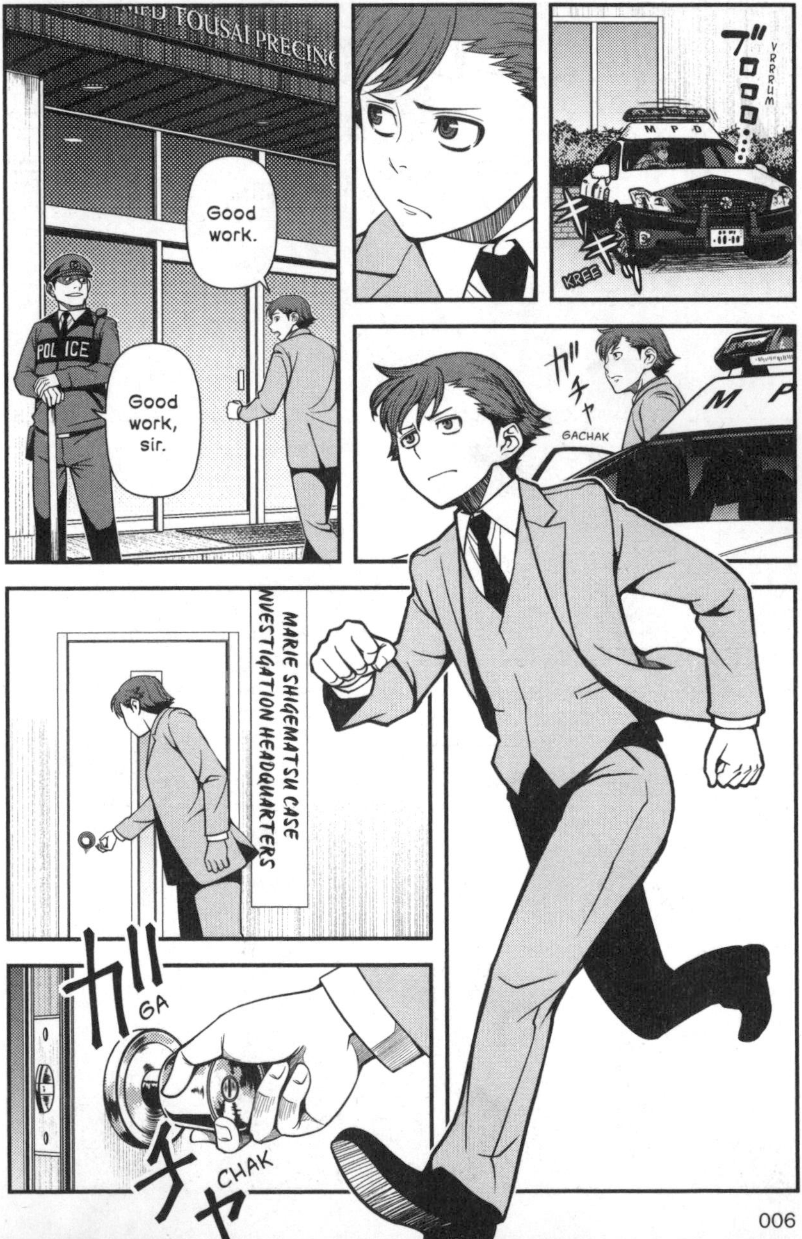
ブロロロ…
VRRRUM
ギギ
KREE
TOUSAI PRECINC
Good work.
Good work, sir.
ガチャ
GACHAK
MARIE SHIGEMATSU CASE
NVESTIGATION HEADQUARTERS
ガ
GA
チャ
CHAK

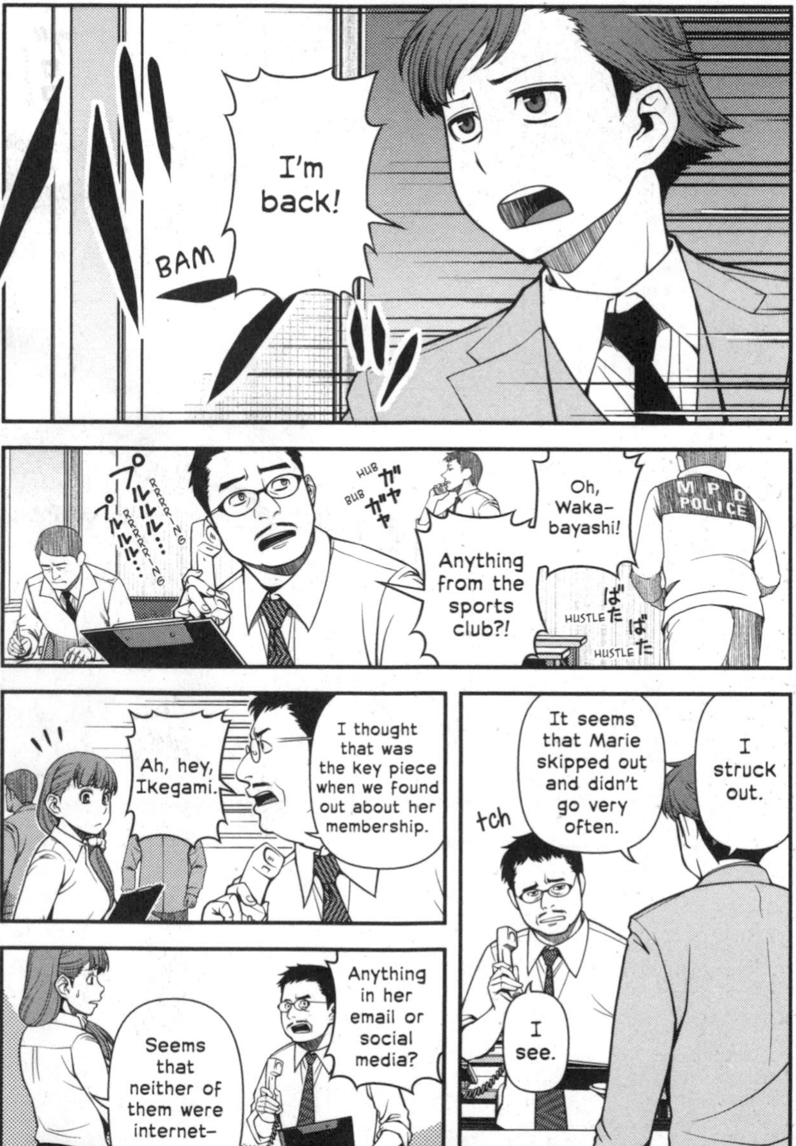

I'm back!
BAM
Oh, Waka-bayashi!
Anything from the sports club?!
HUB BUB
RRRRING RRRRING
HUSTLE HUSTLE
I struck out.
It seems that Marie skipped out and didn't go very often.
tch
I see.
I thought that was the key piece when we found out about her membership.
Ah, hey, Ikegami.
Anything in her email or social media?
Seems that neither of them were internet-savvy.

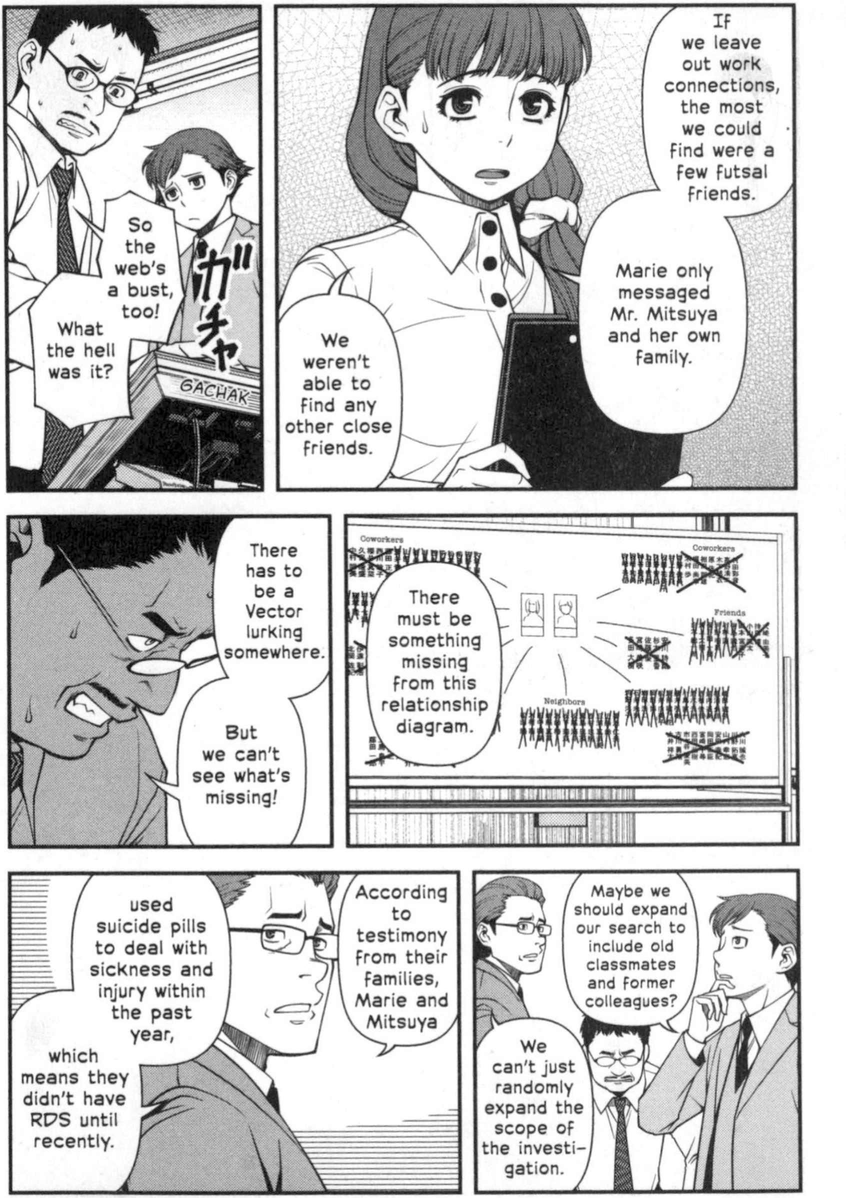
If we leave out work connections, the most we could find were a few futsal friends.
Marie only messaged Mr. Mitsuya and her own family.
We weren't able to find any other close friends.
So the web's a bust, too!
What the hell was it?
ガチャ
GACHAK
Coworkers
Coworkers
Friends
Neighbors
There must be something missing from this relationship diagram.
There has to be a Vector lurking somewhere.
But we can't see what's missing!
Maybe we should expand our search to include old classmates and former colleagues?
We can't just randomly expand the scope of the investigation.
According to testimony from their families, Marie and Mitsuya
used suicide pills to deal with sickness and injury within the past year,
which means they didn't have RDS until recently.

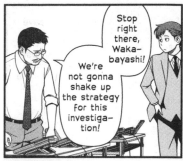

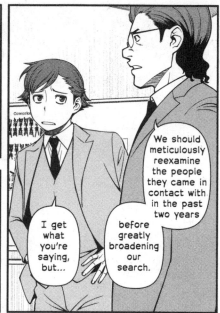

We should meticulously reexamine the people they came in contact with in the past two years
before greatly broadening our search.
I get what you're saying, but...
Stop right there, Waka-bayashi!
We're not gonna shake up the strategy for this investiga-tion!
A reexam-ination is top priority!
We'll only manage to confuse everyone on the scene by changing course now!
I'm just saying, if that doesn't work,
then we should change our methods.
RAAGE
Shut up!
Where is Kenzaki, anyway?!
Why are you the only member of the Vector Unit around
when the detective division is assisting your investi-gation?!
Well, I just got back myself,
and I don't know where the Chief is...
GA CHIK

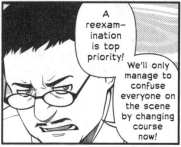

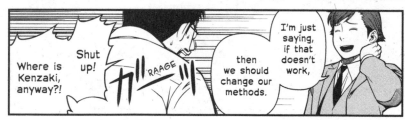

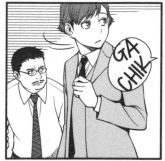

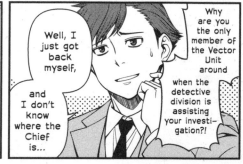

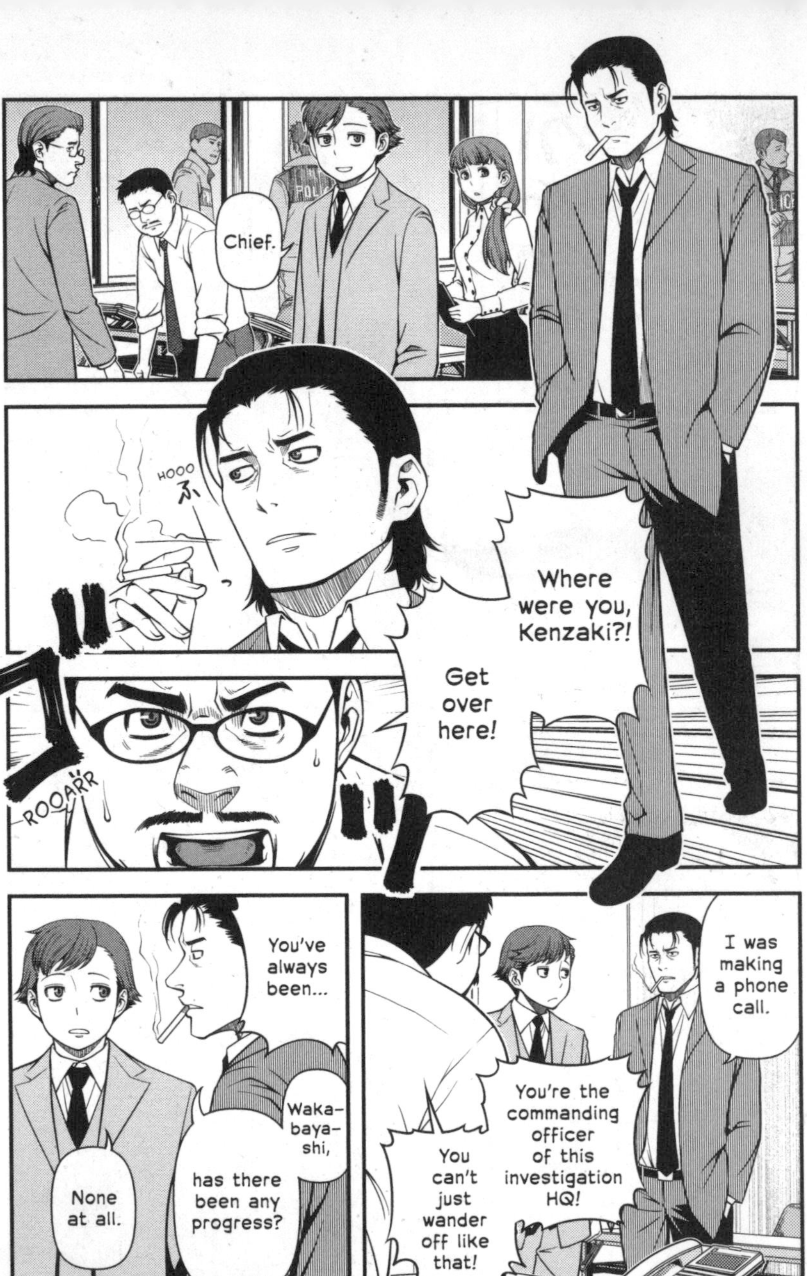
Chief.
HOOO ふ
Where were you, Kenzaki?!
Get over here!
ROOARR
I was making a phone call.
You're the commanding officer of this investigation HQ!
You can't just wander off like that!
You've always been...
Waka-bayashi,
has there been any progress?
None at all.

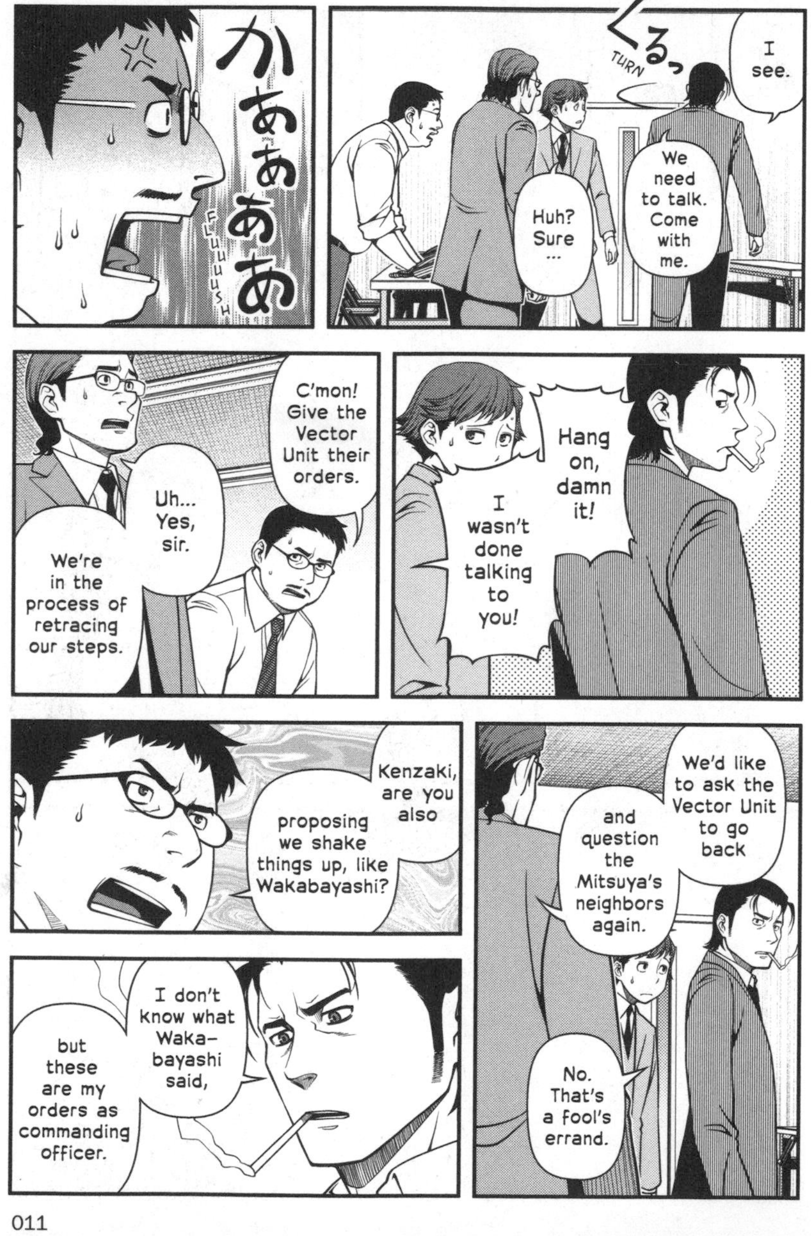
I see.
くるっ
TURN
We need to talk. Come with me.
Huh? Sure ...
かあああ
FLUUUUSH
Hang on, damn it!
I wasn't done talking to you!
C'mon! Give the Vector Unit their orders.
Uh... Yes, sir.
We're in the process of retracing our steps.
We'd like to ask the Vector Unit to go back
and question the Mitsuya's neighbors again.
No. That's a fool's errand.
Kenzaki, are you also
proposing we shake things up, like Wakabayashi?
I don't know what Waka-bayashi said,
but these are my orders as commanding officer.

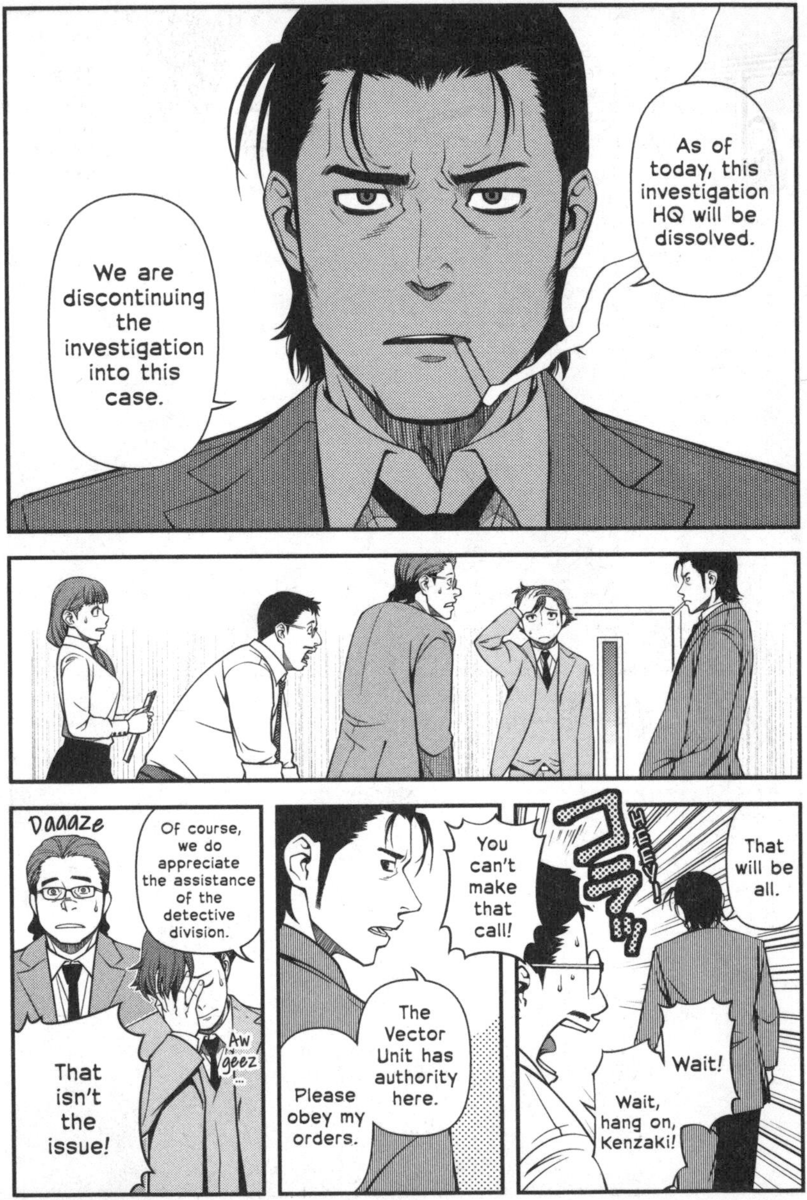
As of today, this investigation HQ will be dissolved.
We are discontinuing the investigation into this case.
That will be all.
HEY!
Wait!
Wait, hang on, Kenzaki!
You can't make that call!
The Vector Unit has authority here.
Please obey my orders.
Of course, we do appreciate the assistance of the detective division.
Daaaze
Aw geez...
That isn't the issue!

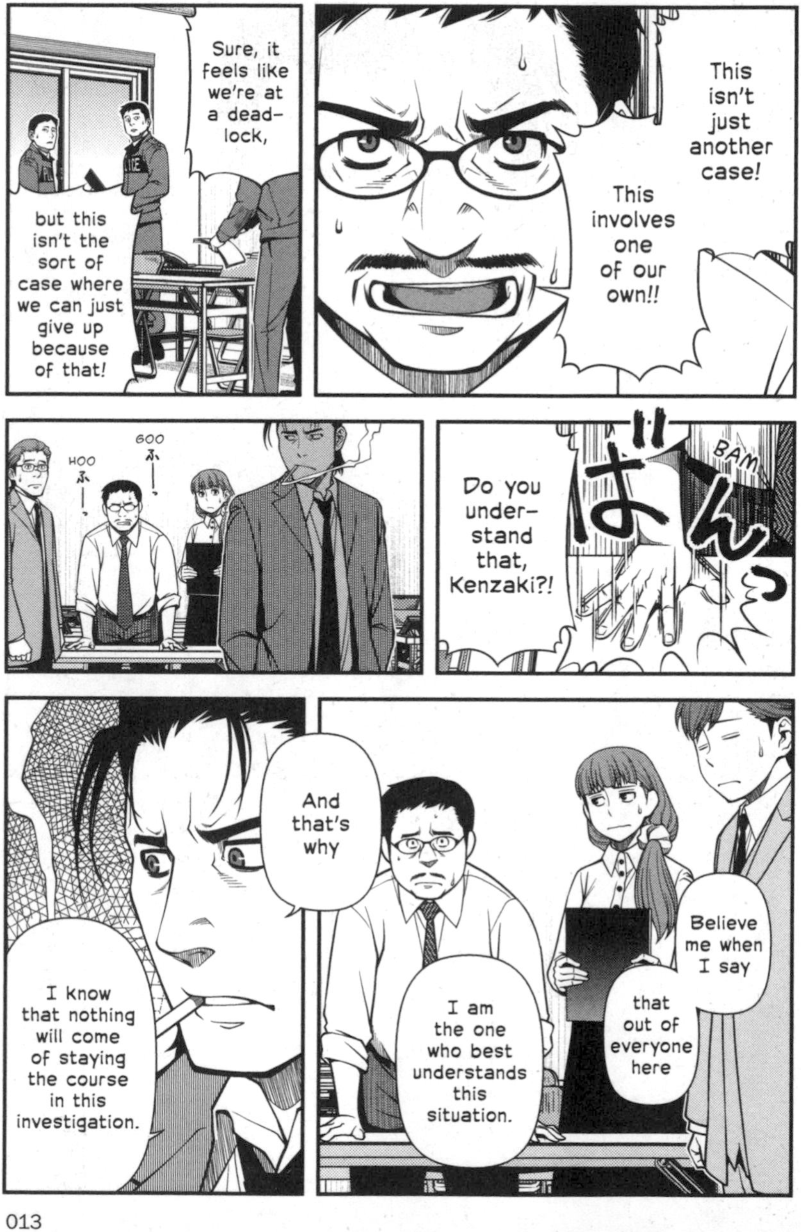
This isn't just another case!
This involves one of our own!!
Sure, it feels like we're at a dead-lock,
but this isn't the sort of case where we can just give up because of that!
BAM
ばんっ
Do you under-stand that, Kenzaki?!
GOO
ふーっ
HOO
ふーっ
Believe me when I say
that out of everyone here
I am the one who best understands this situation.
And that's why
I know that nothing will come of staying the course in this investigation.

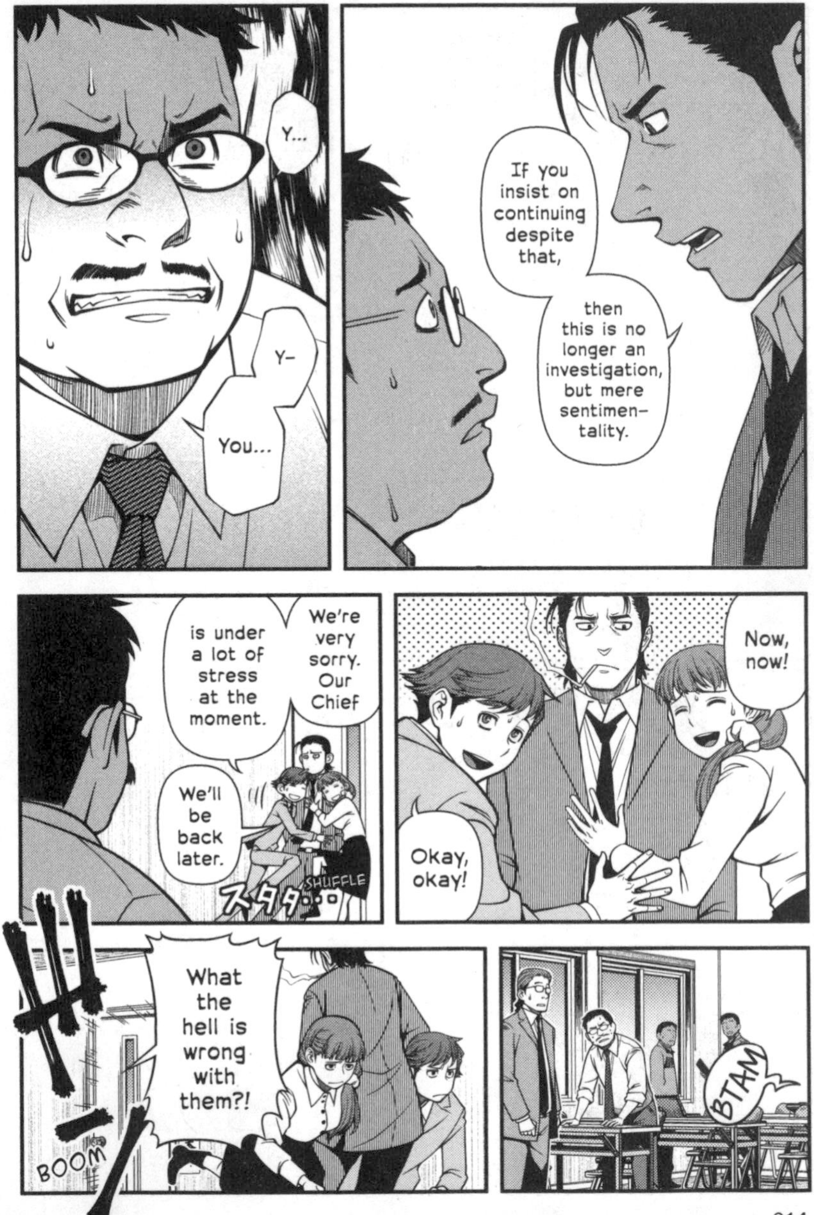
If you insist on continuing despite that,
then this is no longer an investigation, but mere sentimentality.
Y...
Y-
You...
Now, now!
Okay, okay!
We're very sorry. Our Chief
is under a lot of stress at the moment.
We'll be back later.
SHUFFLE
BTAM
What the hell is wrong with them?!
BOOM

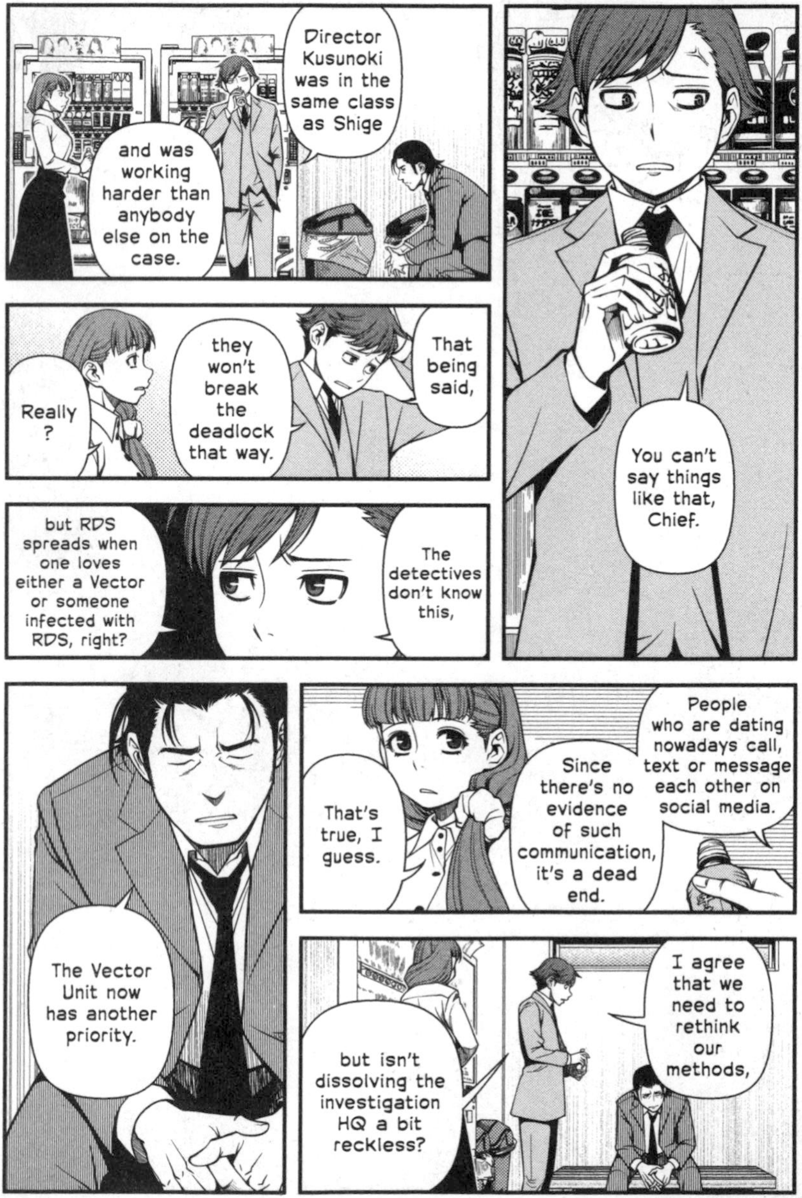
You can't say things like that, Chief.
Director Kusunoki was in the same class as Shige
and was working harder than anybody else on the case.
That being said,
they won't break the deadlock that way.
Really?
The detectives don't know this,
but RDS spreads when one loves either a Vector or someone infected with RDS, right?
People who are dating nowadays call, text or message each other on social media.
Since there's no evidence of such communication, it's a dead end.
That's true, I guess.
I agree that we need to rethink our methods,
but isn't dissolving the investigation HQ a bit reckless?
The Vector Unit now has another priority.

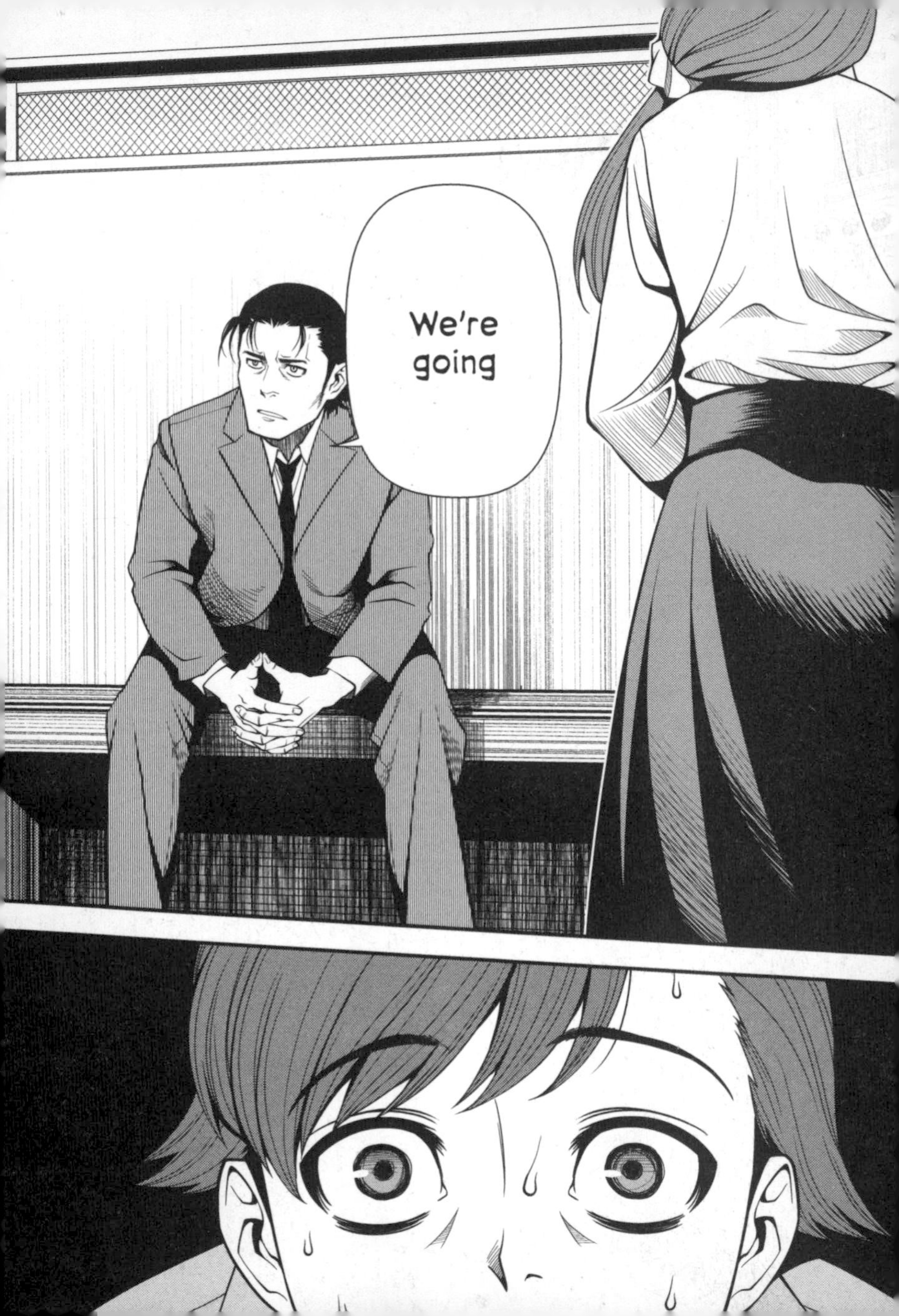
We're going

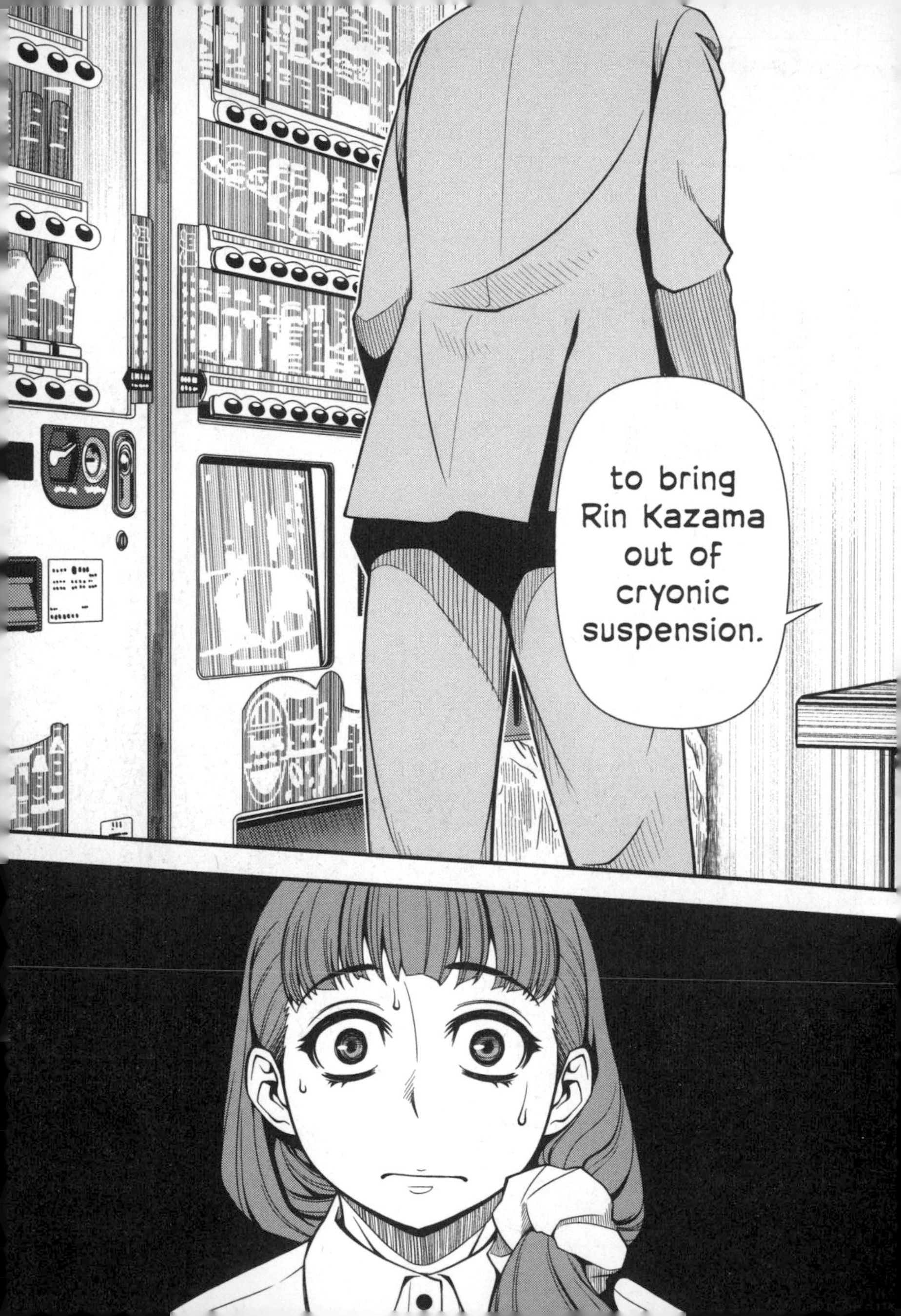
to bring Rin Kazama out of cryonic suspension.

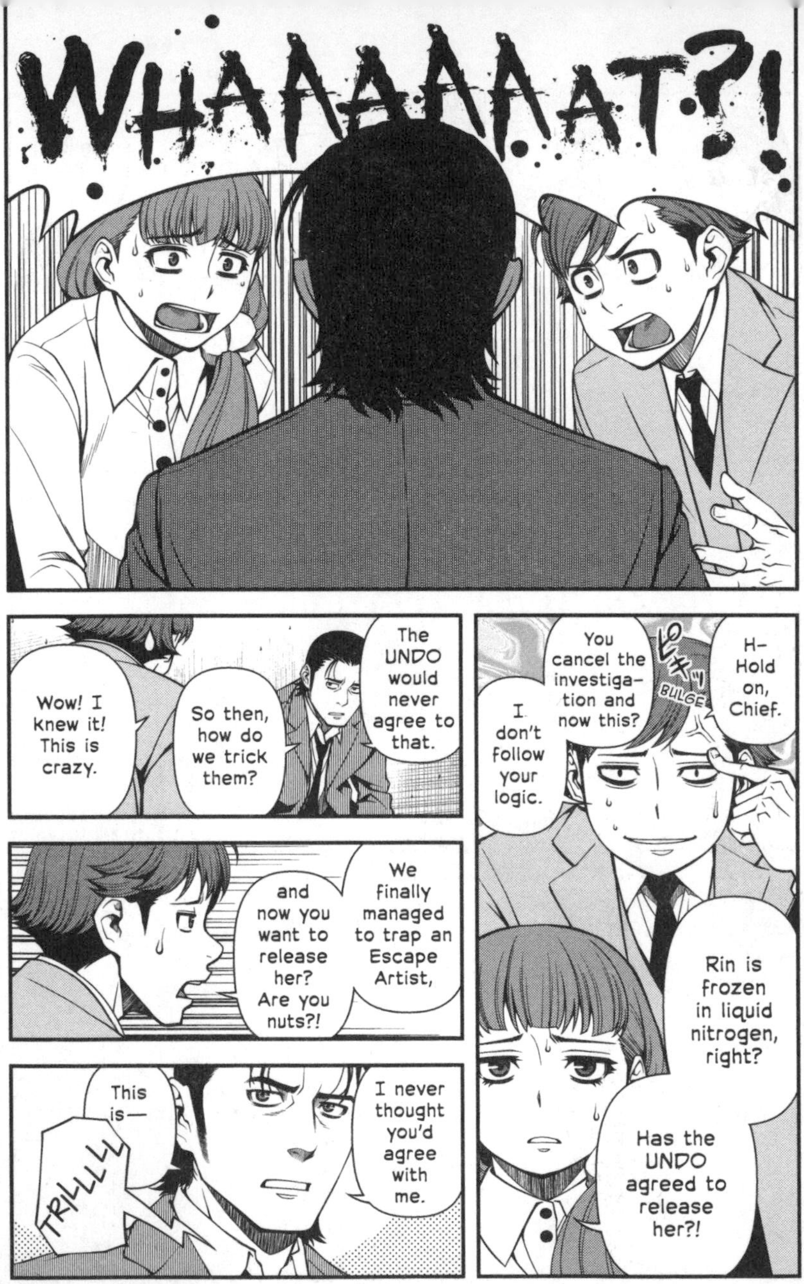
WHAAAAAAT?!
H-Hold on, Chief.
BULGE
You cancel the investigation and now this?
I don't follow your logic.
Rin is frozen in liquid nitrogen, right?
Has the UNDO agreed to release her?!
The UNDO would never agree to that.
So then, how do we trick them?
Wow! I knew it! This is crazy.
We finally managed to trap an Escape Artist,
and now you want to release her? Are you nuts?!
I never thought you'd agree with me.
This is—
TRILLLL

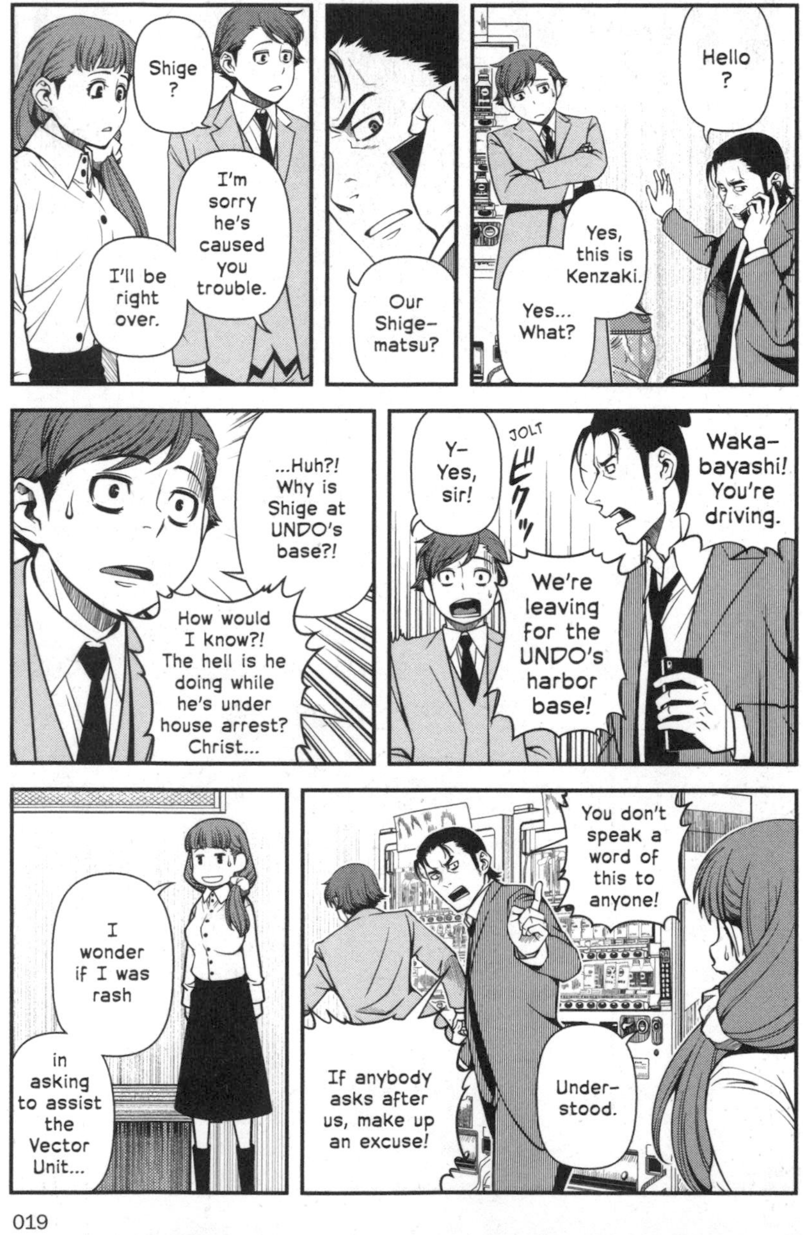
Hello?
Yes, this is Kenzaki.
Yes... What?
Our Shigematsu?
I'm sorry he's caused you trouble.
I'll be right over.
Shige?
Wakabayashi! You're driving.
JOLT
ビクッ
Y- Yes, sir!
We're leaving for the UNDO's harbor base!
...Huh?! Why is Shige at UNDO's base?!
How would I know?! The hell is he doing while he's under house arrest? Christ...
You don't speak a word of this to anyone!
Understood.
If anybody asks after us, make up an excuse!
I wonder if I was rash
in asking to assist the Vector Unit...

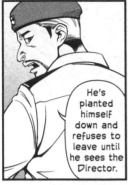

UNDO Harbor Base
Yes, that's right.
He came here without any notice.
He's planted himself down and refuses to leave until he sees the Director.
We're sorry for the trouble.
He wouldn't leave even after I warned him.
It's a real pain, dealing with people like that.
I wonder what hap-pened.
This isn't like Shige.
He might've had the same idea I did.
We're keeping him in here.
Director! Lieutenant Kenzaki is here to see you.

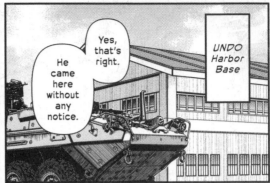

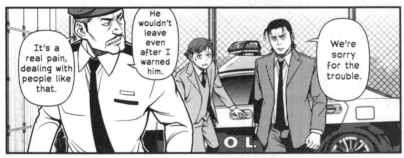

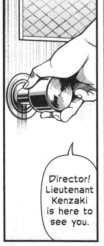

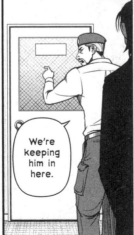

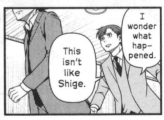

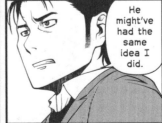

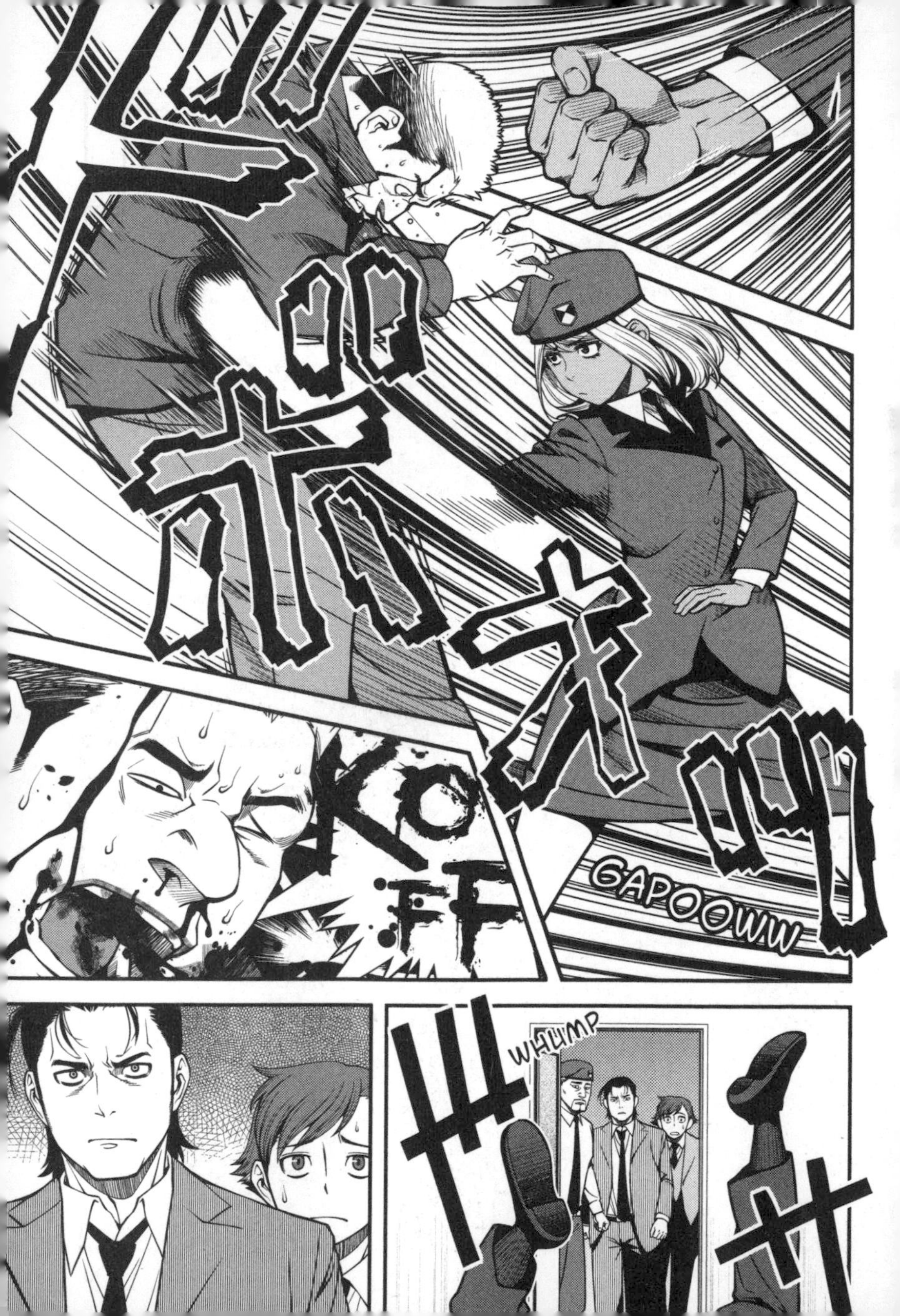
GAPOOOWW
KOFF
WHUMP

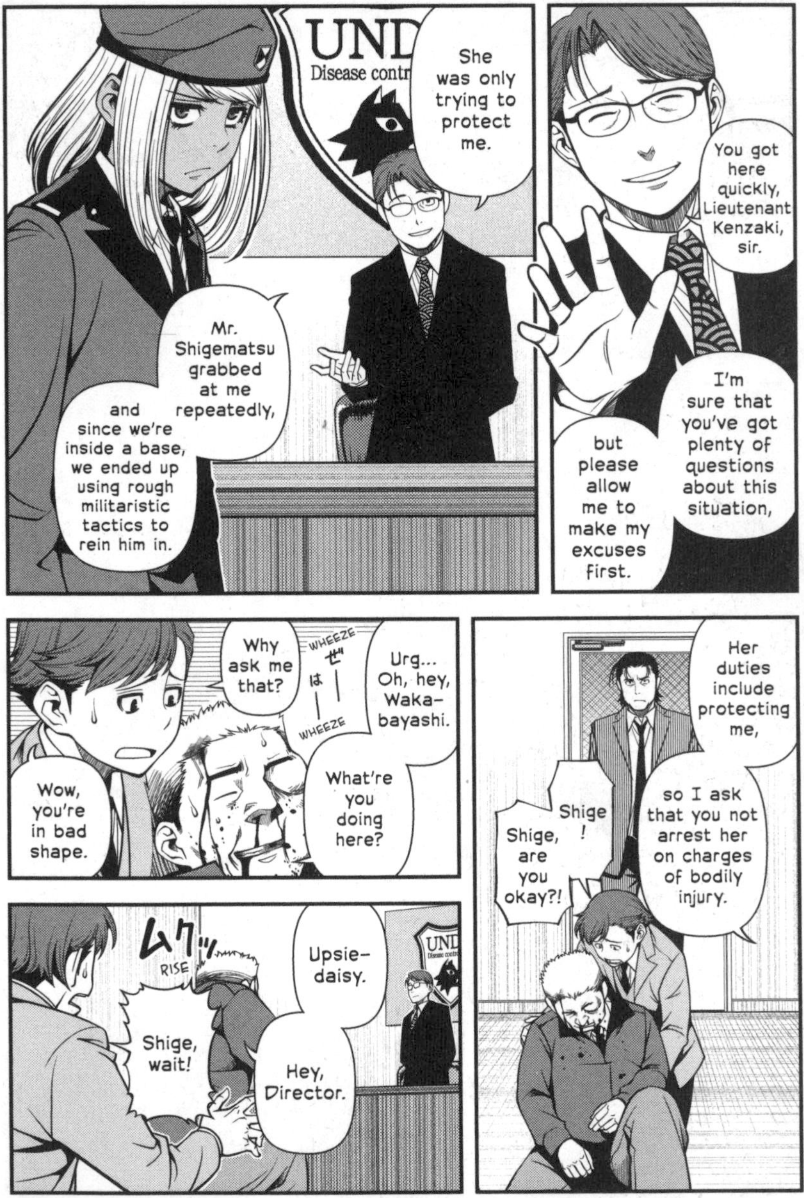
You got here quickly, Lieutenant Kenzaki, sir.
I'm sure that you've got plenty of questions about this situation,
but please allow me to make my excuses first.
UND
Disease contr
She was only trying to protect me.
Mr. Shigematsu grabbed at me repeatedly,
and since we're inside a base, we ended up using rough militaristic tactics to rein him in.
Her duties include protecting me,
so I ask that you not arrest her on charges of bodily injury.
Shige!
Shige, are you okay?!
Urg... Oh, hey, Wakabayashi.
ぜー WHEEZE
はー WHEEZE
What're you doing here?
Why ask me that?
Wow, you're in bad shape.
Upsie-daisy.
ムクッ RISE
Hey, Director.
Shige, wait!

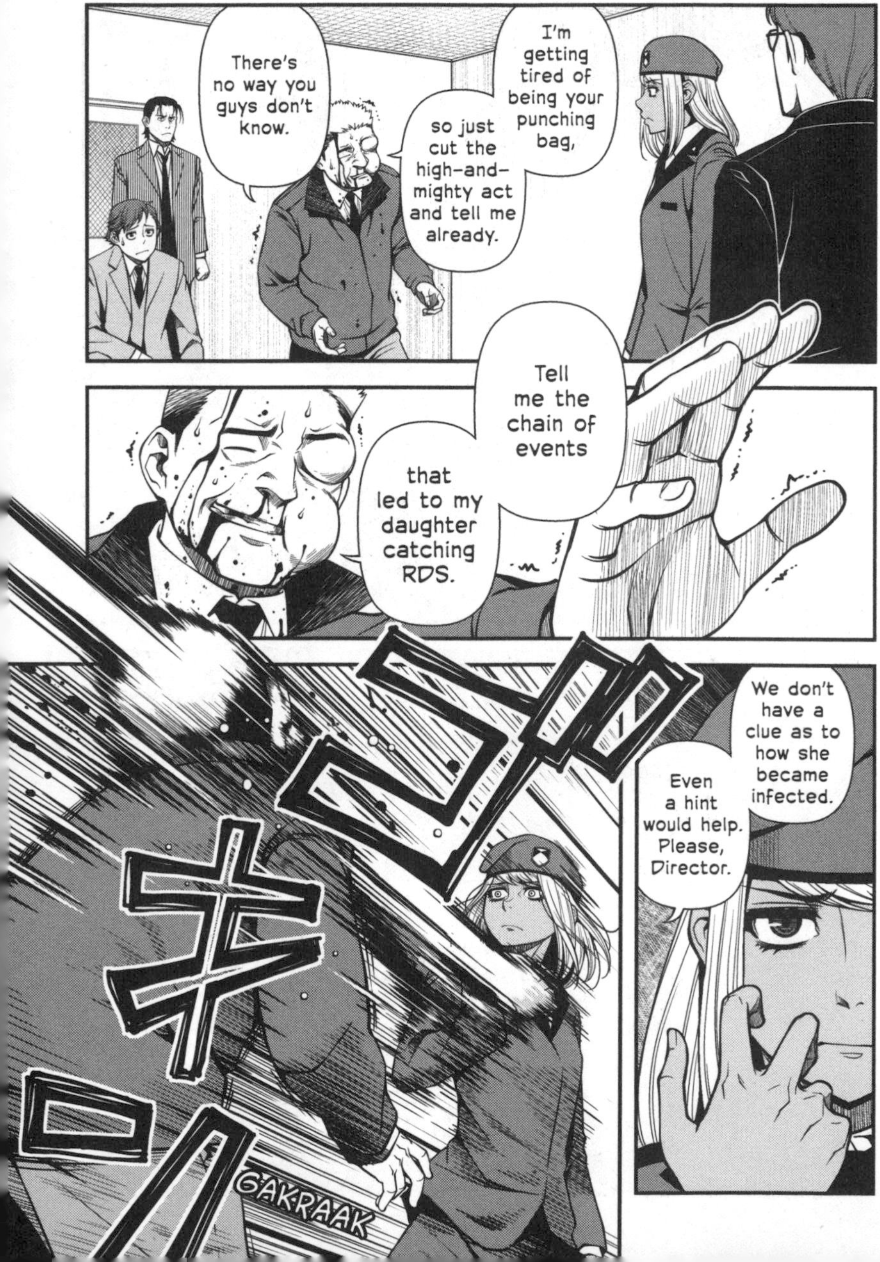
I'm getting tired of being your punching bag,
so just cut the high-and-mighty act and tell me already.
There's no way you guys don't know.
Tell me the chain of events
that led to my daughter catching RDS.
We don't have a clue as to how she became infected.
Even a hint would help. Please, Director.
GAKRAAK

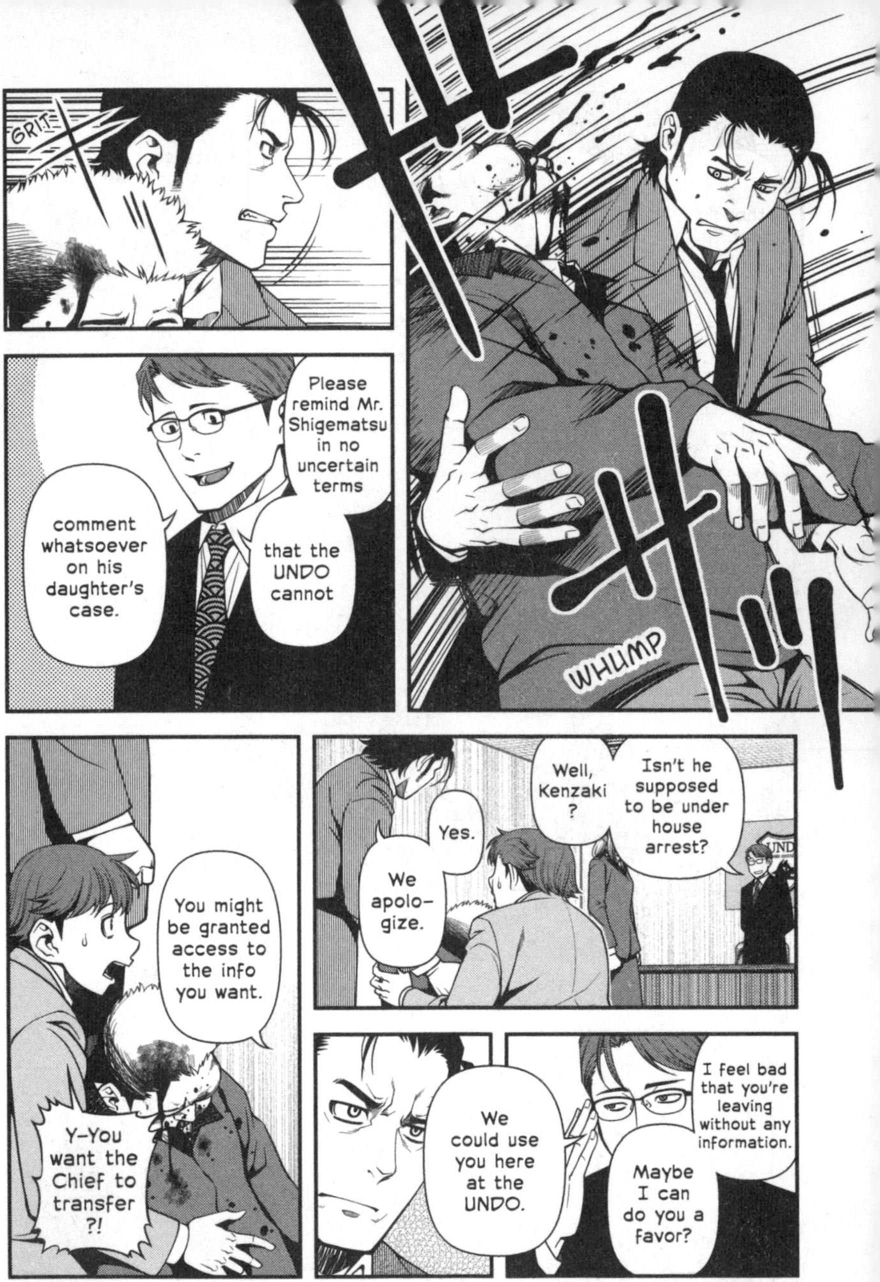
WHUMP
GRIT
Please remind Mr. Shigematsu in no uncertain terms
that the UNDO cannot
comment whatsoever on his daughter's case.
Isn't he supposed to be under house arrest?
Well, Kenzaki?
Yes.
We apolo-gize.
I feel bad that you're leaving without any information.
Maybe I can do you a favor?
We could use you here at the UNDO.
You might be granted access to the info you want.
Y-You want the Chief to transfer?!

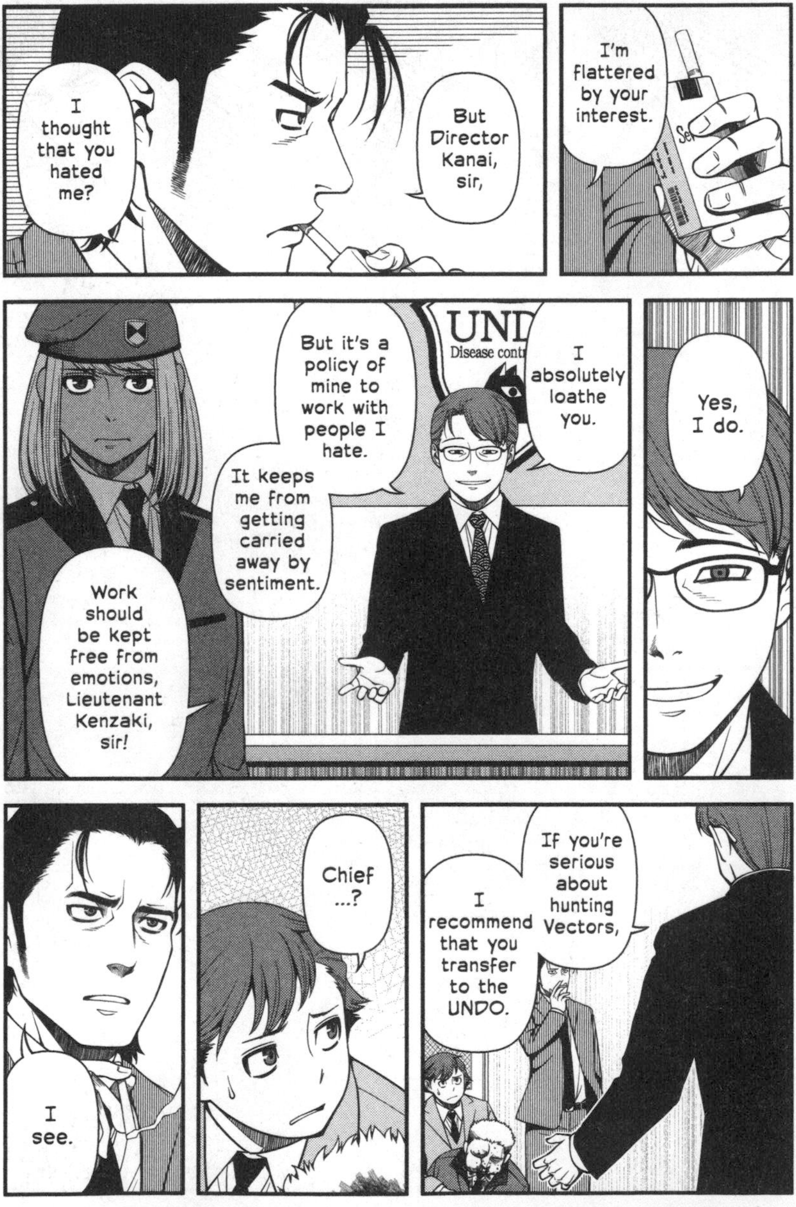
I'm flattered by your interest.
But Director Kanai, sir,
I thought that you hated me?
Yes, I do.
I absolutely loathe you.
But it's a policy of mine to work with people I hate.
It keeps me from getting carried away by sentiment.
Work should be kept free from emotions, Lieutenant Kenzaki, sir!
If you're serious about hunting Vectors,
I recommend that you transfer to the UNDO.
Chief ...?
I see.

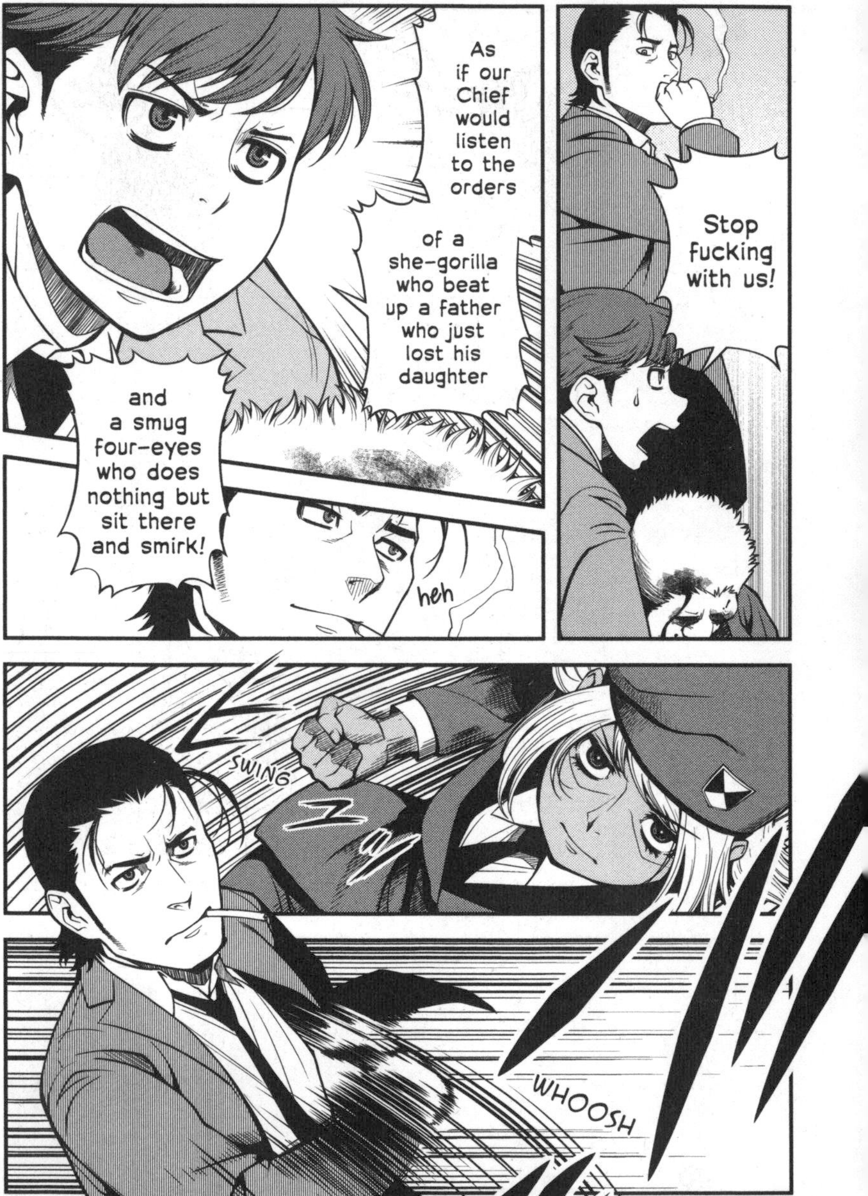
Stop fucking with us!
As if our Chief would listen to the orders
of a she-gorilla who beat up a father who just lost his daughter
and a smug four-eyes who does nothing but sit there and smirk!
heh
SWING
WHOOSH

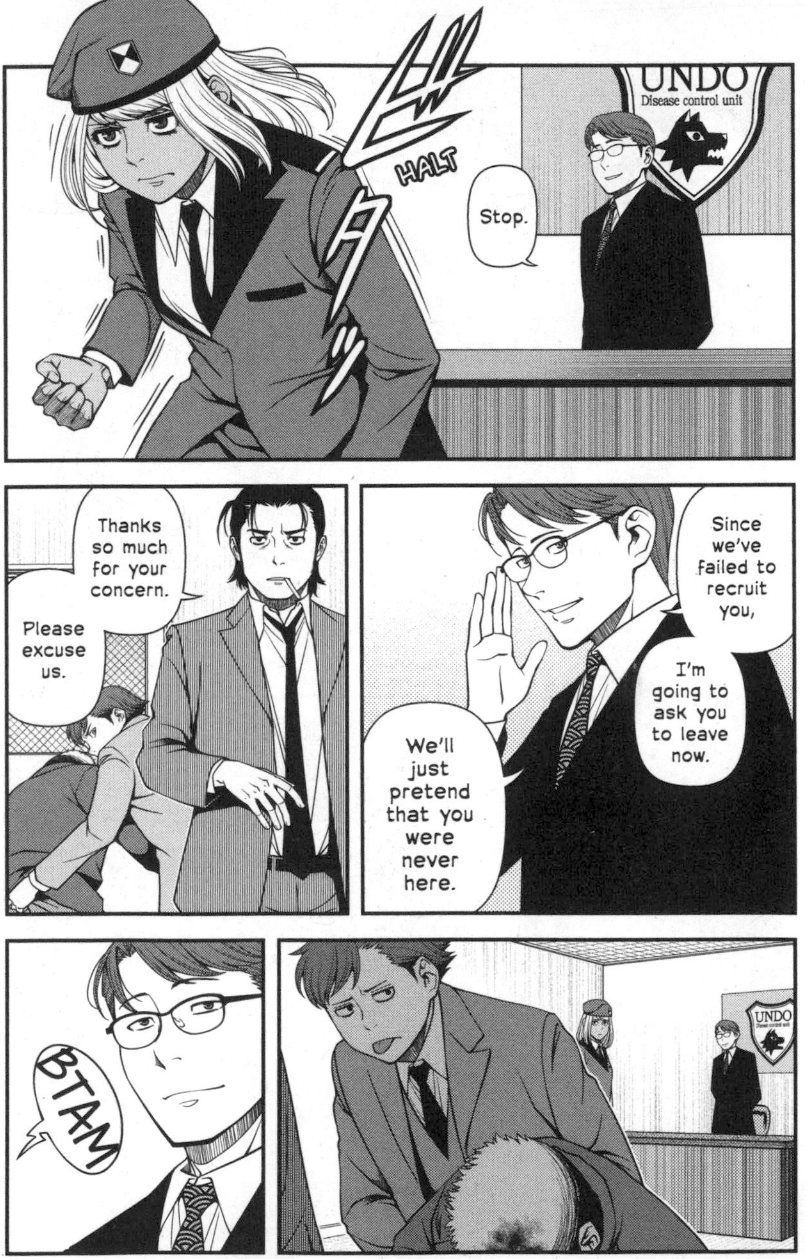
UNDO
Disease control unit
HALT
Stop.
Since we've failed to recruit you,
I'm going to ask you to leave now.
We'll just pretend that you were never here.
Thanks so much for your concern.
Please excuse us.
UNDO
BTAM

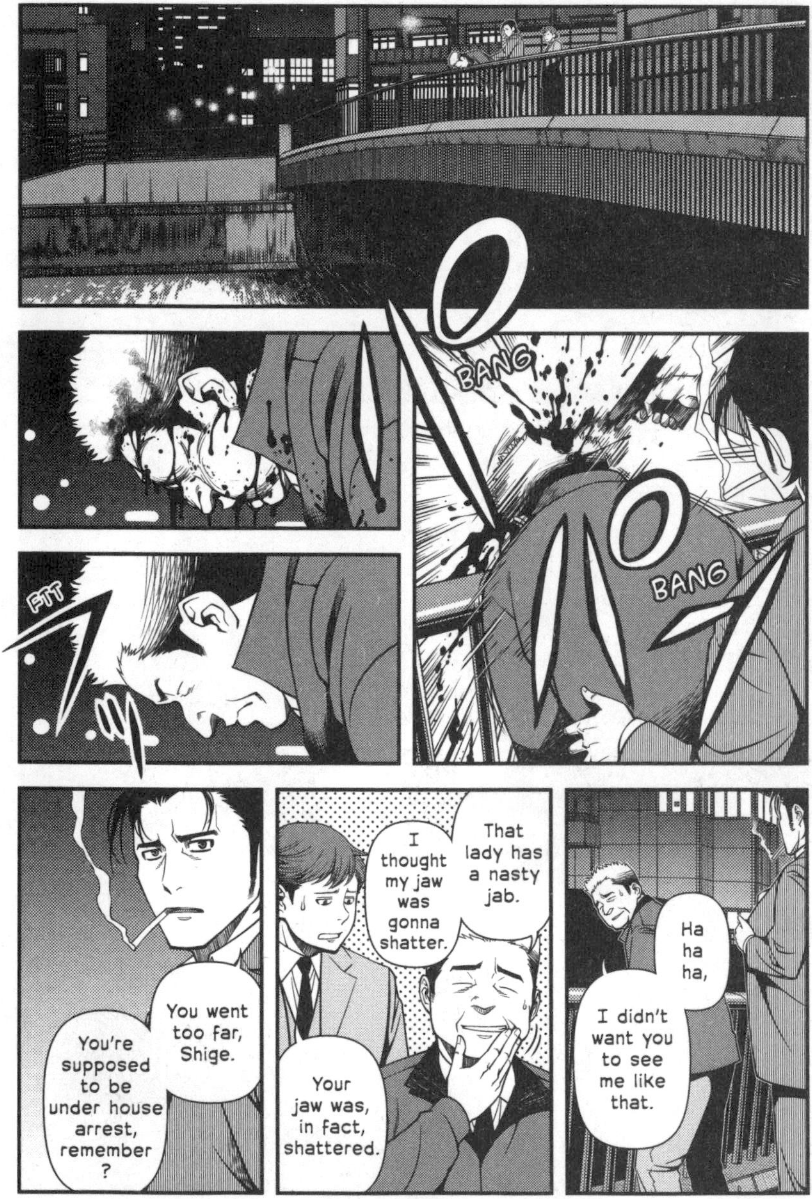
BANG
BANG
FTT
Ha ha ha,
I didn't want you to see me like that.
That lady has a nasty jab.
I thought my jaw was gonna shatter.
Your jaw was, in fact, shattered.
You went too far, Shige.
You're supposed to be under house arrest, remember?

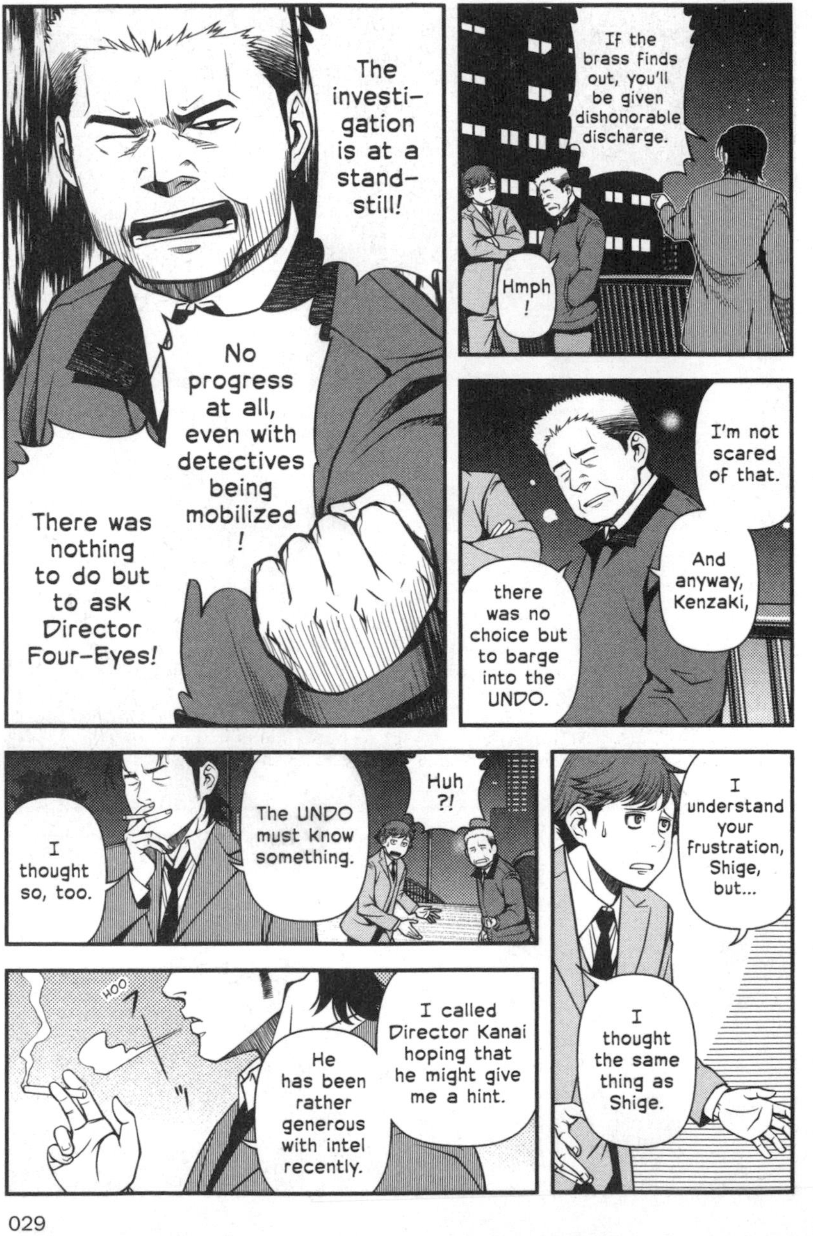
If the brass finds out, you'll be given dishonorable discharge.
Hmph!
I'm not scared of that.
And anyway, Kenzaki,
there was no choice but to barge into the UNDO.
The investigation is at a standstill!
No progress at all, even with detectives being mobilized!
There was nothing to do but to ask Director Four-Eyes!
I understand your frustration, Shige, but...
I thought the same thing as Shige.
Huh?!
The UNDO must know something.
I thought so, too.
HOO
I called Director Kanai hoping that he might give me a hint.
He has been rather generous with intel recently.

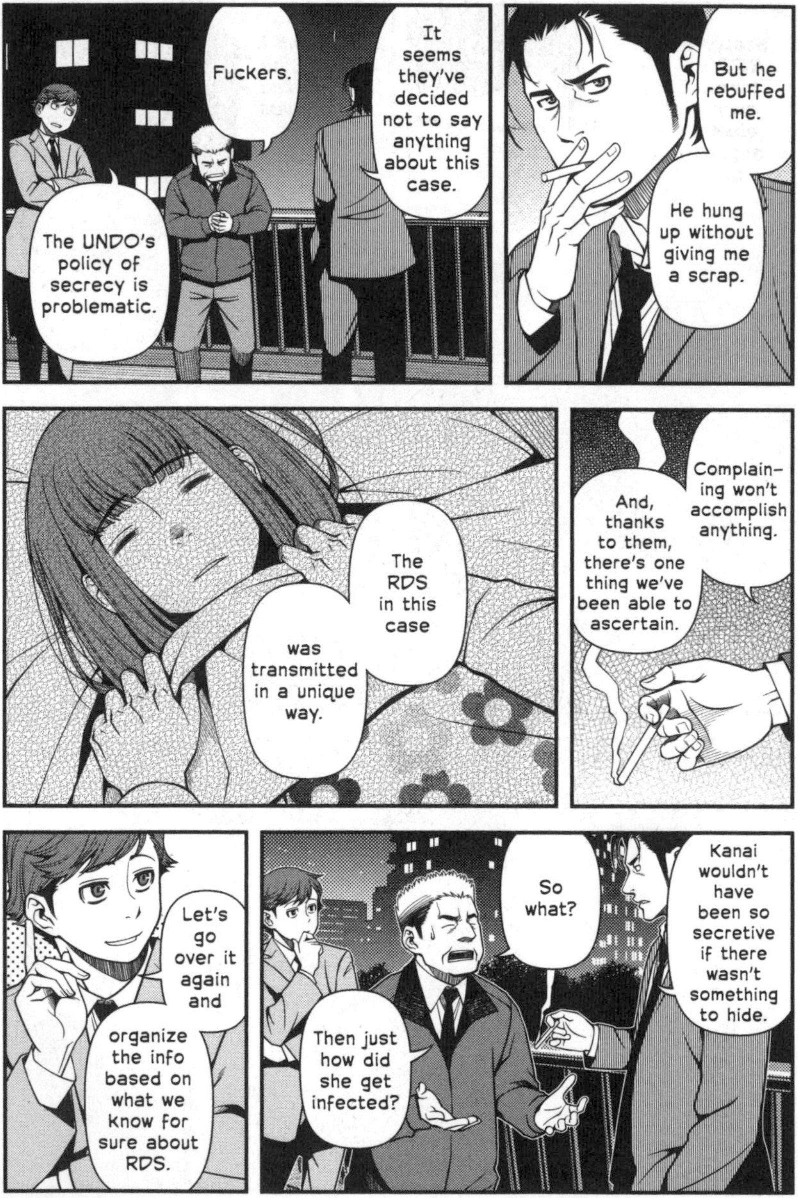
But he rebuffed me.
He hung up without giving me a scrap.
It seems they've decided not to say anything about this case.
Fuckers.
The UNDO's policy of secrecy is problematic.
Complaining won't accomplish anything.
And, thanks to them, there's one thing we've been able to ascertain.
The RDS in this case
was transmitted in a unique way.
Kanai wouldn't have been so secretive if there wasn't something to hide.
So what?
Then just how did she get infected?
Let's go over it again and
organize the info based on what we know for sure about RDS.

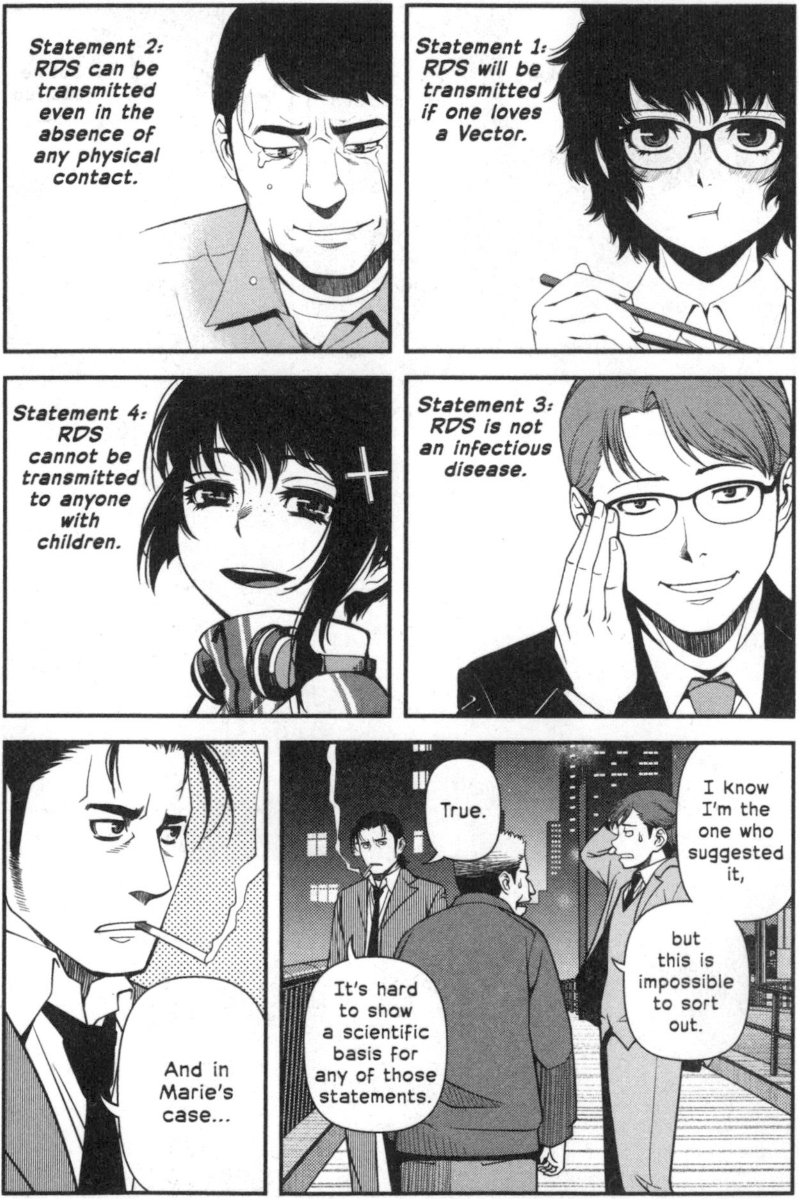
Statement 1: RDS will be transmitted if one loves a Vector.
Statement 2: RDS can be transmitted even in the absence of any physical contact.
Statement 3: RDS is not an infectious disease.
Statement 4: RDS cannot be transmitted to anyone with children.
I know I'm the one who suggested it,
but this is impossible to sort out.
True.
It's hard to show a scientific basis for any of those statements.
And in Marie's case...

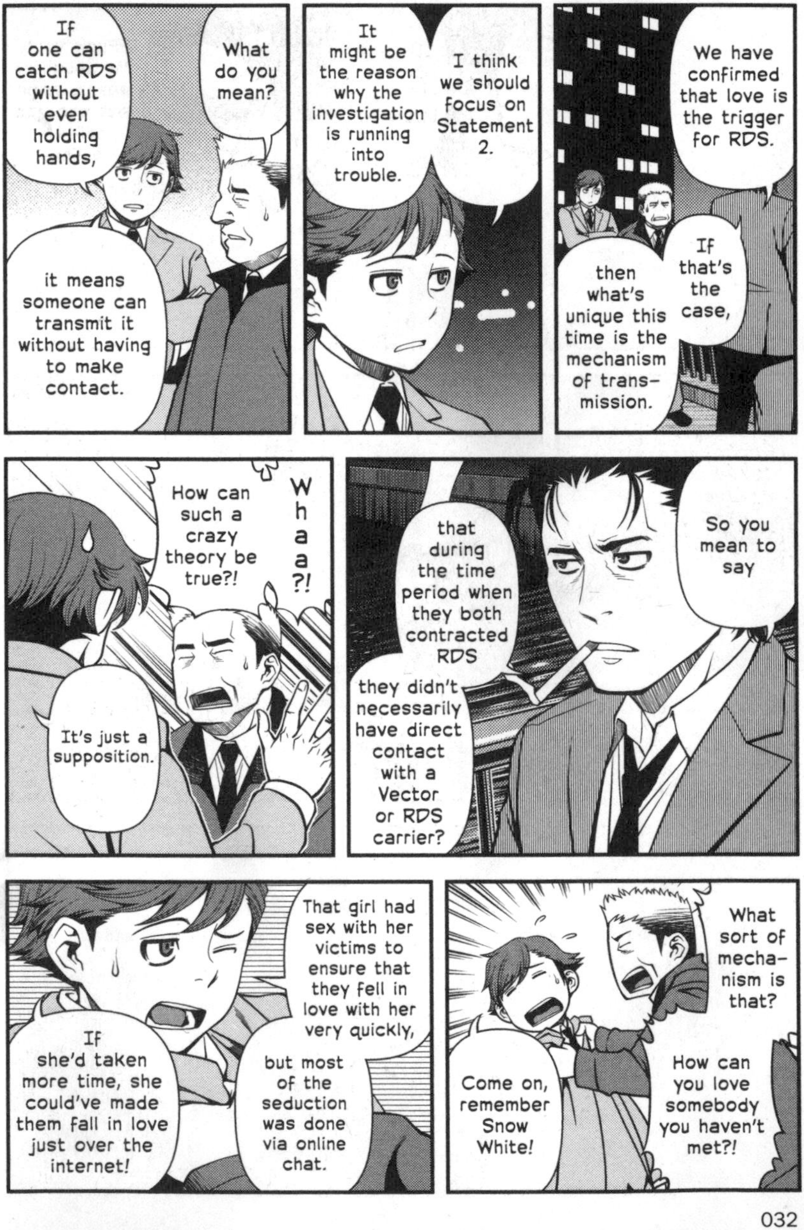
We have confirmed that love is the trigger for RDS.
If that's the case,
then what's unique this time is the mechanism of trans-mission.
I think we should focus on Statement 2.
It might be the reason why the investigation is running into trouble.
What do you mean?
If one can catch RDS without even holding hands,
it means someone can transmit it without having to make contact.
So you mean to say
that during the time period when they both contracted RDS
they didn't necessarily have direct contact with a Vector or RDS carrier?
Whaa?!
How can such a crazy theory be true?!
It's just a supposition.
What sort of mecha-nism is that?
How can you love somebody you haven't met?!
Come on, remember Snow White!
That girl had sex with her victims to ensure that they fell in love with her very quickly,
but most of the seduction was done via online chat.
If she'd taken more time, she could've made them fall in love just over the internet!

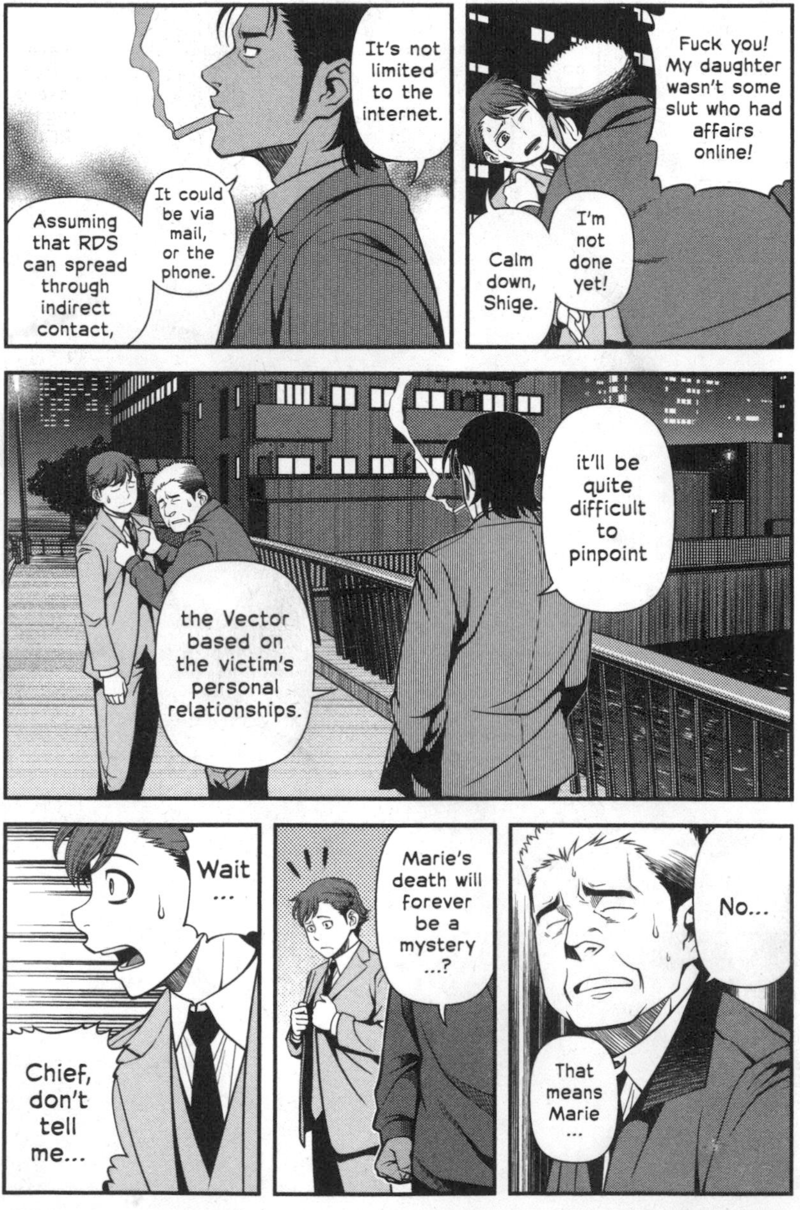

Fuck you! My daughter wasn't some slut who had affairs online!
I'm not done yet!
Calm down, Shige.
It's not limited to the internet.
It could be via mail, or the phone.
Assuming that RDS can spread through indirect contact,
it'll be quite difficult to pinpoint
the Vector based on the victim's personal relationships.
No...
That means Marie ...
Marie's death will forever be a mystery ...?
Wait ...
Chief, don't tell me...

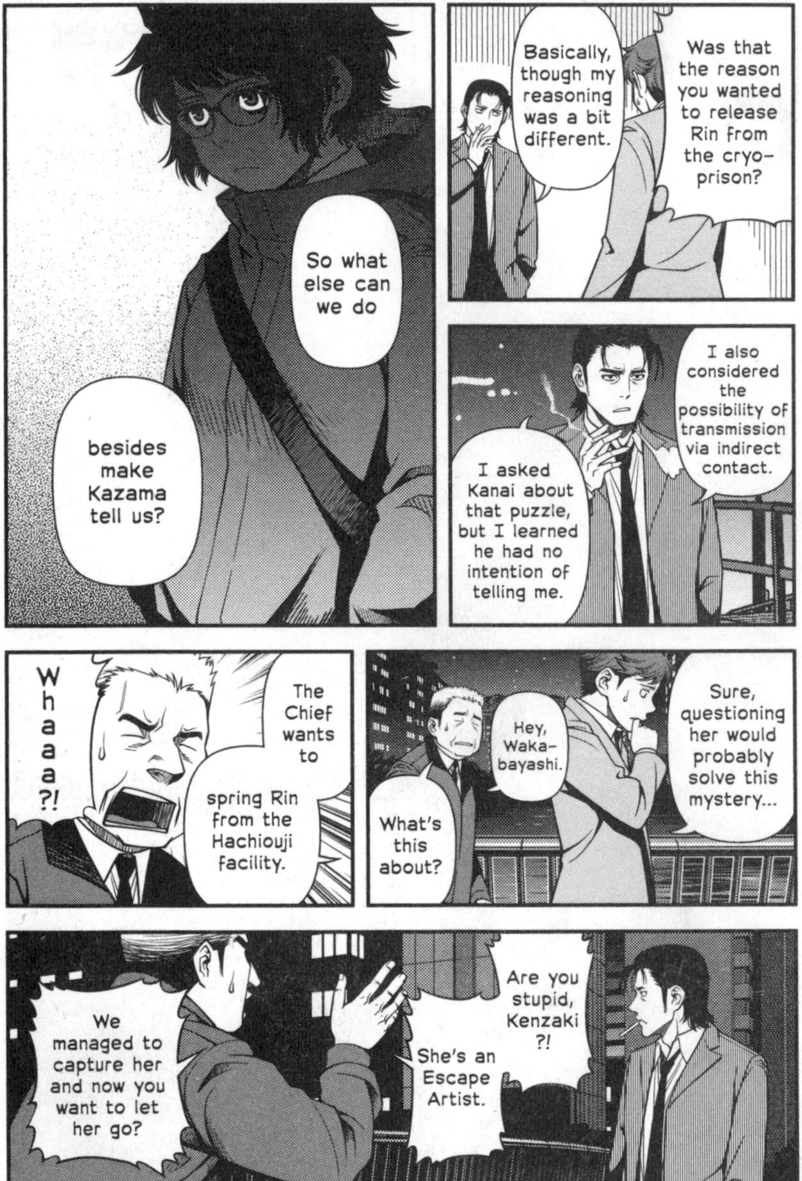
Was that the reason you wanted to release Rin from the cryo-prison?
Basically, though my reasoning was a bit different.
I also considered the possibility of transmission via indirect contact.
I asked Kanai about that puzzle, but I learned he had no intention of telling me.
So what else can we do
besides make Kazama tell us?
Sure, questioning her would probably solve this mystery...
Hey, Waka-bayashi.
What's this about?
The Chief wants to
spring Rin from the Hachiouji facility.
Whaaaa?!
Are you stupid, Kenzaki?!
She's an Escape Artist.
We managed to capture her and now you want to let her go?

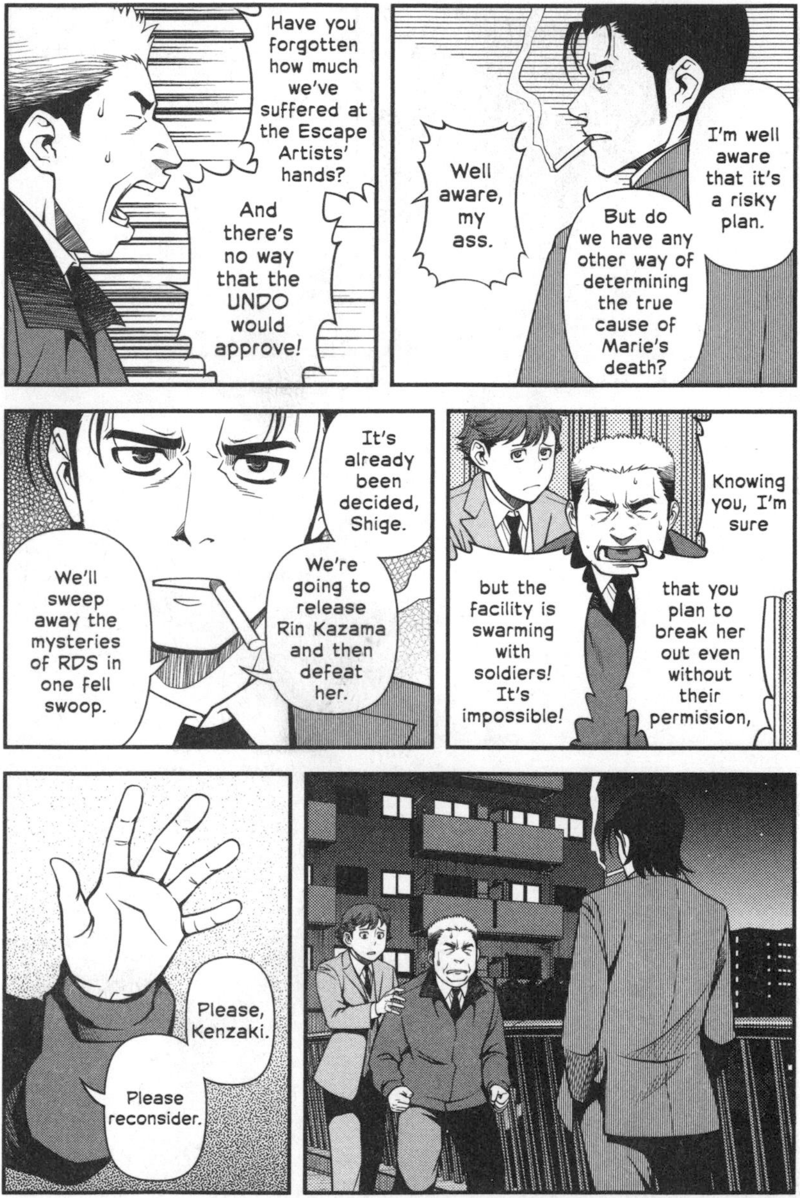
I'm well aware that it's a risky plan.
But do we have any other way of determining the true cause of Marie's death?
Well aware, my ass.
Have you forgotten how much we've suffered at the Escape Artists' hands?
And there's no way that the UNDO would approve!
Knowing you, I'm sure
that you plan to break her out even without their permission,
but the facility is swarming with soldiers! It's impossible!
It's already been decided, Shige.
We're going to release Rin Kazama and then defeat her.
We'll sweep away the mysteries of RDS in one fell swoop.
Please, Kenzaki.
Please reconsider.

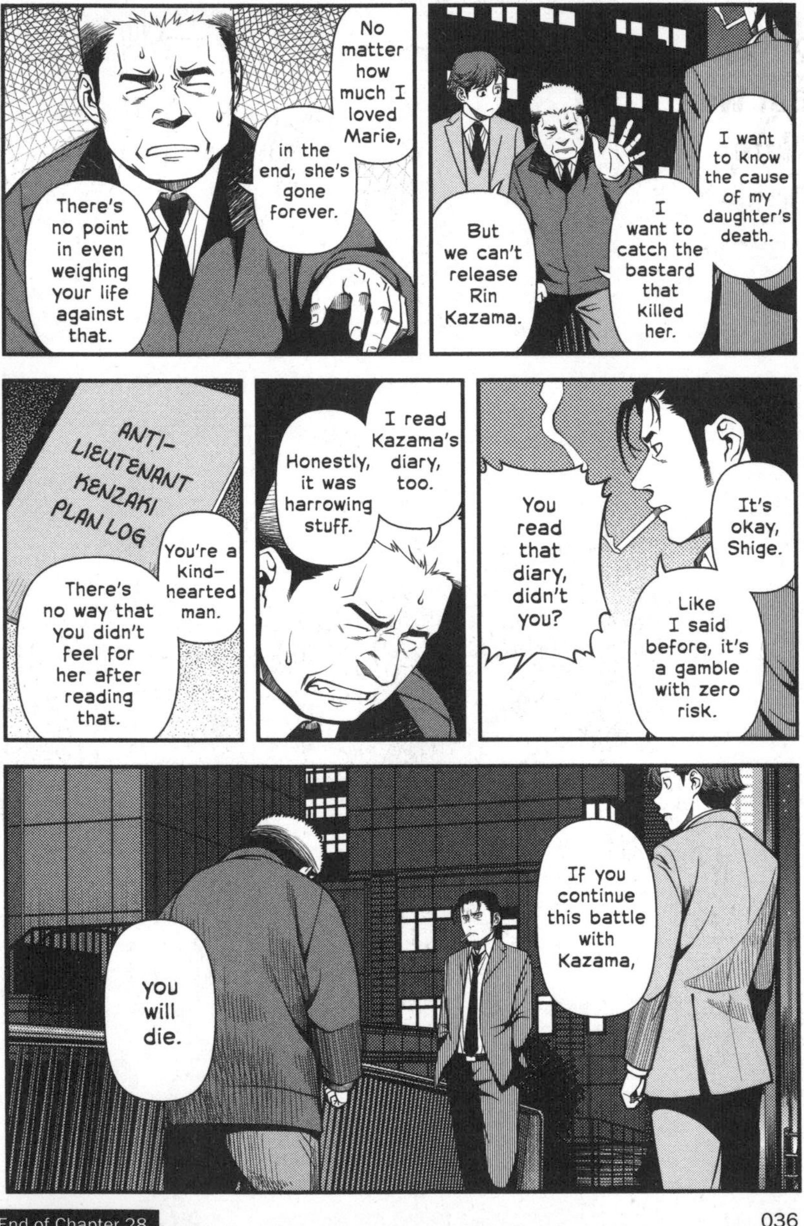
I want to know the cause of my daughter's death.
I want to catch the bastard that killed her.
But we can't release Rin Kazama.
No matter how much I loved Marie,
in the end, she's gone forever.
There's no point in even weighing your life against that.
It's okay, Shige.
Like I said before, it's a gamble with zero risk.
You read that diary, didn't you?
I read Kazama's diary, too.
Honestly, it was harrowing stuff.
ANTI-LIEUTENANT KENZAKI PLAN LOG
You're a kind-hearted man.
There's no way that you didn't feel for her after reading that.
If you continue this battle with Kazama,
you will die.

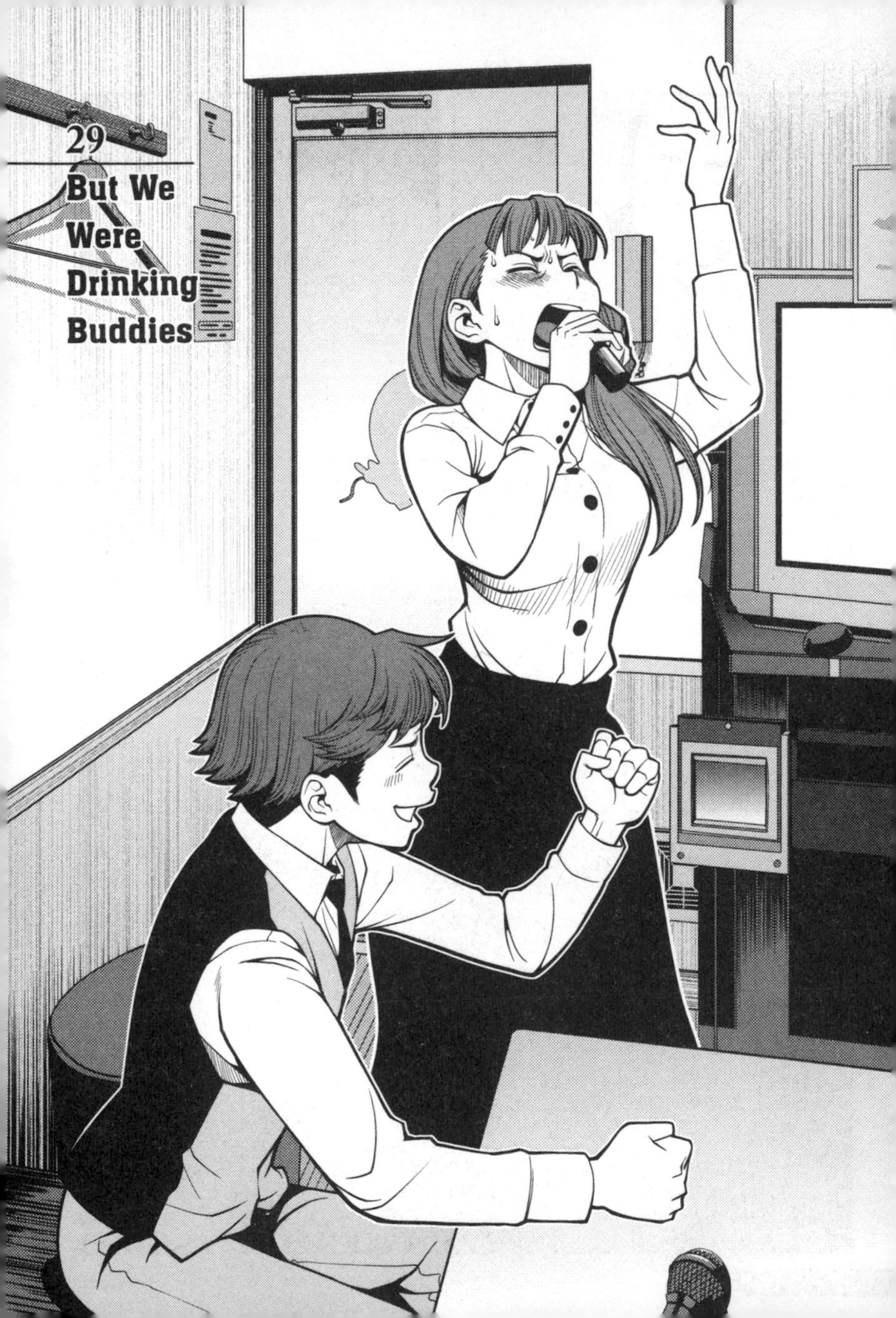
29
But We Were Drinking Buddies

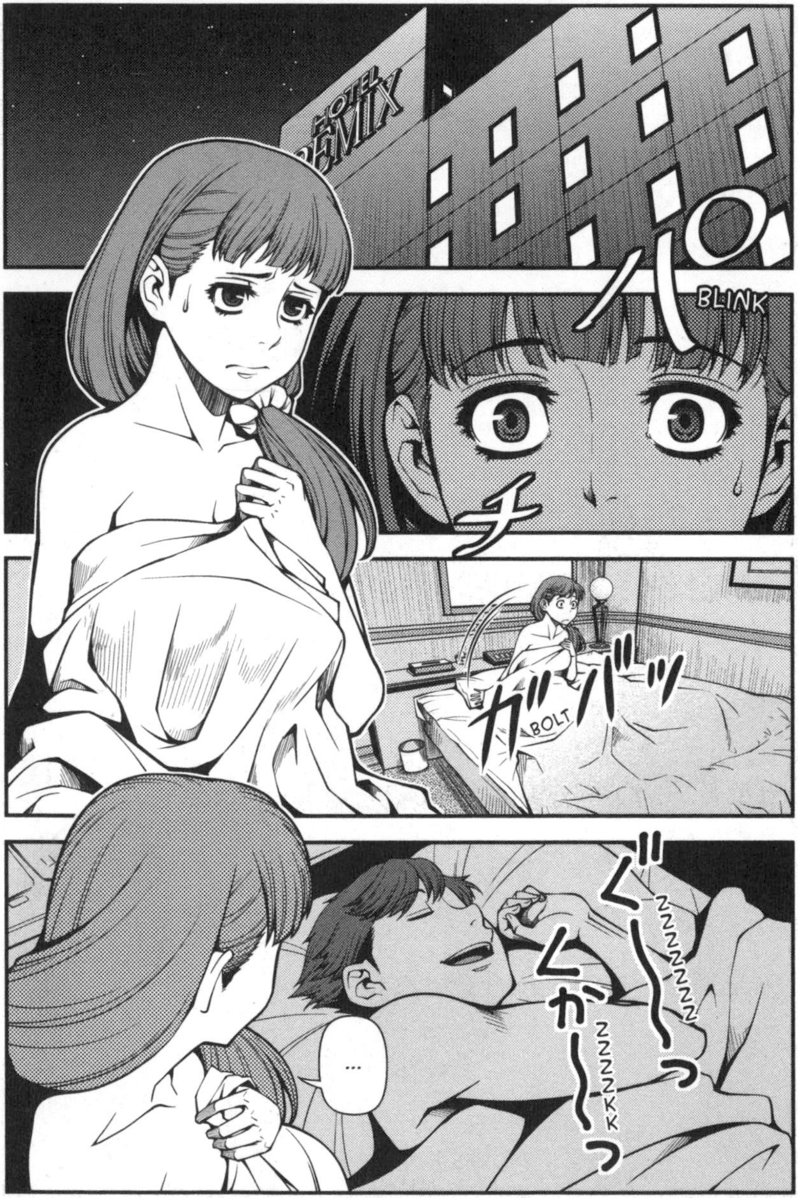
HOTEL
パ
チ
BLINK
ガバッ
BOLT
ぐ～～っ
ZZZZZZZZ
くか～～っ
ZZZZKK
...

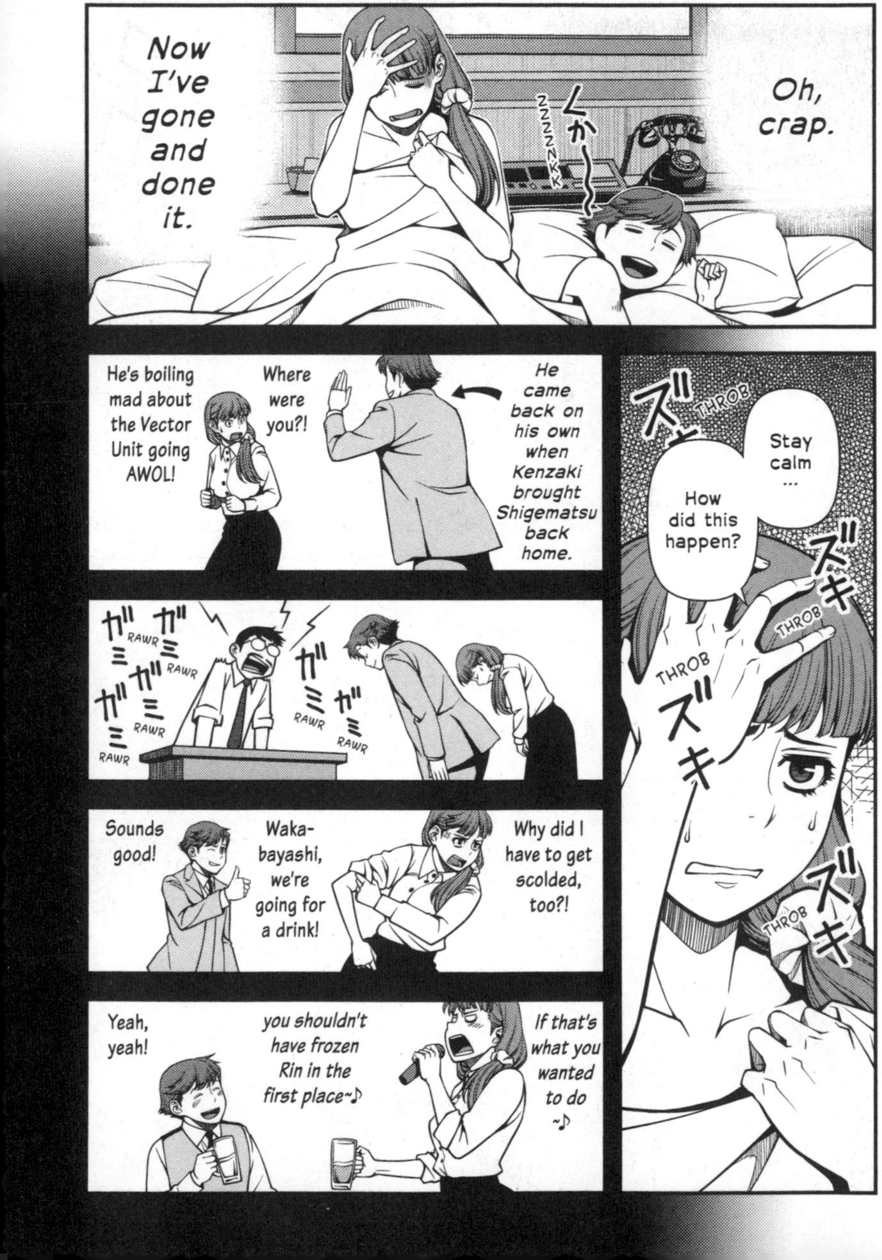

Oh, crap.
ZZZZNKK
Now I've gone and done it.
THROB
Stay calm ...
How did this happen?
THROB
THROB
THROB
He came back on his own when Kenzaki brought Shigematsu back home.
Where were you?!
He's boiling mad about the Vector Unit going AWOL!
RAWR
RAWR
RAWR
RAWR
RAWR
RAWR
Why did I have to get scolded, too?!
Waka-bayashi, we're going for a drink!
Sounds good!
If that's what you wanted to do ~♪
you shouldn't have frozen Rin in the first place~♪
Yeah, yeah!

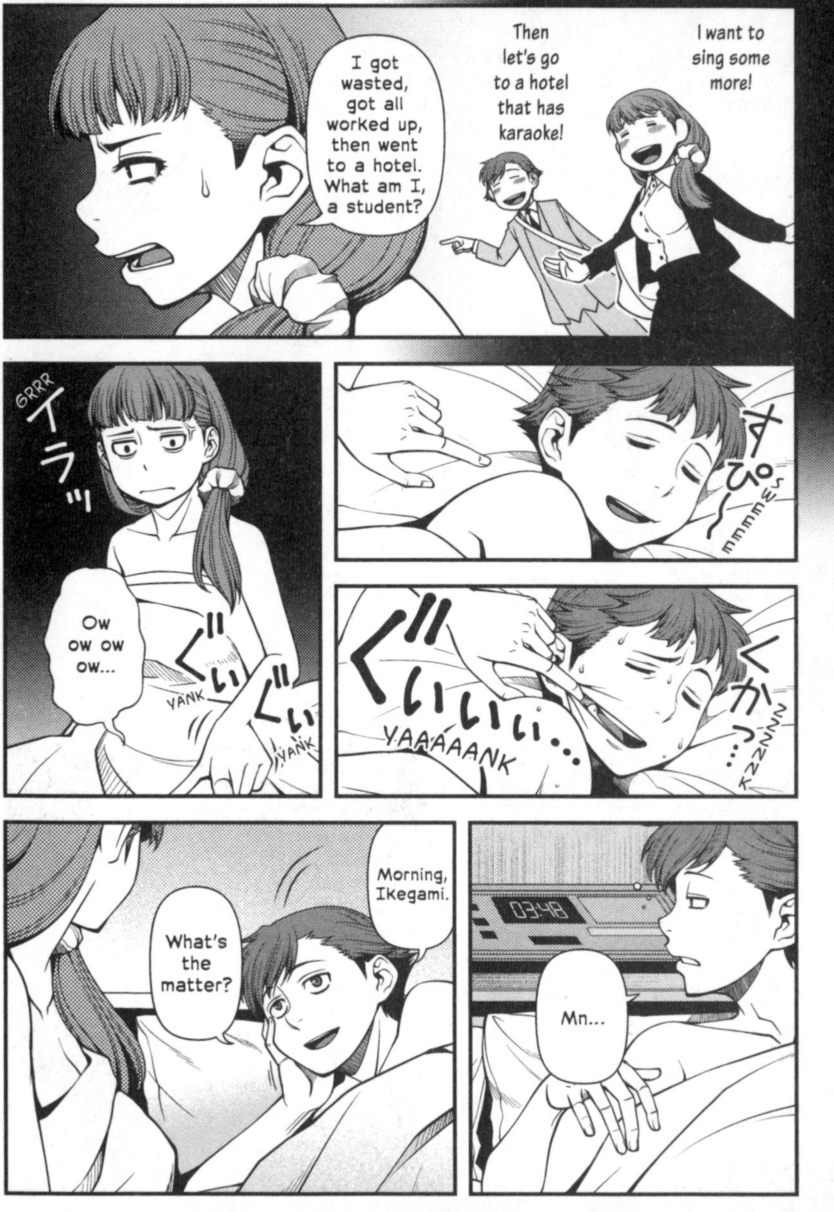

I want to sing some more!
Then let's go to a hotel that has karaoke!
I got wasted, got all worked up, then went to a hotel. What am I, a student?
すぴ〜
SWEEEEEEEE
ぐいいい…
YAAAAAANK
くかっ…
KZZNNNN
イラッ
GRRR
Ow ow ow ow...
ぐい
YANK
ぐい
YANK
Mn...
Morning, Ikegami.
What's the matter?

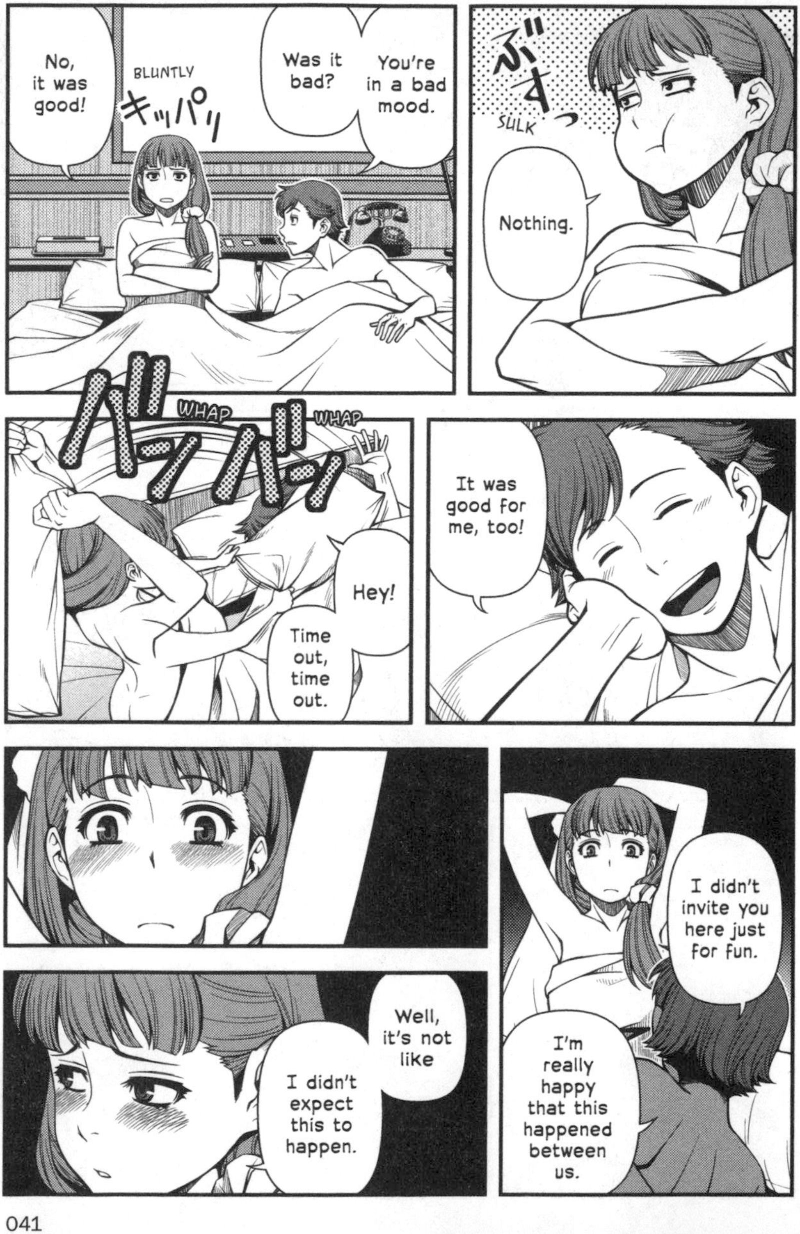
ぶすっ
SULK
Nothing.
You're in a bad mood.
Was it bad?
BLUNTLY
キッパリ
No, it was good!
It was good for me, too!
バッバッ
WHAP
WHAP
Hey!
Time out, time out.
I didn't invite you here just for fun.
I'm really happy that this happened between us.
Well, it's not like
I didn't expect this to happen.

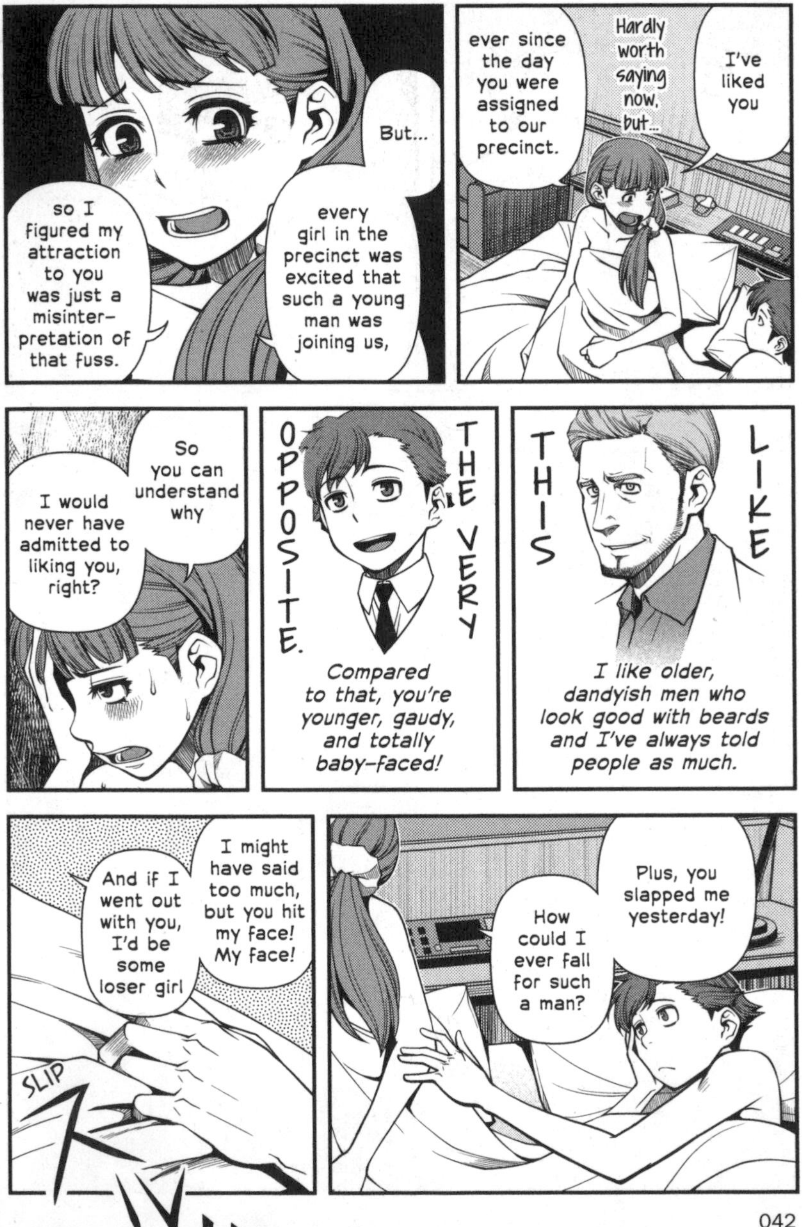
I've liked you
Hardly worth saying now, but...
ever since the day you were assigned to our precinct.
But...
every girl in the precinct was excited that such a young man was joining us,
so I figured my attraction to you was just a misinterpretation of that fuss.
LIKE THIS
I like older, dandyish men who look good with beards and I've always told people as much.
THE VERY OPPOSITE.
Compared to that, you're younger, gaudy, and totally baby-faced!
So you can understand why
I would never have admitted to liking you, right?
Plus, you slapped me yesterday!
How could I ever fall for such a man?
I might have said too much, but you hit my face! My face!
And if I went out with you, I'd be some loser girl
SLIP

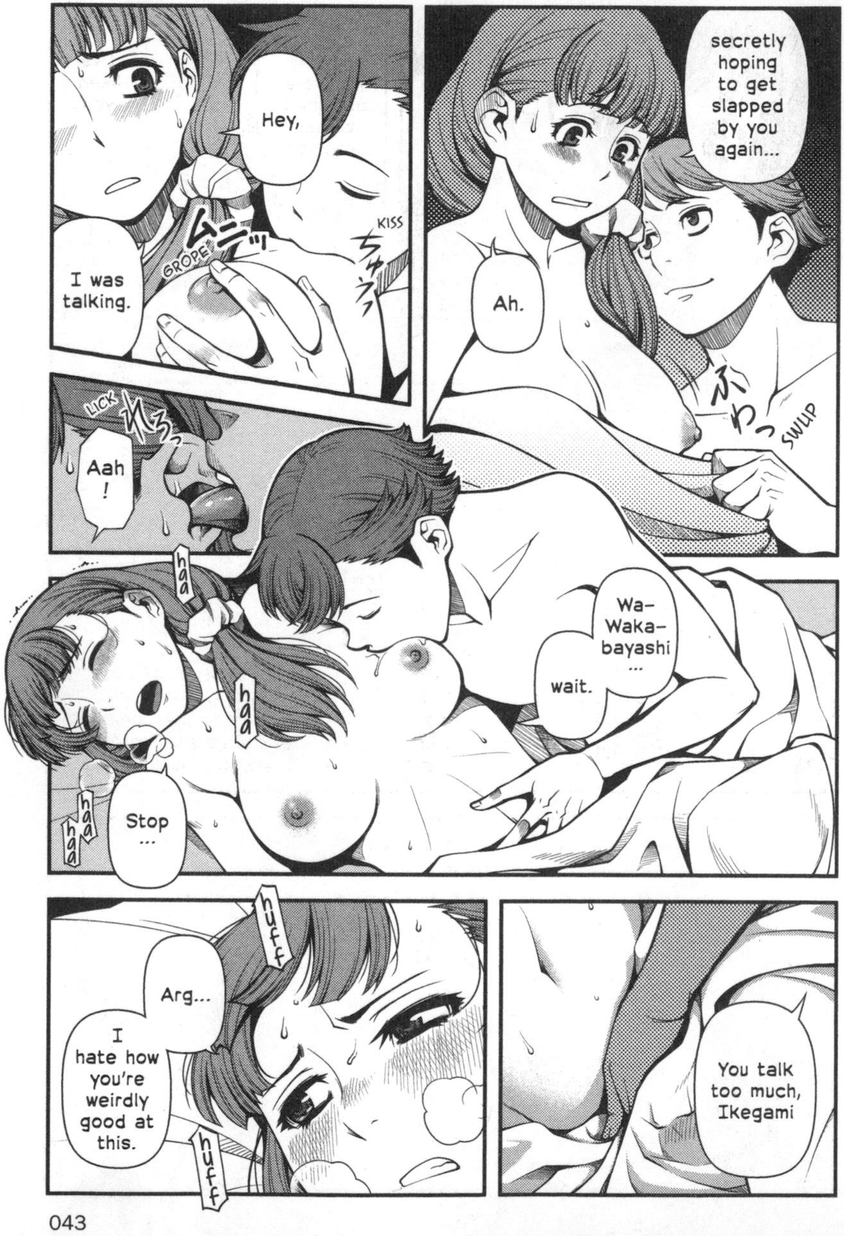
secretly hoping to get slapped by you again...
Ah.
SWLP
Hey,
I was talking.
KISS
GROPE
LICK
Aah!
Wa-Wakabayashi...
wait.
haa
haa
Stop...
haa
haa
You talk too much, Ikegami
huff
Arg...
I hate how you're weirdly good at this.
huff

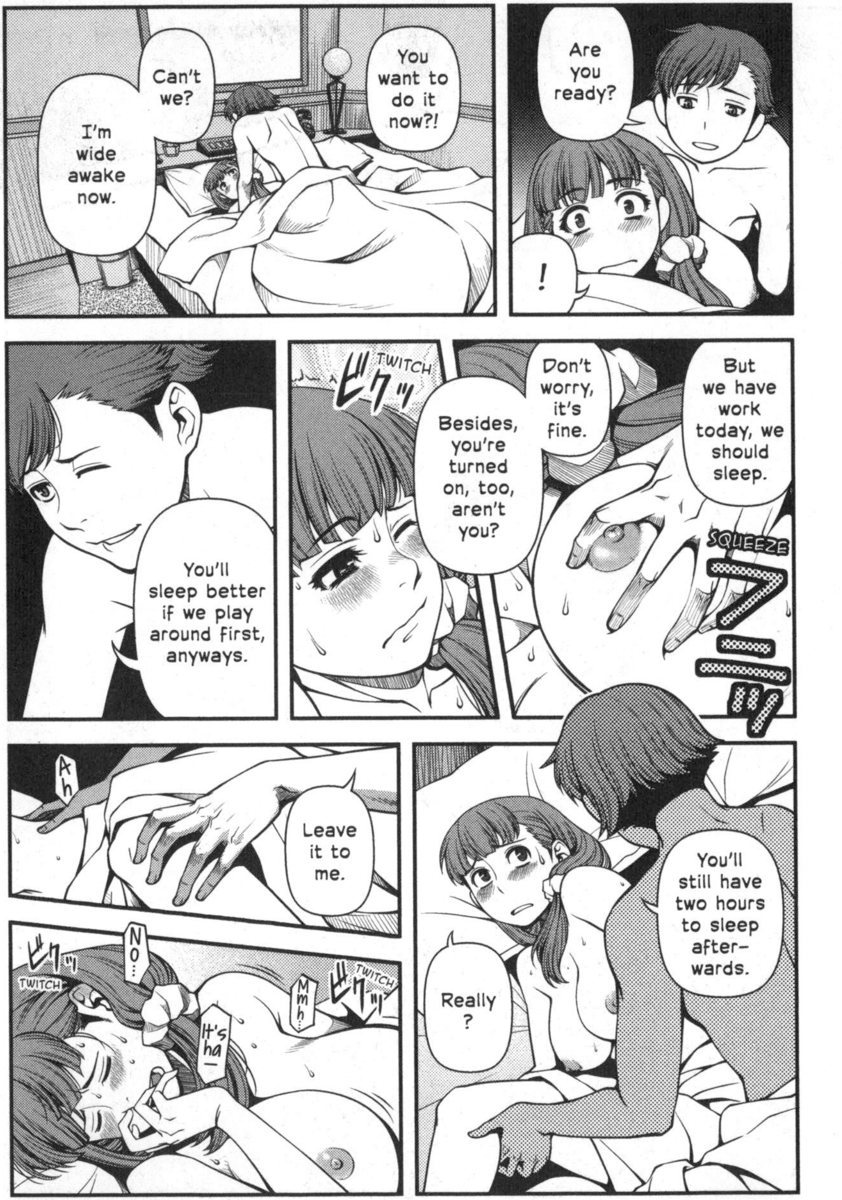
Are you ready?
!
You want to do it now?!
Can't we?
I'm wide awake now.
But we have work today, we should sleep.
Don't worry, it's fine.
SQUEEZE
TWITCH
Besides, you're turned on, too, aren't you?
You'll sleep better if we play around first, anyways.
You'll still have two hours to sleep after-wards.
Really?
Ah
Leave it to me.
TWITCH
Mmh...
It's ha—
NO...
TWITCH

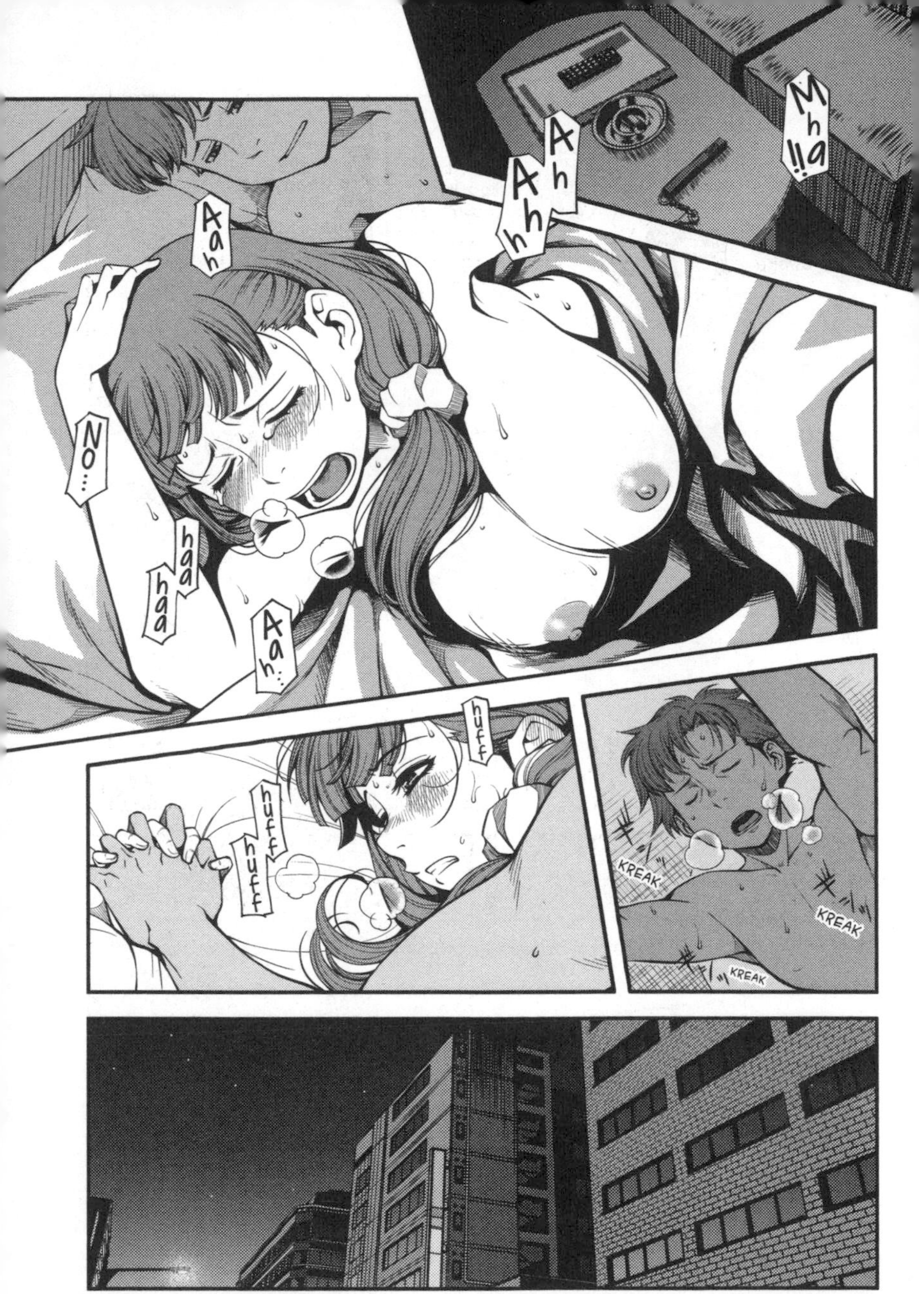
Mha!!
Ah
Ahh
Aah
No...
haa
haa
Aah...
KREAK
KREAK
KREAK
huff
huff
huff

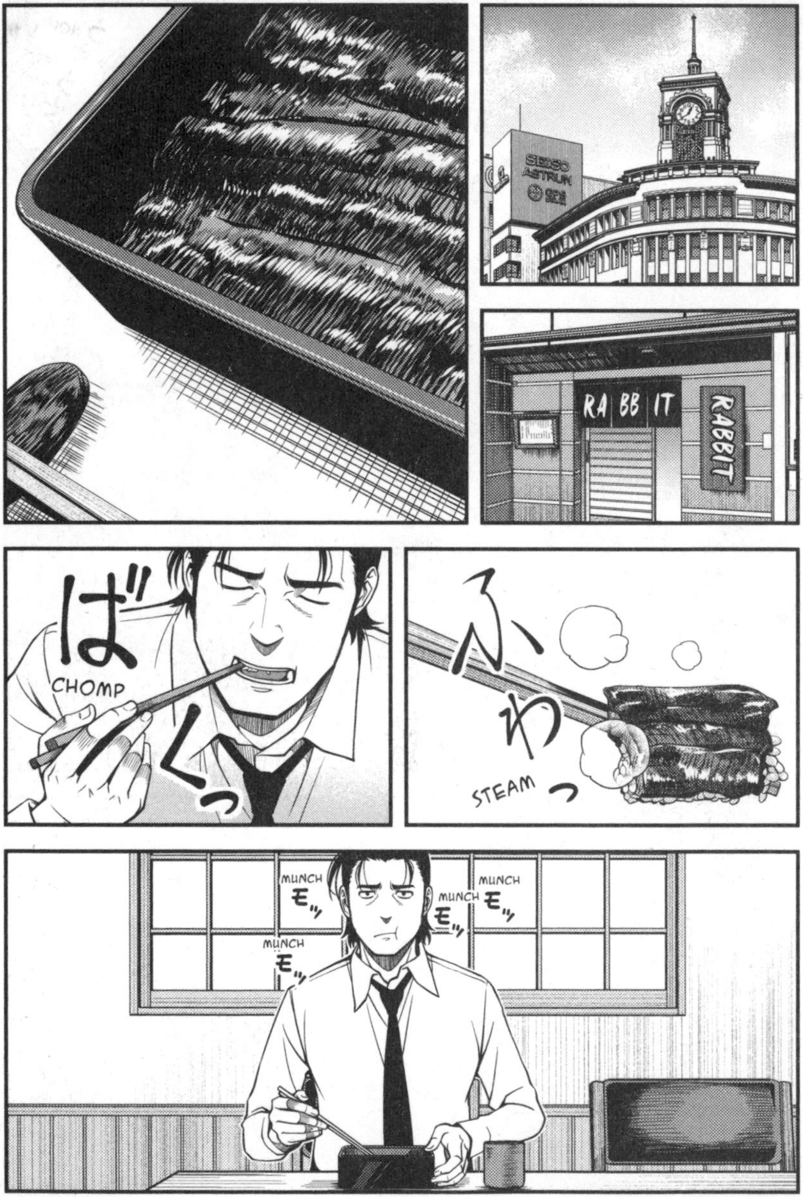
SEISO ASTRUM
RA BB IT
RABBIT
ふわっ
STEAM
ばくっ
CHOMP
MUNCH
モッ
MUNCH
モッ
MUNCH
モッ
MUNCH
モッ

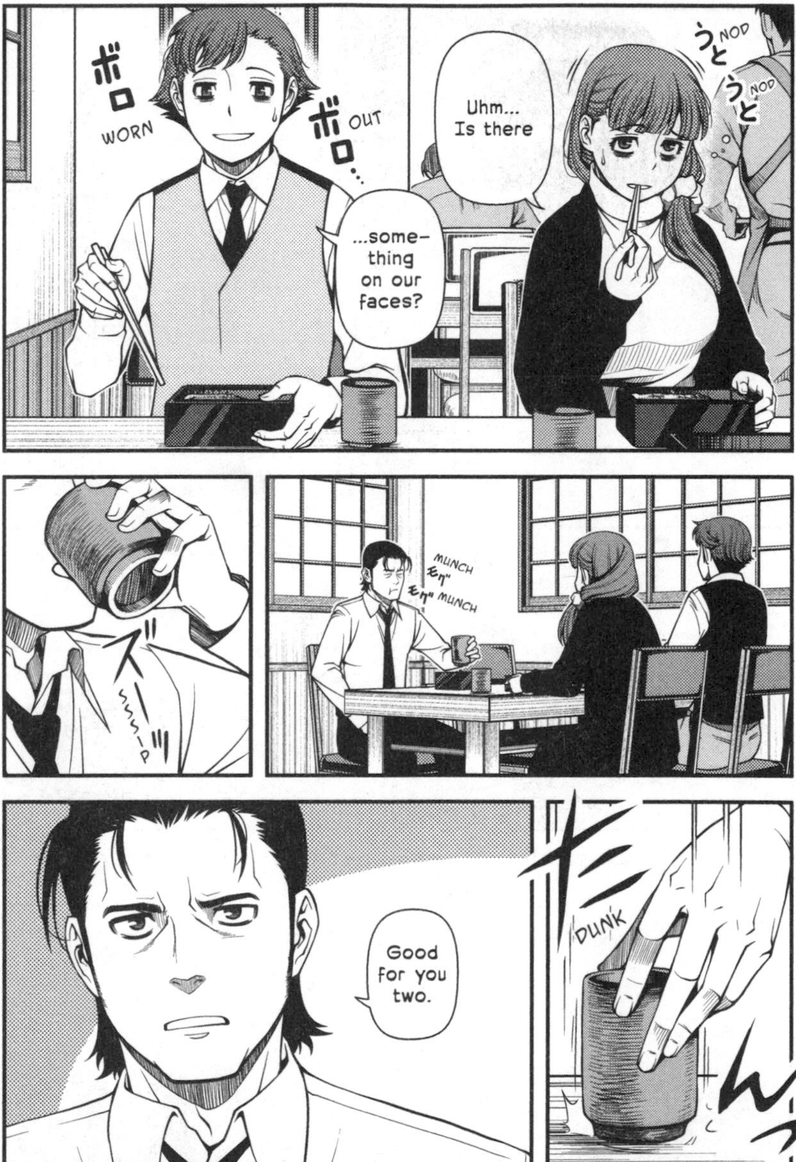
うと NOD
うと NOD
Uhm... Is there
...some-thing on our faces?
ボロ WORN
ボロ... OUT
MUNCH モグ
モグ MUNCH
ズー
SSSIP
DUNK
Good for you two.

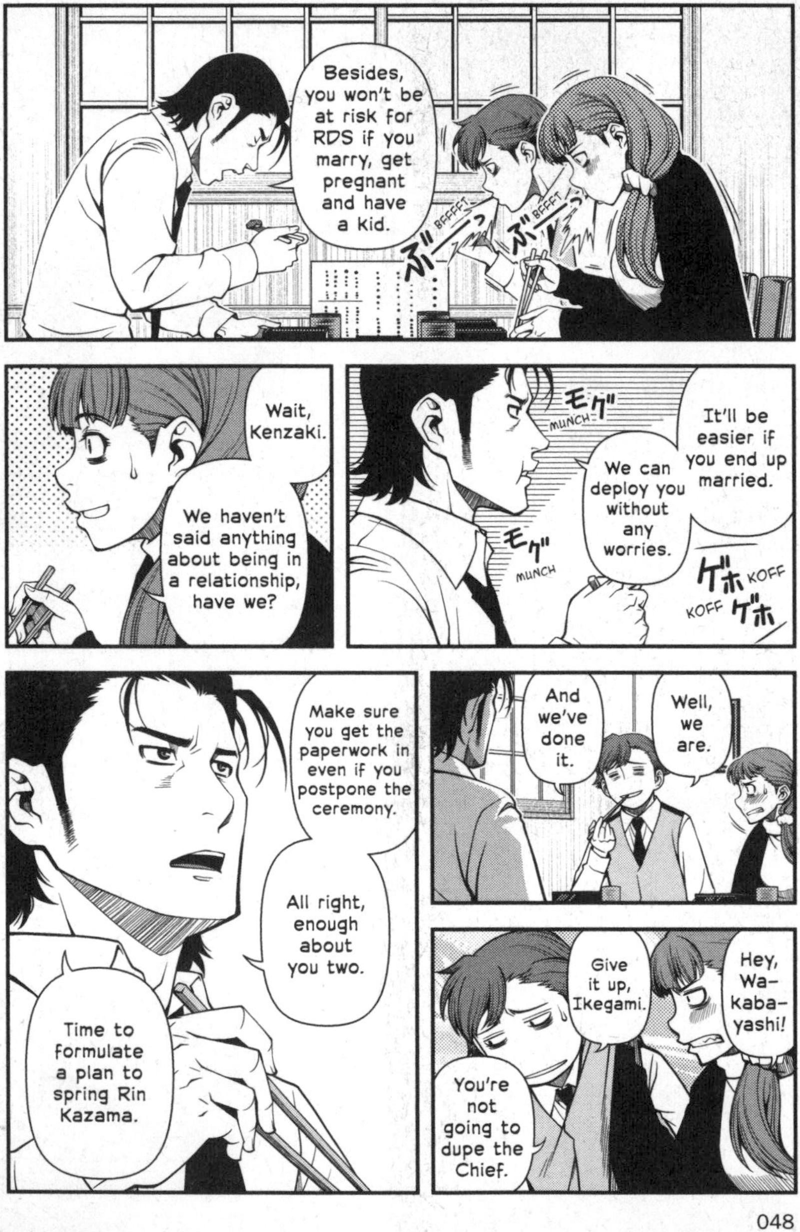
BFFFT
ぶーっ
BFFFFT
ぶーっ
Besides, you won't be at risk for RDS if you marry, get pregnant and have a kid.
It'll be easier if you end up married.
モグ
MUNCH
We can deploy you without any worries.
モグ
MUNCH
ゲホ KOFF
KOFF ゲホ
Wait, Kenzaki.
We haven't said anything about being in a relationship, have we?
Well, we are.
And we've done it.
Hey, Wa-kaba-yashi!
Give it up, Ikegami.
You're not going to dupe the Chief.
Make sure you get the paperwork in even if you postpone the ceremony.
All right, enough about you two.
Time to formulate a plan to spring Rin Kazama.

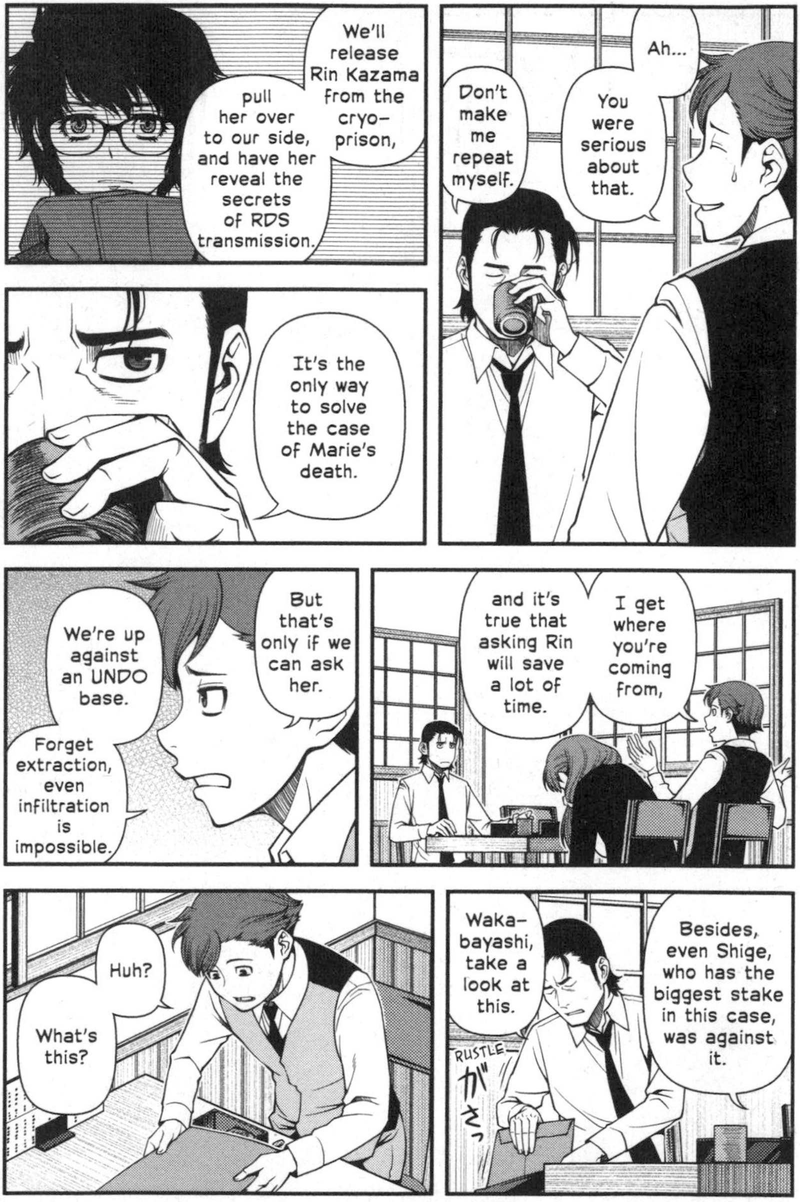
Ah...
You were serious about that.
Don't make me repeat myself.
We'll release Rin Kazama from the cryo-prison,
pull her over to our side, and have her reveal the secrets of RDS transmission.
It's the only way to solve the case of Marie's death.
I get where you're coming from,
and it's true that asking Rin will save a lot of time.
But that's only if we can ask her.
We're up against an UNDO base.
Forget extraction, even infiltration is impossible.
Besides, even Shige, who has the biggest stake in this case, was against it.
Waka-bayashi, take a look at this.
RUSTLE
がさっ
Huh?
What's this?

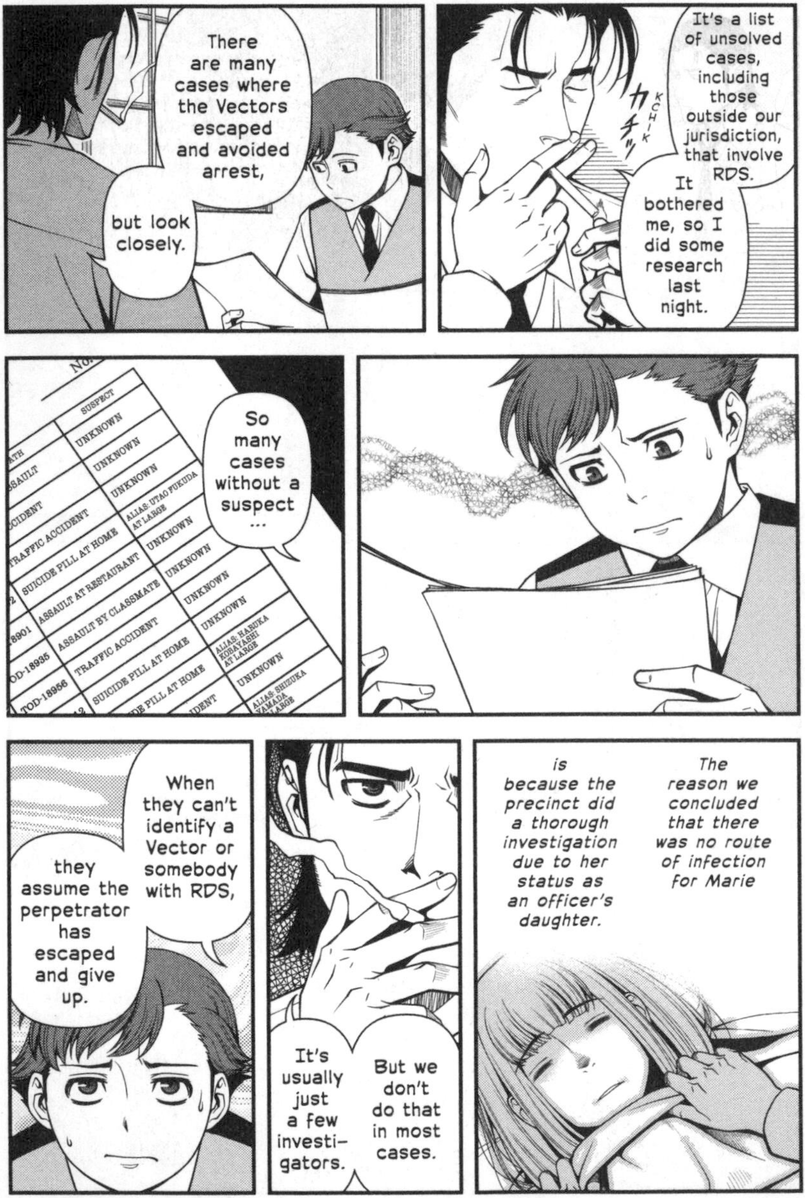
It's a list of unsolved cases, including those outside our jurisdiction, that involve RDS.
カチッ
KCHIK
It bothered me, so I did some research last night.
There are many cases where the Vectors escaped and avoided arrest,
but look closely.
So many cases without a suspect ...
The reason we concluded that there was no route of infection for Marie
is because the precinct did a thorough investigation due to her status as an officer's daughter.
But we don't do that in most cases.
It's usually just a few investi-gators.
When they can't identify a Vector or somebody with RDS,
they assume the perpetrator has escaped and give up.

*Suspect may be listed as "unknown" in cases where no suspects were identified at all.

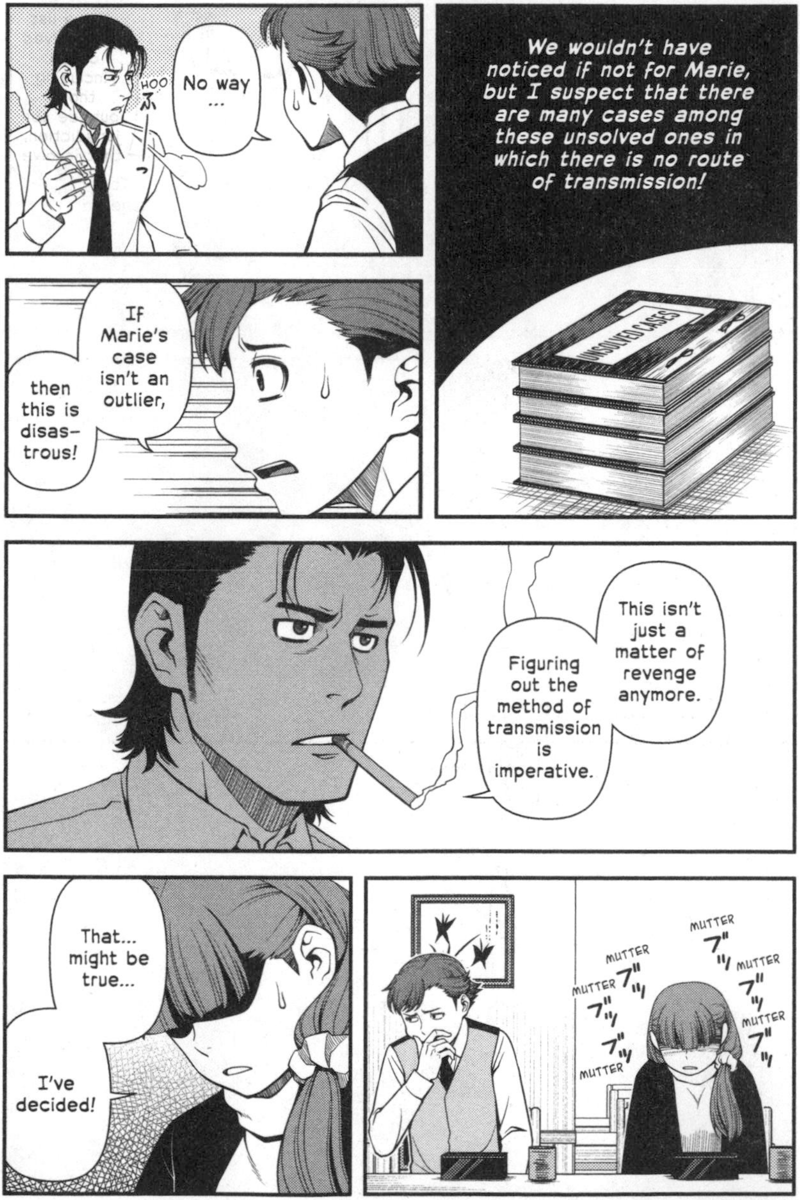
We wouldn't have noticed if not for Marie, but I suspect that there are many cases among these unsolved ones in which there is no route of transmission!
UNSOLVED CASES
No way ...
HOO ふ
If Marie's case isn't an outlier,
then this is disastrous!
This isn't just a matter of revenge anymore.
Figuring out the method of transmission is imperative.
MUTTER ブツ
MUTTER ブツ
MUTTER ブツ
MUTTER ブツ
MUTTER ブツ
MUTTER ブツ
That... might be true...
I've decided!

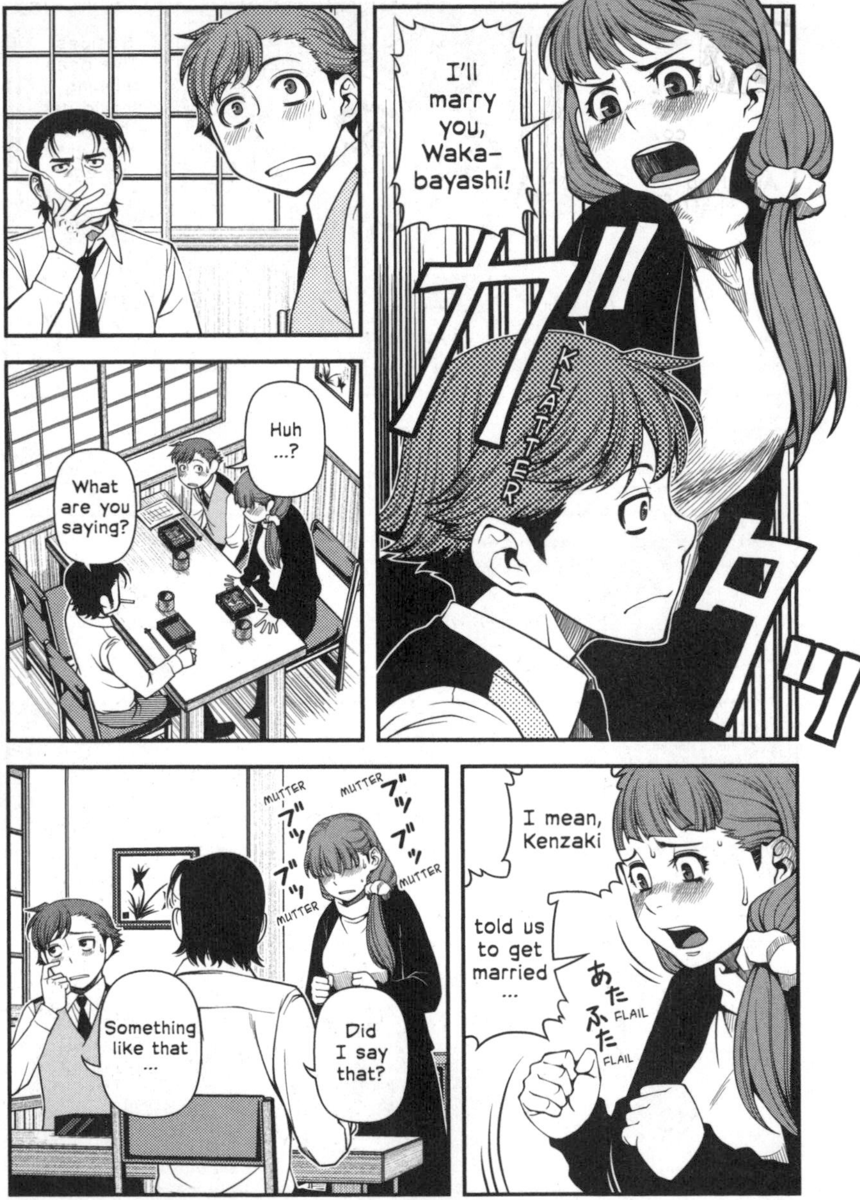
I'll marry you, Waka-bayashi!
ガタッ
KLATTER
Huh ...?
What are you saying?
I mean, Kenzaki
told us to get married ...
あたふた
FLAIL
FLAIL
MUTTER
ブツブツ
MUTTER
ブツブツ
MUTTER
MUTTER
Did I say that?
Something like that ...

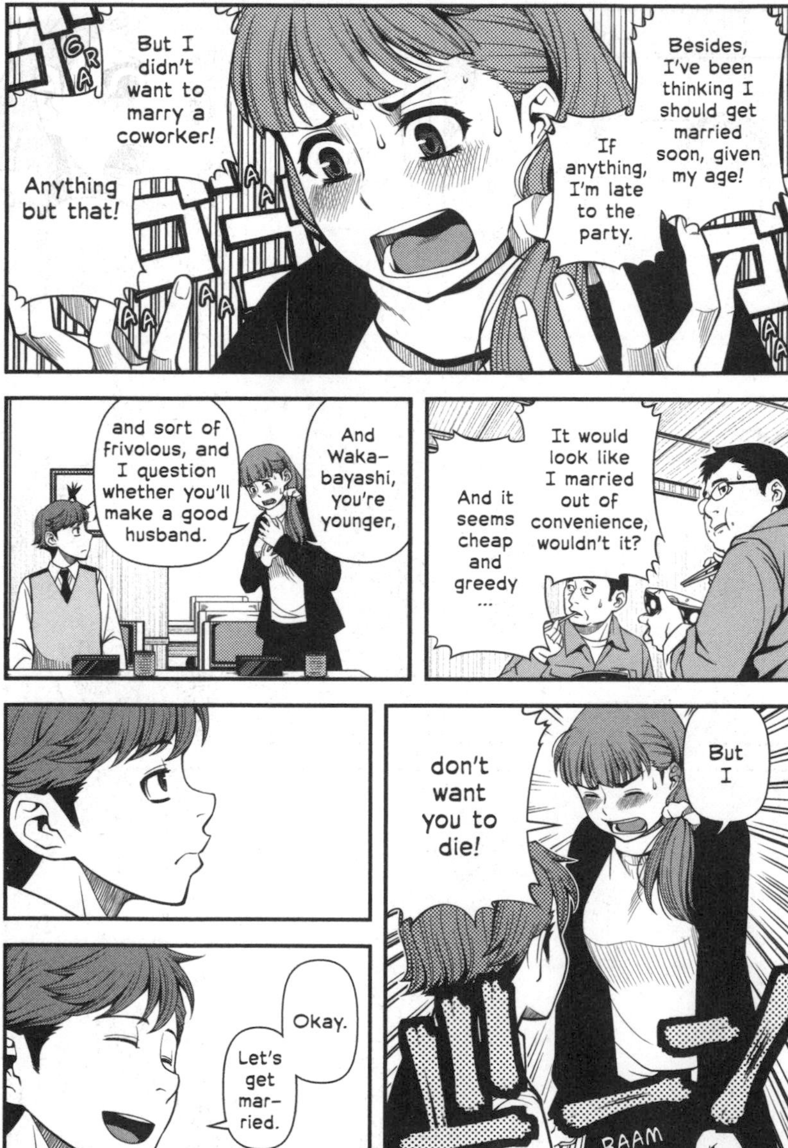
Besides, I've been thinking I should get married soon, given my age!
If anything, I'm late to the party.
But I didn't want to marry a coworker!
Anything but that!
GRA
It would look like I married out of convenience, wouldn't it?
And it seems cheap and greedy ...
And Waka-bayashi, you're younger,
and sort of frivolous, and I question whether you'll make a good husband.
But I
don't want you to die!
BAAM
Okay.
Let's get mar-ried.

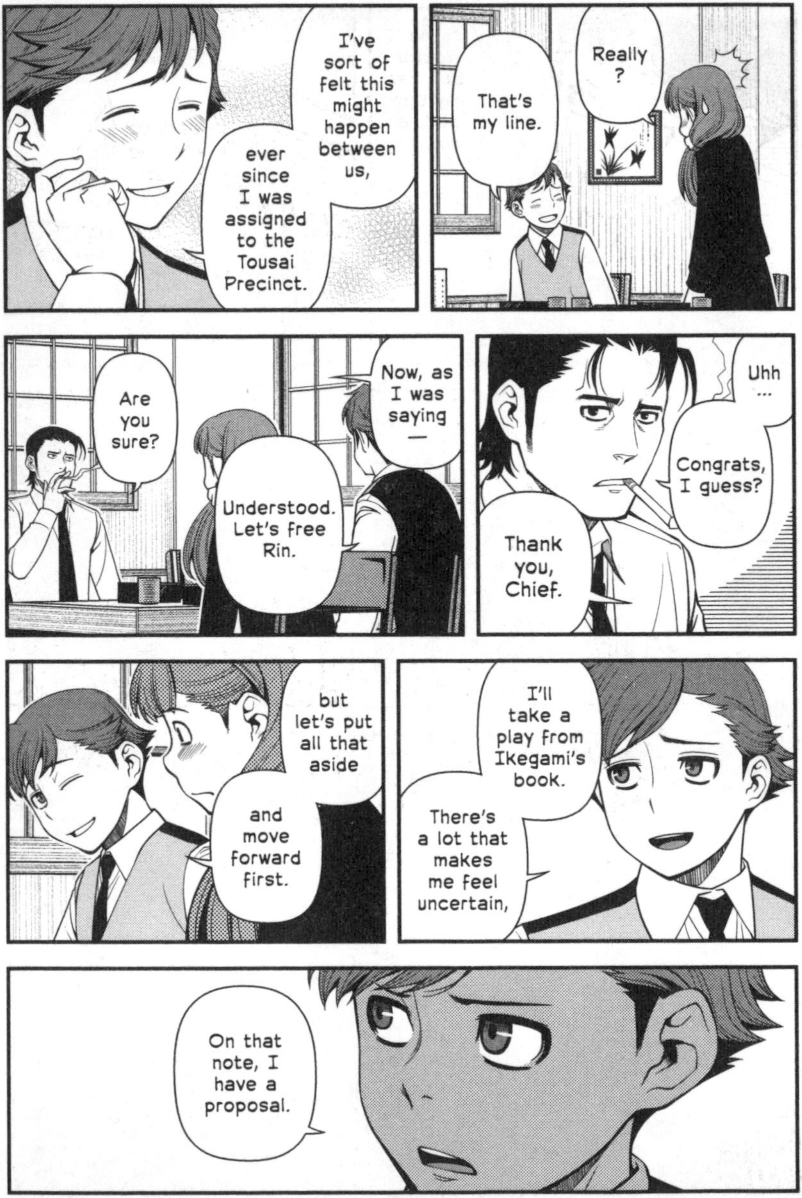
Really?
That's my line.
I've sort of felt this might happen between us,
ever since I was assigned to the Tousai Precinct.
Uhh...
Congrats, I guess?
Thank you, Chief.
Now, as I was saying —
Are you sure?
Understood. Let's free Rin.
I'll take a play from Ikegami's book.
There's a lot that makes me feel uncertain,
but let's put all that aside
and move forward first.
On that note, I have a proposal.

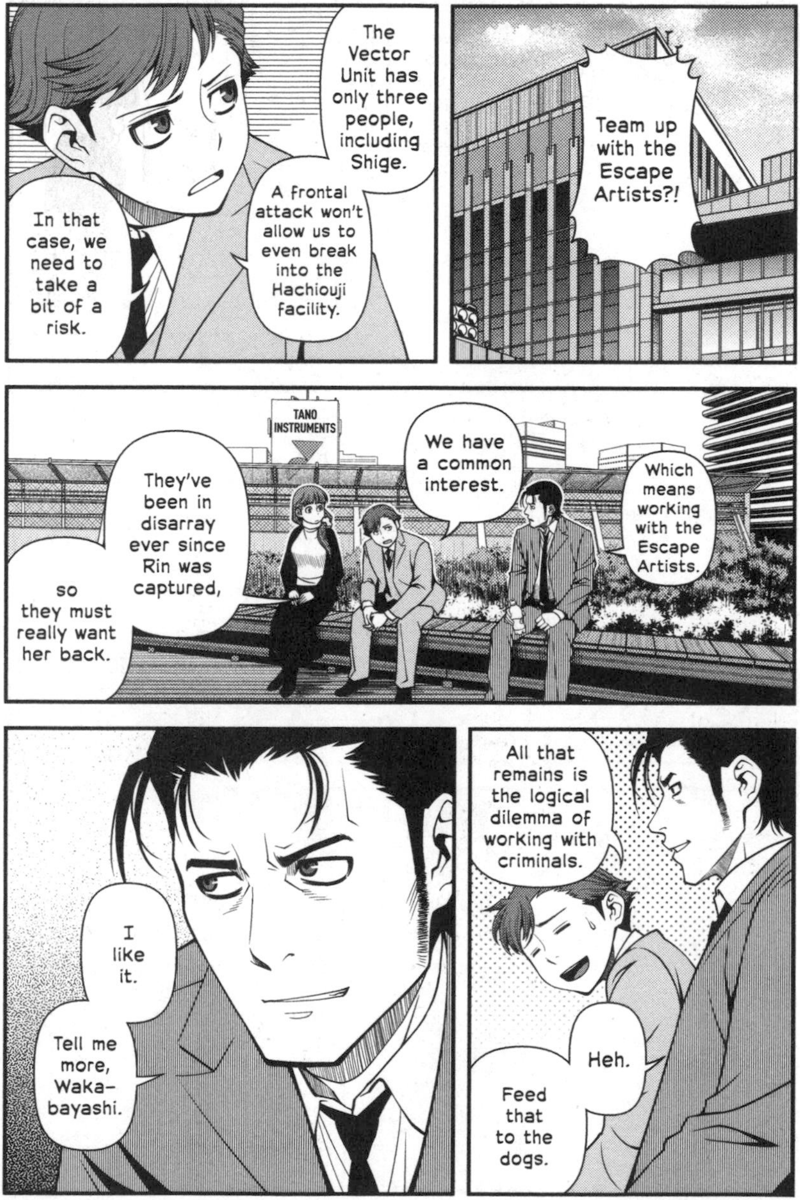
Team up with the Escape Artists?!
The Vector Unit has only three people, including Shige.
A frontal attack won't allow us to even break into the Hachiouji facility.
In that case, we need to take a bit of a risk.
Which means working with the Escape Artists.
We have a common interest.
TANO INSTRUMENTS
They've been in disarray ever since Rin was captured,
so they must really want her back.
All that remains is the logical dilemma of working with criminals.
Heh.
Feed that to the dogs.
I like it.
Tell me more, Waka-bayashi.

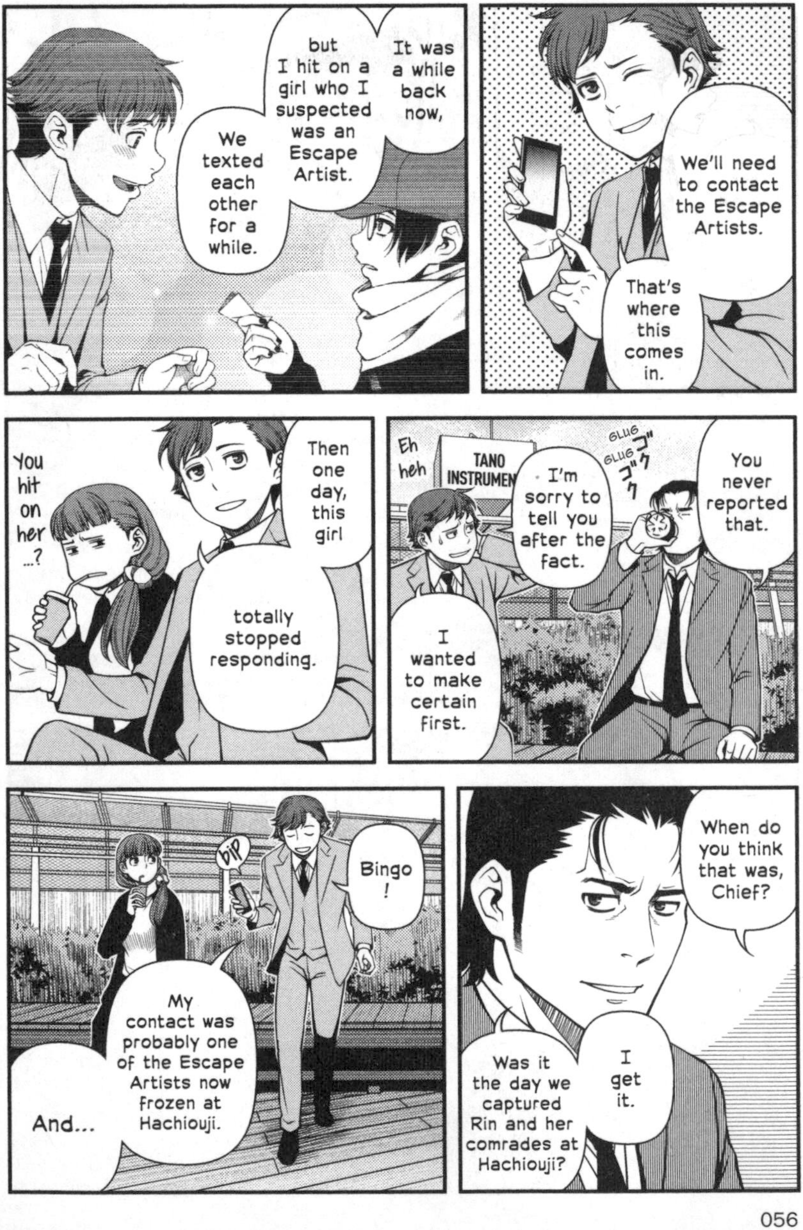
We'll need to contact the Escape Artists.
That's where this comes in.
It was a while back now,
but I hit on a girl who I suspected was an Escape Artist.
We texted each other for a while.
You never reported that.
GLUG GLUG
ゴクゴク
TANO INSTRUMEN
Eh heh
I'm sorry to tell you after the fact.
I wanted to make certain first.
Then one day, this girl
totally stopped responding.
You hit on her ...?
When do you think that was, Chief?
I get it.
Was it the day we captured Rin and her comrades at Hachiouji?
Bingo!
bip
My contact was probably one of the Escape Artists now frozen at Hachiouji.
And...

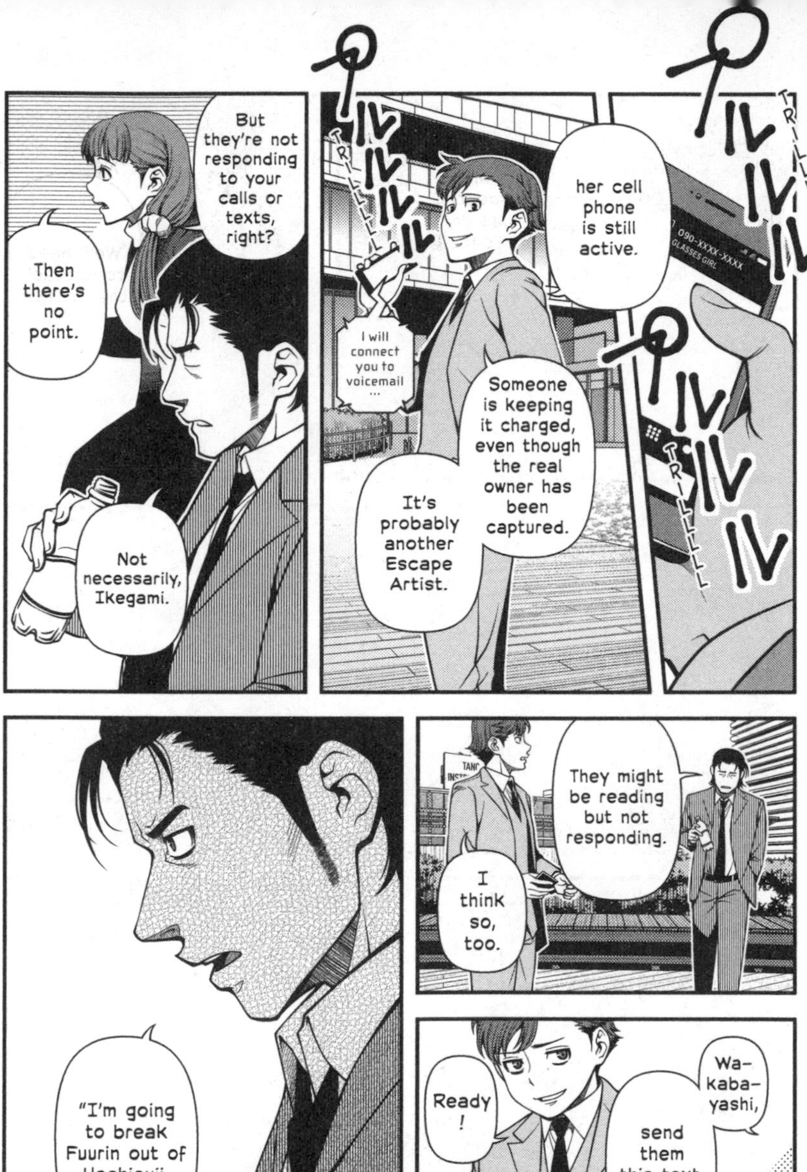
TRILLLLL
090-XXXX-XXXX
GLASSES GIRL
her cell phone is still active.
TRILLLL
TRILLLL
I will connect you to voicemail ...
Someone is keeping it charged, even though the real owner has been captured.
It's probably another Escape Artist.
But they're not responding to your calls or texts, right?
Then there's no point.
Not necessarily, Ikegami.
They might be reading but not responding.
I think so, too.
Wa-kaba-yashi,
send them this text, verbatim.
Ready!
bip
"I'm going to break Fuurin out of Hachiouji.

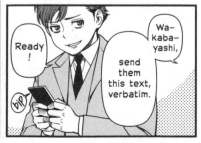

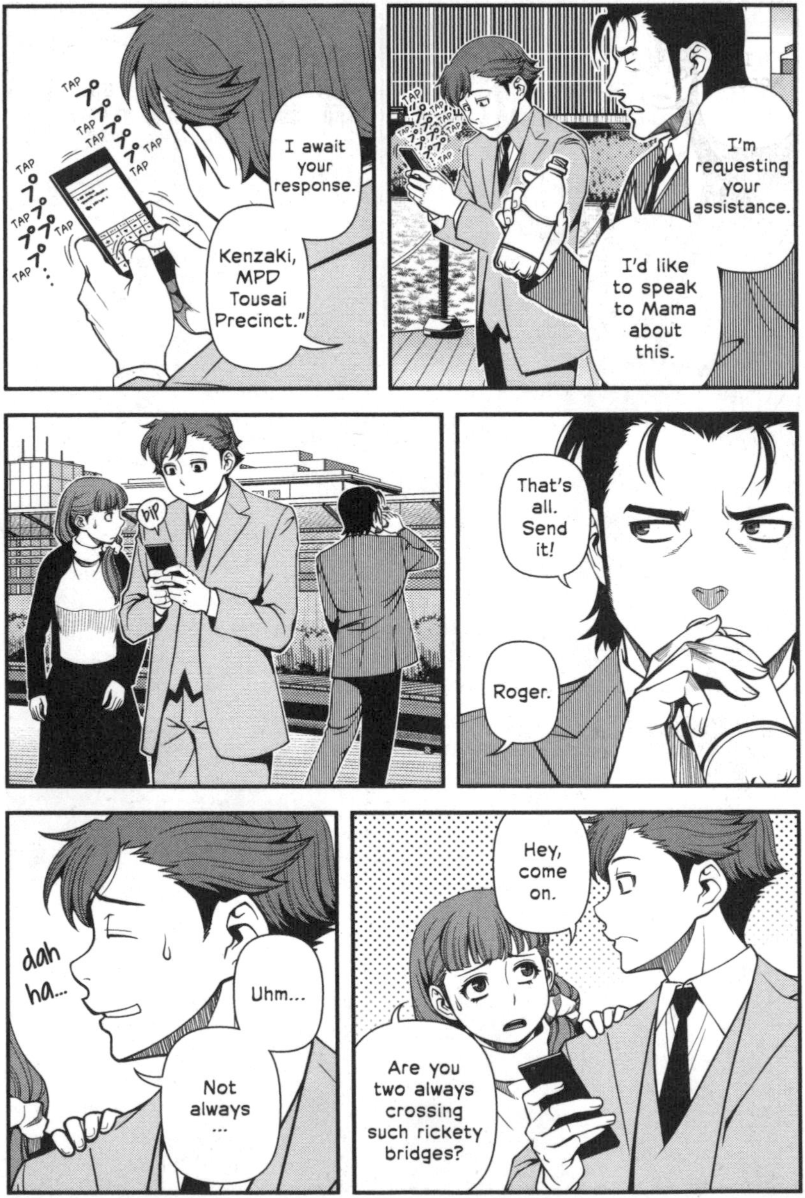
TAP
I'm requesting your assistance.
I'd like to speak to Mama about this.
TAP
I await your response.
Kenzaki, MPD Tousai Precinct."
That's all. Send it!
Roger.
bip
Hey, come on.
Are you two always crossing such rickety bridges?
Uhm...
dah ha...
Not always ...

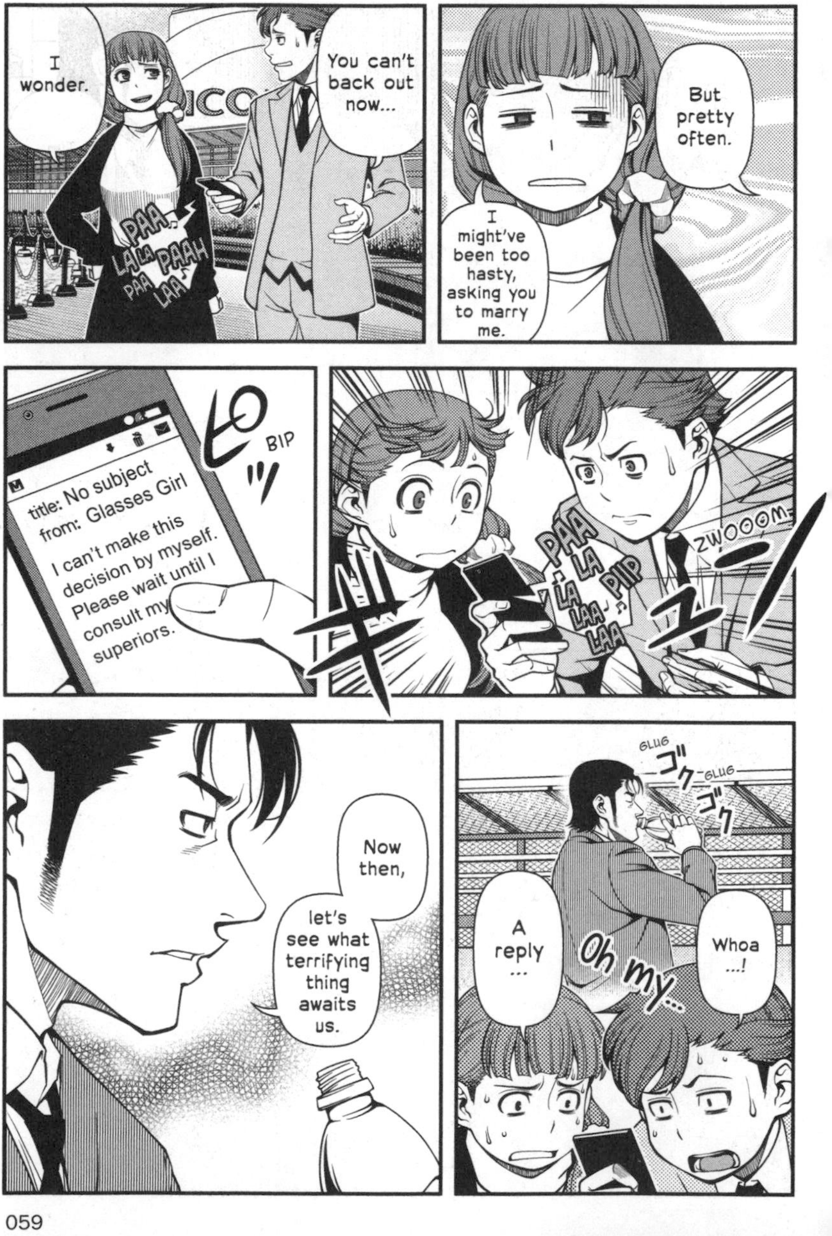
But pretty often.
I might've been too hasty, asking you to marry me.
You can't back out now...
PAA LA LA PAAH PAA LAA
I wonder.
ZWOOOM
PAA LA PIP LA LAA LAA
BIP
title: No subject
from: Glasses Girl
I can't make this decision by myself. Please wait until I consult my superiors.
GLUG GLUG
Whoa ...!
Oh my...
A reply ...
Now then,
let's see what terrifying thing awaits us.

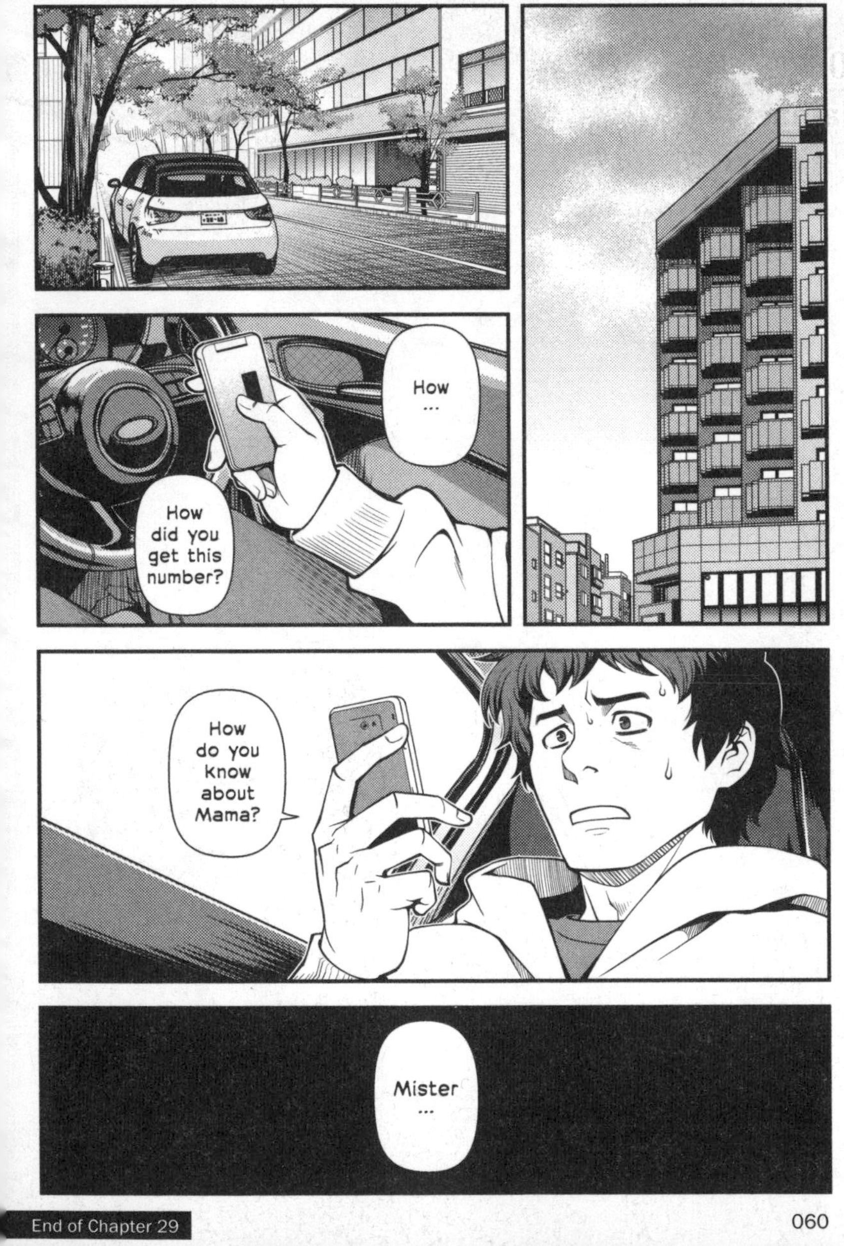
How ...
How did you get this number?
How do you know about Mama?
Mister ...

End of Chapter 29

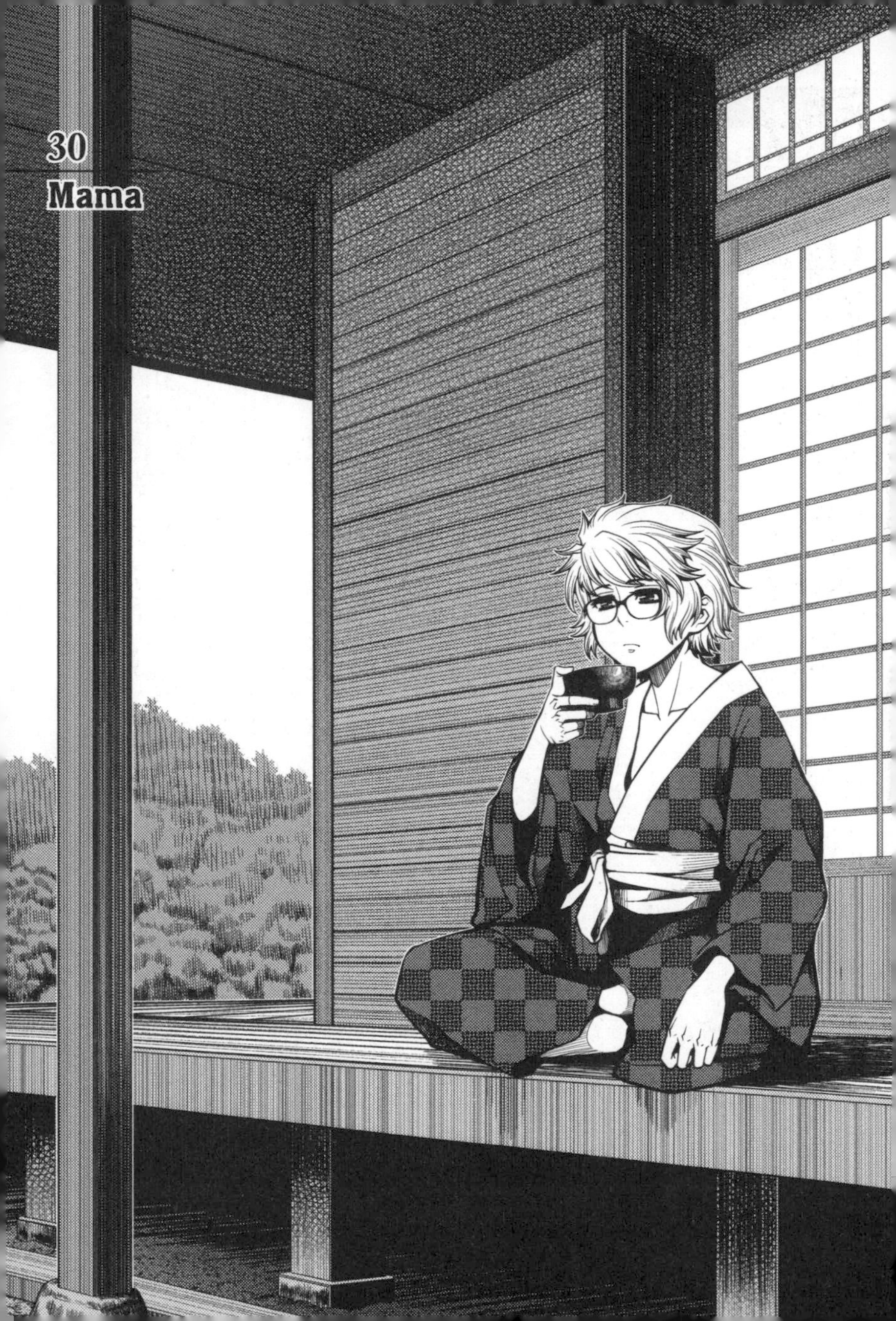
30
Mama

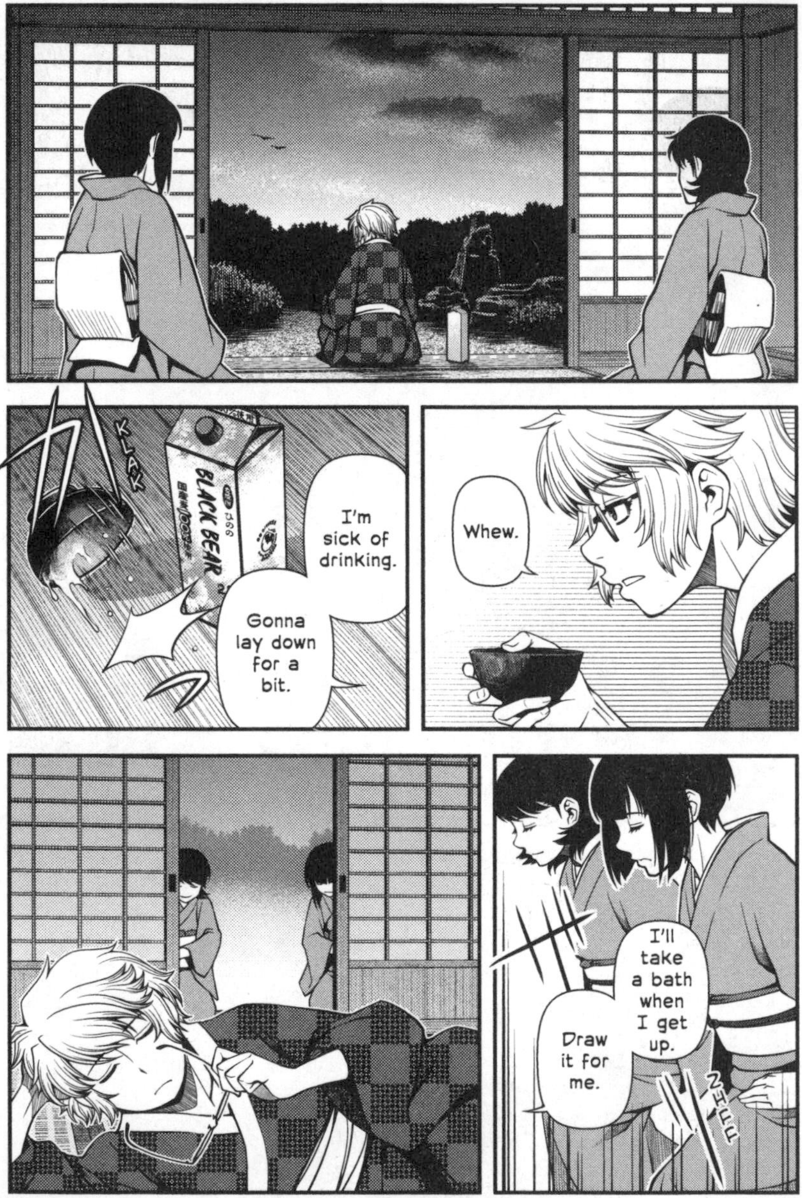

Whew.
I'm sick of drinking.
KLAK
BLACK BEAR
Gonna lay down for a bit.
I'll take a bath when I get up.
Draw it for me.

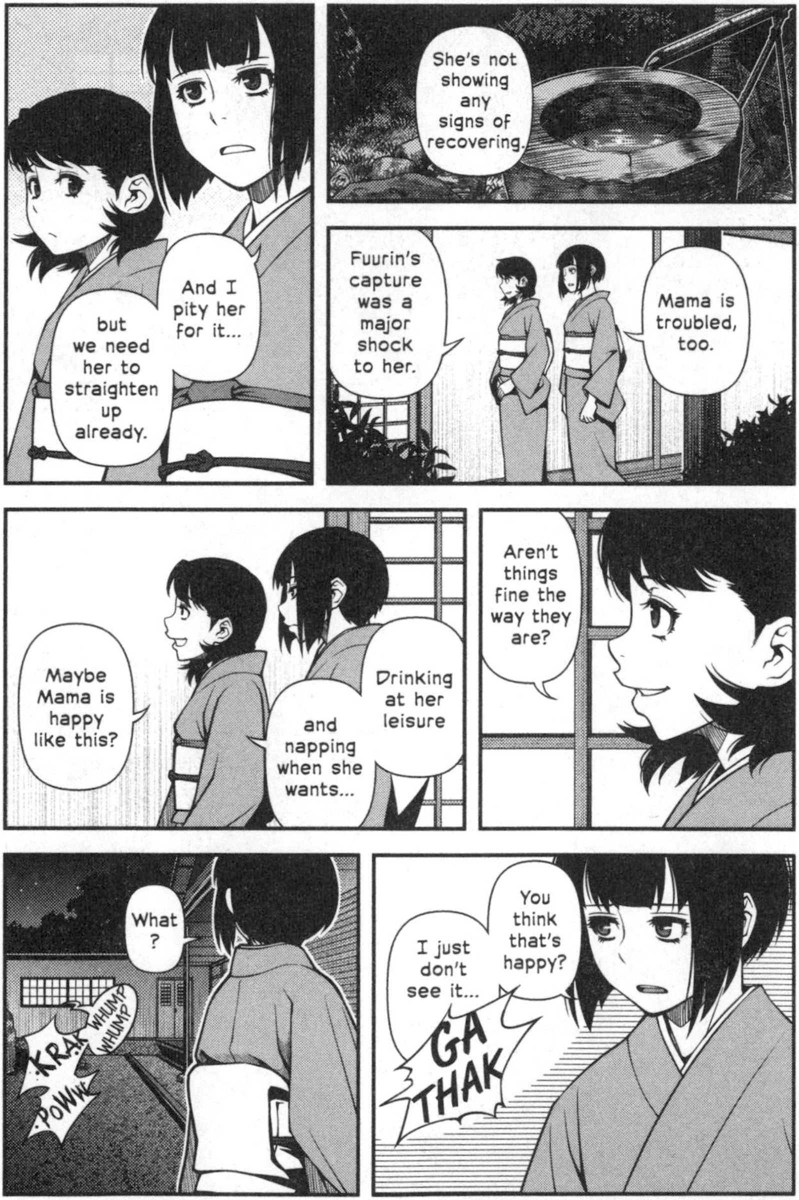

She's not showing any signs of recovering.
Mama is troubled, too.
Fuurin's capture was a major shock to her.
And I pity her for it...
but we need her to straighten up already.
Aren't things fine the way they are?
Drinking at her leisure
and napping when she wants...
Maybe Mama is happy like this?
You think that's happy?
I just don't see it...
GA THAK
What?
WHUMP WHUMP
KRAK
POWW

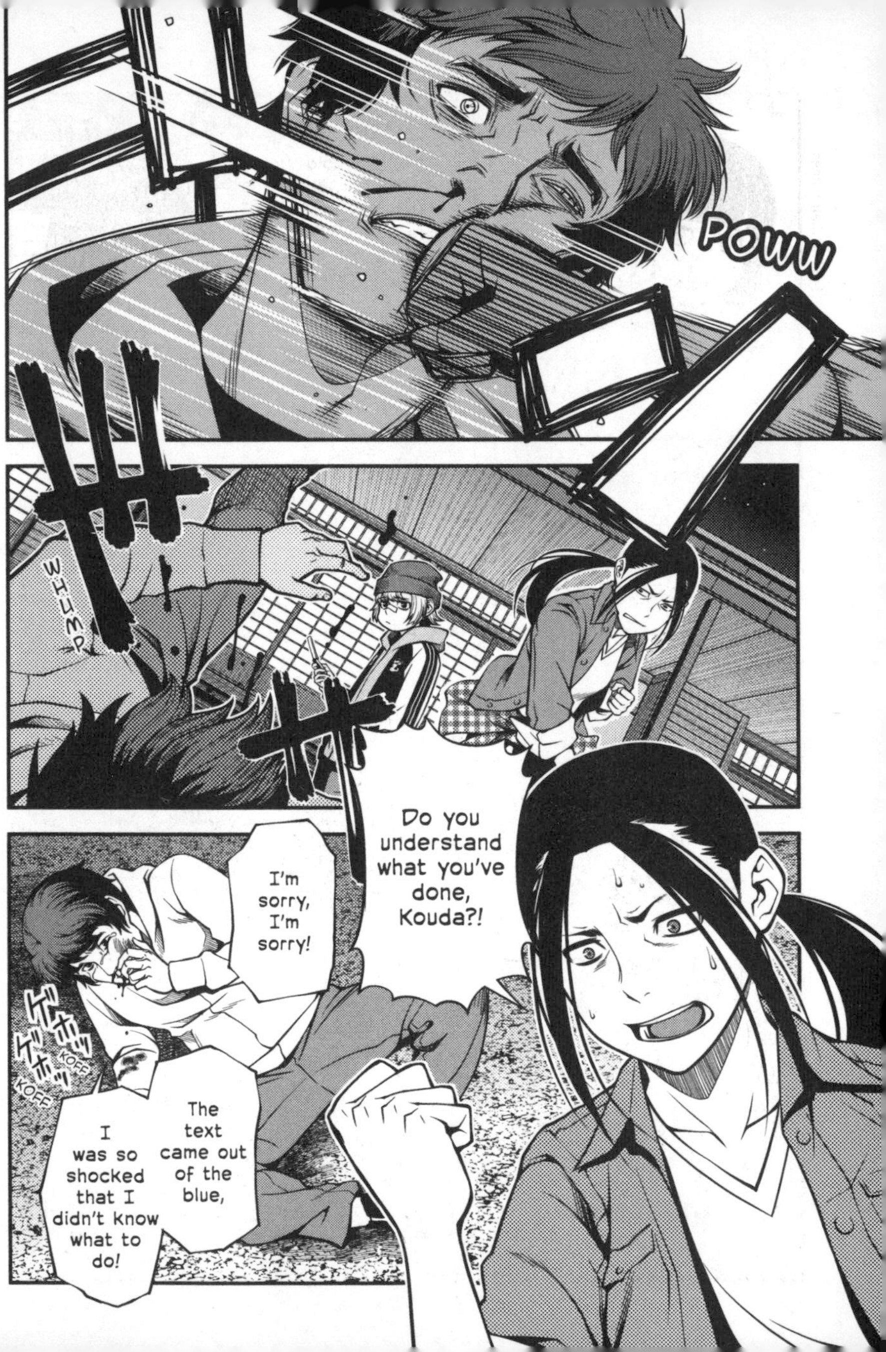
POWW
WHUMP
Do you understand what you've done, Kouda?!
I'm sorry, I'm sorry!
ゲホッ KOFF
ゲホッ KOFF
The text came out of the blue,
I was so shocked that I didn't know what to do!

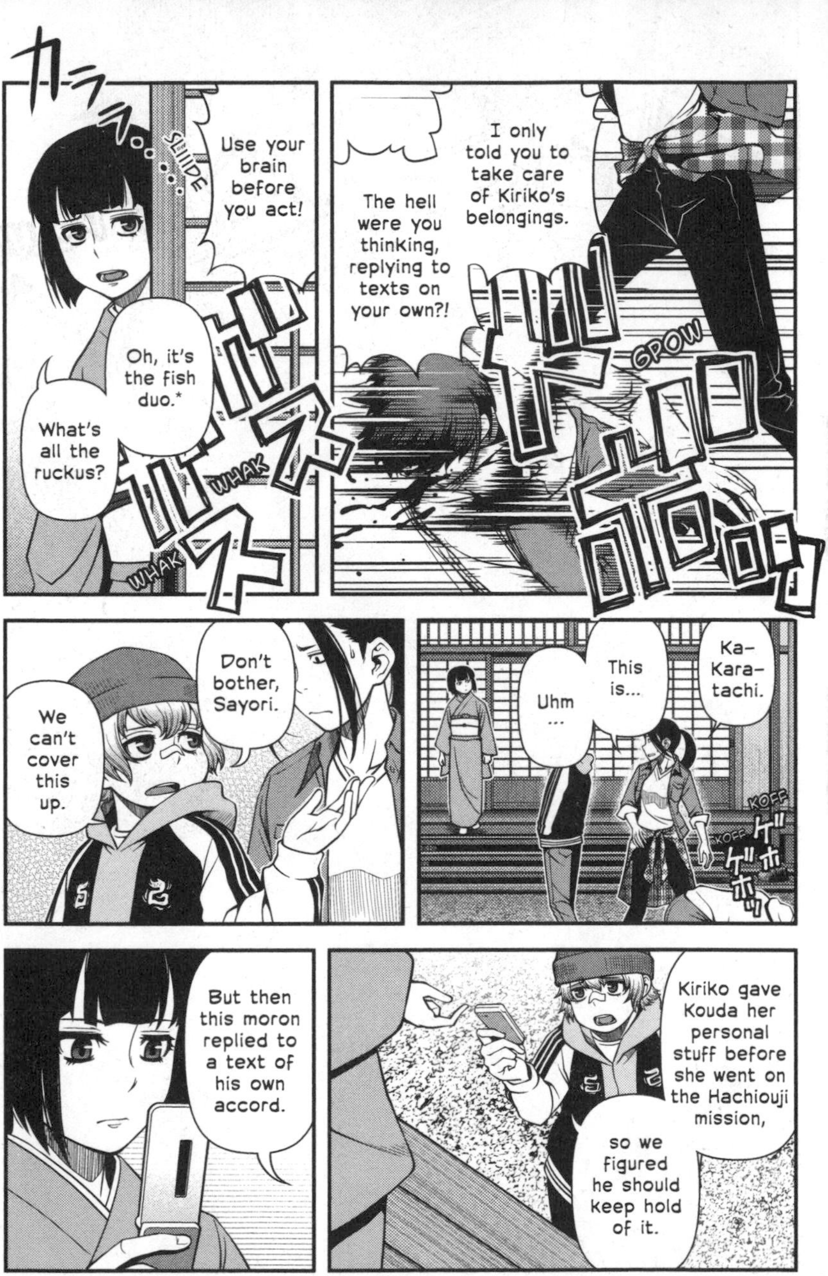
I only told you to take care of Kiriko's belongings.
The hell were you thinking, replying to texts on your own?!
GPOW
SLIIIDE
Use your brain before you act!
WHAK
WHAK
Oh, it's the fish duo.*
What's all the ruckus?
Ka-Kara-tachi.
This is...
Uhm ...
KOFF
KOFF
Don't bother, Sayori.
We can't cover this up.
Kiriko gave Kouda her personal stuff before she went on the Hachiouji mission,
so we figured he should keep hold of it.
But then this moron replied to a text of his own accord.

*Misago and Sayori have the character for "fish" in their names.

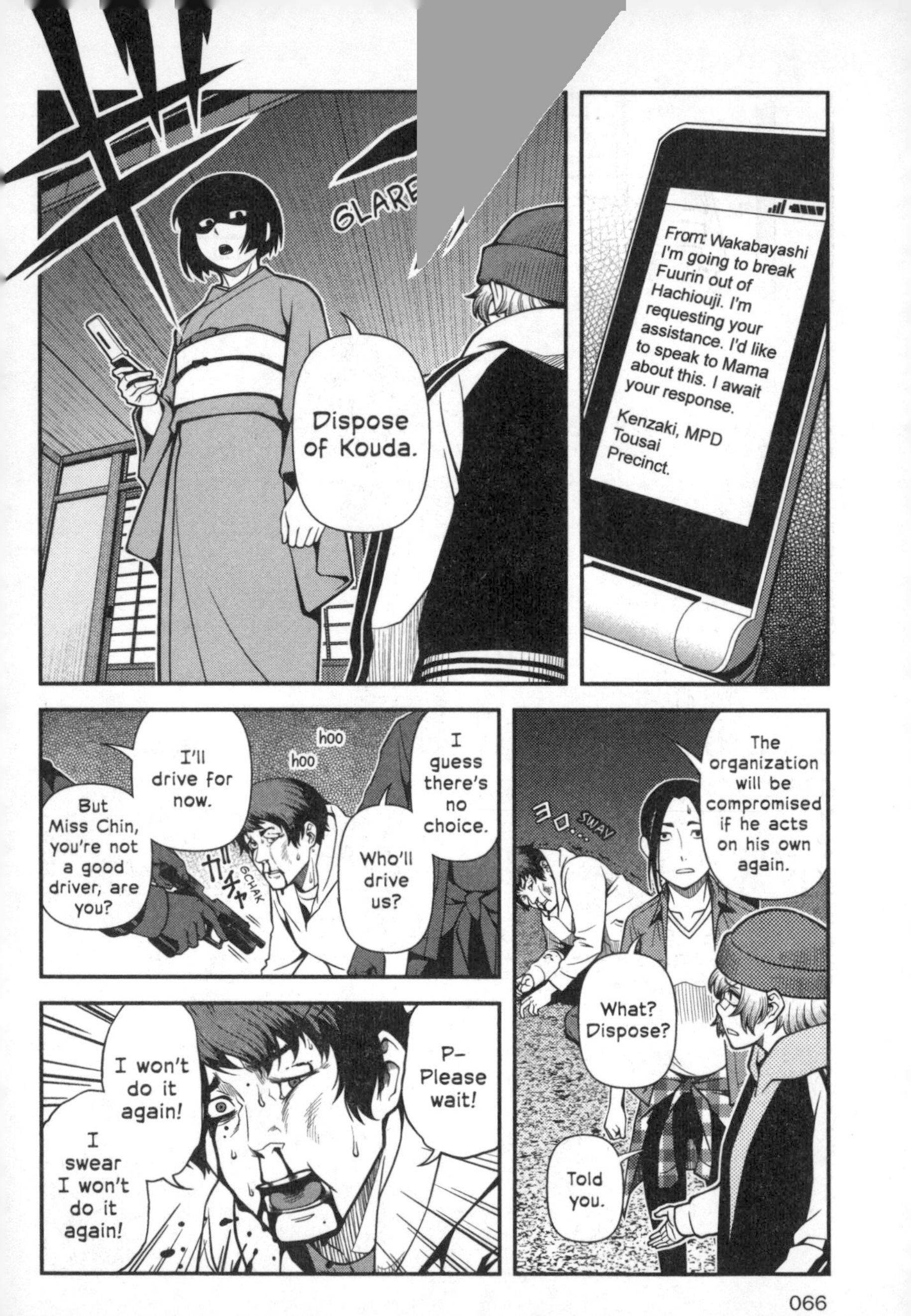
From: Wakabayashi
I'm going to break Fuurin out of Hachiouji. I'm requesting your assistance. I'd like to speak to Mama about this. I await your response.
Kenzaki, MPD Tousai Precinct.
GLARE
Dispose of Kouda.
The organization will be compromised if he acts on his own again.
ヨロ… SWAY
What? Dispose?
Told you.
I guess there's no choice.
Who'll drive us?
hoo
hoo
I'll drive for now.
But Miss Chin, you're not a good driver, are you?
ガチャ GCHAK
P- Please wait!
I won't do it again!
I swear I won't do it again!

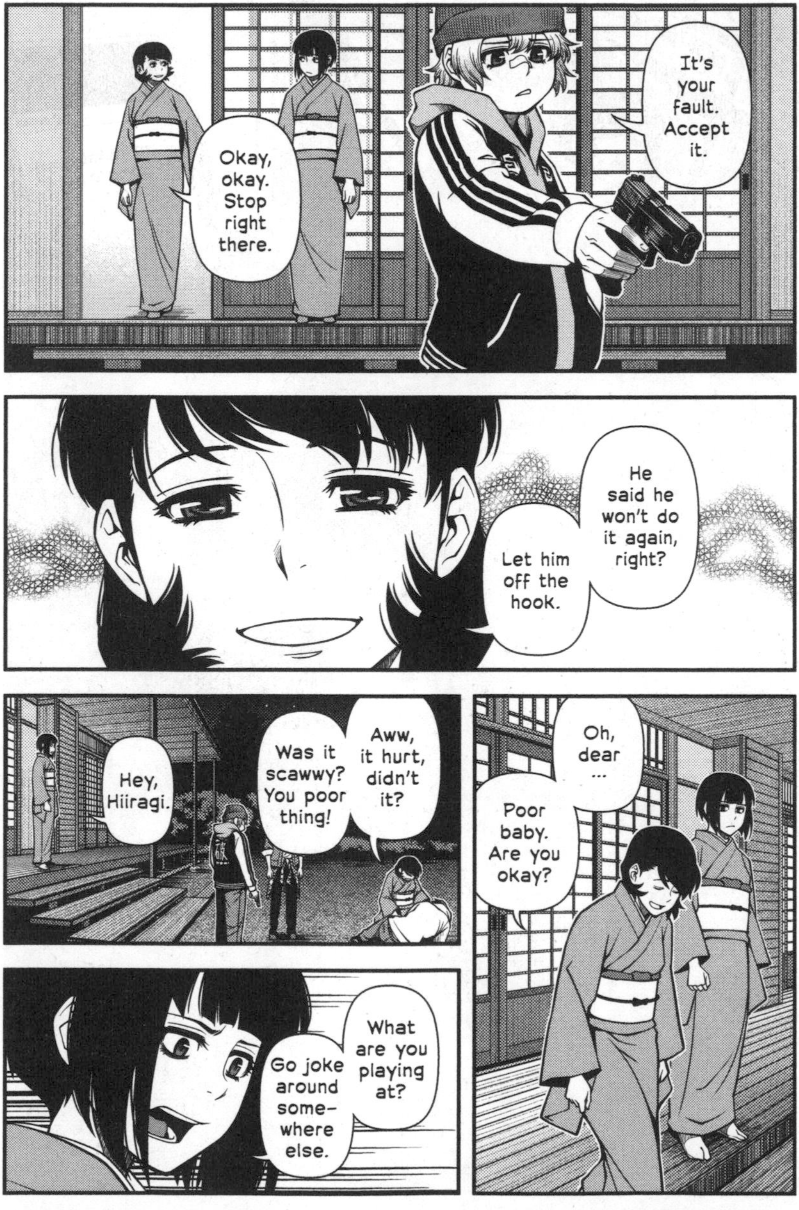
It's your fault. Accept it.
Okay, okay. Stop right there.
He said he won't do it again, right?
Let him off the hook.
Oh, dear ...
Poor baby. Are you okay?
Aww, it hurt, didn't it?
Was it scawwy? You poor thing!
Hey, Hiiragi.
What are you playing at?
Go joke around some-where else.

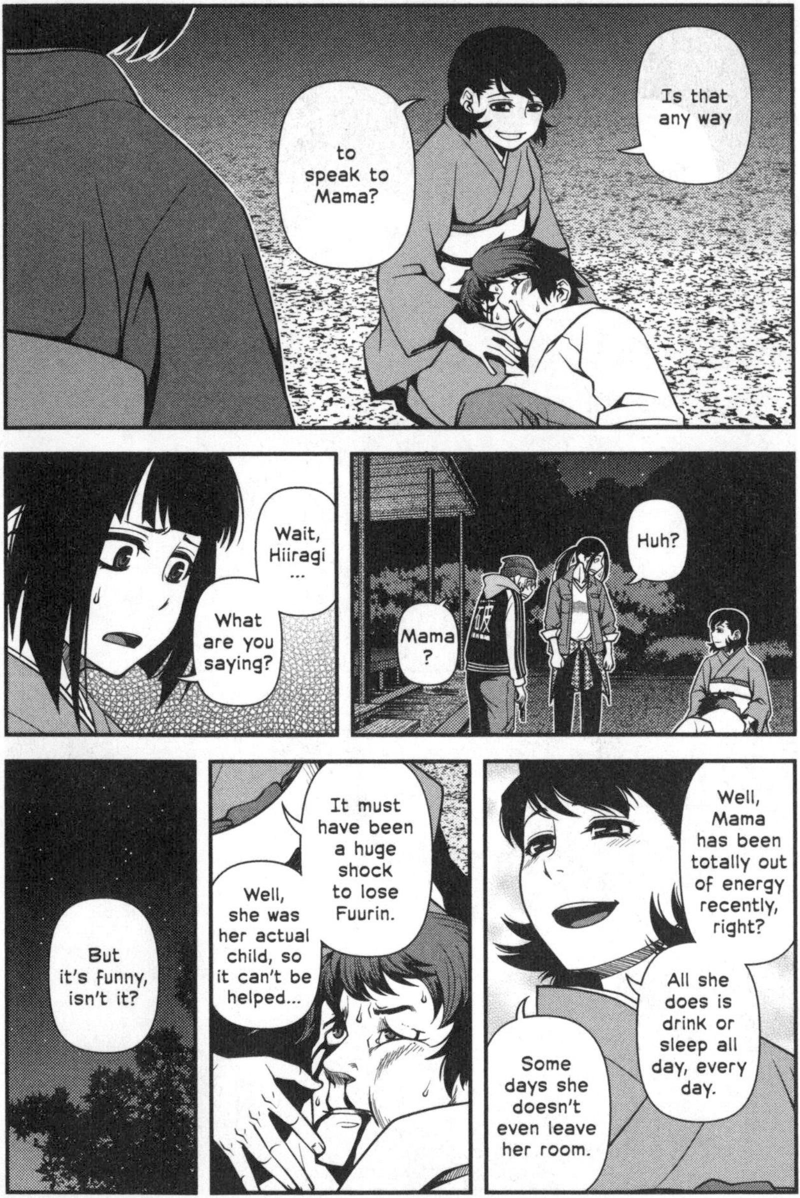
Is that any way
to speak to Mama?
Huh?
Mama ?
Wait, Hiiragi ...
What are you saying?
Well, Mama has been totally out of energy recently, right?
All she does is drink or sleep all day, every day.
Some days she doesn't even leave her room.
It must have been a huge shock to lose Fuurin.
Well, she was her actual child, so it can't be helped...
But it's funny, isn't it?

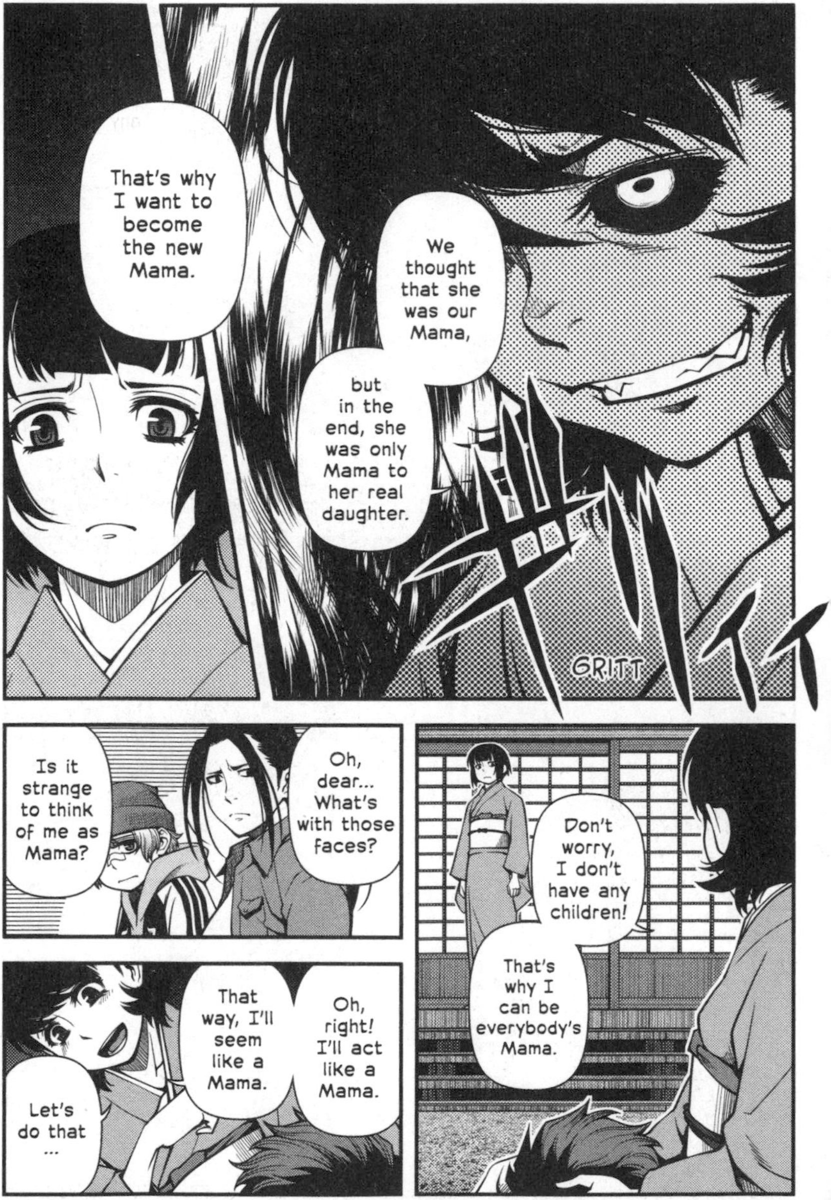

We thought that she was our Mama,
but in the end, she was only Mama to her real daughter.
GRITT
That's why I want to become the new Mama.
Don't worry, I don't have any children!
That's why I can be everybody's Mama.
Oh, dear... What's with those faces?
Is it strange to think of me as Mama?
Oh, right! I'll act like a Mama.
That way, I'll seem like a Mama.
Let's do that ...

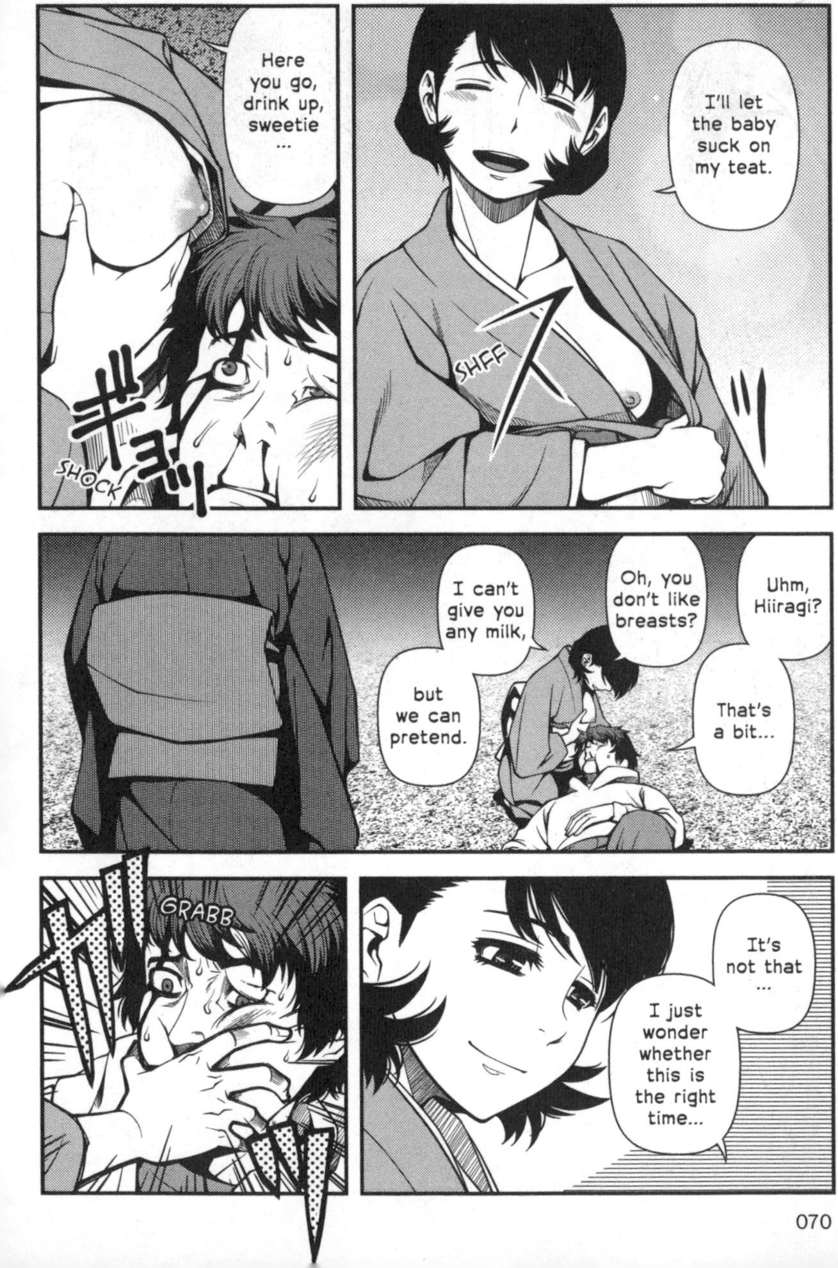
I'll let the baby suck on my teat.
SHFF
Here you go, drink up, sweetie ...
ギョッ
SHOCK
Uhm, Hiiragi?
That's a bit...
Oh, you don't like breasts?
I can't give you any milk,
but we can pretend.
It's not that ...
I just wonder whether this is the right time...
GRABB

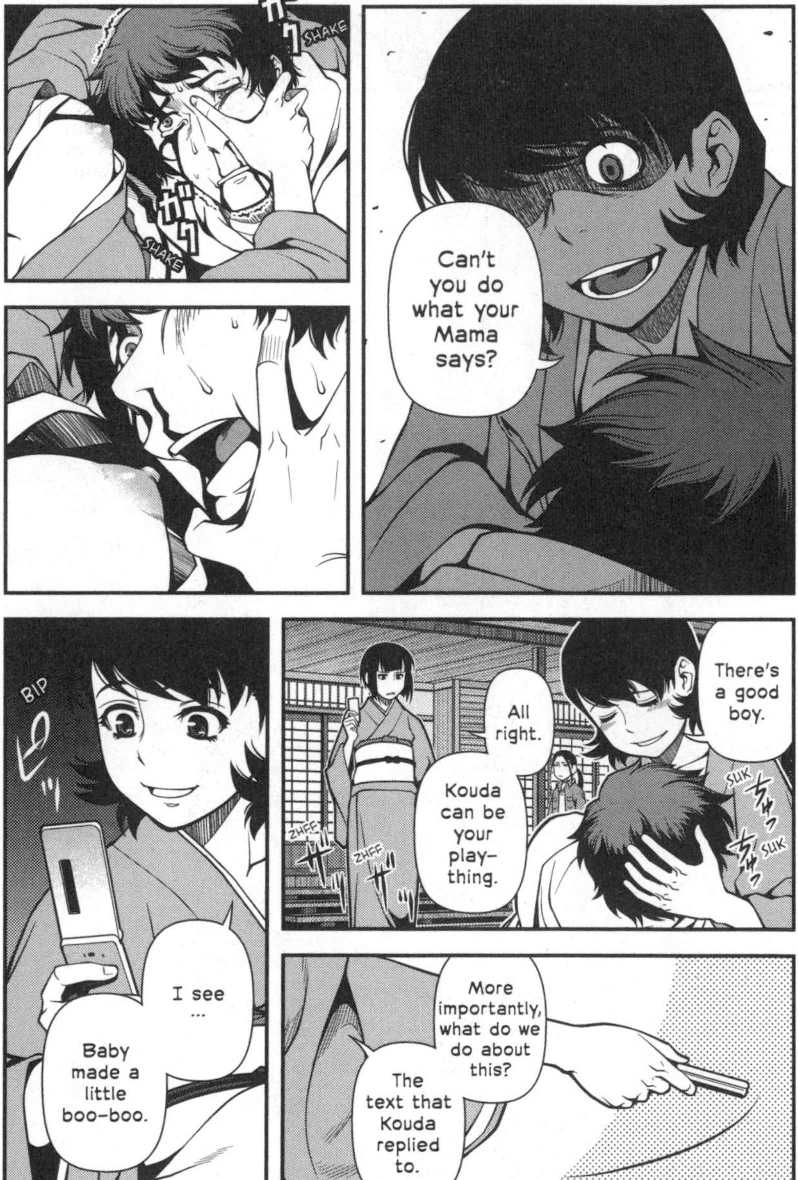
Can't you do what your Mama says?
SHAKE
SHAKE
There's a good boy.
SUK
SUK
All right.
Kouda can be your play-thing.
ZHFF
ZHFF
More importantly, what do we do about this?
The text that Kouda replied to.
BIP
I see ...
Baby made a little boo-boo.

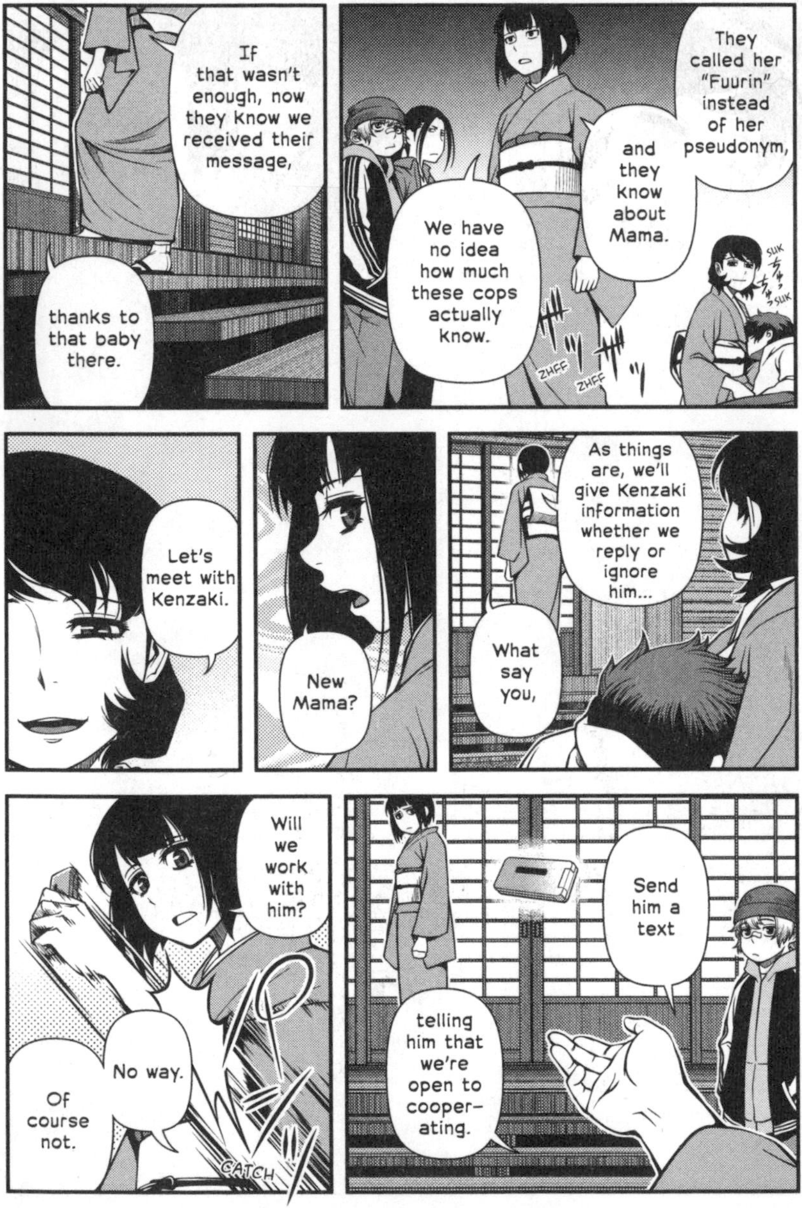
They called her "Fuurin" instead of her pseudonym,
and they know about Mama.
SUK
SUK
We have no idea how much these cops actually know.
ZHFF
ZHFF
If that wasn't enough, now they know we received their message,
thanks to that baby there.
As things are, we'll give Kenzaki information whether we reply or ignore him...
What say you,
New Mama?
Let's meet with Kenzaki.
Send him a text
telling him that we're open to cooperating.
Will we work with him?
No way.
Of course not.
CATCH

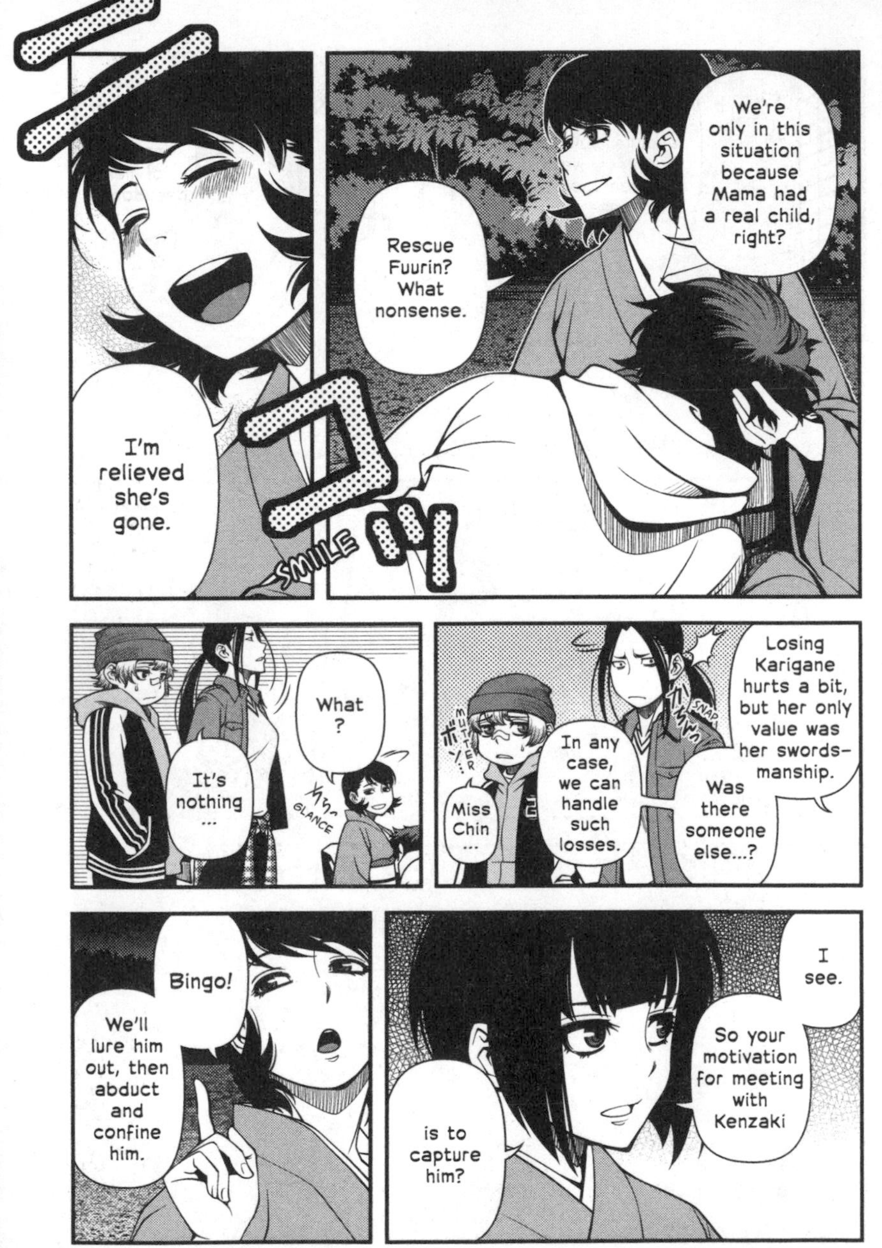
We're only in this situation because Mama had a real child, right?
Rescue Fuurin? What nonsense.
I'm relieved she's gone.
SMILE
Losing Karigane hurts a bit, but her only value was her swordsmanship.
SNAP
Was there someone else...?
In any case, we can handle such losses.
MUTTER
Miss Chin...
What?
GLANCE
It's nothing...
I see.
So your motivation for meeting with Kenzaki
is to capture him?
Bingo!
We'll lure him out, then abduct and confine him.

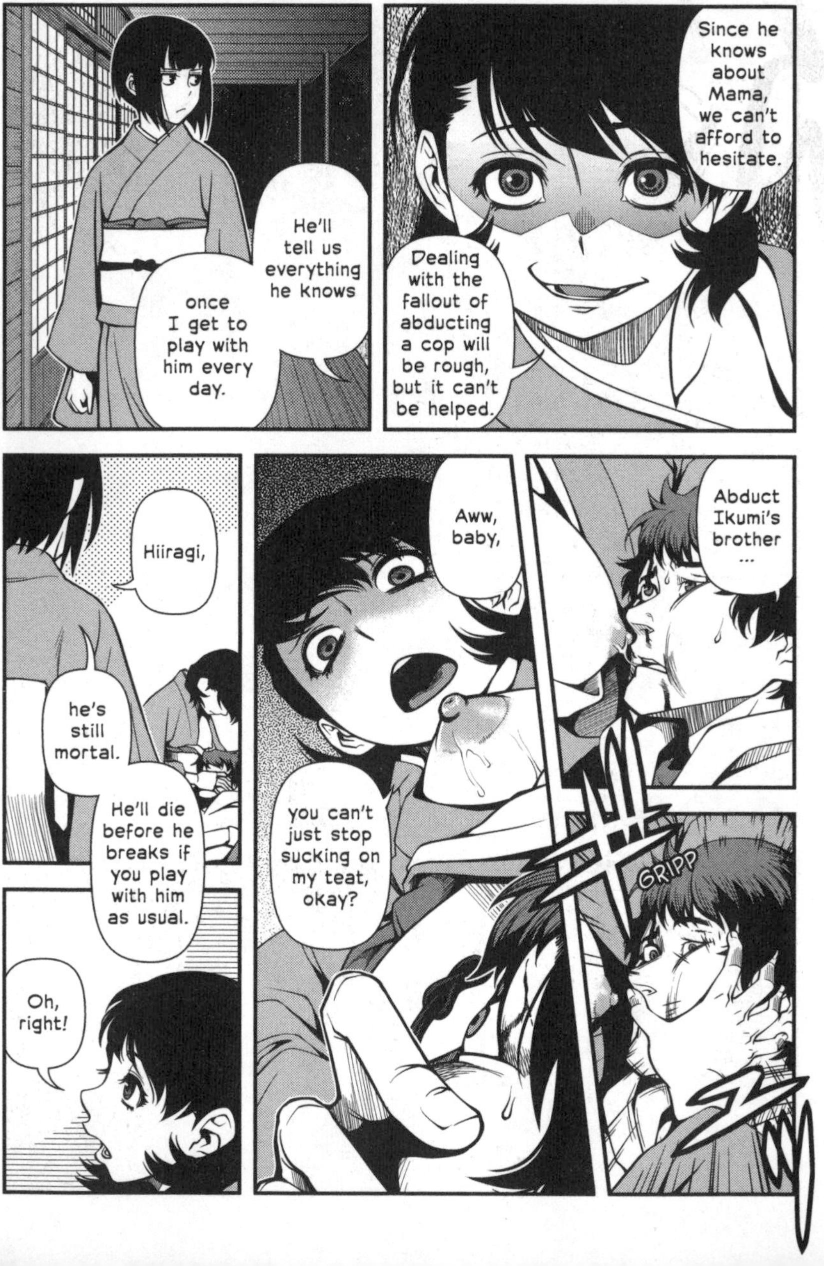
Since he knows about Mama, we can't afford to hesitate.
Dealing with the fallout of abducting a cop will be rough, but it can't be helped.
He'll tell us everything he knows
once I get to play with him every day.
Abduct Ikumi's brother ...
GRIPP
Aww, baby,
you can't just stop sucking on my teat, okay?
Hiiragi,
he's still mortal.
He'll die before he breaks if you play with him as usual.
Oh, right!

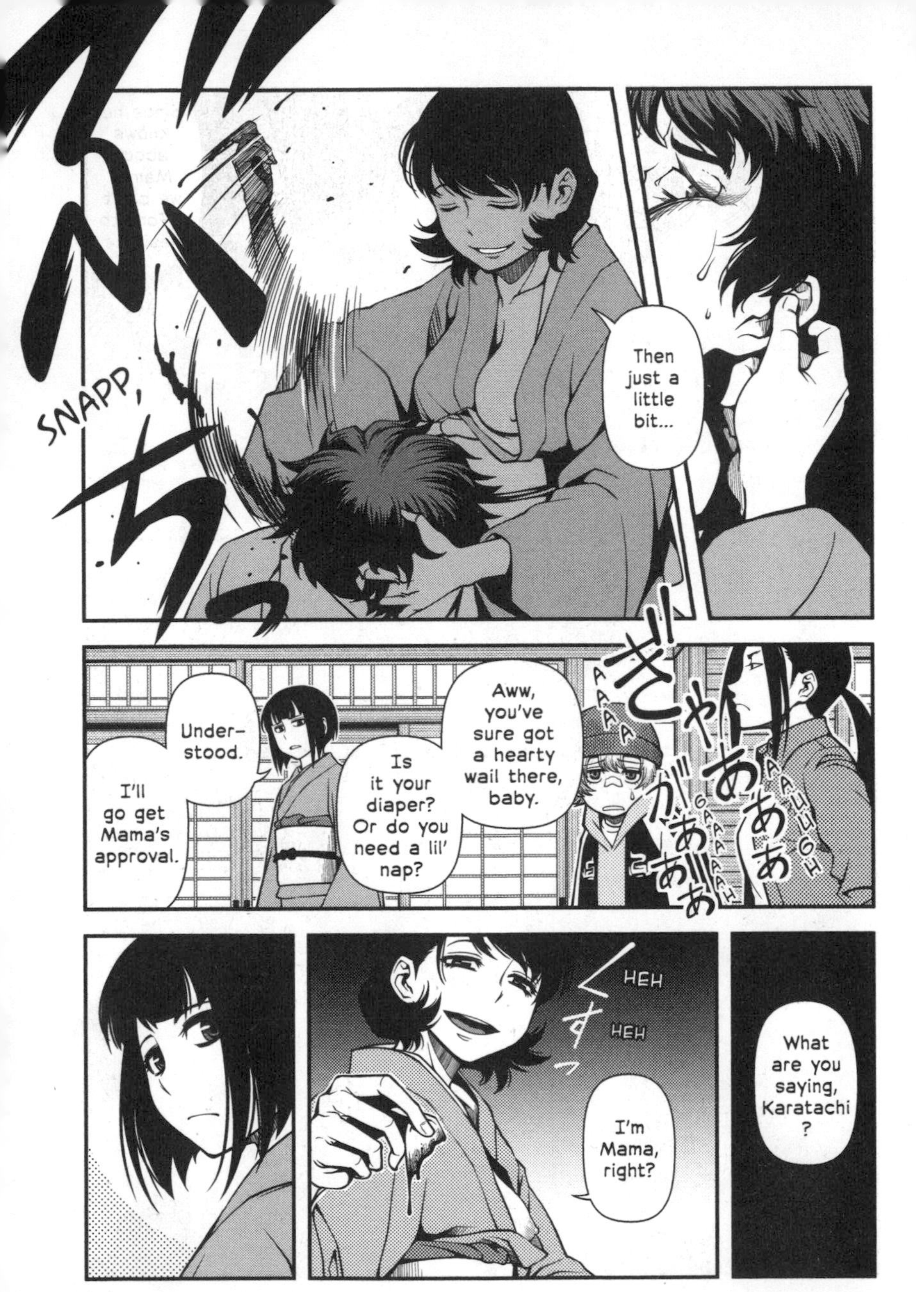
Then just a little bit...
SNAPP
AAAAA
AAUGH
GAAAAAH
Aww, you've sure got a hearty wail there, baby.
Is it your diaper? Or do you need a lil' nap?
Under-stood.
I'll go get Mama's approval.
What are you saying, Karatachi?
HEH HEH
I'm Mama, right?

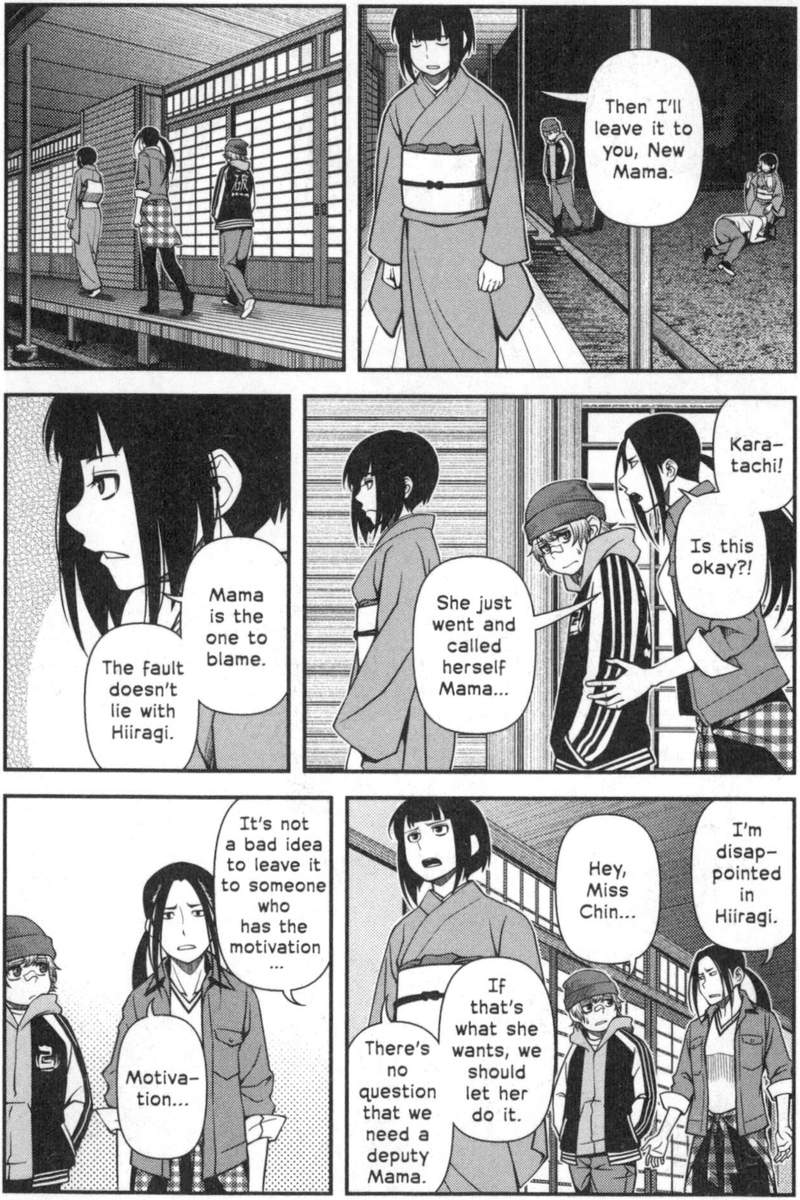
Then I'll leave it to you, New Mama.
Kara-tachi!
Is this okay?!
She just went and called herself Mama...
Mama is the one to blame.
The fault doesn't lie with Hiiragi.
I'm disap-pointed in Hiiragi.
Hey, Miss Chin...
If that's what she wants, we should let her do it.
There's no question that we need a deputy Mama.
It's not a bad idea to leave it to someone who has the motivation ...
Motiva-tion...

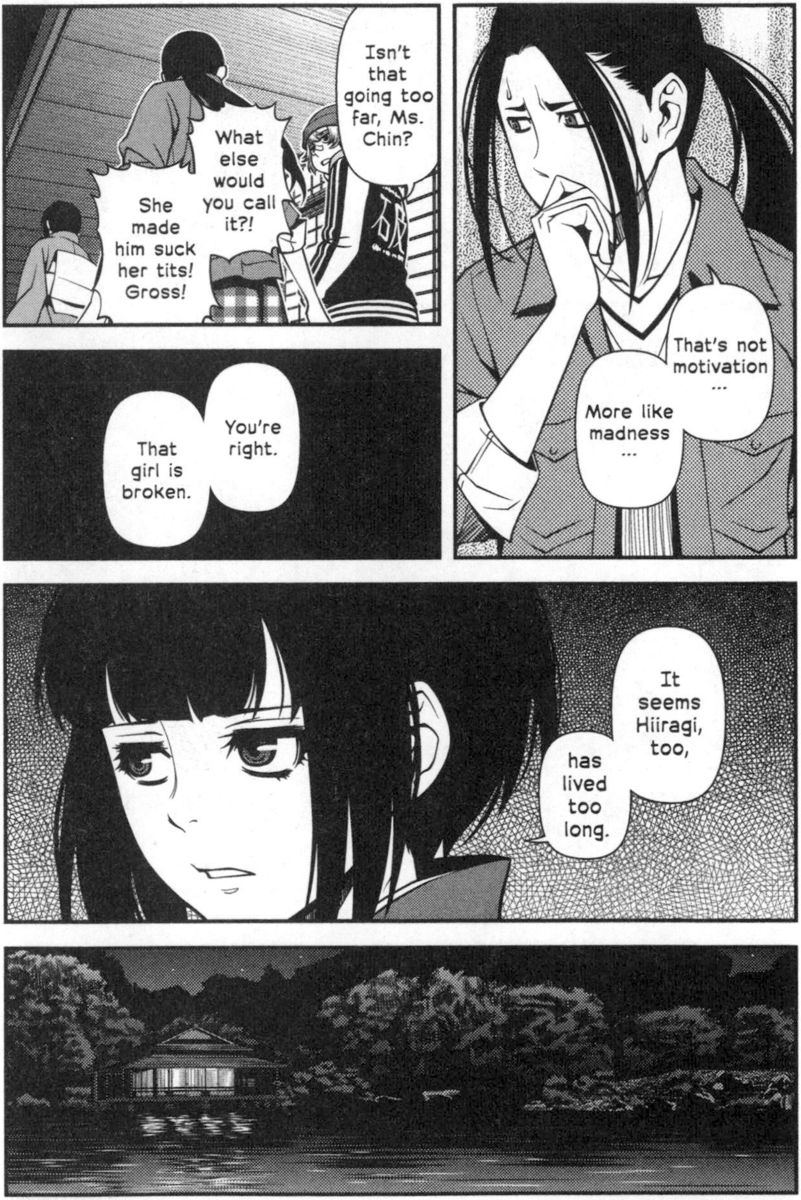
That's not motivation ...
More like madness ...
Isn't that going too far, Ms. Chin?
What else would you call it?!
She made him suck her tits! Gross!
You're right.
That girl is broken.
It seems Hiiragi, too,
has lived too long.

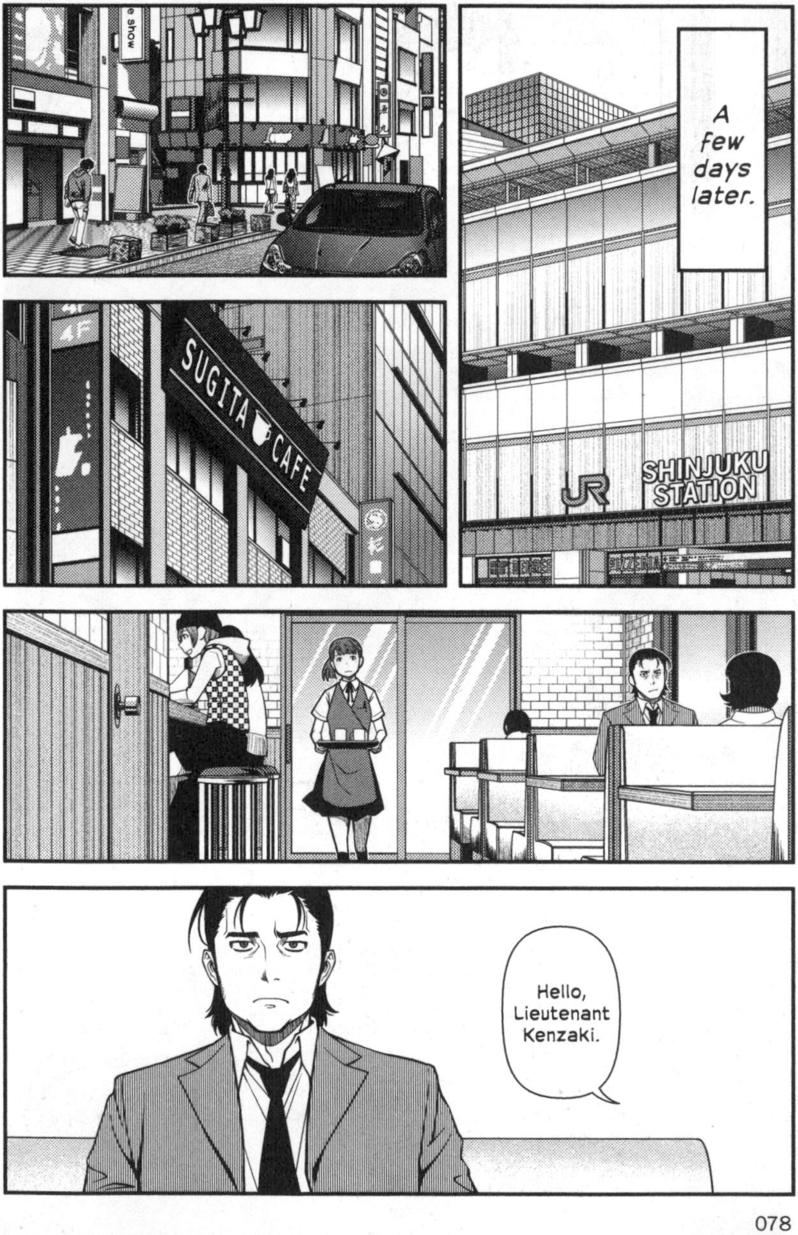
A few days later.
JR
SHINJUKU STATION
PIZZERIA
e show
4F
SUGITA CAFE
Hello, Lieutenant Kenzaki.

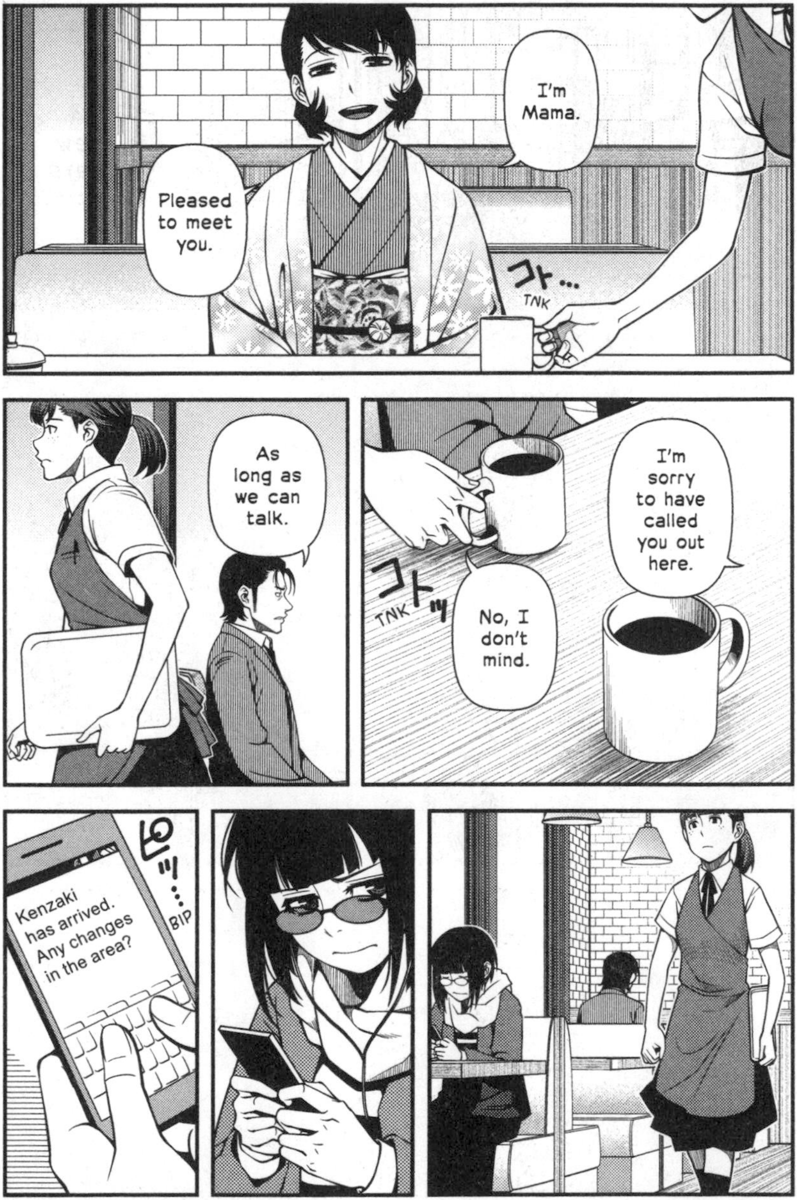

I'm Mama.
Pleased to meet you.
コト...
TNK
I'm sorry to have called you out here.
No, I don't mind.
コトッ
TNK
As long as we can talk.
ピッ...
BIP
Kenzaki has arrived. Any changes in the area?

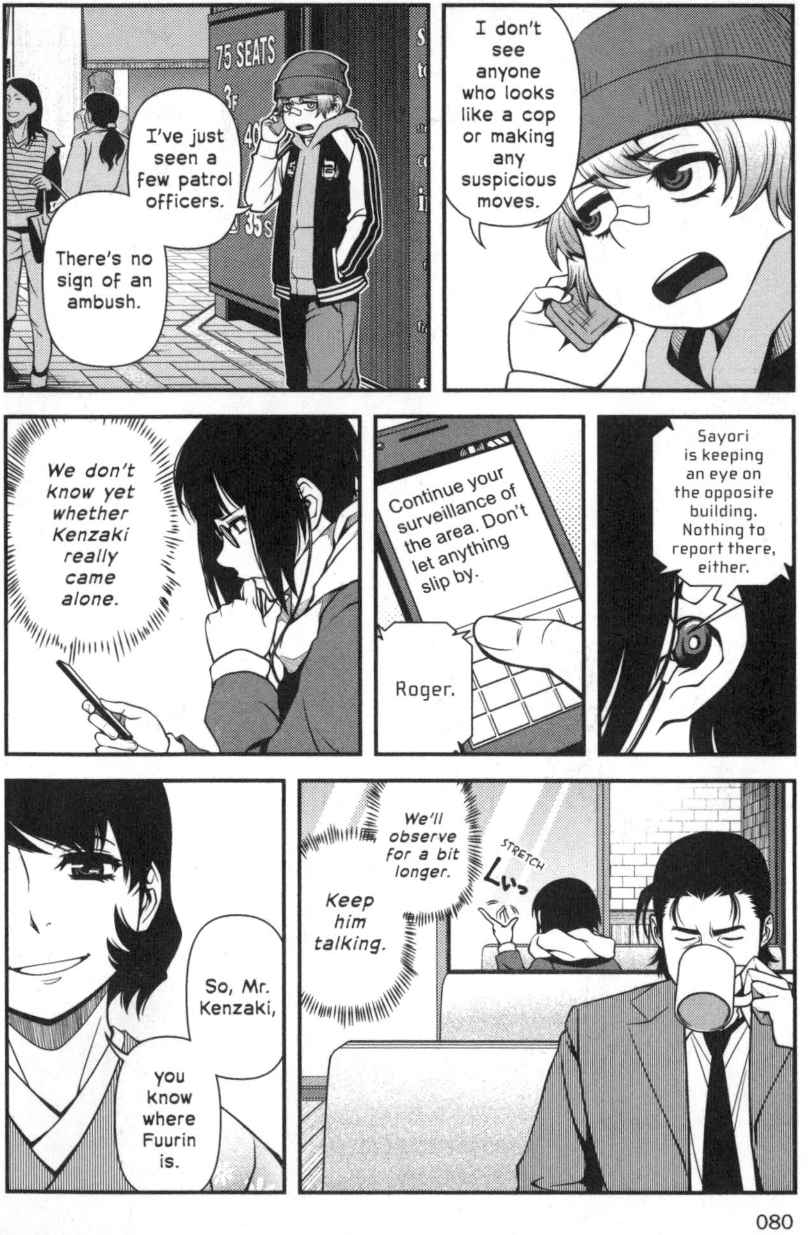
I don't see anyone who looks like a cop or making any suspicious moves.
75 SEATS
I've just seen a few patrol officers.
There's no sign of an ambush.
Sayori is keeping an eye on the opposite building. Nothing to report there, either.
Continue your surveillance of the area. Don't let anything slip by.
Roger.
We don't know yet whether Kenzaki really came alone.
We'll observe for a bit longer.
Keep him talking.
STRETCH
So, Mr. Kenzaki,
you know where Fuurin is.

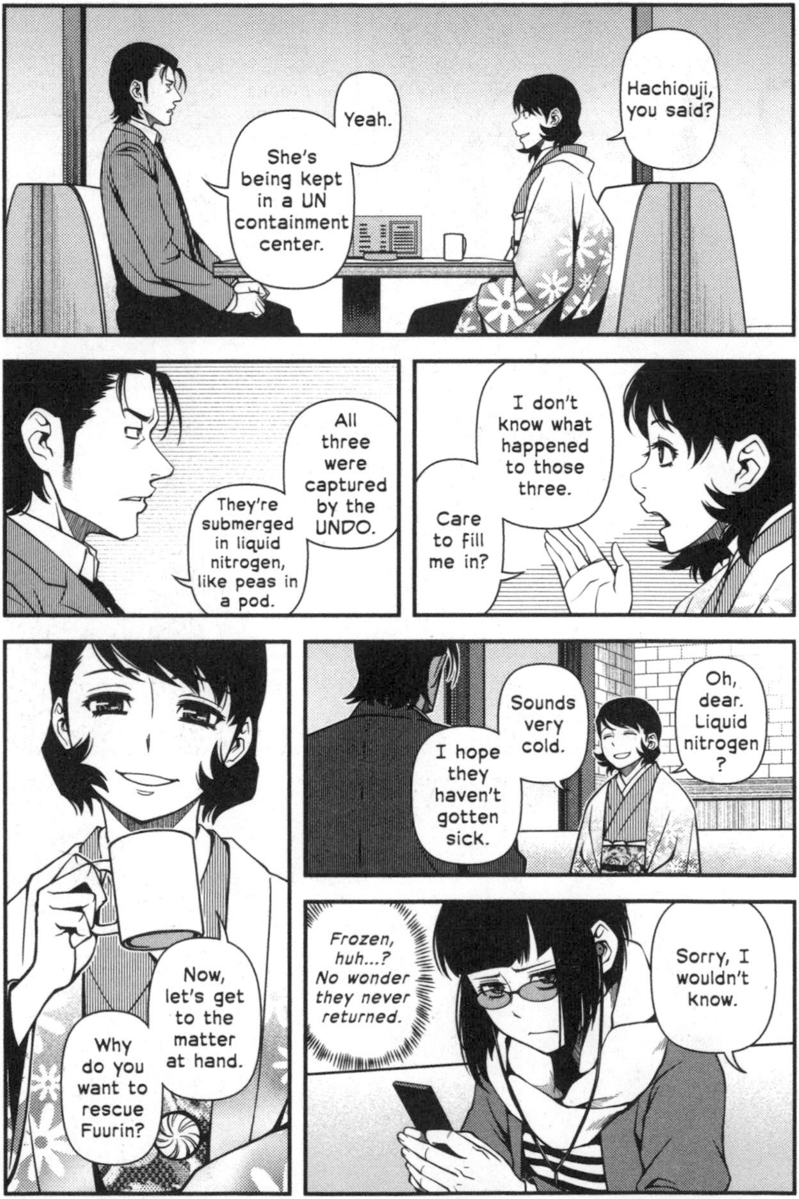
Hachiouji, you said?
Yeah.
She's being kept in a UN containment center.
I don't know what happened to those three.
Care to fill me in?
All three were captured by the UNDO.
They're submerged in liquid nitrogen, like peas in a pod.
Oh, dear. Liquid nitrogen?
Sounds very cold.
I hope they haven't gotten sick.
Sorry, I wouldn't know.
Frozen, huh...? No wonder they never returned.
Now, let's get to the matter at hand.
Why do you want to rescue Fuurin?

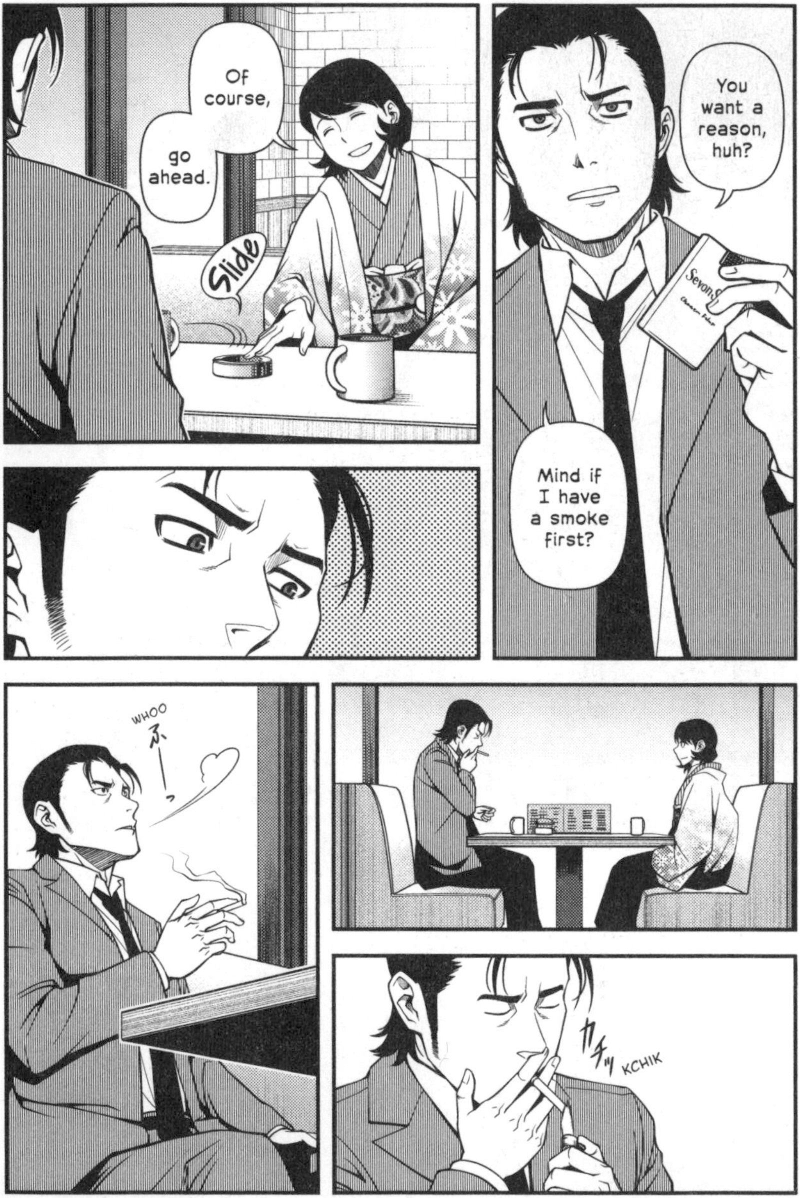
You want a reason, huh?
Mind if I have a smoke first?
Of course,
go ahead.
Slide
カチッ
KCHIK
WHOO
ふーっ

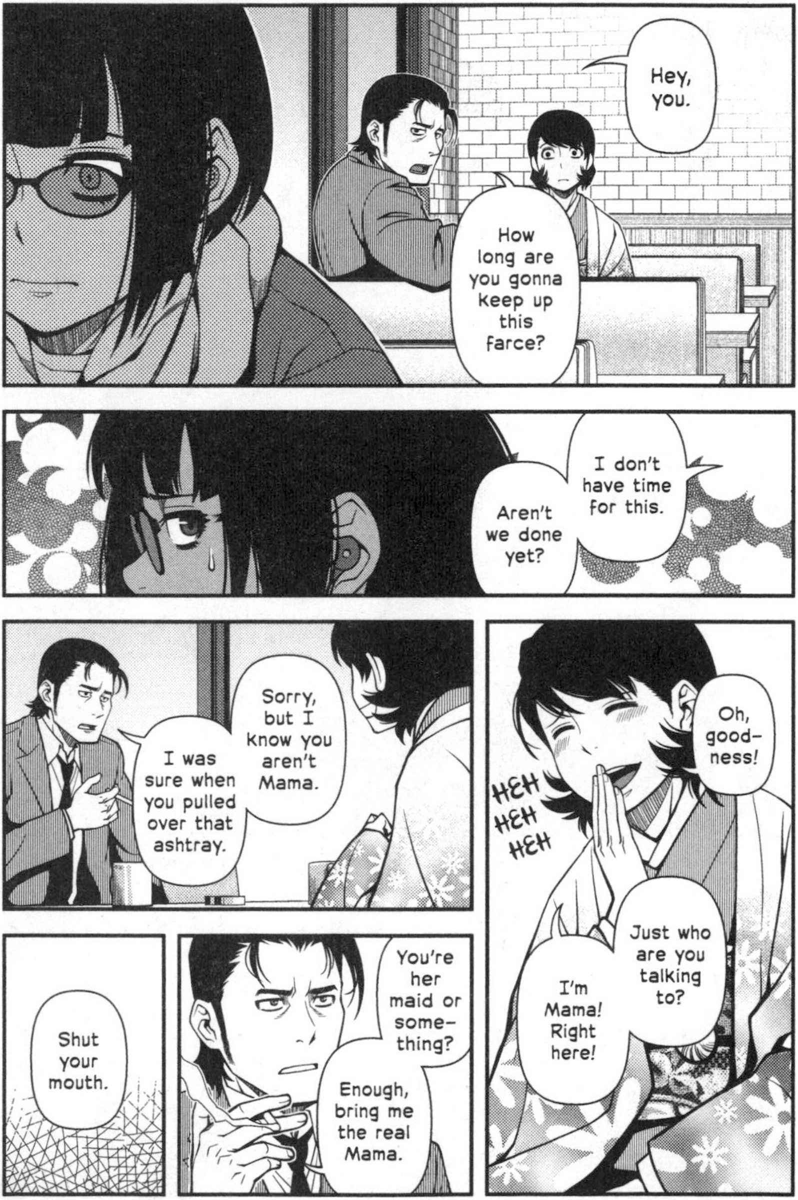

Hey, you.
How long are you gonna keep up this farce?
I don't have time for this.
Aren't we done yet?
Oh, goodness!
HEH HEH HEH
Just who are you talking to?
I'm Mama! Right here!
Sorry, but I know you aren't Mama.
I was sure when you pulled over that ashtray.
You're her maid or something?
Enough, bring me the real Mama.
Shut your mouth.

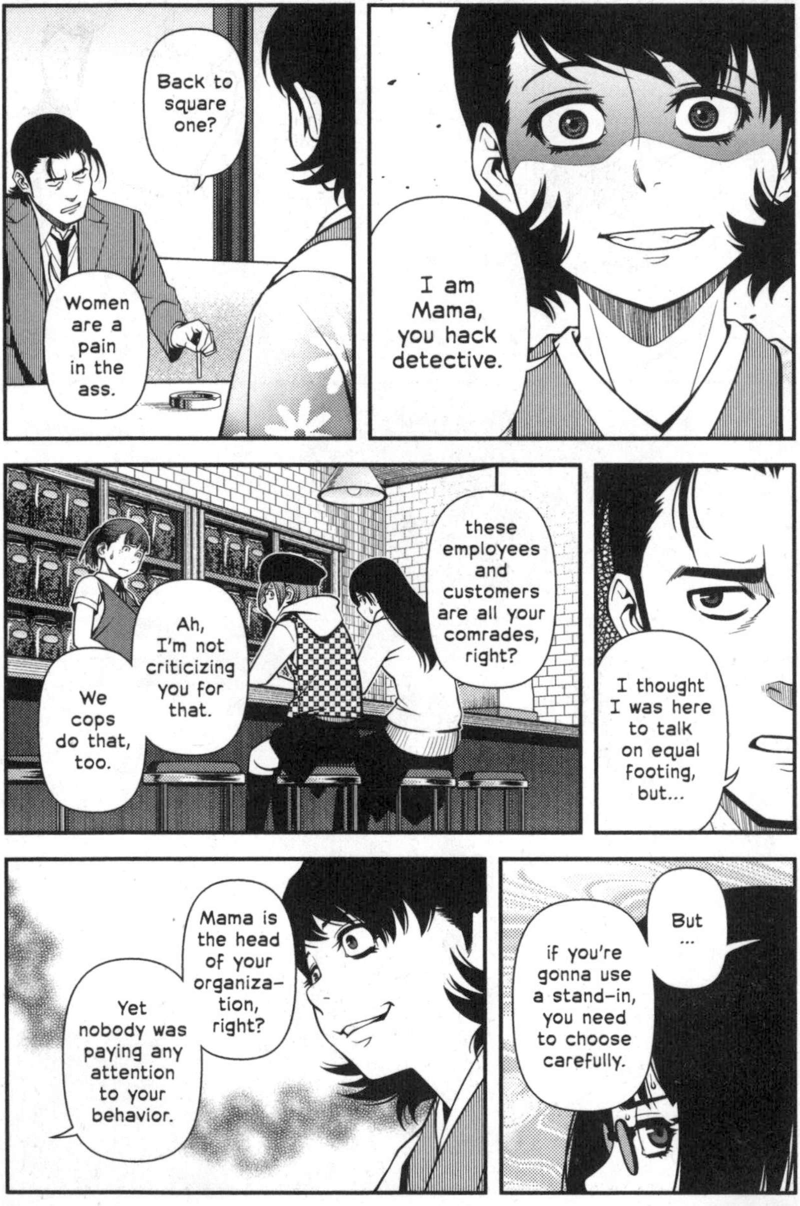
I am Mama, you hack detective.
Back to square one?
Women are a pain in the ass.
I thought I was here to talk on equal footing, but...
these employees and customers are all your comrades, right?
Ah, I'm not criticizing you for that.
We cops do that, too.
But ...
if you're gonna use a stand-in, you need to choose carefully.
Mama is the head of your organiza-tion, right?
Yet nobody was paying any attention to your behavior.

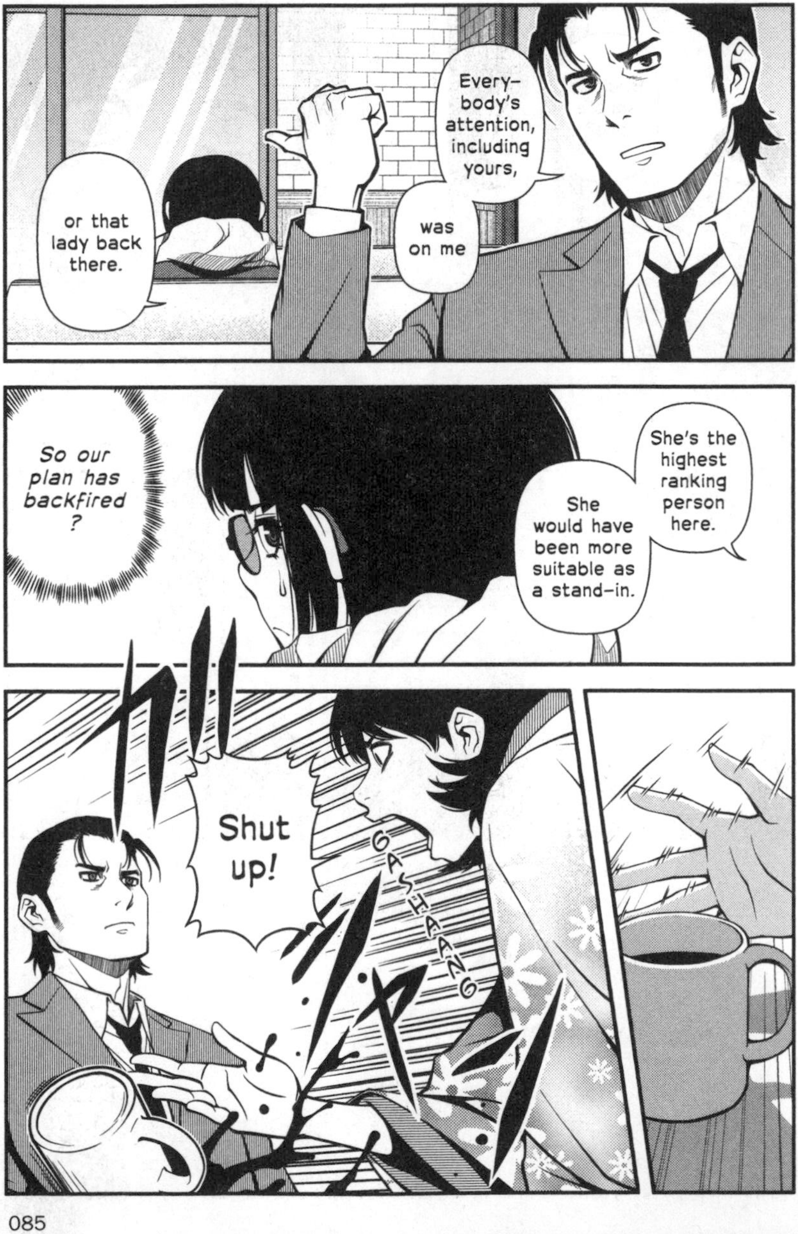
Every-body's attention, including yours,
was on me
or that lady back there.
She's the highest ranking person here.
She would have been more suitable as a stand-in.
So our plan has backfired?
Shut up!
GASHAANG

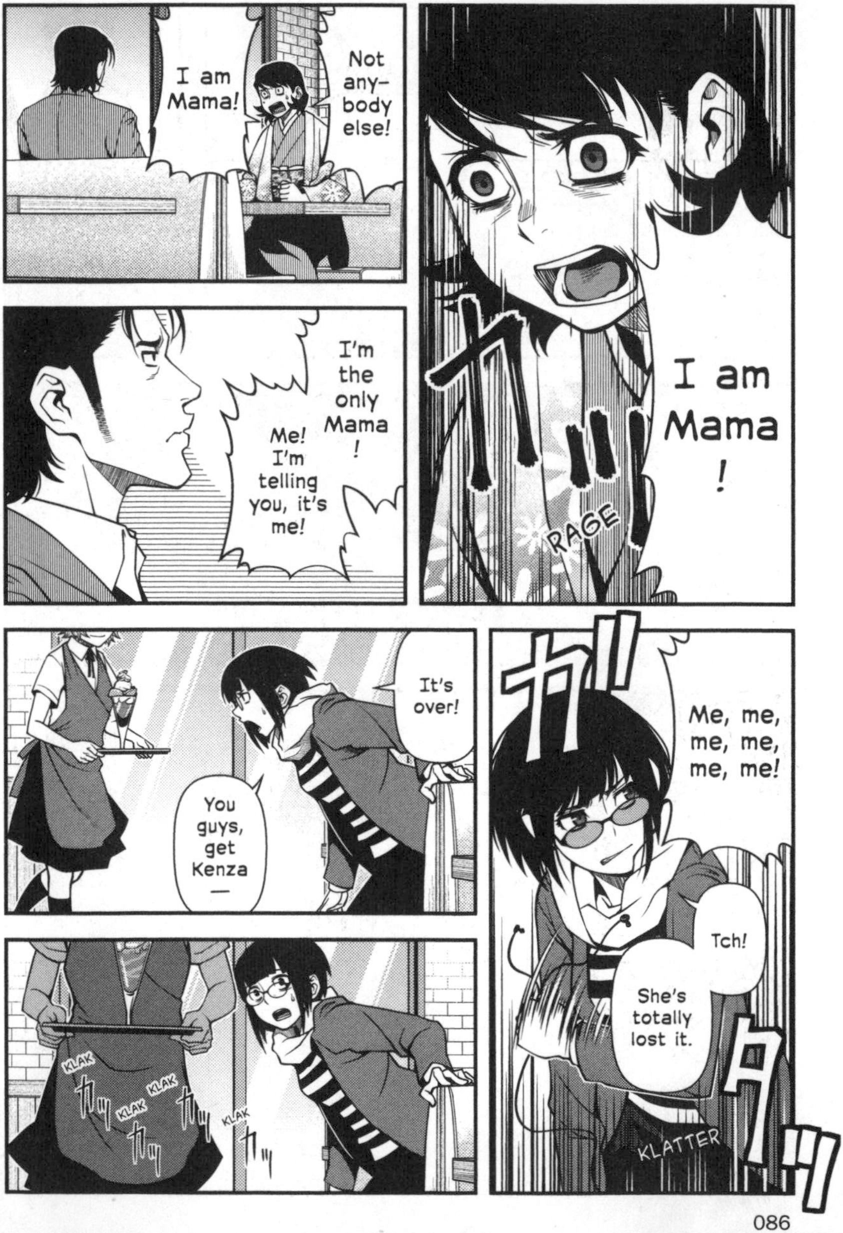

I am Mama!
RAGE
Not any-body else!
I am Mama!
I'm the only Mama!
Me! I'm telling you, it's me!
Me, me, me, me, me, me!
Tch!
She's totally lost it.
KLATTER
It's over!
You guys, get Kenza—
KLAK
KLAK
KLAK
KLAK

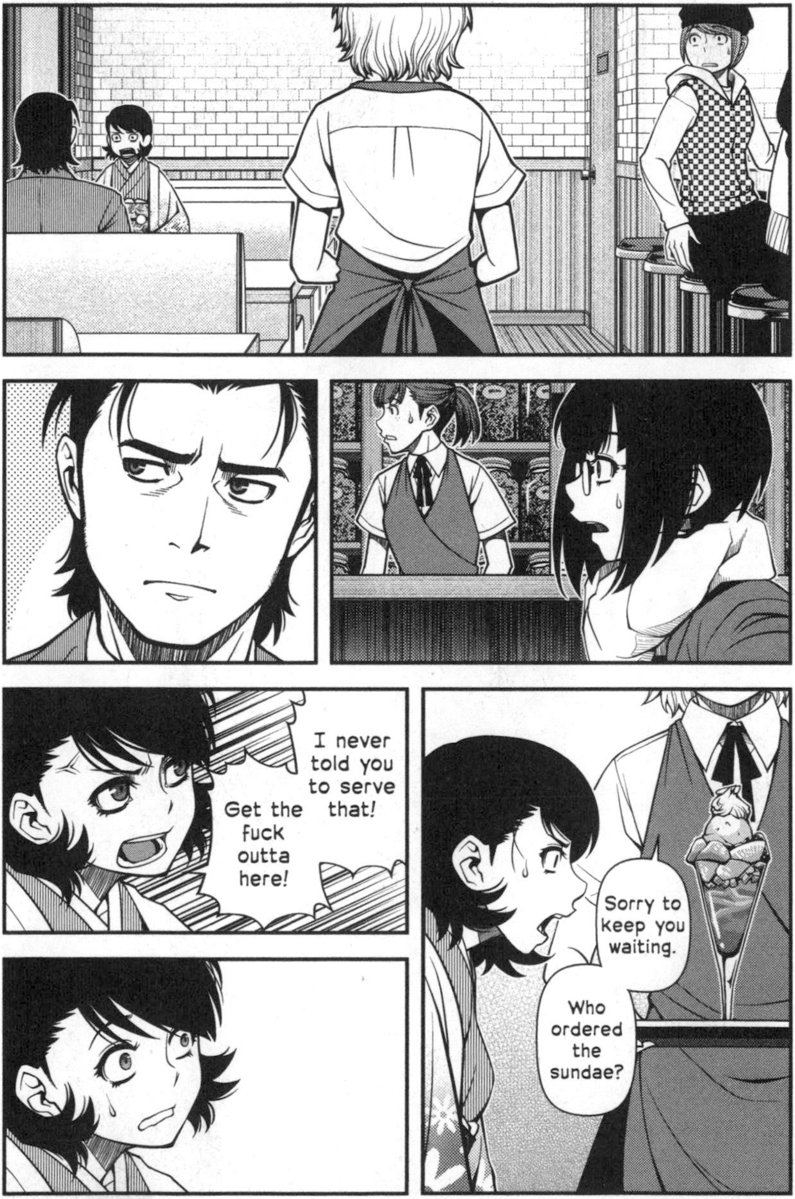
Sorry to keep you waiting.
Who ordered the sundae?
I never told you to serve that!
Get the fuck outta here!

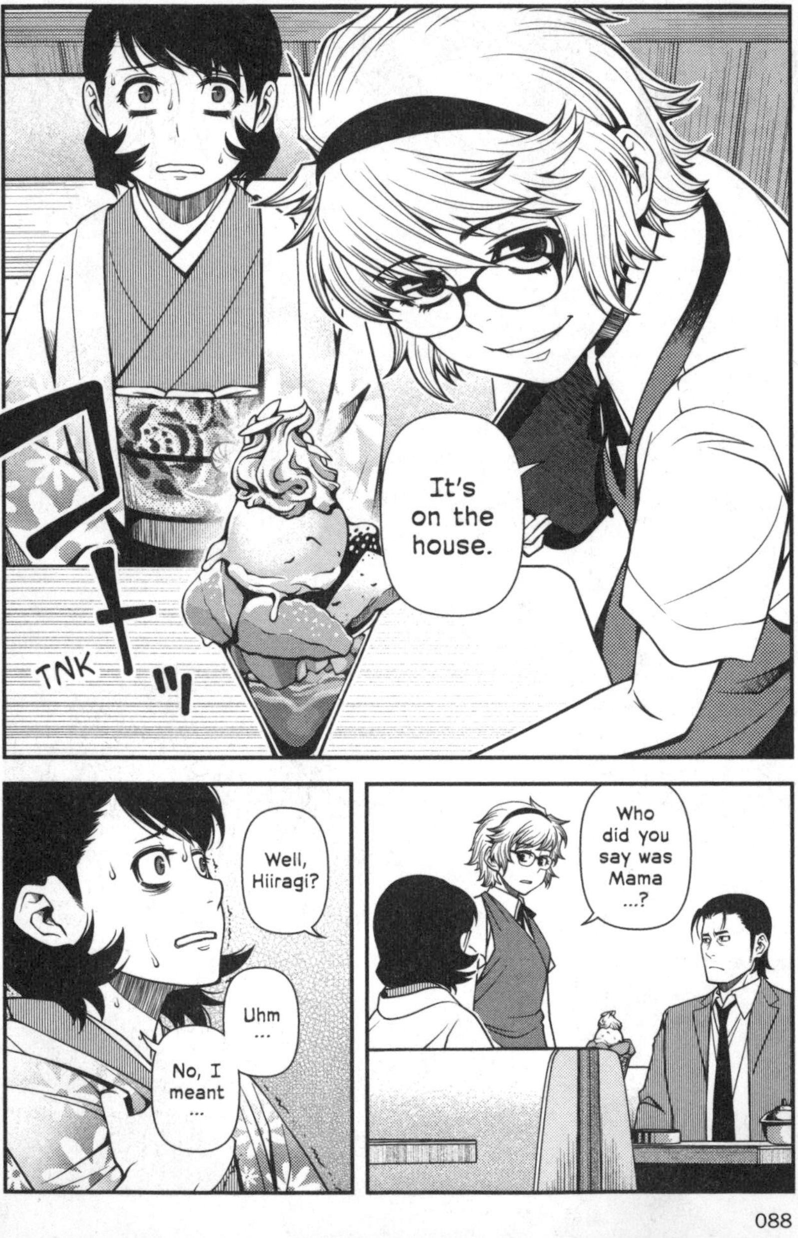
It's on the house.
TNK
Who did you say was Mama ...?
Well, Hiiragi?
Uhm ...
No, I meant ...

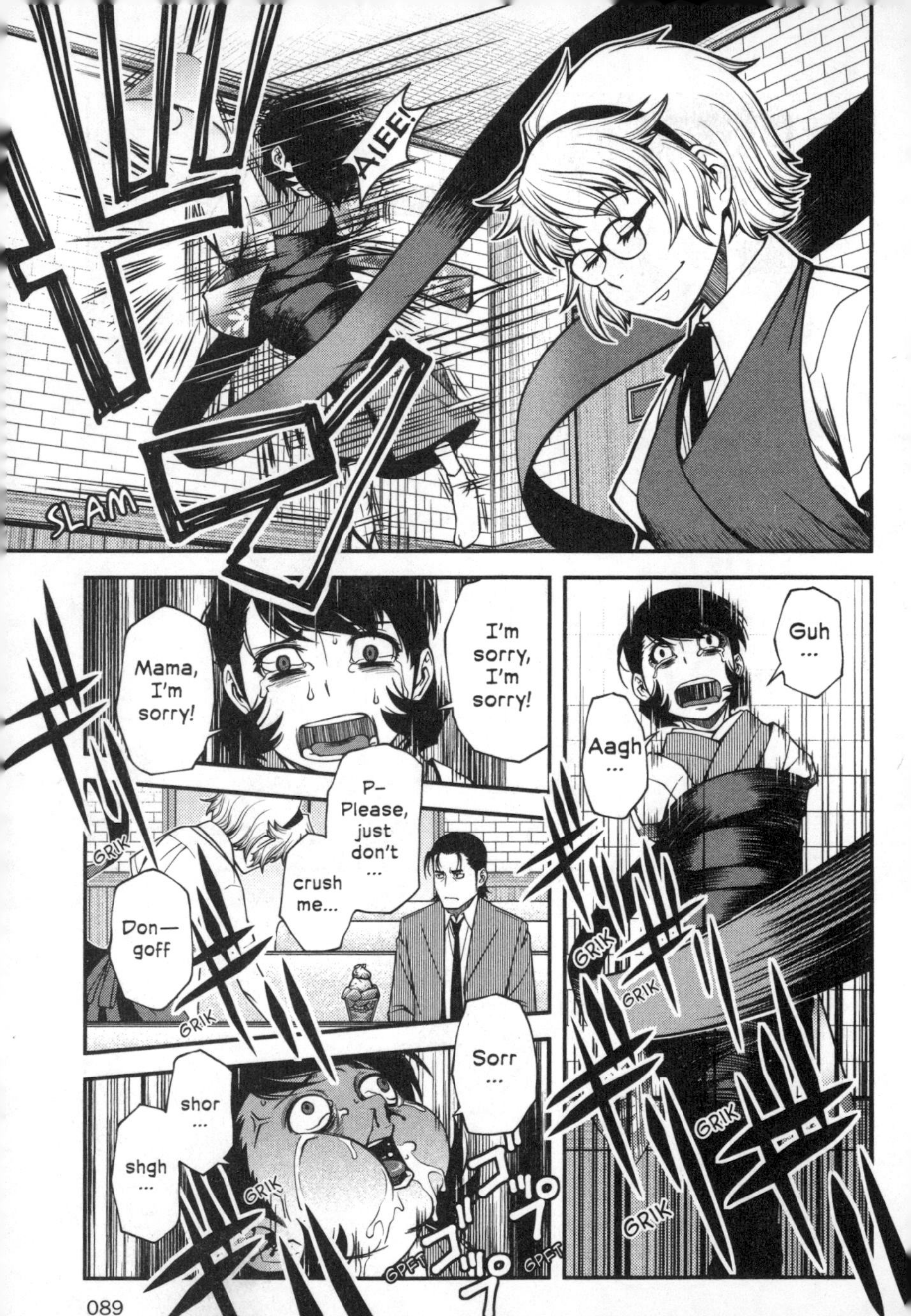
AIEE!
SLAM
Guh ...
Aagh ...
GRIK
GRIK
GRIK
GRIK
I'm sorry, I'm sorry!
Mama, I'm sorry!
P— Please, just don't ... crush me...
GRIK
Don— goff
GRIK
Sorr ...
shor ...
shgh ...
GRIK
GPFT
GPFT

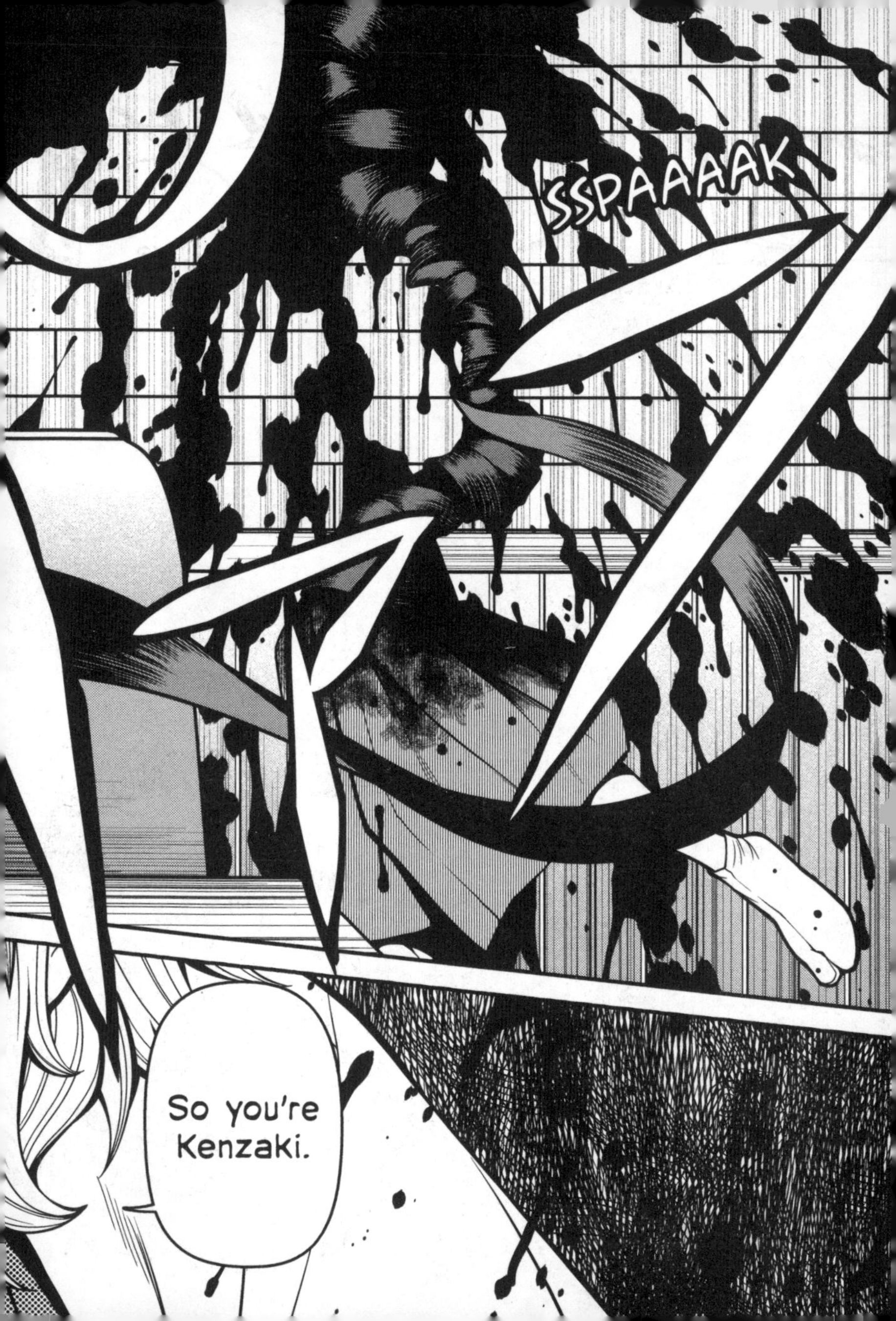
SSPAAAAK
So you're Kenzaki.

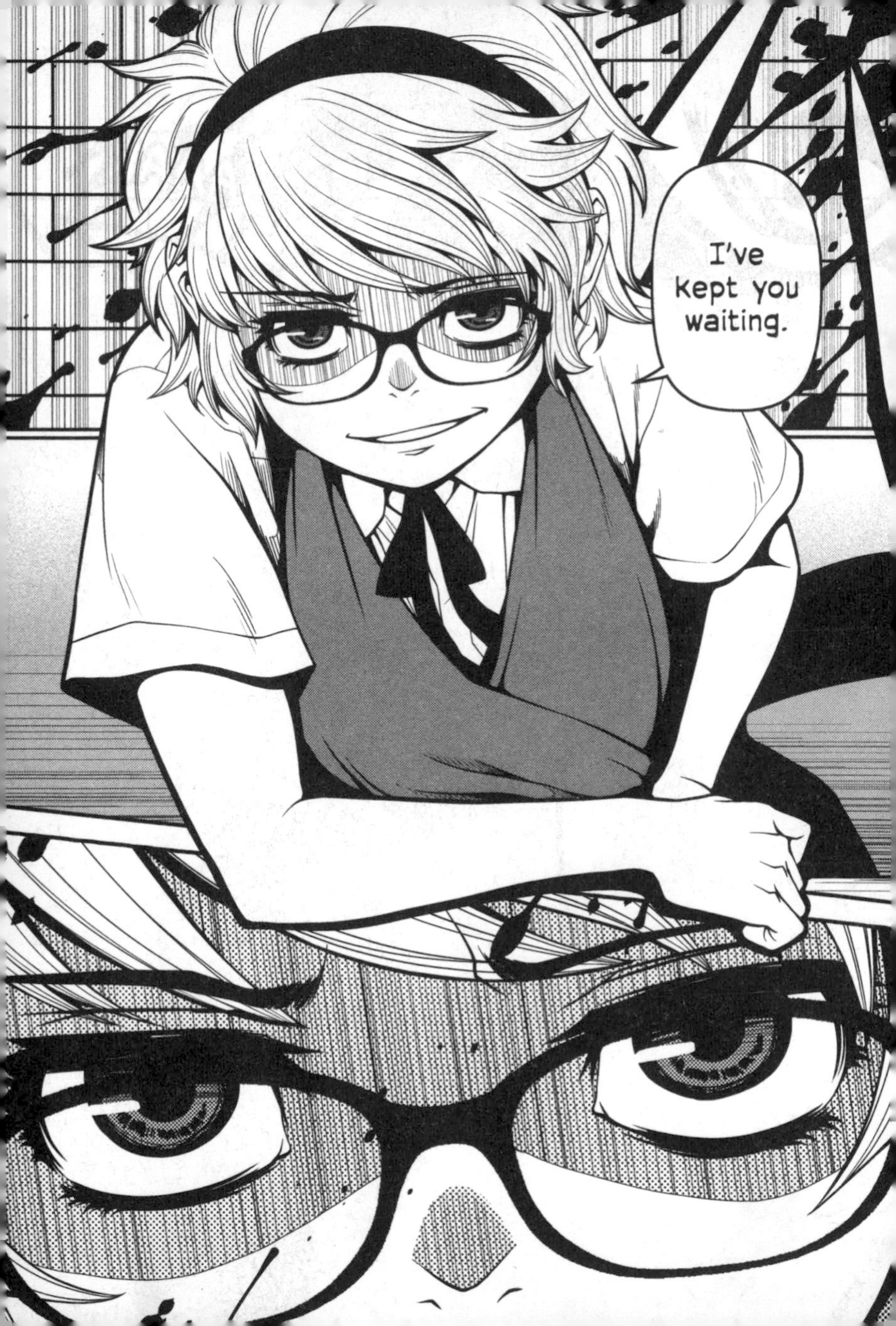
I've kept you waiting.

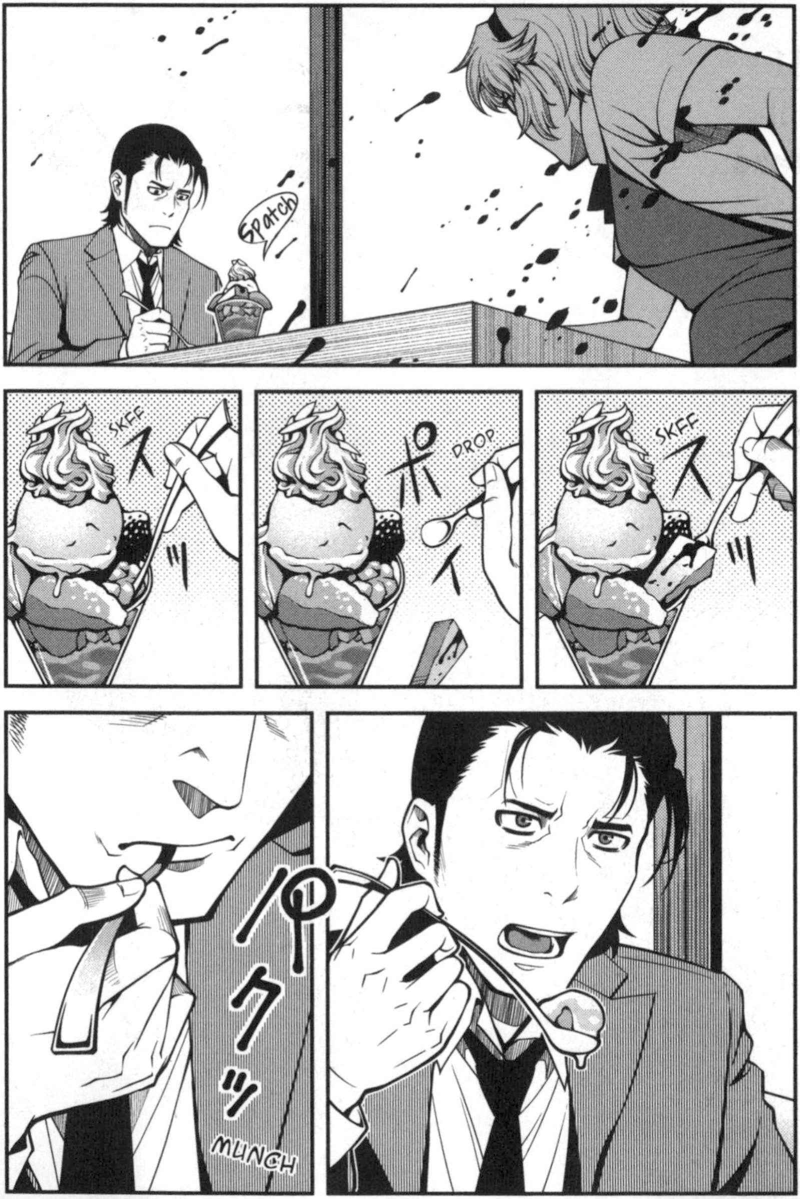
Spatch
スッ
SKFF
ポイ
DROP
スッ
SKFF
パクッ
MUNCH

31

I'll Take Her

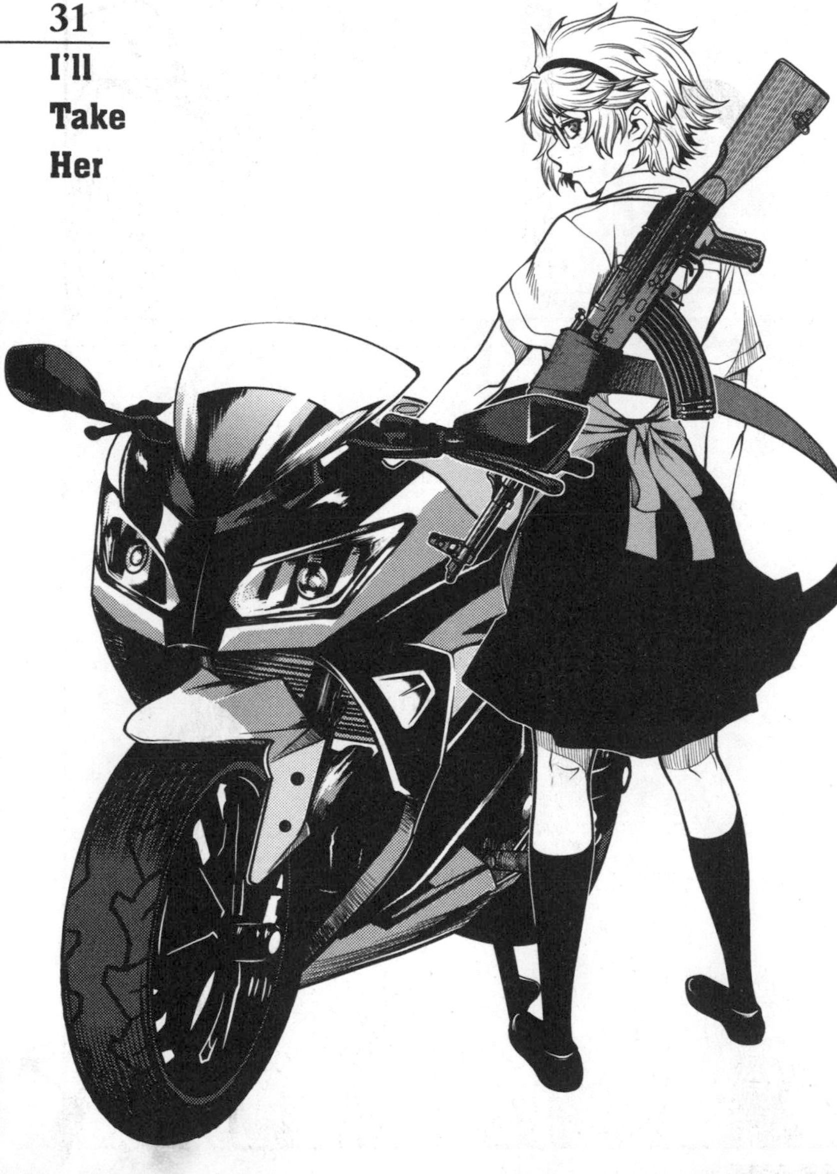

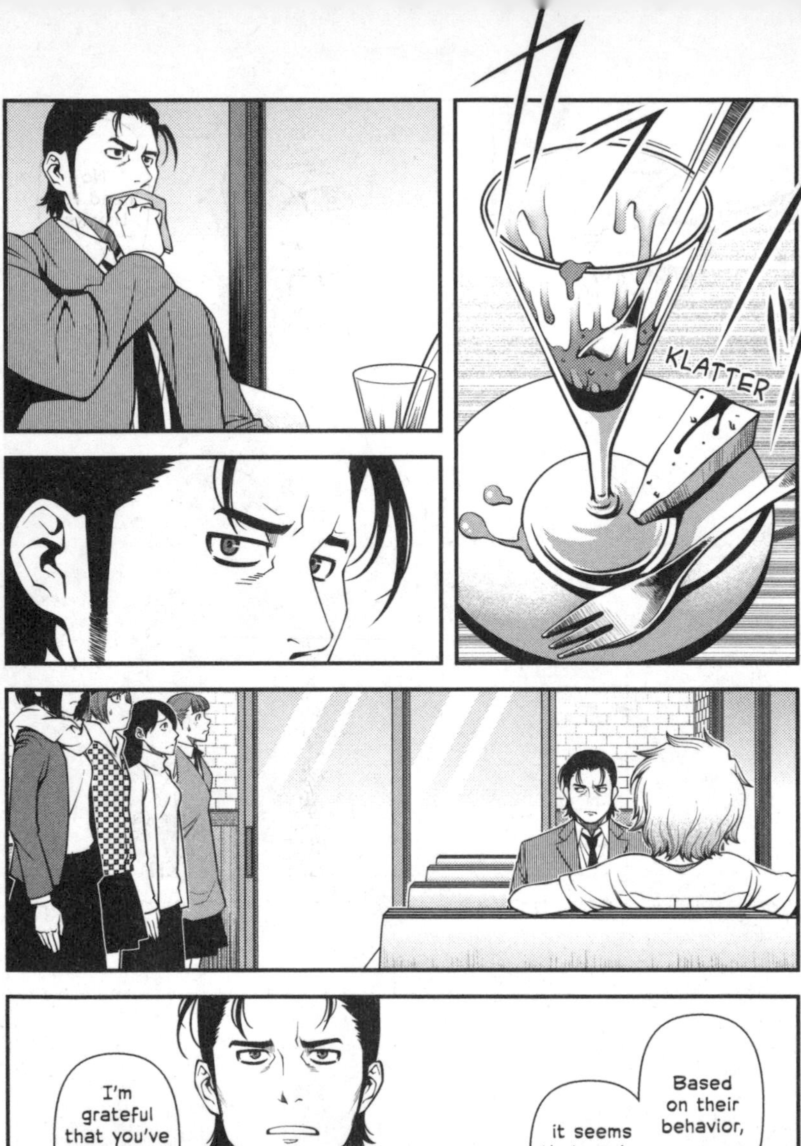
KLATTER
Based on their behavior,
it seems that you're the real Mama.
I'm grateful that you've agreed to speak with me.

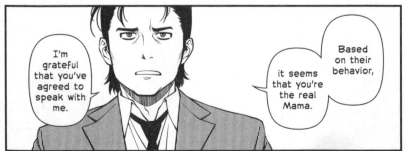

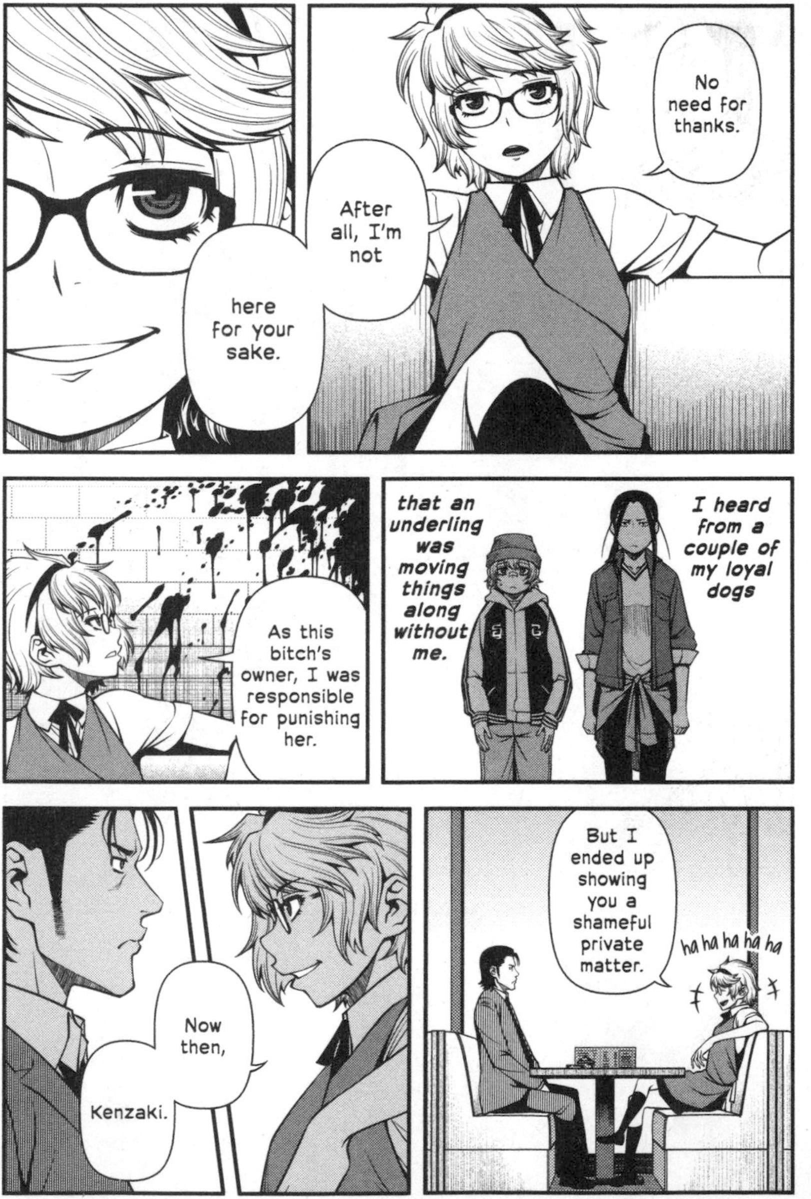
No need for thanks.
After all, I'm not
here for your sake.
I heard from a couple of my loyal dogs
that an underling was moving things along without me.
As this bitch's owner, I was responsible for punishing her.
But I ended up showing you a shameful private matter.
ha ha ha ha ha
Now then,
Kenzaki.

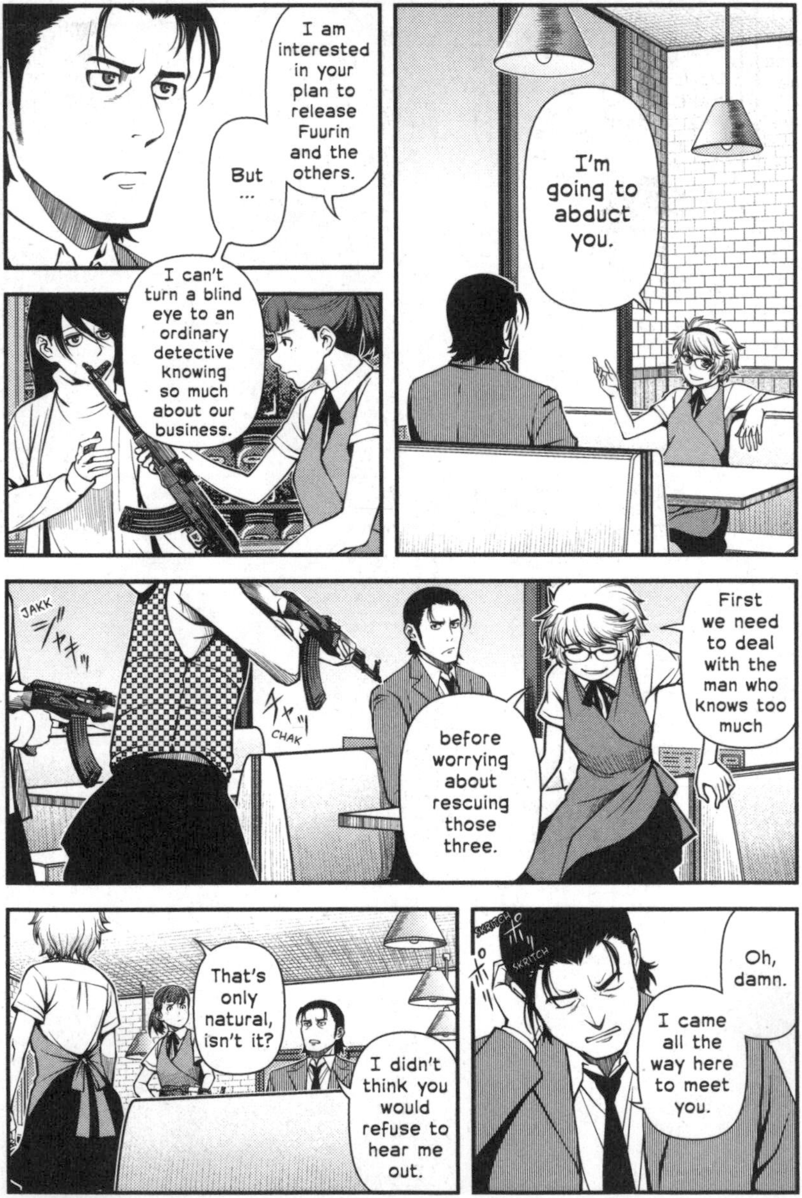
I'm going to abduct you.
I am interested in your plan to release Fuurin and the others.
But ...
I can't turn a blind eye to an ordinary detective knowing so much about our business.
First we need to deal with the man who knows too much
before worrying about rescuing those three.
JAKK
CHAK
SKRITCH
SKRITCH
Oh, damn.
I came all the way here to meet you.
I didn't think you would refuse to hear me out.
That's only natural, isn't it?

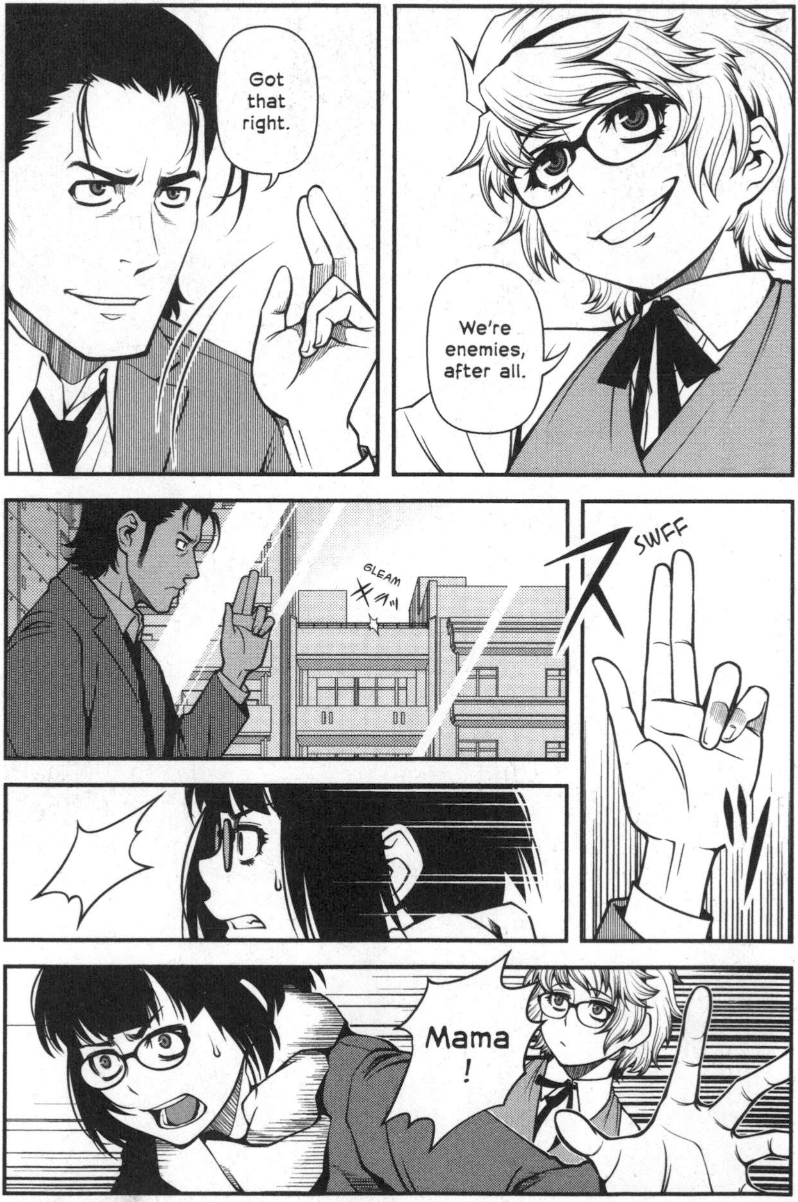
We're enemies, after all.
Got that right.
SWFF
GLEAM
Mama
!

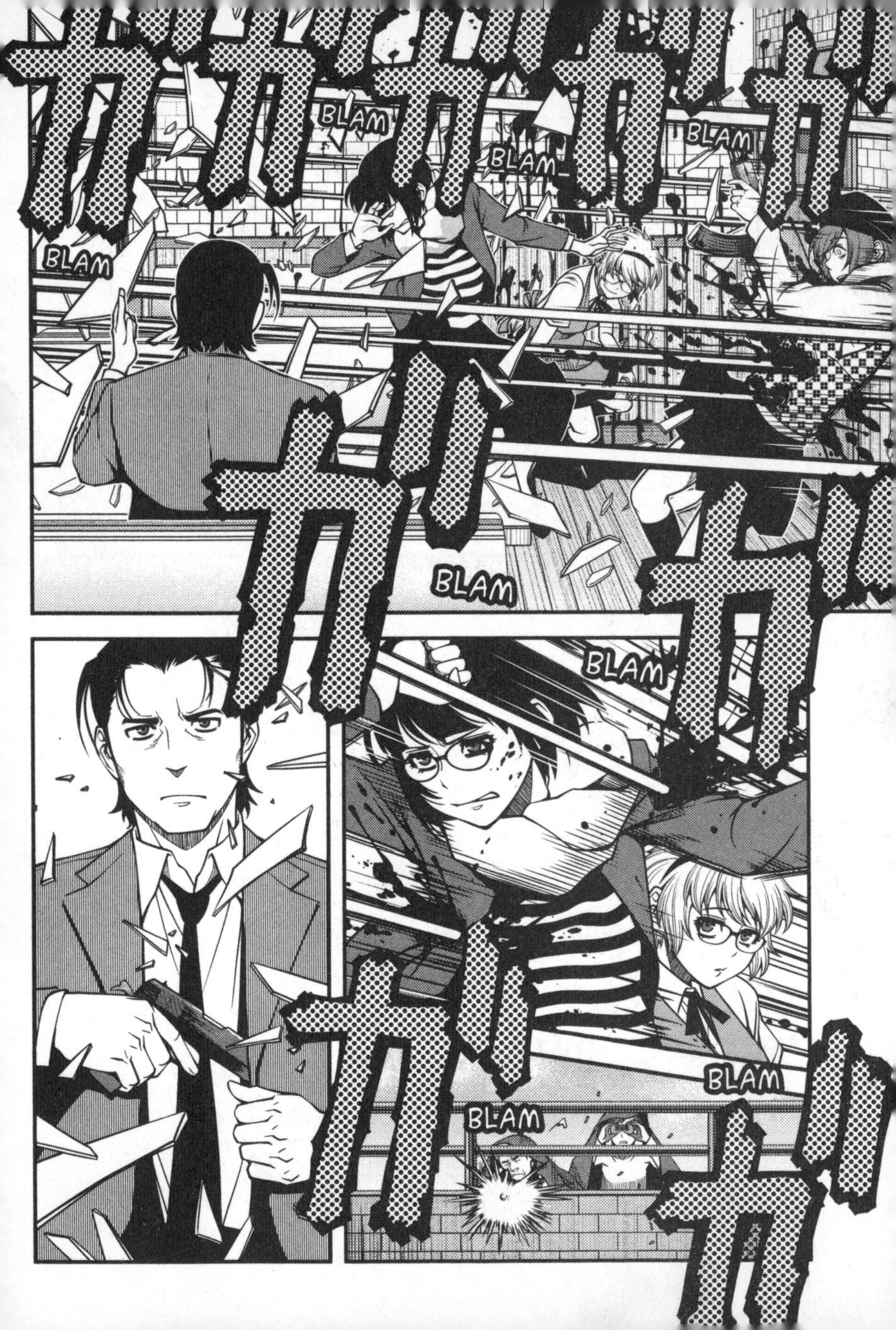
BLAM
BLAM
BLAM
BLAM
BLAM
BLAM
BLAM
BLAM

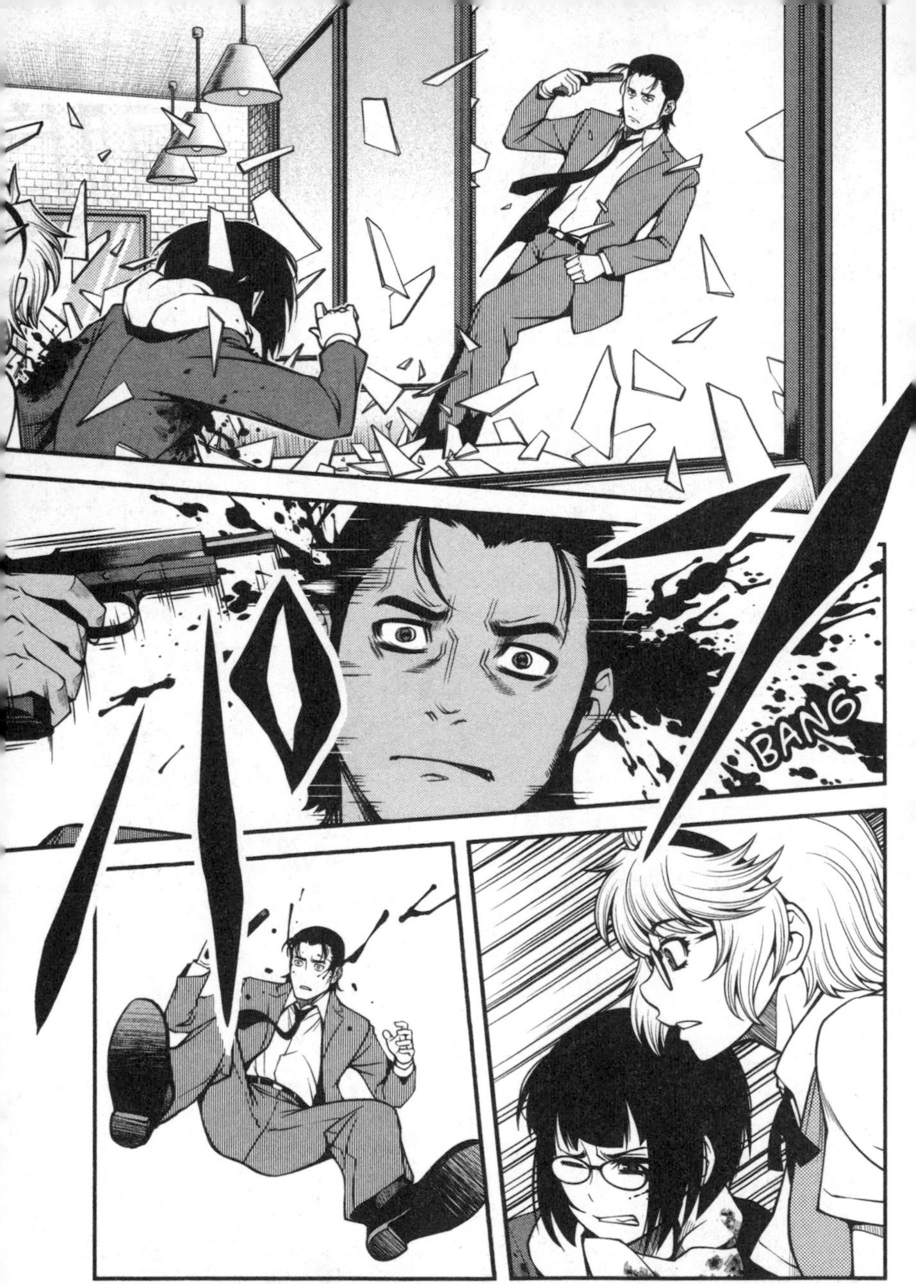
BANG

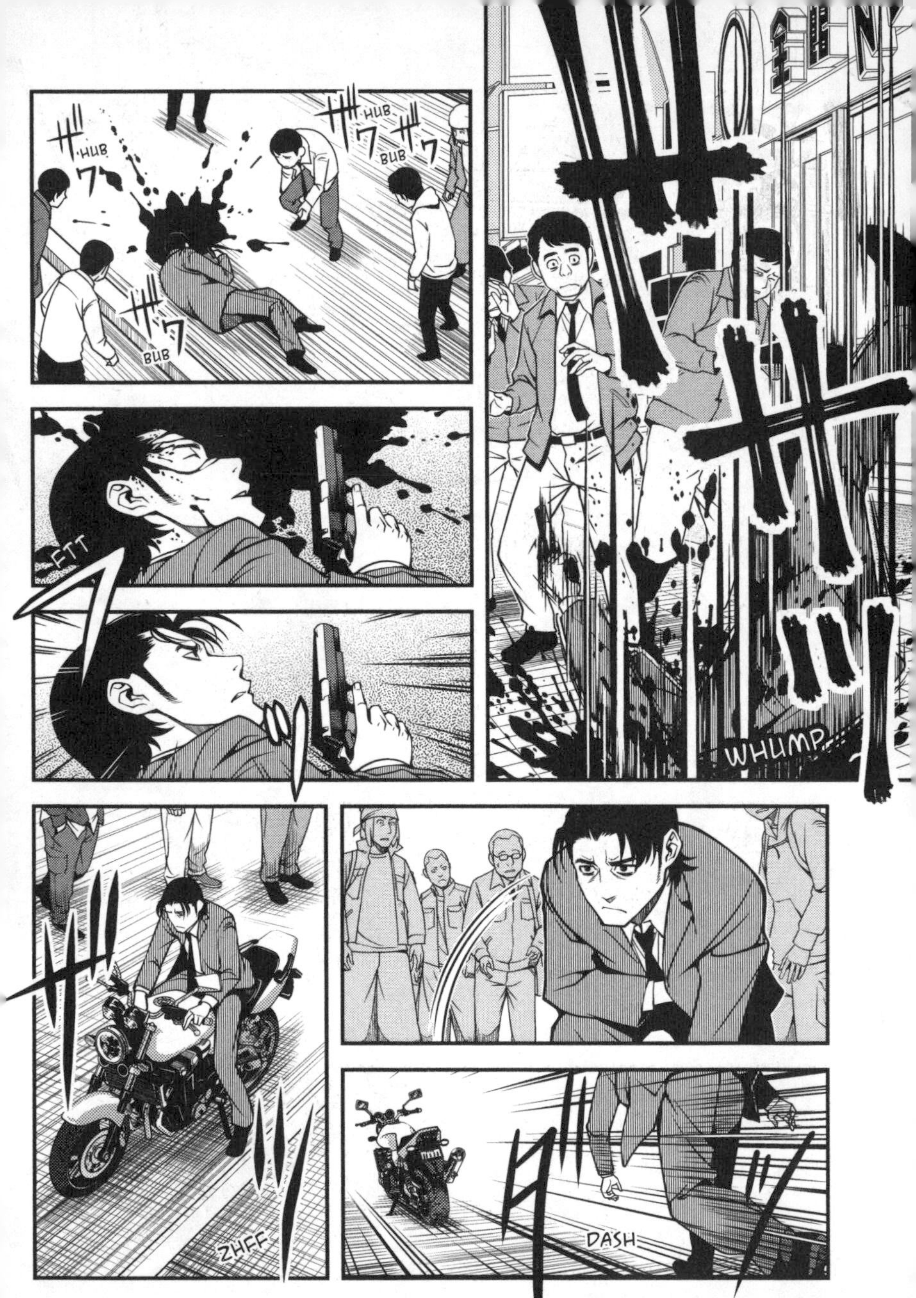
WHUMP
HUB
BUB
HUB
BUB
FTT
DASH
ZHFF

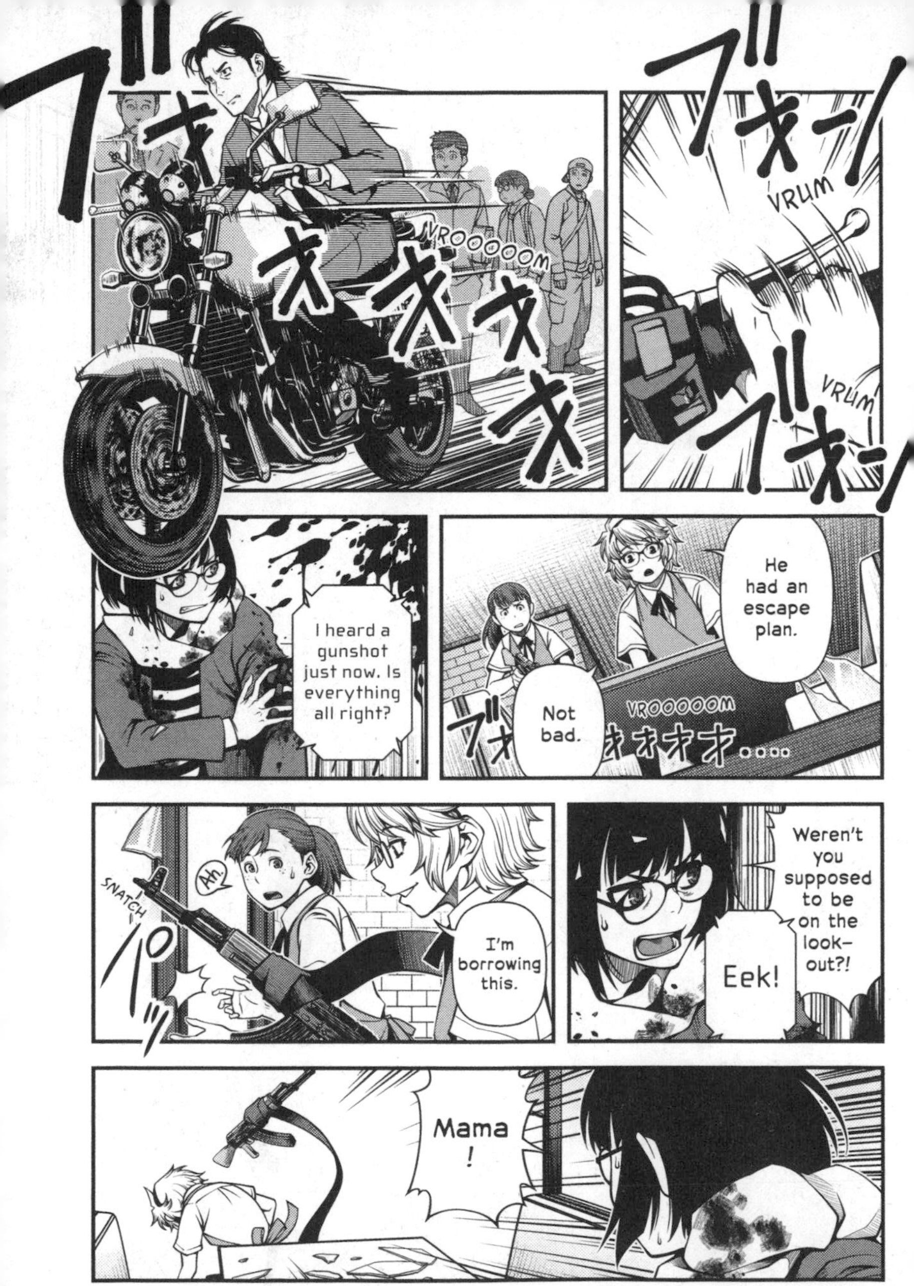
VRUM
VRUM
VROOOOOM
He had an escape plan.
Not bad.
VROOOOOM
I heard a gunshot just now. Is everything all right?
Weren't you supposed to be on the look-out?!
Eek!
Ah.
I'm borrowing this.
SNATCH
Mama!

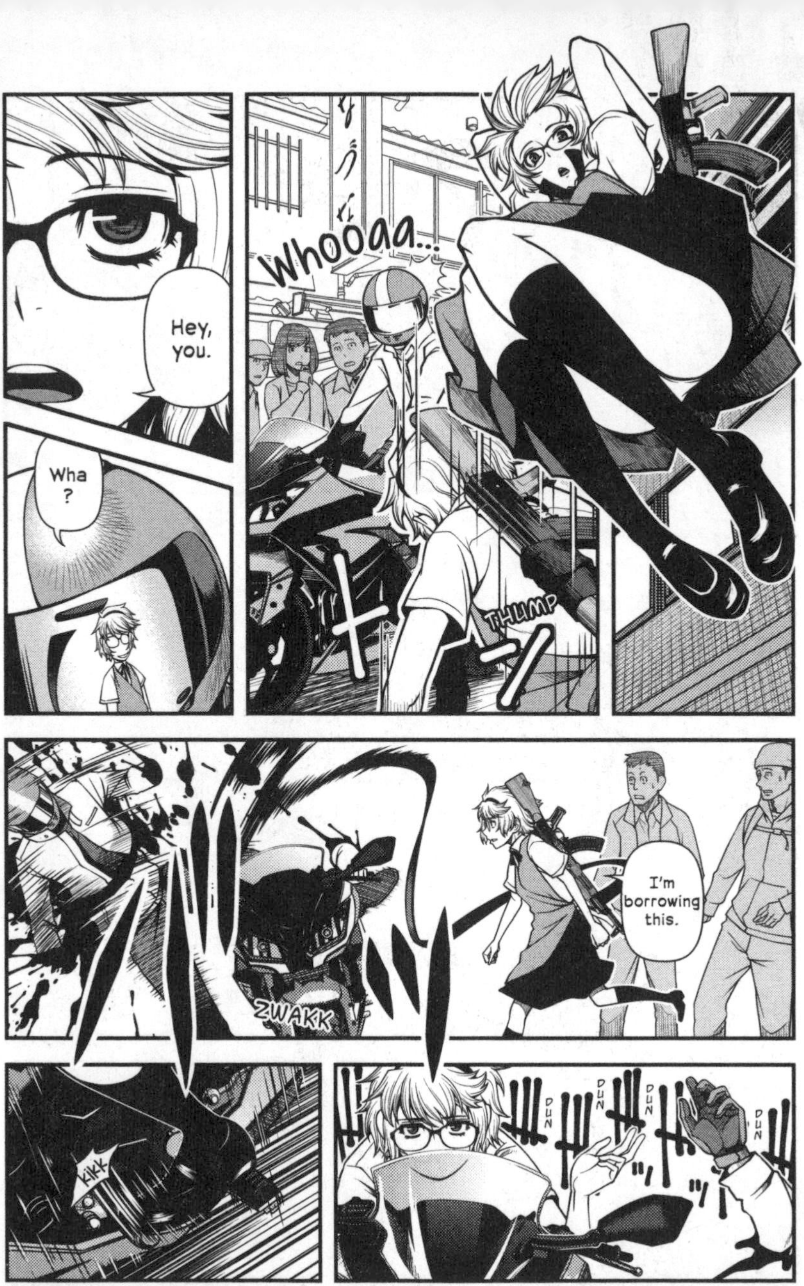
Whooaa...
THUMP
Hey, you.
Wha ?
I'm borrowing this.
ZWAKK
DUN
DUN
DUN
DUN
KIKK

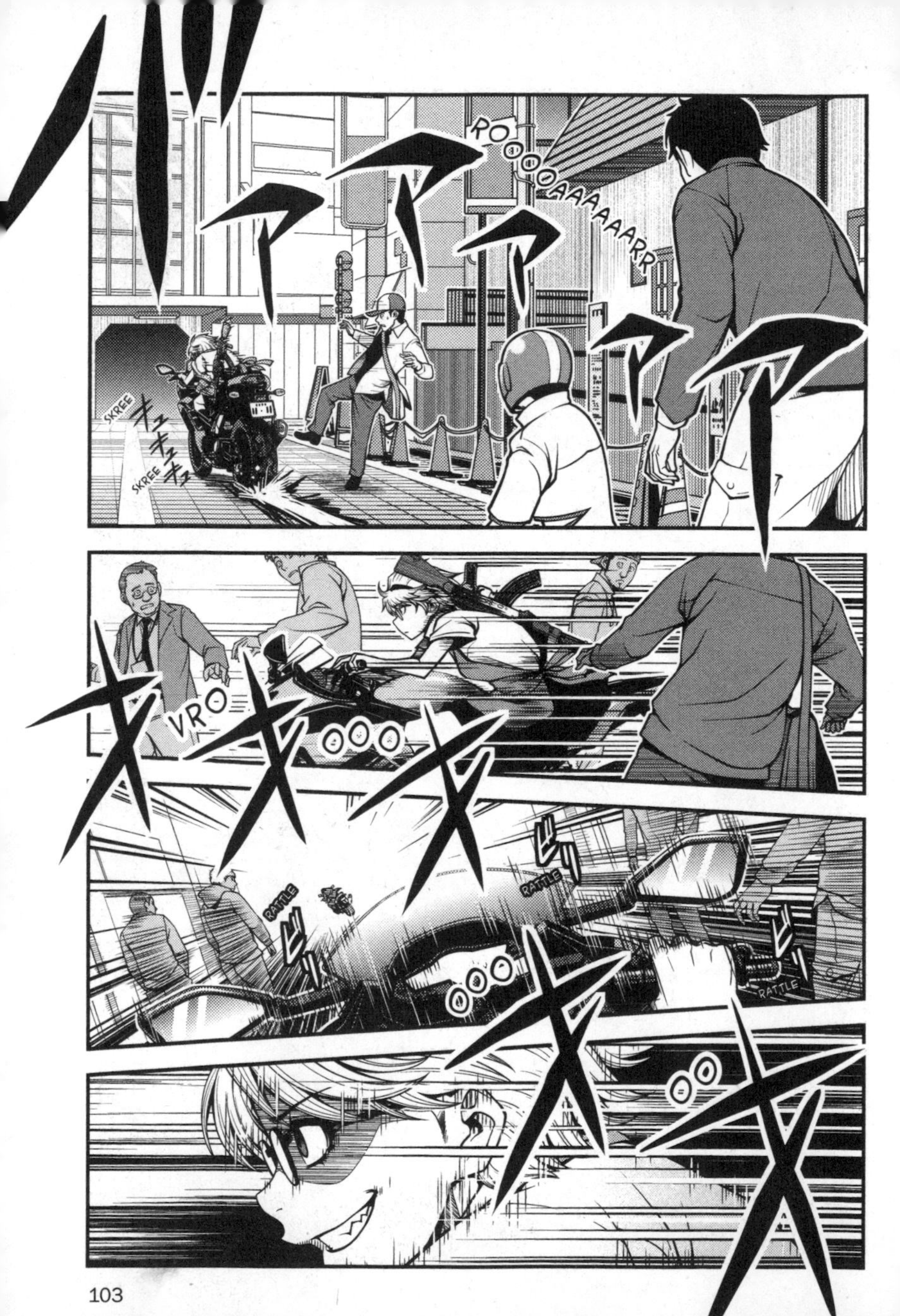
ROOOOAAAAAARR
SKREE
SKREE
VROOOO
RATTLE
RATTLE
RATTLE

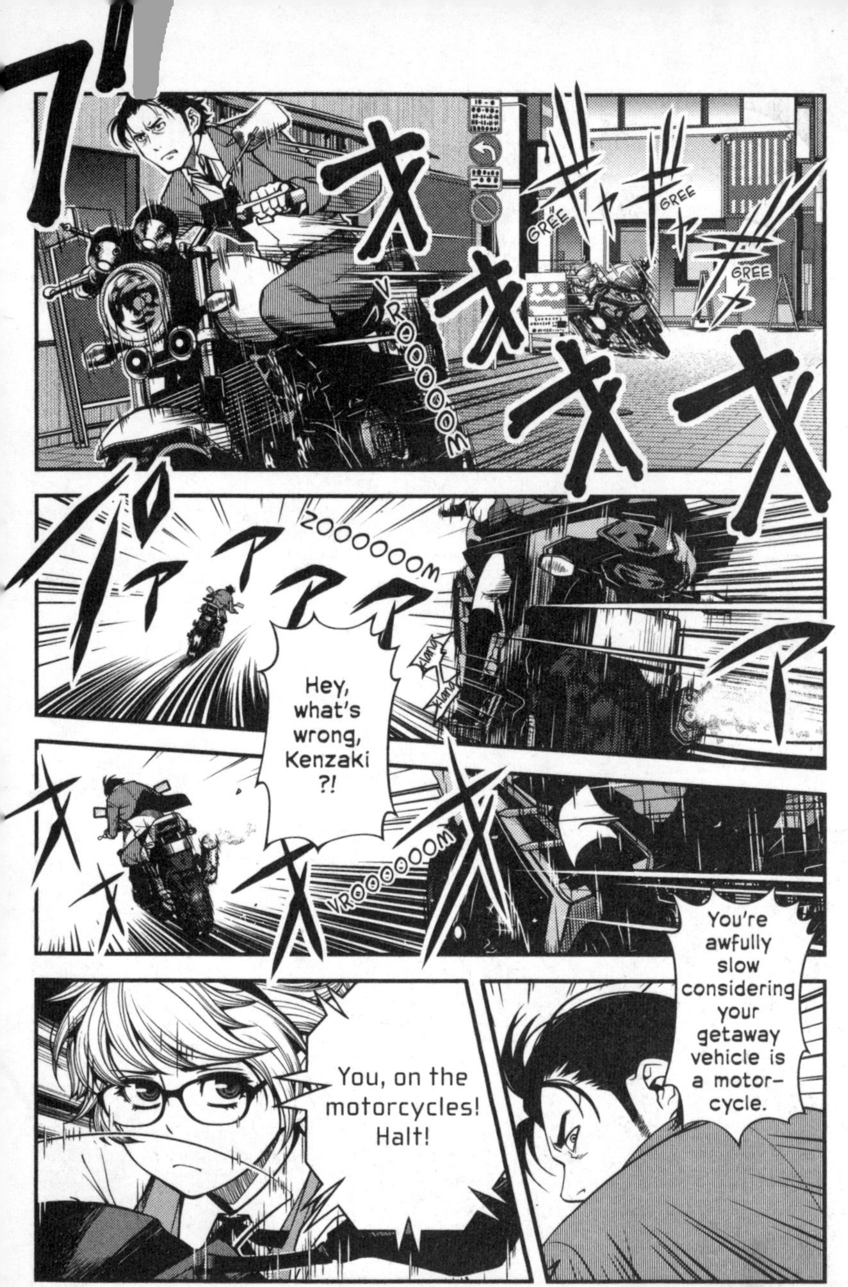
GREE
GREE
GREE
VROOOOOOOM
ZOOOOOOOM
klang
klang
Hey, what's wrong, Kenzaki ?!
VROOOOOOOM
You're awfully slow considering your getaway vehicle is a motor-cycle.
You, on the motorcycles! Halt!

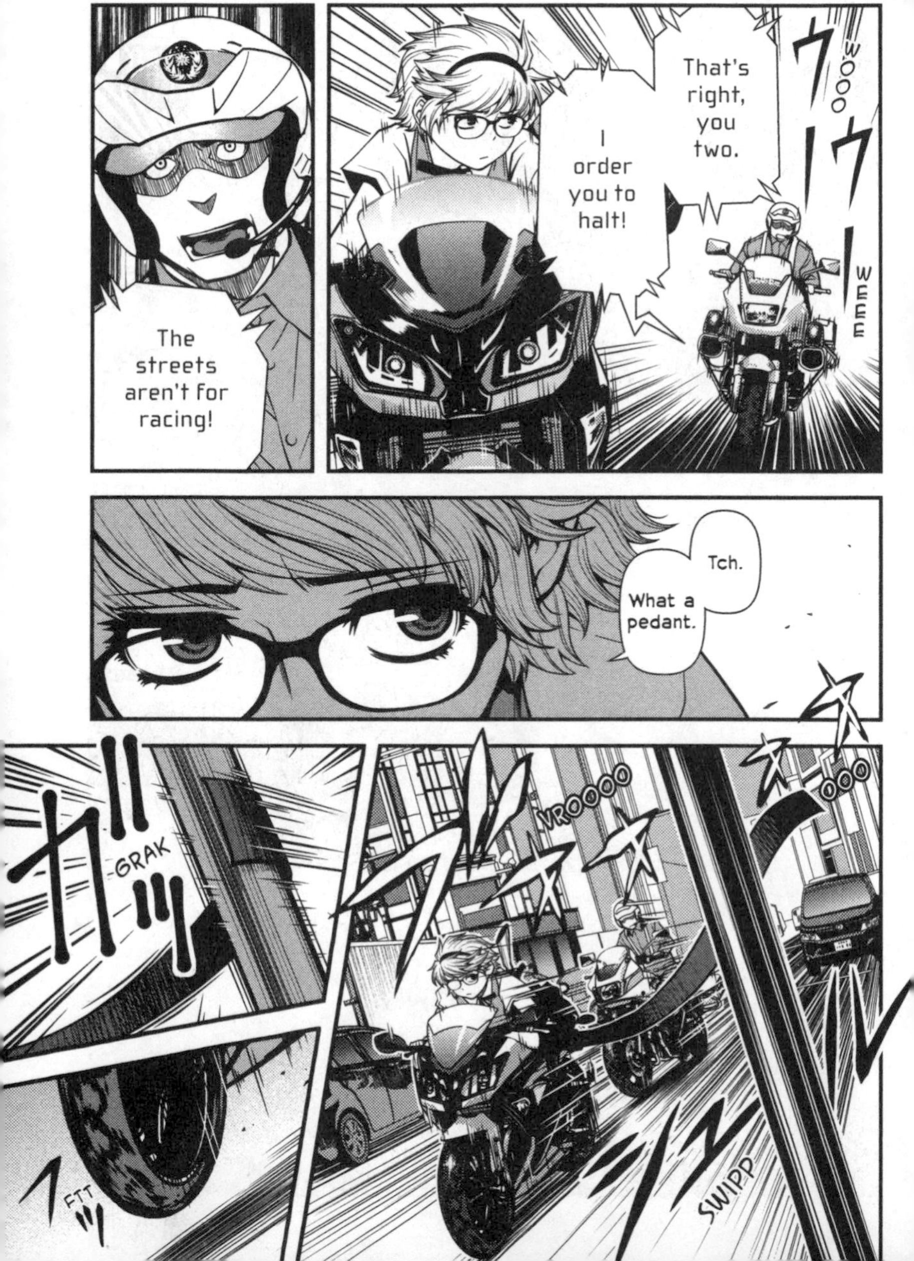

That's right, you two.
I order you to halt!
ウーウー
WOOO
WEEE
The streets aren't for racing!
Tch.
What a pedant.
VROOOO
OOO
SWIPP
カッ
GRAK
FTT

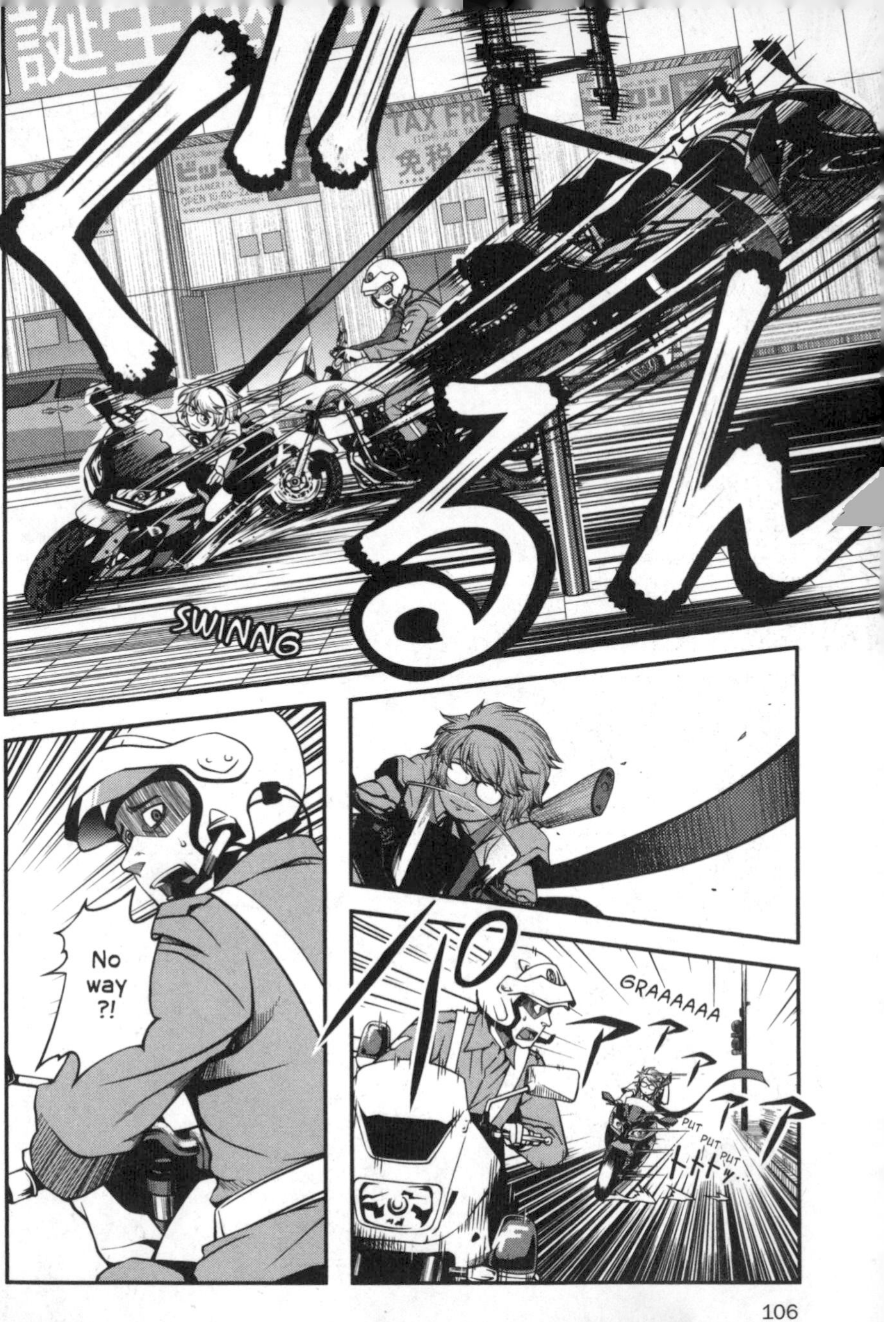
SWINNG
GRAAAAAA
PUT PUT PUT
トトトッ…
No way ?!

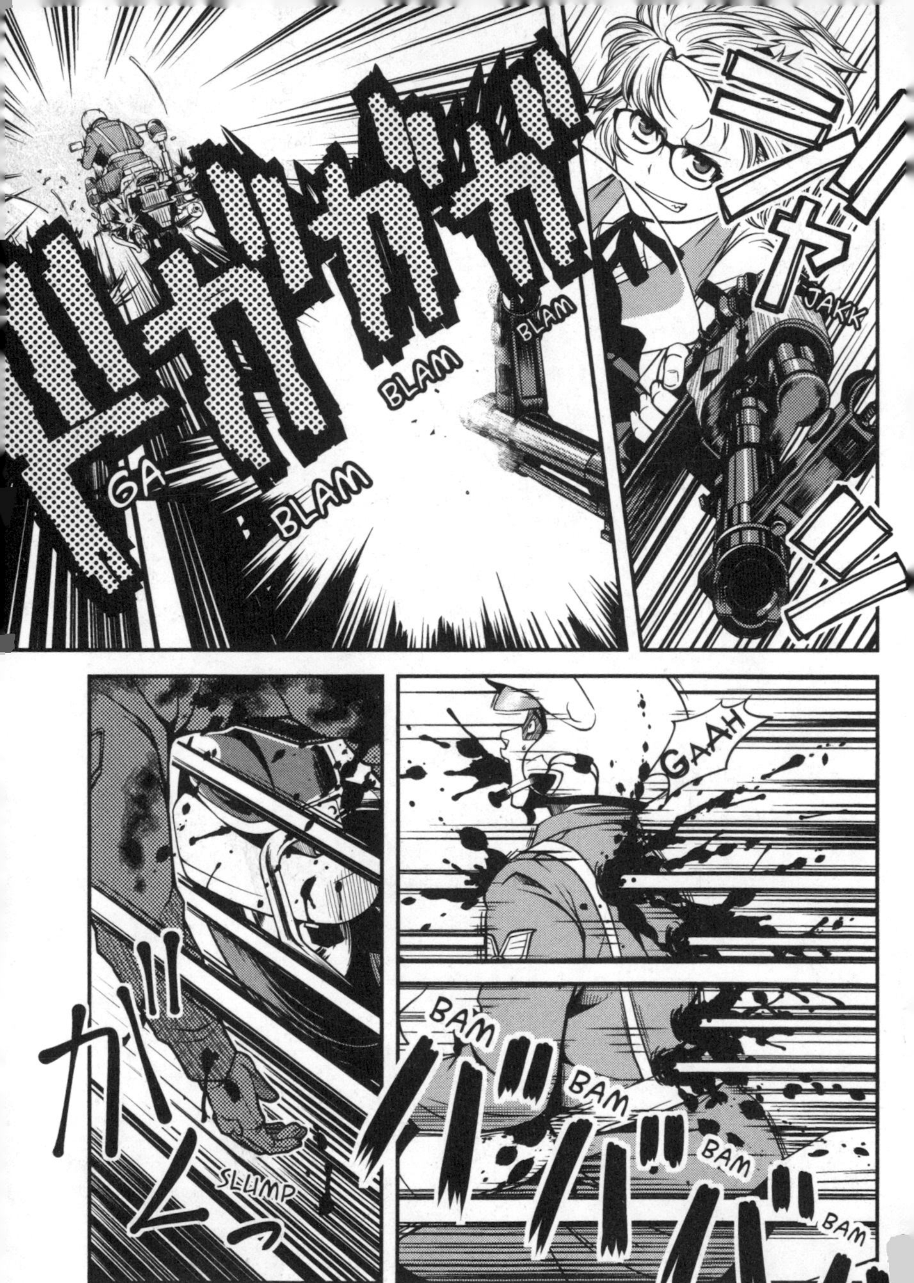
JAKK
BLAM
BLAM
BLAM
BLAM
GA
GAAH
BAM
BAM
BAM
BAM
SLUMP

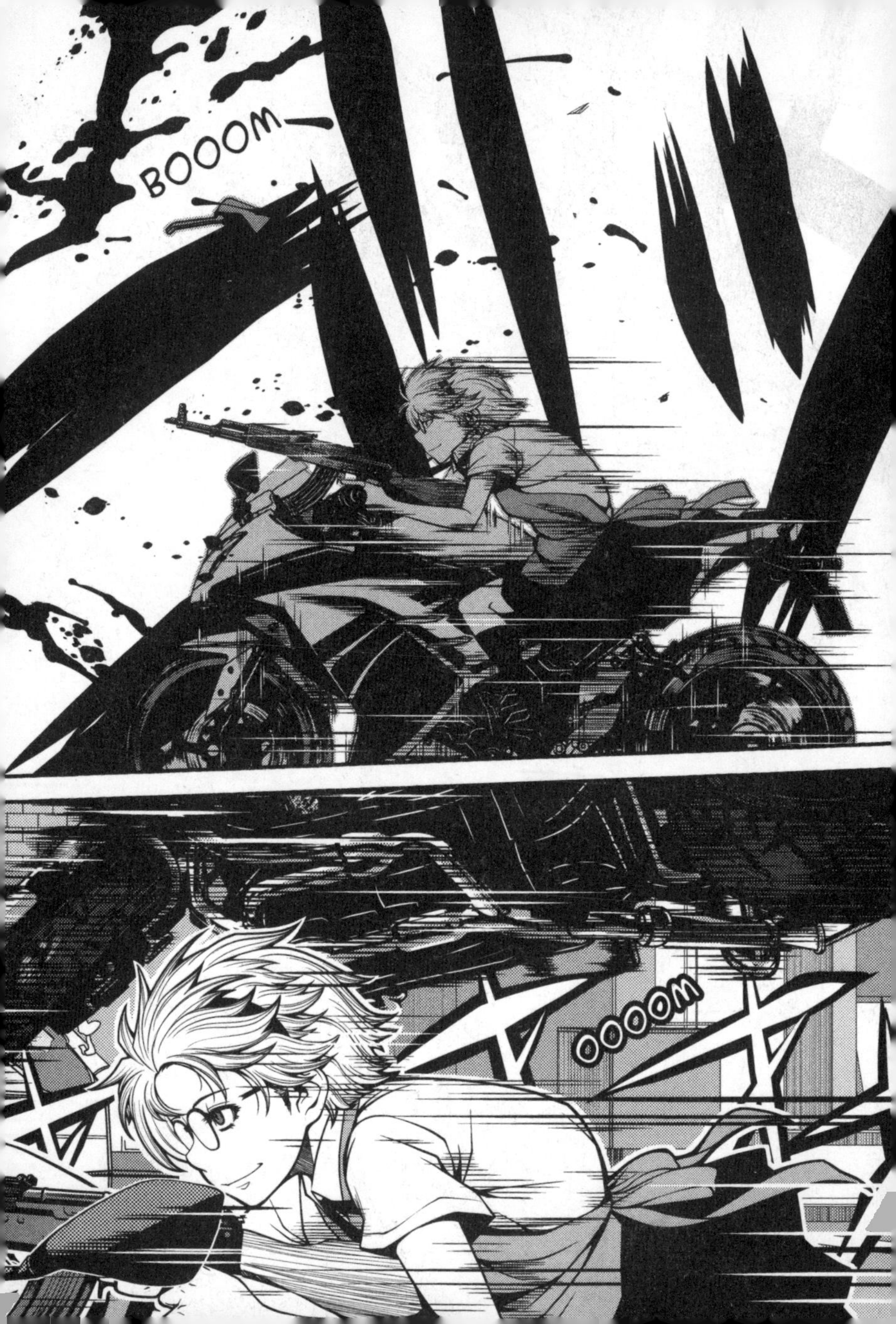
BOOOM
OOOOM

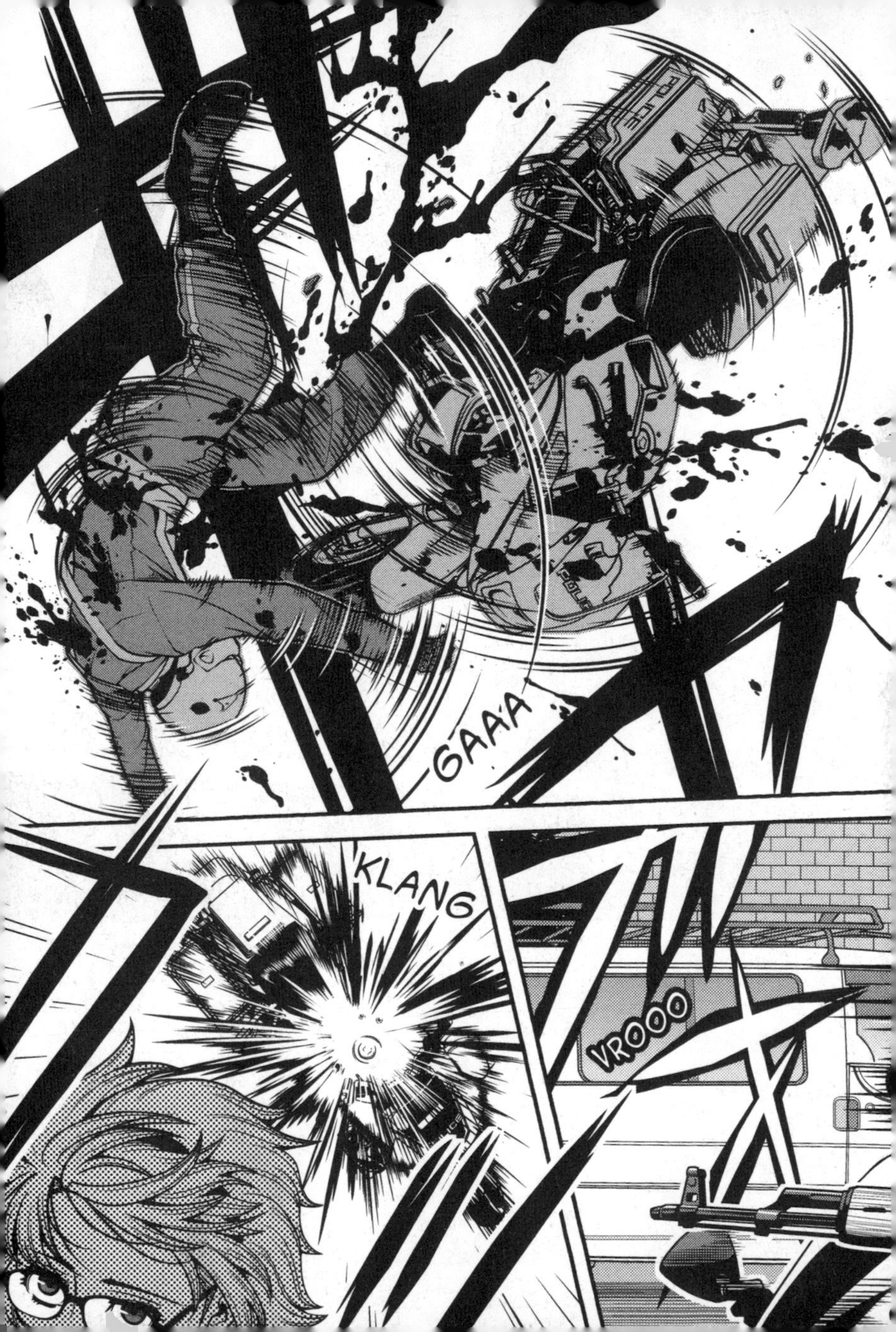
GAAA
VROOO
KLANG

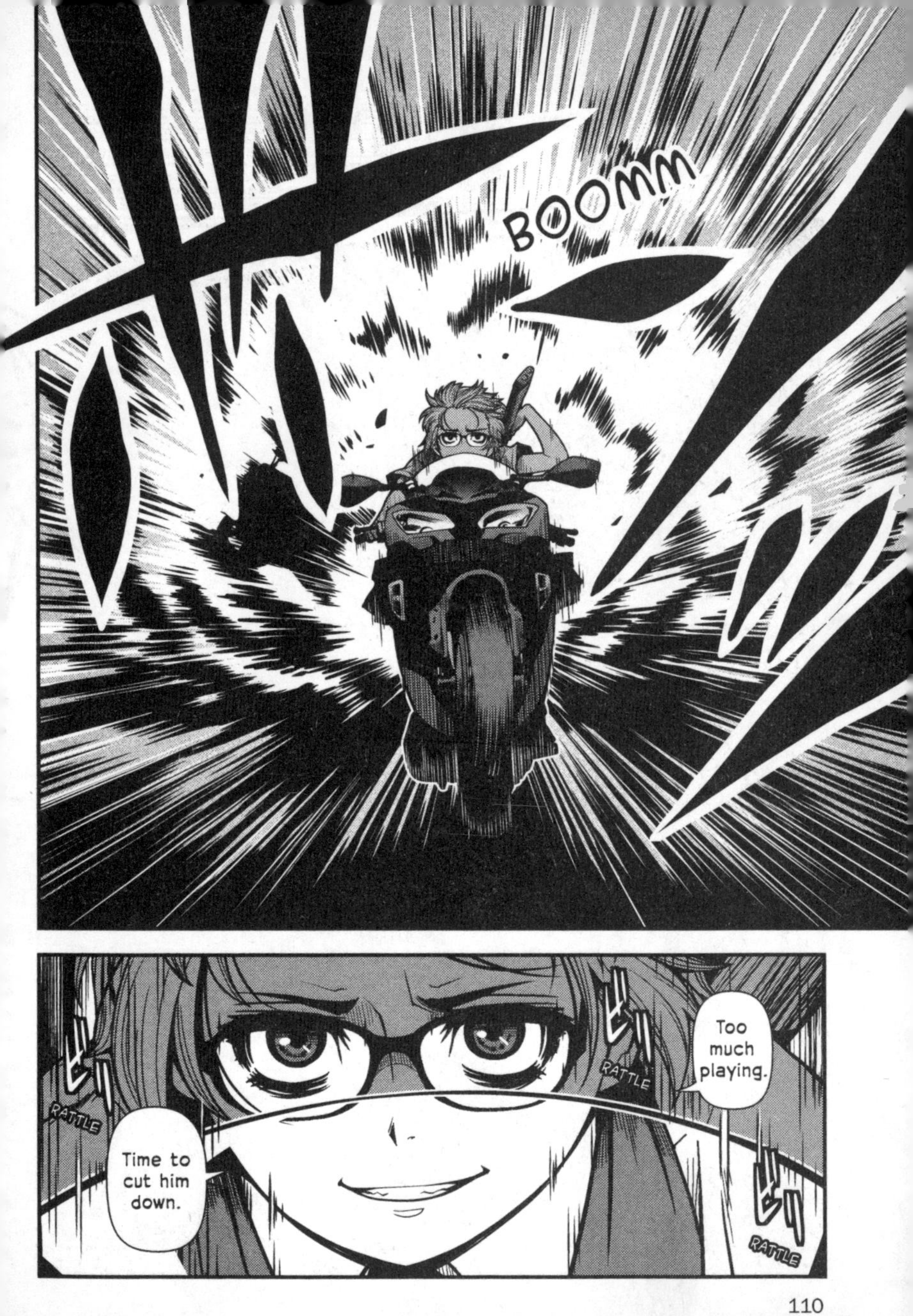
BOOMM
Too much playing.
RATTLE
RATTLE
RATTLE
Time to cut him down.

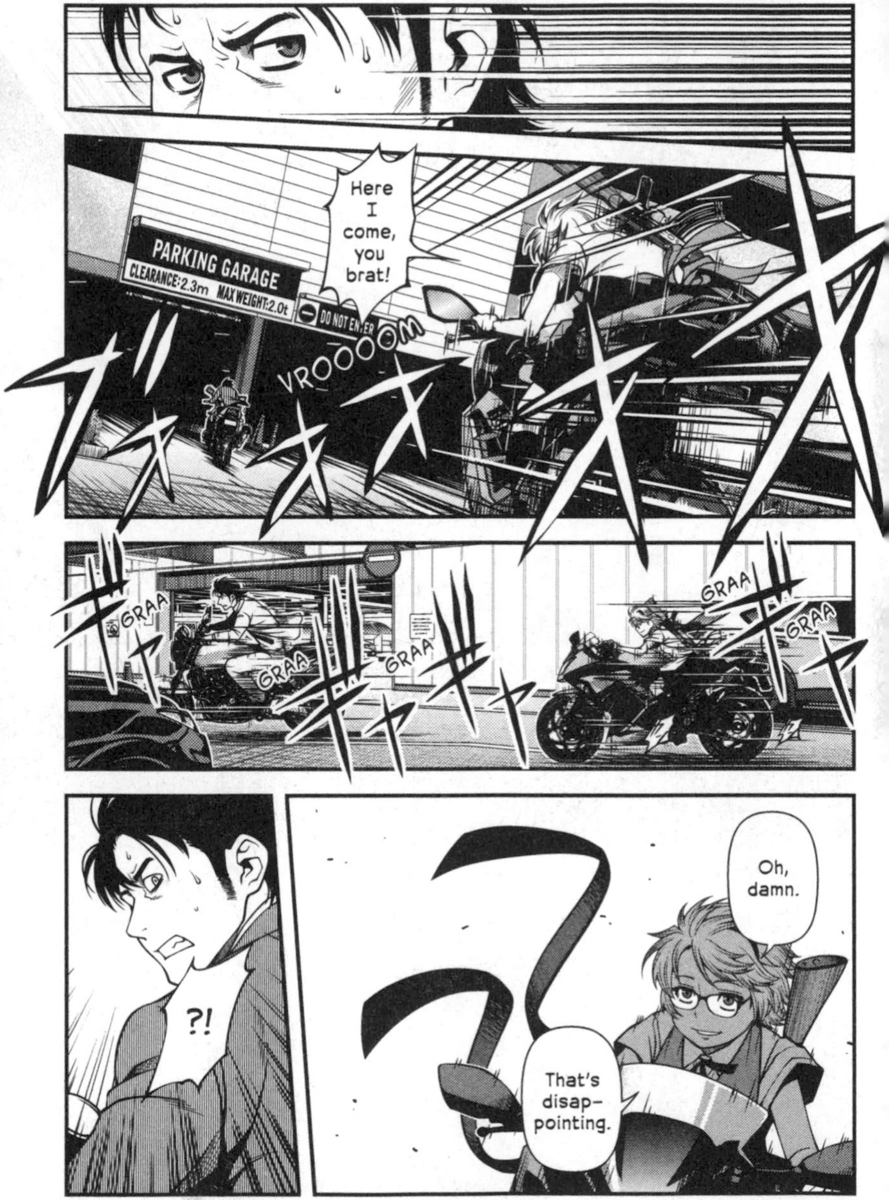
Here I come, you brat!
PARKING GARAGE
CLEARANCE:2.3m MAX WEIGHT:2.0t
DO NOT EN ER
VROOOOM
GRAA
GRAA
GRAA
GRAA
GRAA
Oh, damn.
That's disap-pointing.
?!

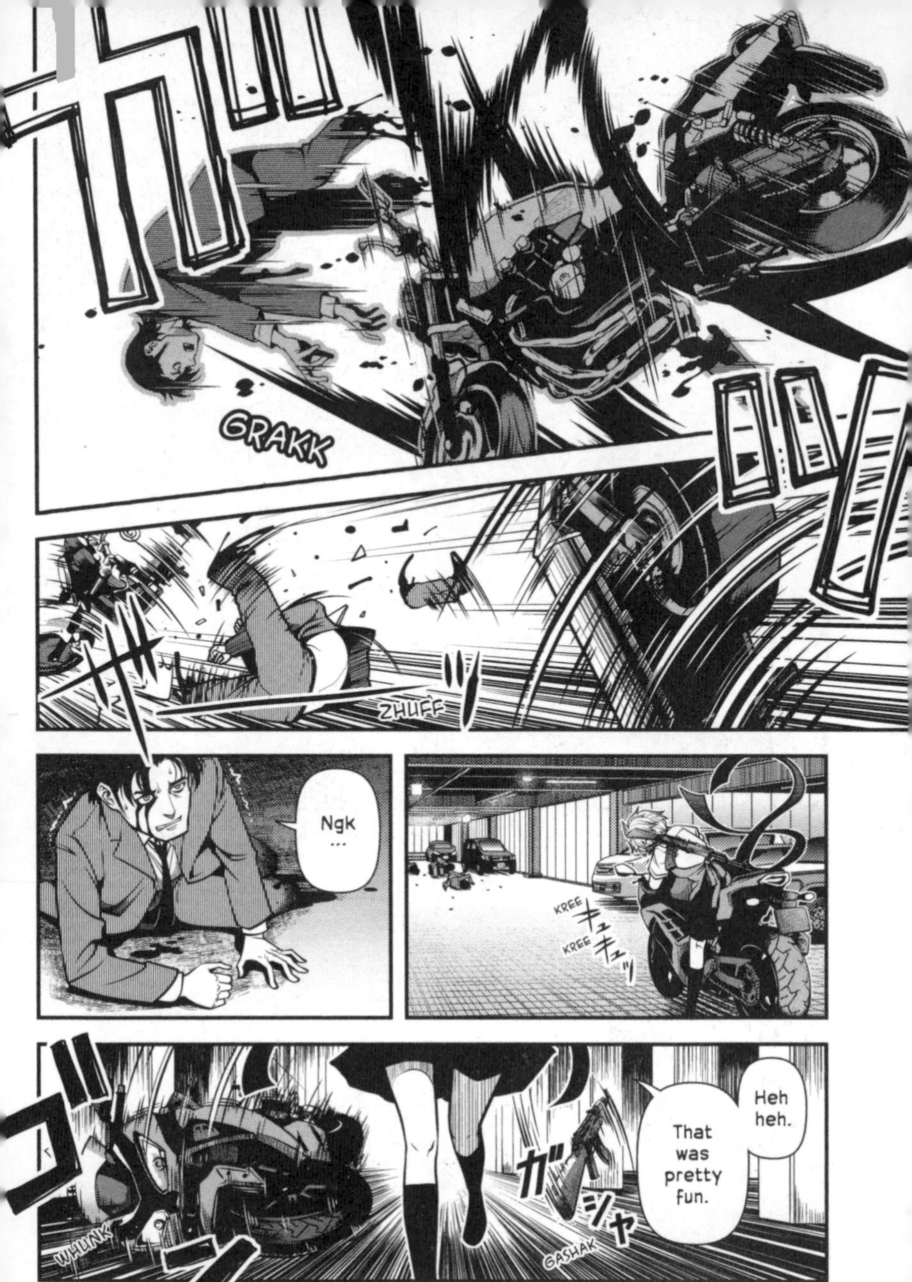
GRAKK
ZHUFF
KREE
KREE
Ngk ...
Heh heh.
That was pretty fun.
GASHAK
WHUNK

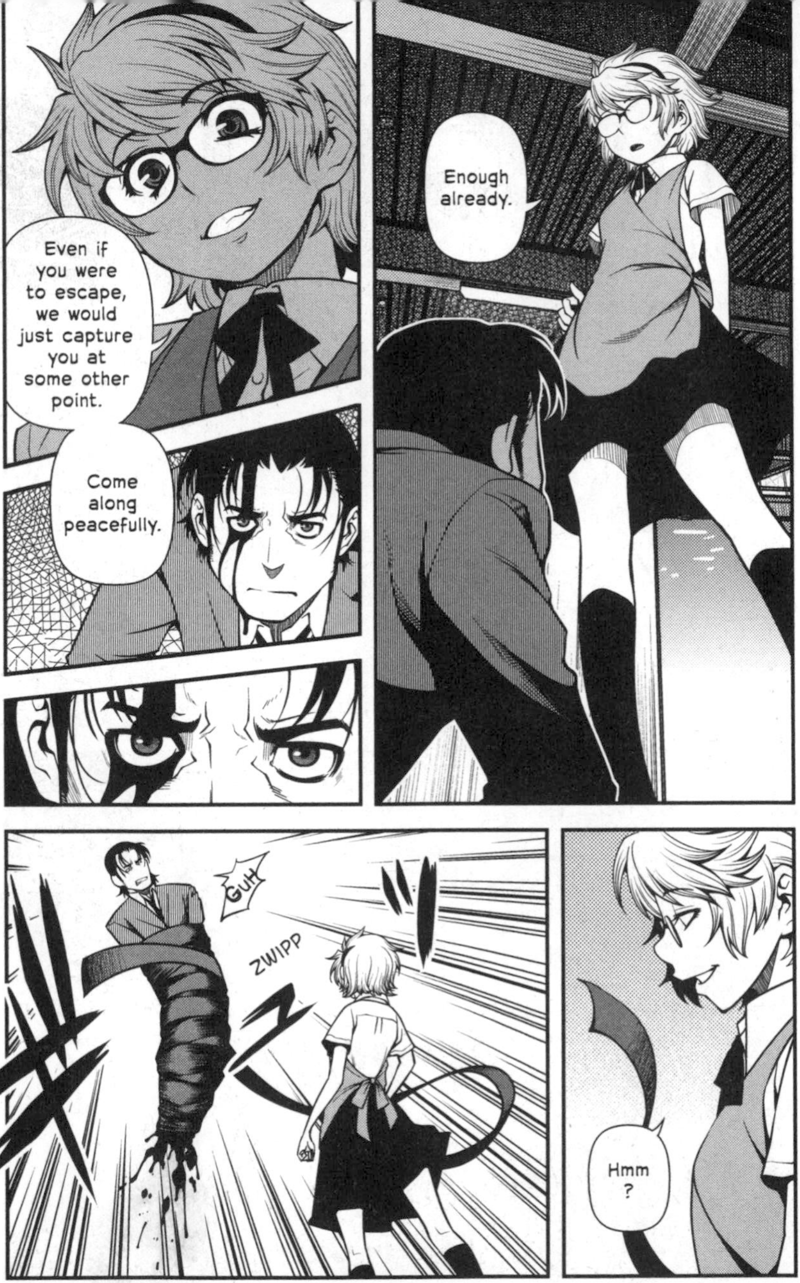
Enough already.
Even if you were to escape, we would just capture you at some other point.
Come along peacefully.
Hmm?
GUH
ZWIPP

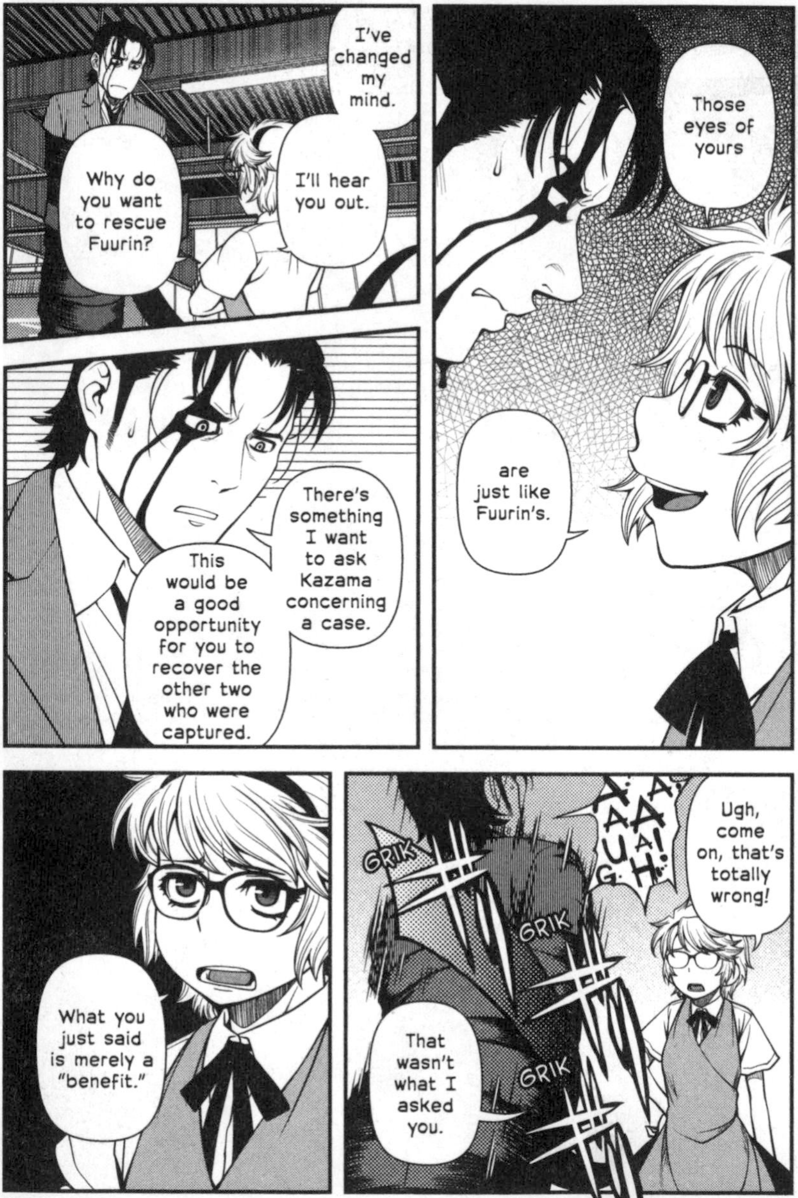
Those eyes of yours
are just like Fuurin's.
I've changed my mind.
I'll hear you out.
Why do you want to rescue Fuurin?
There's something I want to ask Kazama concerning a case.
This would be a good opportunity for you to recover the other two who were captured.
AAAAAUGH!
Ugh, come on, that's totally wrong!
GRIK
GRIK
GRIK
That wasn't what I asked you.
What you just said is merely a "benefit."

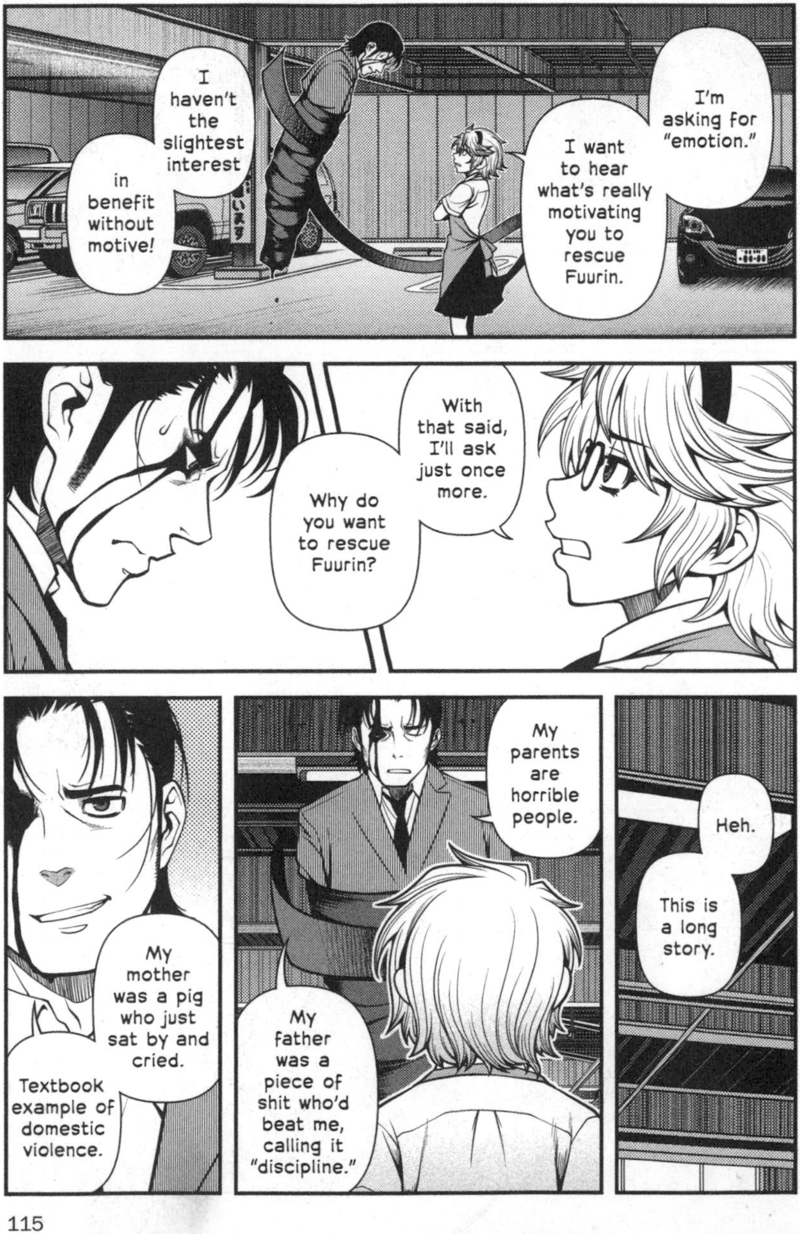
I'm asking for "emotion."
I want to hear what's really motivating you to rescue Fuurin.
I haven't the slightest interest
in benefit without motive!
With that said, I'll ask just once more.
Why do you want to rescue Fuurin?
Heh.
This is a long story.
My parents are horrible people.
My father was a piece of shit who'd beat me, calling it "discipline."
My mother was a pig who just sat by and cried.
Textbook example of domestic violence.

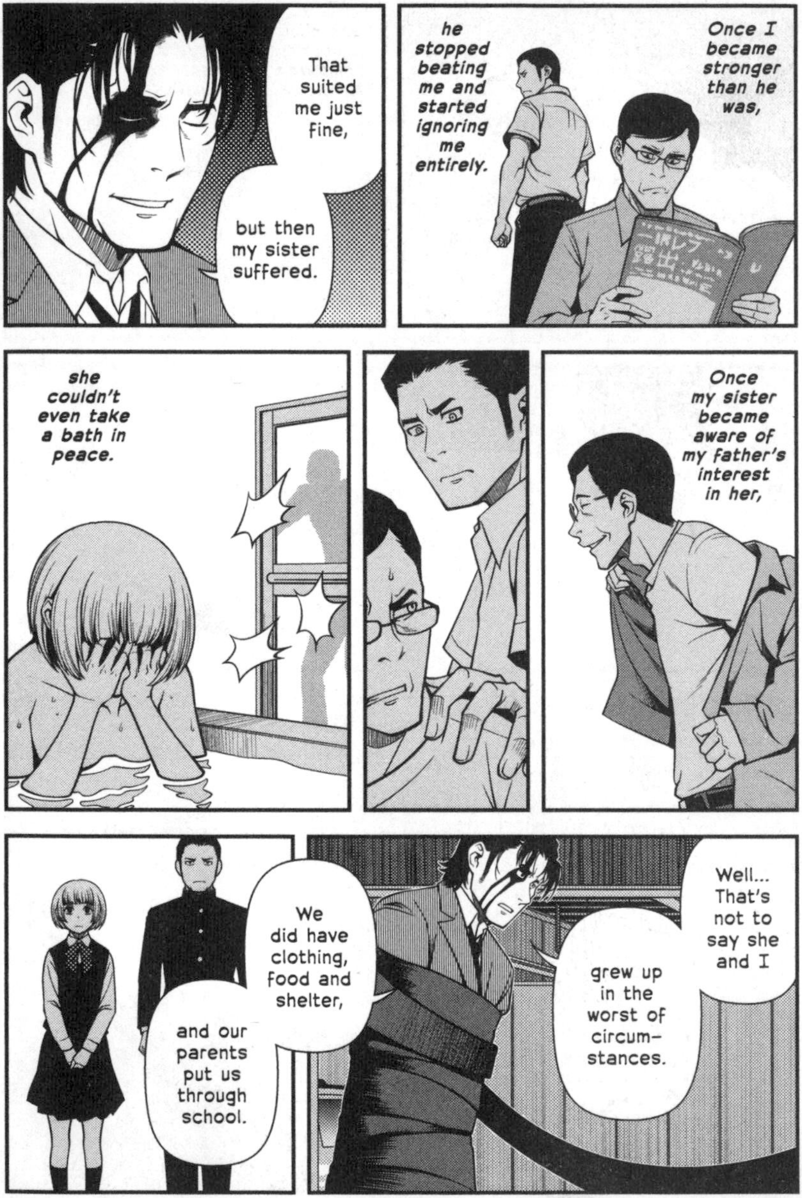
Once I became stronger than he was,
he stopped beating me and started ignoring me entirely.
That suited me just fine,
but then my sister suffered.
Once my sister became aware of my father's interest in her,
she couldn't even take a bath in peace.
Well... That's not to say she and I
grew up in the worst of circum-stances.
We did have clothing, food and shelter,
and our parents put us through school.

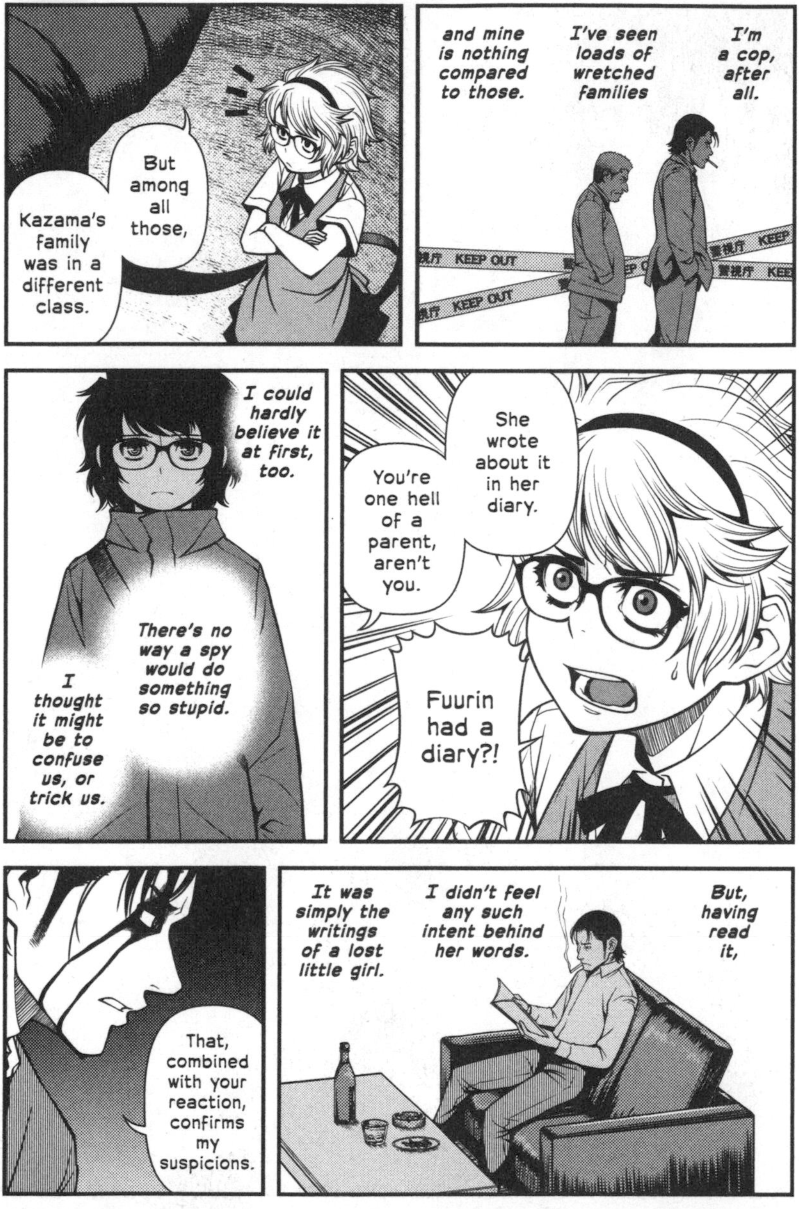
I'm a cop, after all.
I've seen loads of wretched families
and mine is nothing compared to those.
KEEP OUT
KEEP OUT
But among all those,
Kazama's family was in a different class.
She wrote about it in her diary.
You're one hell of a parent, aren't you.
Fuurin had a diary?!
I could hardly believe it at first, too.
There's no way a spy would do something so stupid.
I thought it might be to confuse us, or trick us.
But, having read it,
I didn't feel any such intent behind her words.
It was simply the writings of a lost little girl.
That, combined with your reaction, confirms my suspicions.

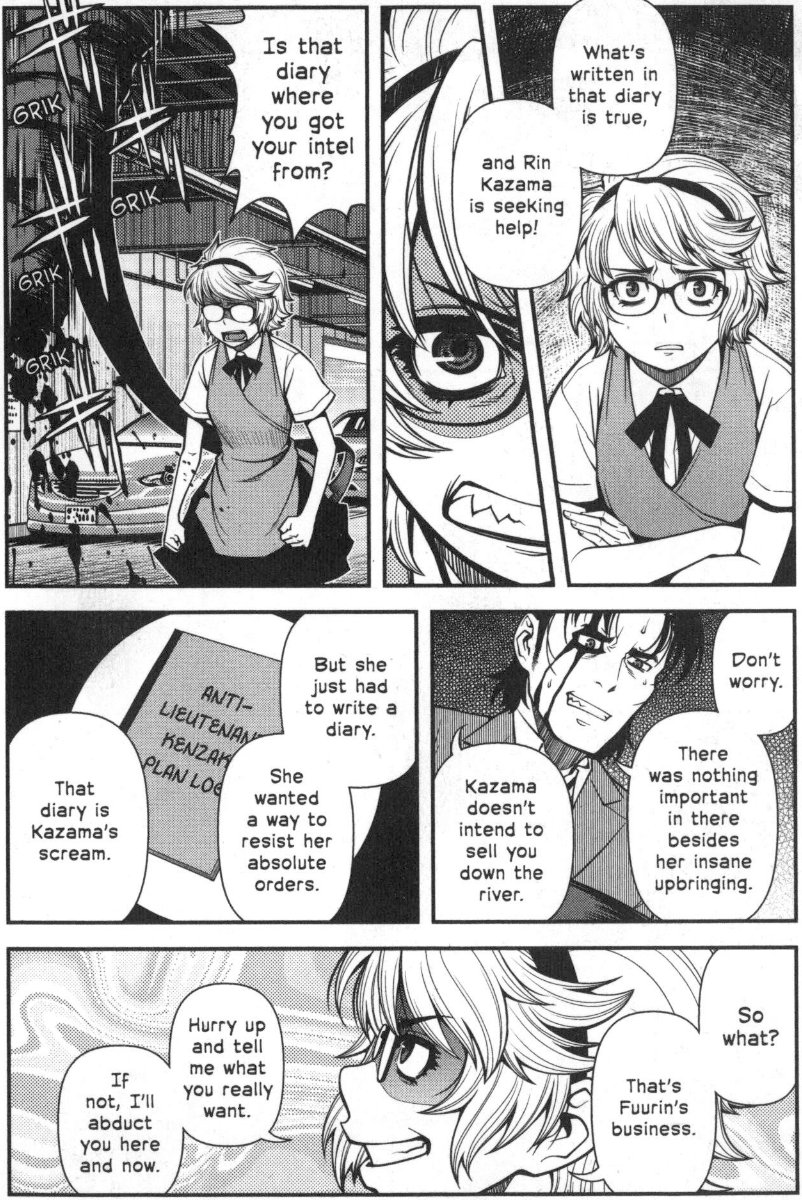
What's written in that diary is true,
and Rin Kazama is seeking help!
Is that diary where you got your intel from?
GRIK
GRIK
GRIK
GRIK
Don't worry.
There was nothing important in there besides her insane upbringing.
Kazama doesn't intend to sell you down the river.
But she just had to write a diary.
ANTI-
LIEUTENAN
KENZAK
PLAN LOG
She wanted a way to resist her absolute orders.
That diary is Kazama's scream.
So what?
That's Fuurin's business.
Hurry up and tell me what you really want.
If not, I'll abduct you here and now.

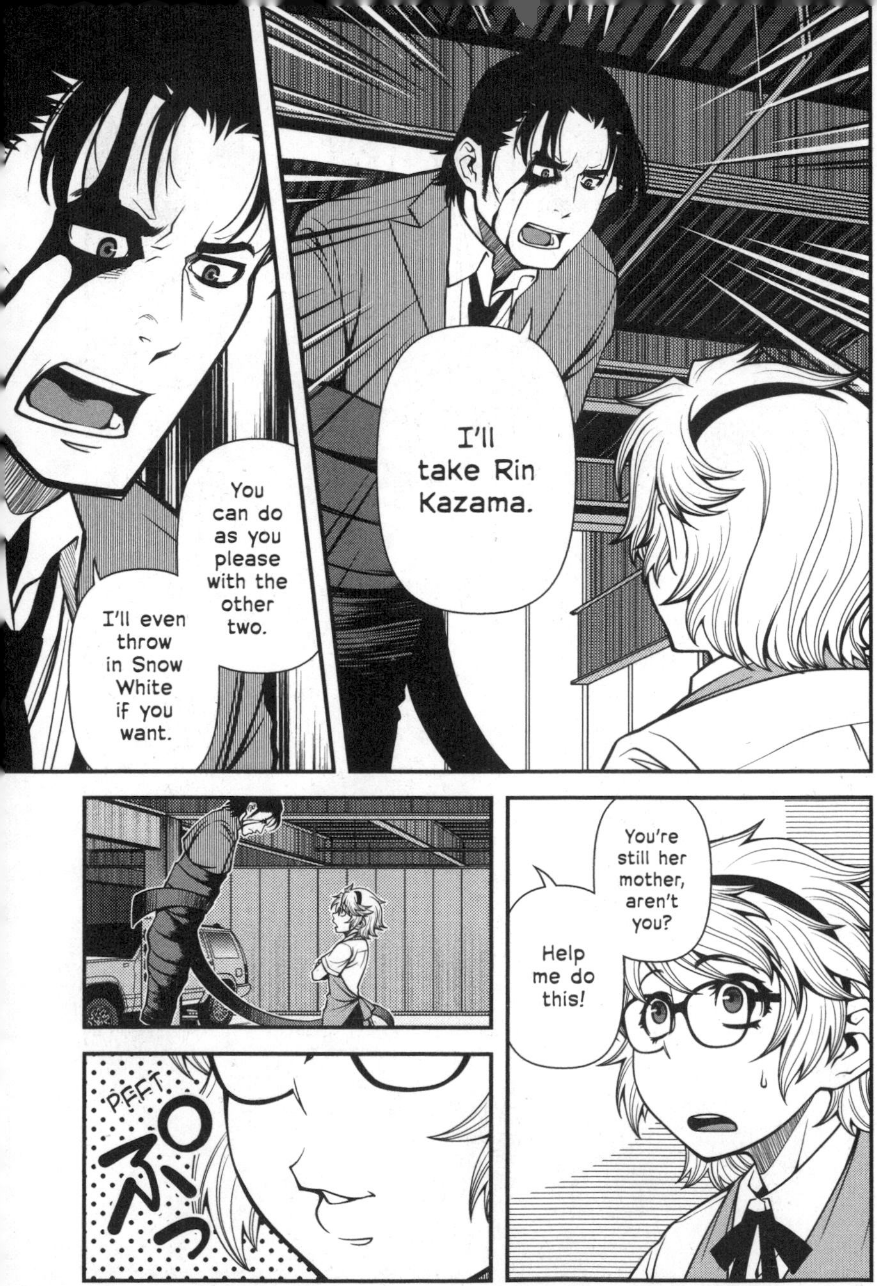

I'll take Rin Kazama.
You can do as you please with the other two.
I'll even throw in Snow White if you want.
You're still her mother, aren't you?
Help me do this!
PFFT
ふっ

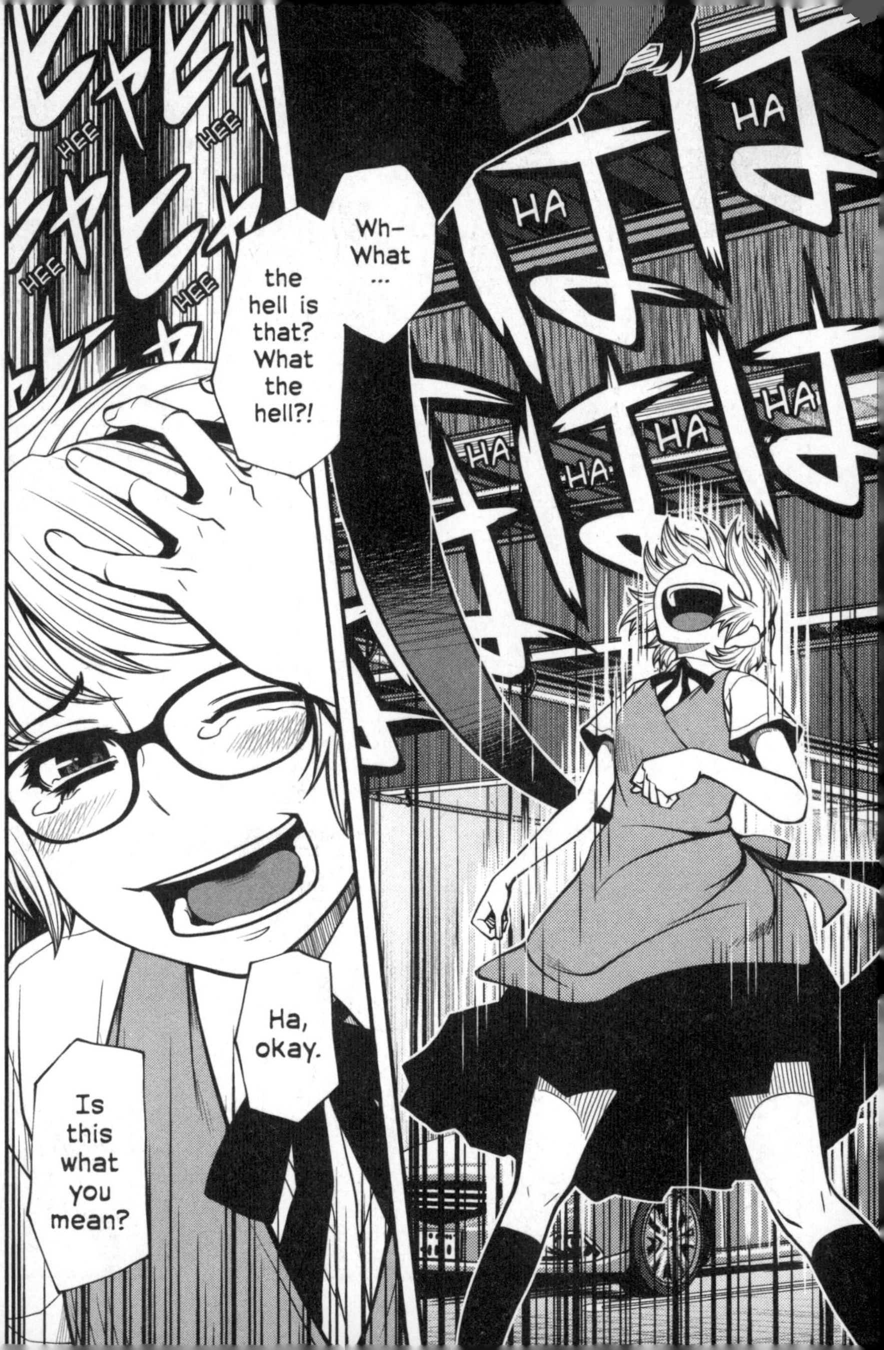

HA
HA
HA
HA
HA
HA
HEE
HEE
HEE
HEE
Wh- What ...
the hell is that? What the hell?!
Ha, okay.
Is this what you mean?

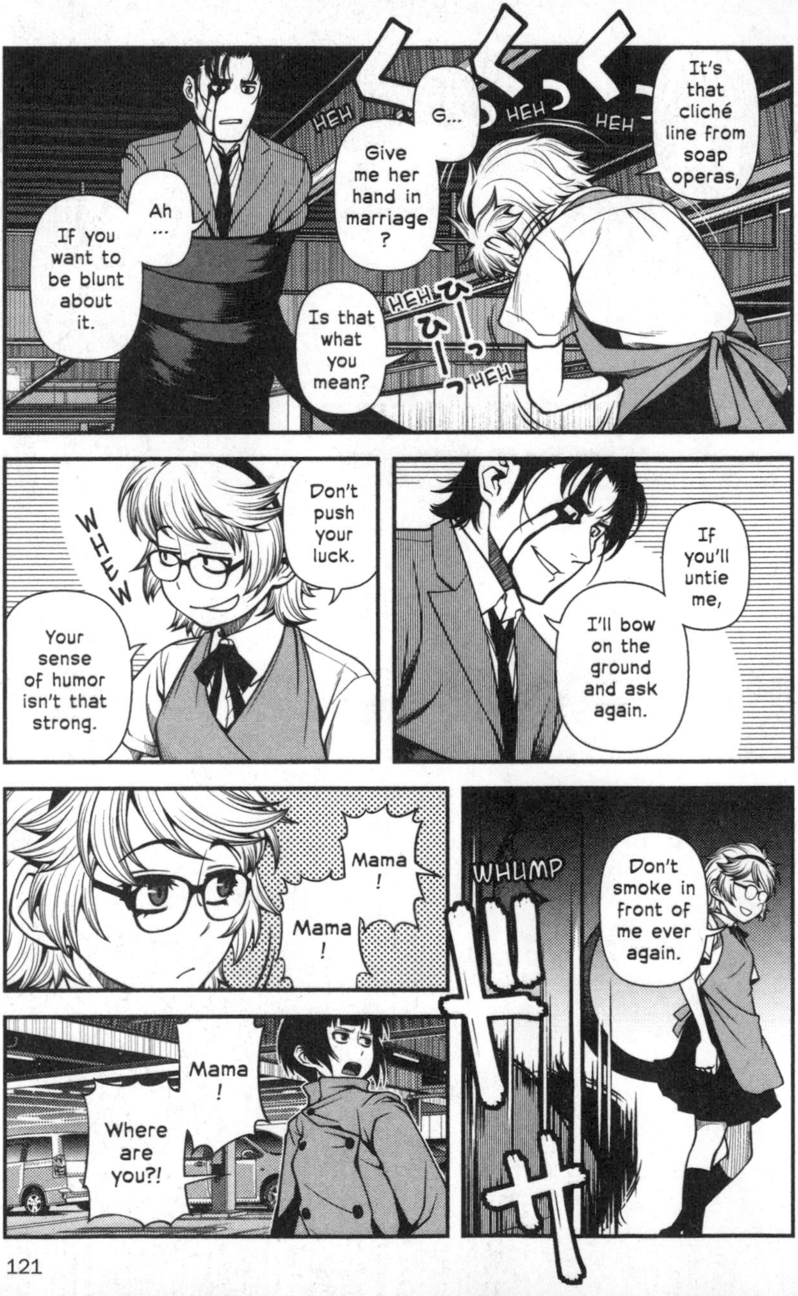
It's that cliché line from soap operas,
HEH HEH HEH
G... Give me her hand in marriage?
HEH HEH
ひーっ ひーっ
Is that what you mean?
Ah ... If you want to be blunt about it.
If you'll untie me,
I'll bow on the ground and ask again.
Don't push your luck.
WHEW
Your sense of humor isn't that strong.
Don't smoke in front of me ever again.
WHUMP
Mama!
Mama!
Mama!
Where are you?!

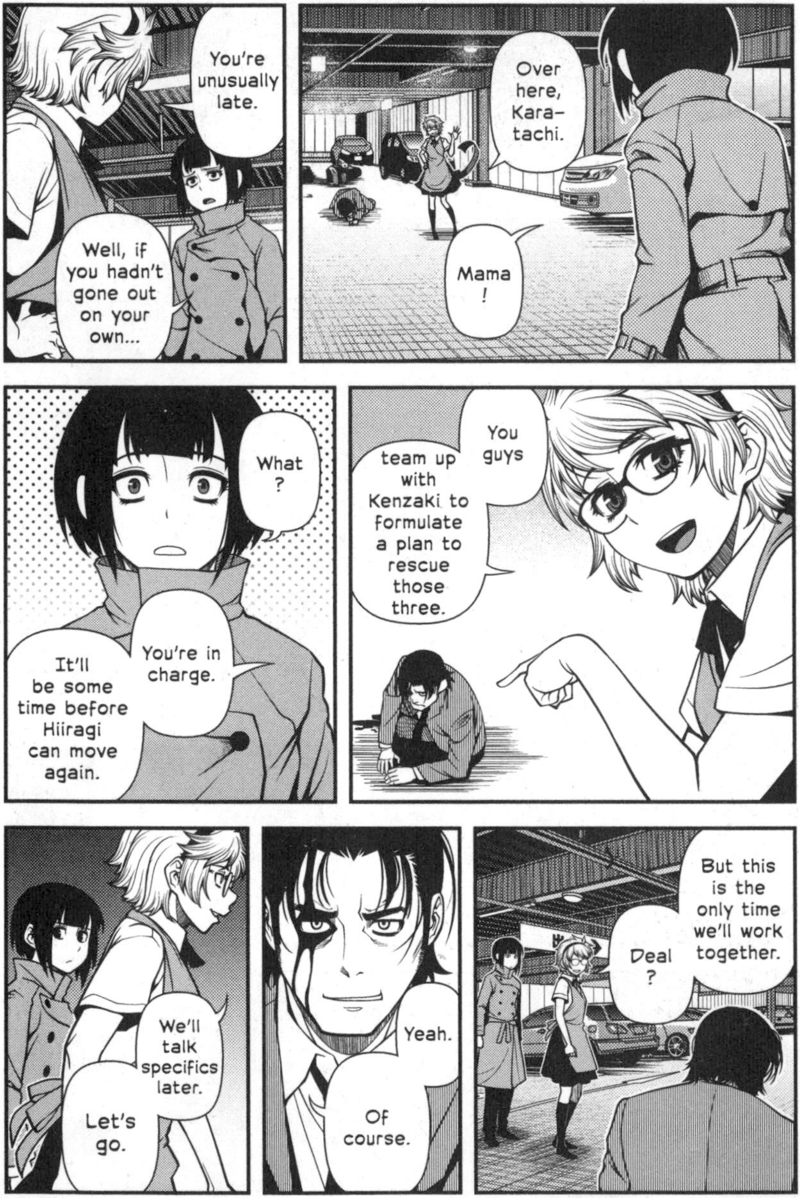
Over here, Karatachi.
Mama!
You're unusually late.
Well, if you hadn't gone out on your own...
You guys
team up with Kenzaki to formulate a plan to rescue those three.
What?
You're in charge.
It'll be some time before Hiiragi can move again.
But this is the only time we'll work together.
Deal?
Yeah.
Of course.
We'll talk specifics later.
Let's go.

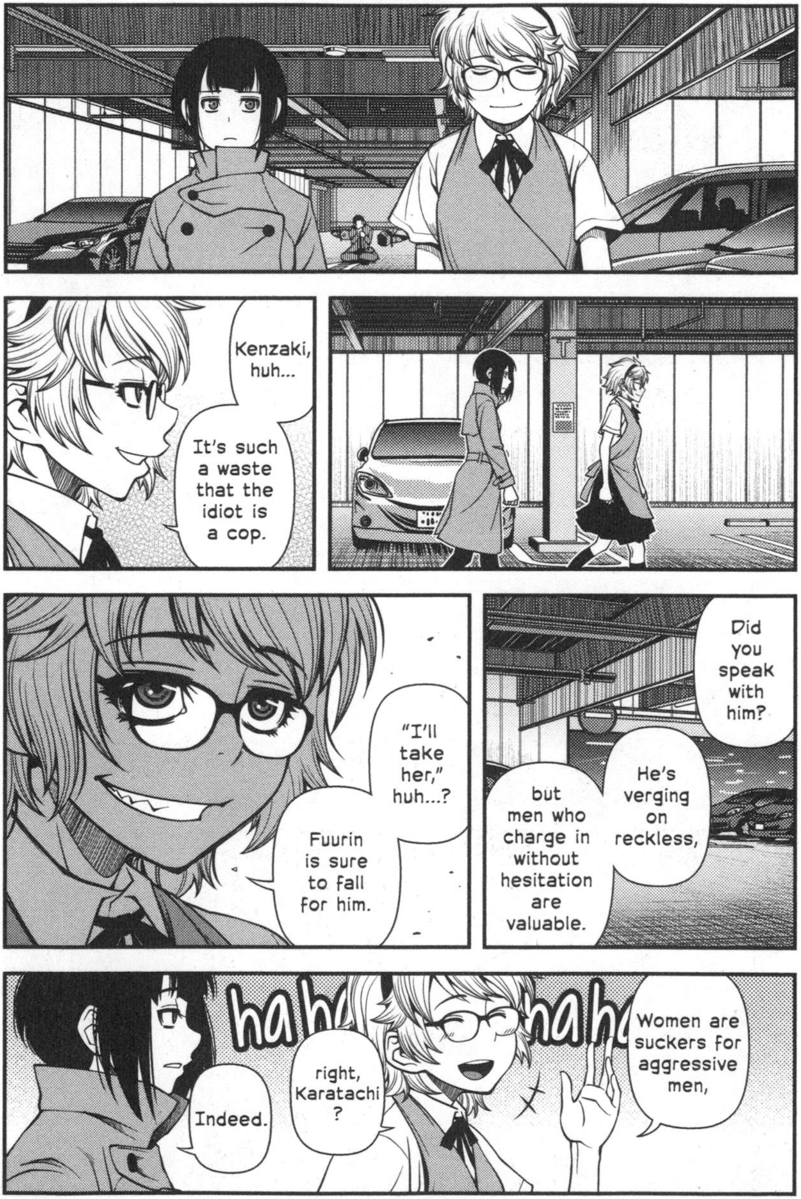
Kenzaki, huh...
It's such a waste that the idiot is a cop.
Did you speak with him?
He's verging on reckless,
but men who charge in without hesitation are valuable.
"I'll take her," huh...?
Fuurin is sure to fall for him.
Women are suckers for aggressive men,
right, Karatachi ?
Indeed.

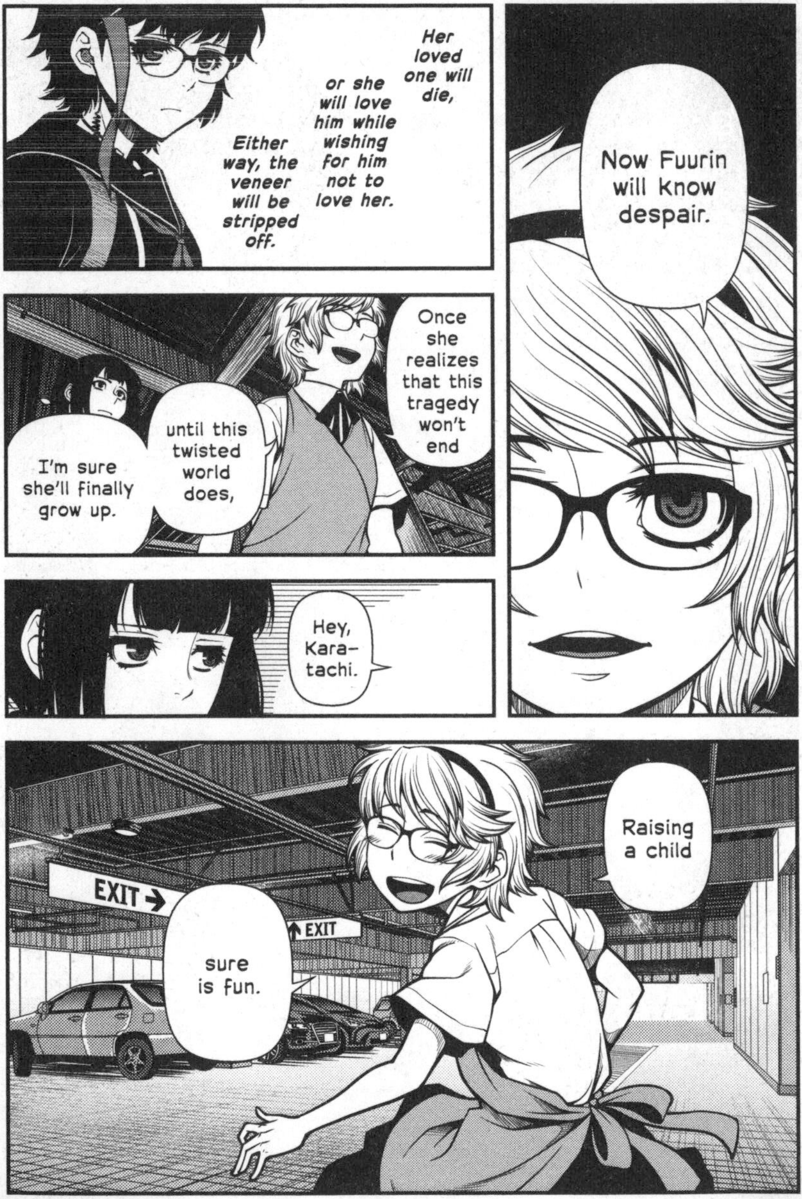
Now Fuurin will know despair.
Her loved one will die,
or she will love him while wishing for him not to love her.
Either way, the veneer will be stripped off.
Once she realizes that this tragedy won't end
until this twisted world does,
I'm sure she'll finally grow up.
Hey, Kara-tachi.
Raising a child
sure is fun.
EXIT
EXIT

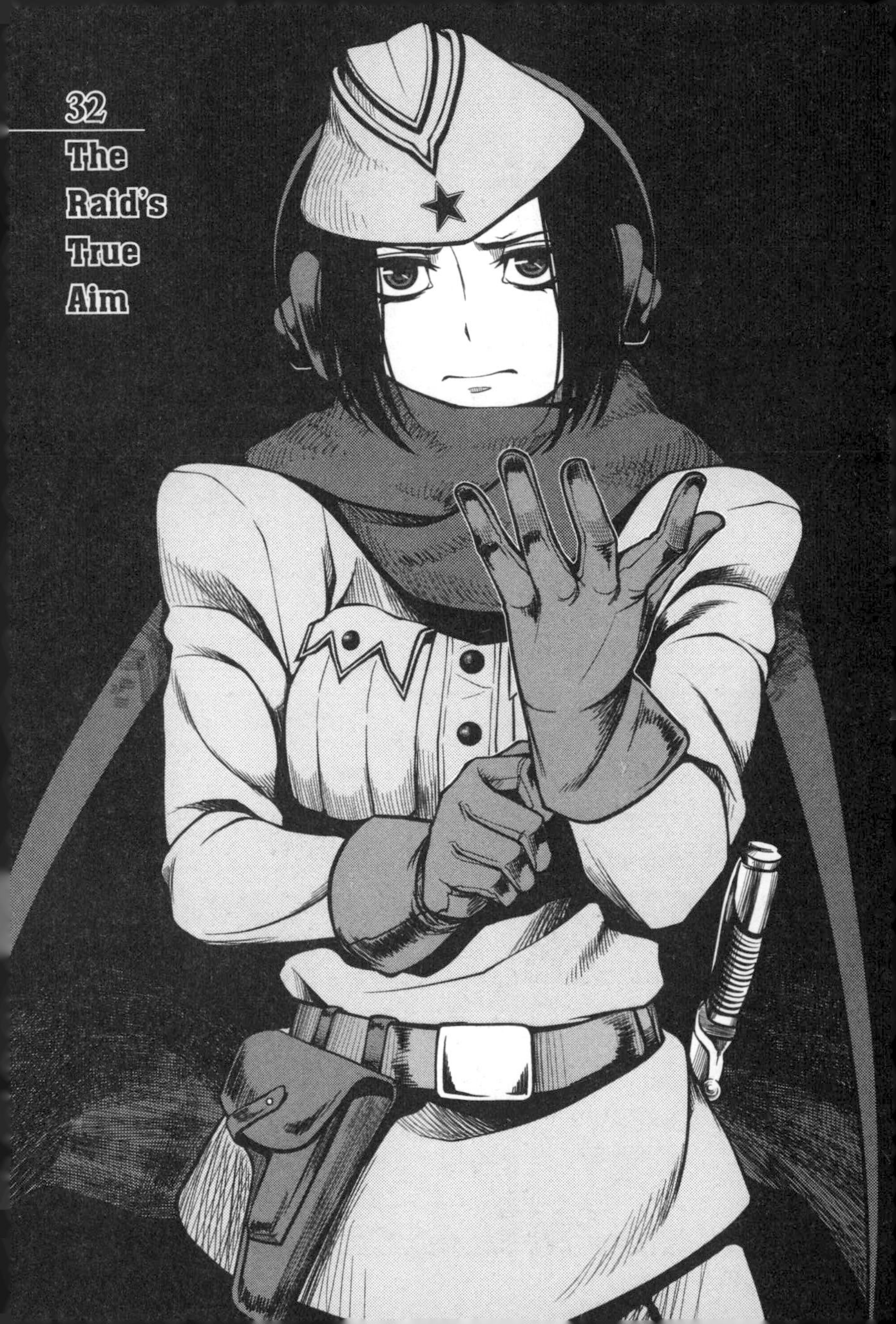
32
The Raid's True Aim

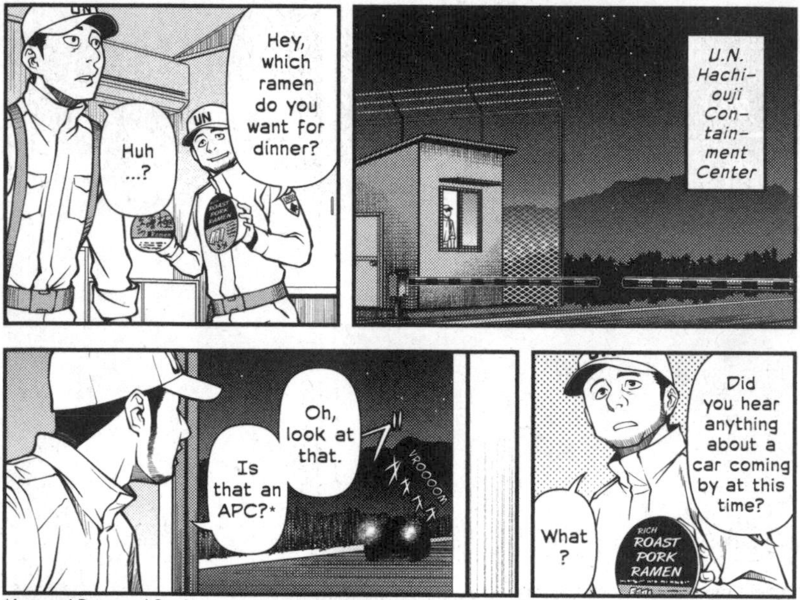
U.N. Hachi-ouji Con-tain-ment Center
Hey, which ramen do you want for dinner?
Huh ...?
ROAST PORK RAMEN
Did you hear anything about a car coming by at this time?
What ?
RICH ROAST PORK RAMEN
VROOOOM
Oh, look at that.
Is that an APC?*

*Armored Personnel Carrier

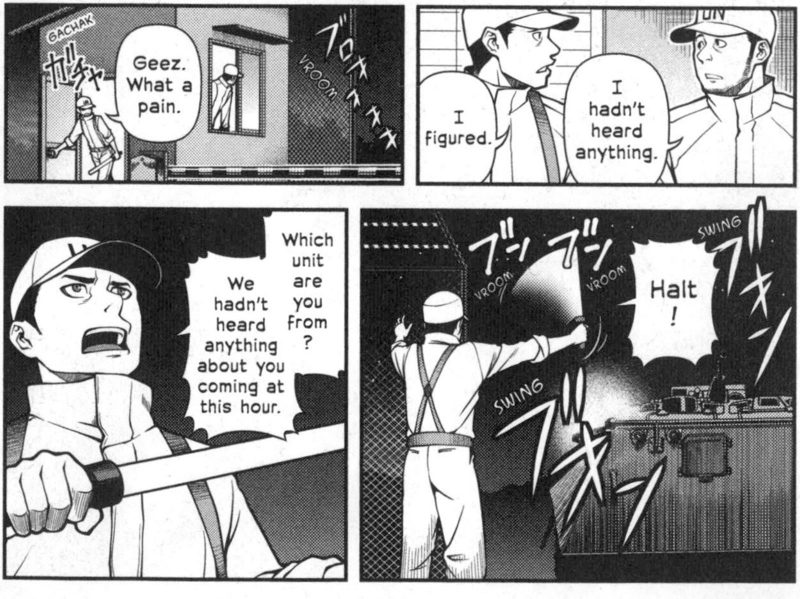
I hadn't heard anything.
I figured.
VROOM
Geez. What a pain.
GACHAK
SWING
Halt !
VROOM
VROOM
SWING
Which unit are you from ?
We hadn't heard anything about you coming at this hour.

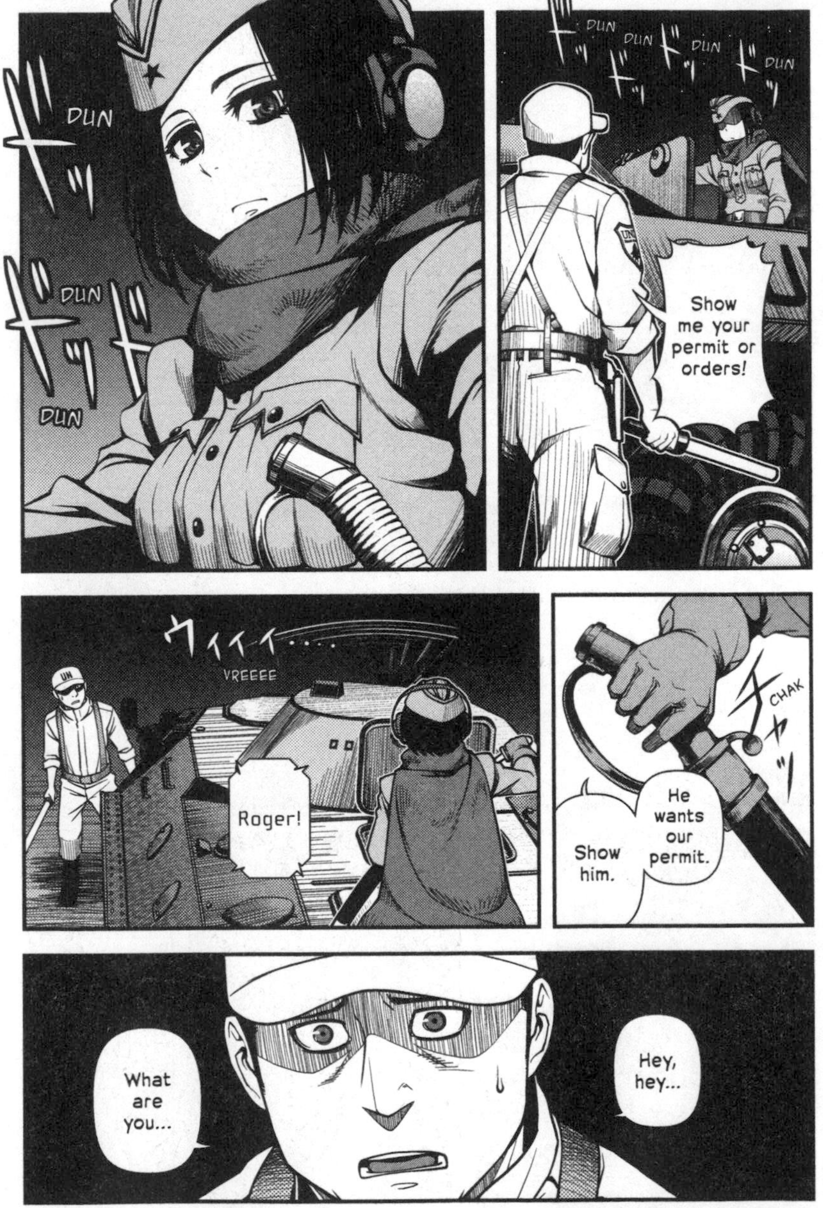
DUN
DUN
DUN
DUN
Show me your permit or orders!
DUN
DUN
DUN
CHAK
He wants our permit.
Show him.
VREEEE
Roger!
Hey, hey...
What are you...

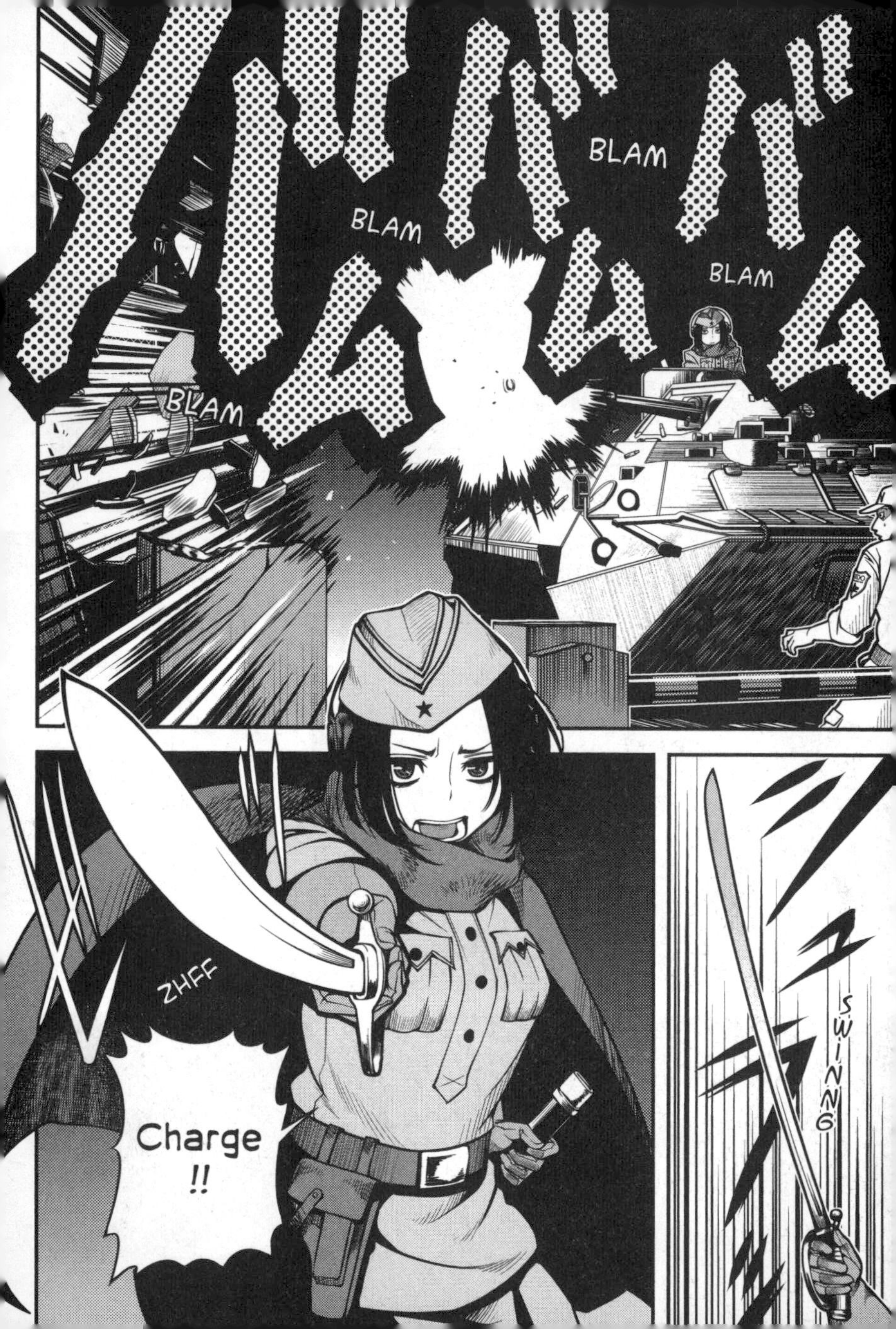
BLAM
BLAM
BLAM
BLAM
SWING
ZHFF
Charge !!

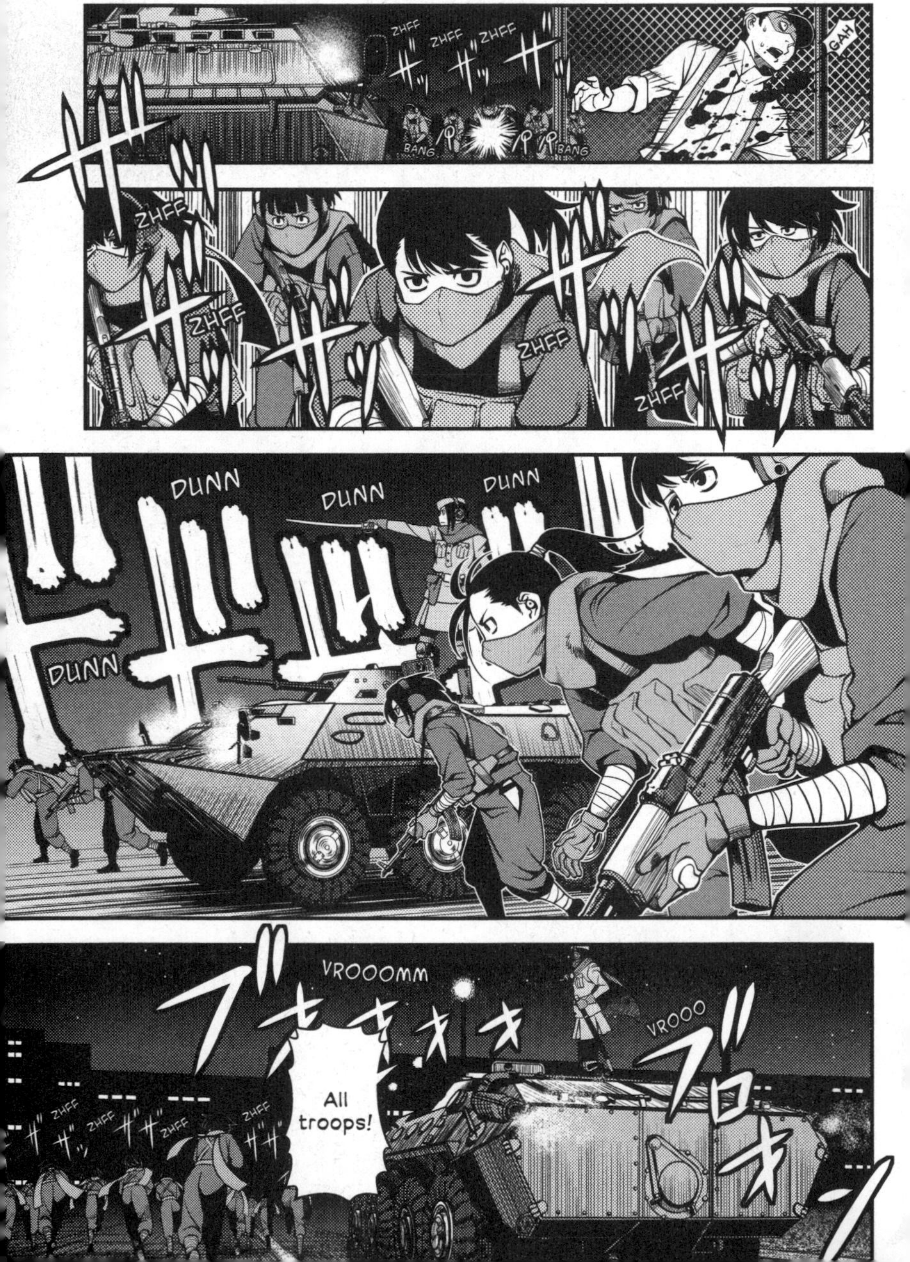
GAH
ZHFF
ZHFF
ZHFF
BANG
BANG
ZHFF
ZHFF
ZHFF
ZHFF
ZHFF
DUNN
DUNN
DUNN
DUNN
VROOO
VROOOMM
All troops!
ZHFF
ZHFF
ZHFF
ZHFF

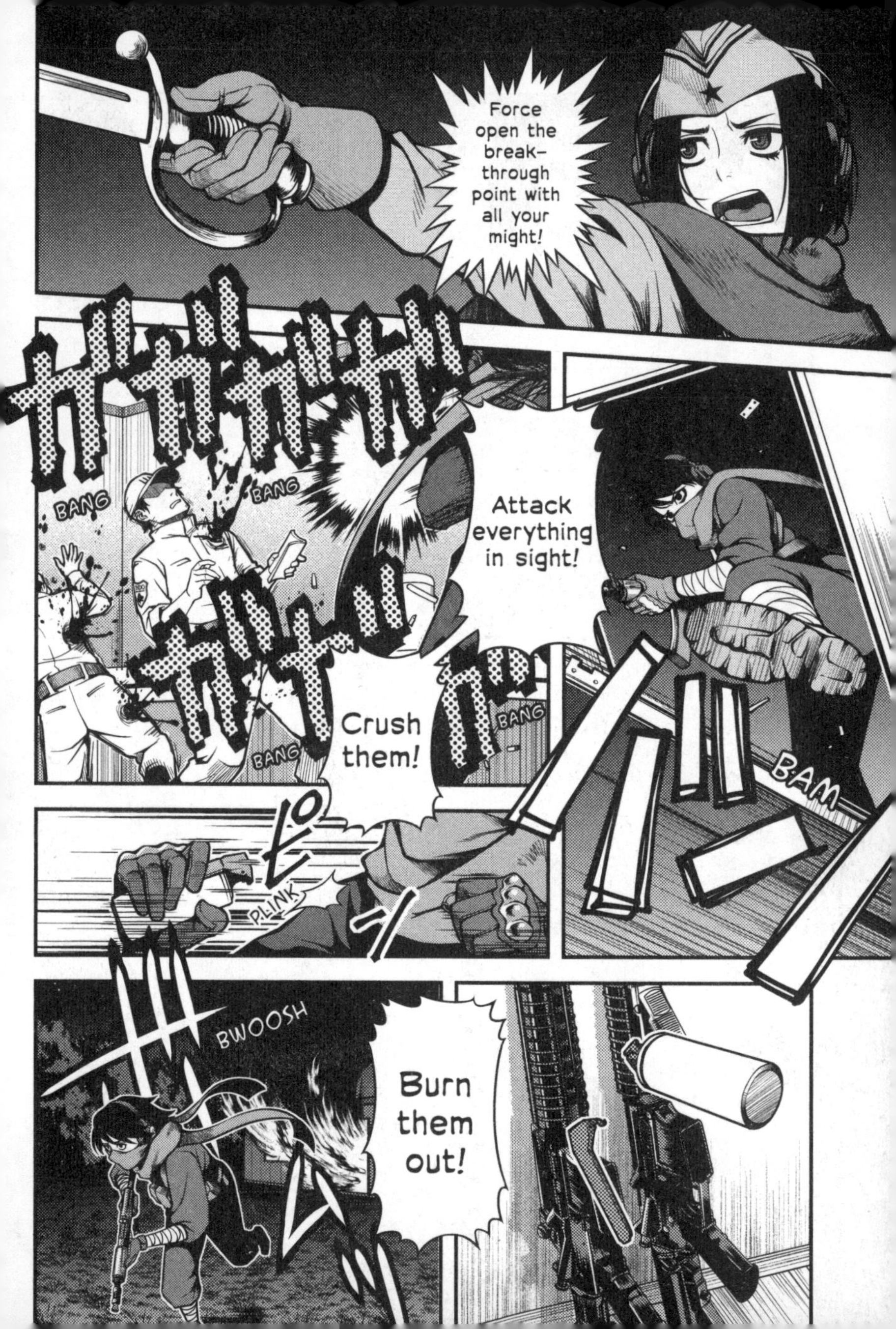
Force open the break-through point with all your might!
Attack everything in sight!
BAM
BANG
BANG
Crush them!
BANG
BANG
PLINK
Burn them out!
BWOOSH

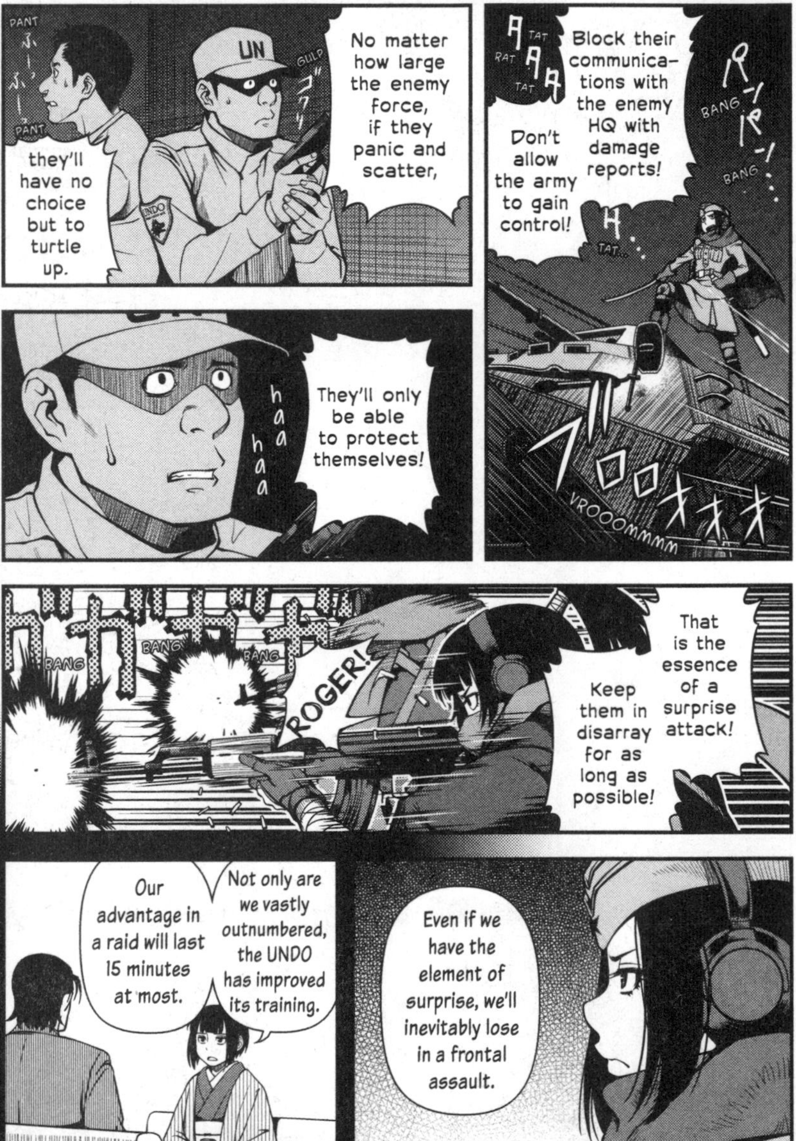
TAT
RAT
TAT
Block their communications with the enemy HQ with damage reports!
Don't allow the army to gain control!
BANG
BANG
TAT
VROOOMMMM
No matter how large the enemy force, if they panic and scatter,
GULP
PANT
PANT
they'll have no choice but to turtle up.
They'll only be able to protect themselves!
haa haa
haa haa
That is the essence of a surprise attack!
Keep them in disarray for as long as possible!
ROGER!
BANG
BANG
BANG
Even if we have the element of surprise, we'll inevitably lose in a frontal assault.
Not only are we vastly outnumbered, the UNDO has improved its training.
Our advantage in a raid will last 15 minutes at most.

From there on, we'll have to use brute force,
but we can't allow the enemy to concentrate their forces in Building E, the cryo-prison's location.
They'll have both revival and a stronghold, and we won't stand a chance.
So we'll need a diversion tactic.
Internment Facility
Building E cryo-prison
First, we'll head towards the facility housing the RDS patients.
We'll begin releasing them from the buildings as we secure them.
Internment Facility
Building E cryo-prison
Once that happens, the UNDO will have no choice but to deal with the escaped patients,
and your task force, Kenzaki, will take that chance to infiltrate Building E.
Internment Facility
Building E cryo-prison
After extracting the three prisoners,
you'll merge with the main force and withdraw from the facility.
The main unit will pretend to be the principal force,
but their real goal is to secure an escape route.
I see. It's a good plan.

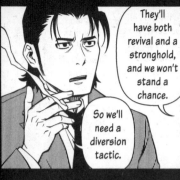

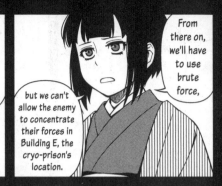

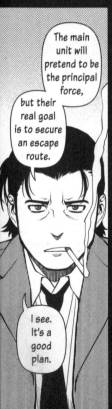

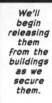

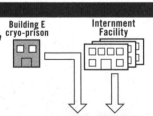

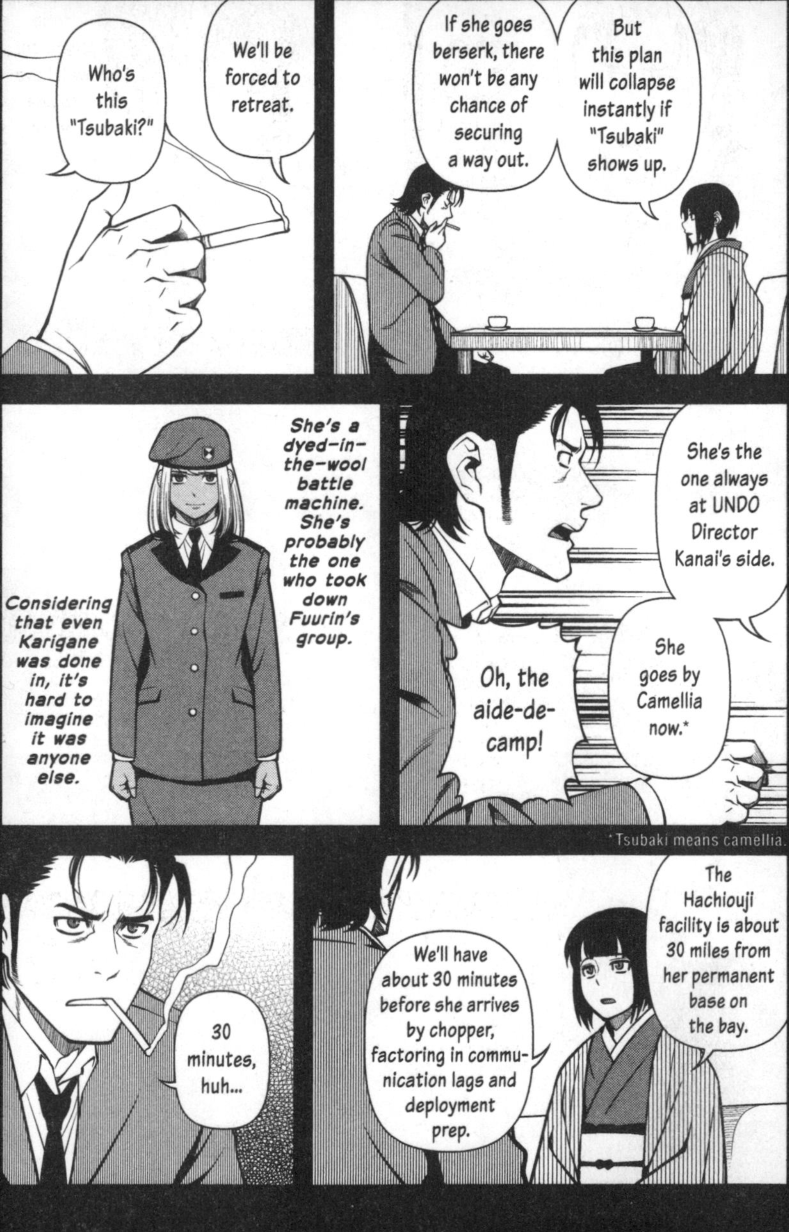
But this plan will collapse instantly if "Tsubaki" shows up.
If she goes berserk, there won't be any chance of securing a way out.
We'll be forced to retreat.
Who's this "Tsubaki?"
She's the one always at UNDO Director Kanai's side.
She goes by Camellia now.*
Oh, the aide-de-camp!
She's a dyed-in-the-wool battle machine. She's probably the one who took down Fuurin's group.
Considering that even Karigane was done in, it's hard to imagine it was anyone else.
The Hachiouji facility is about 30 miles from her permanent base on the bay.
We'll have about 30 minutes before she arrives by chopper, factoring in communication lags and deployment prep.
30 minutes, huh...

*Tsubaki means camellia.

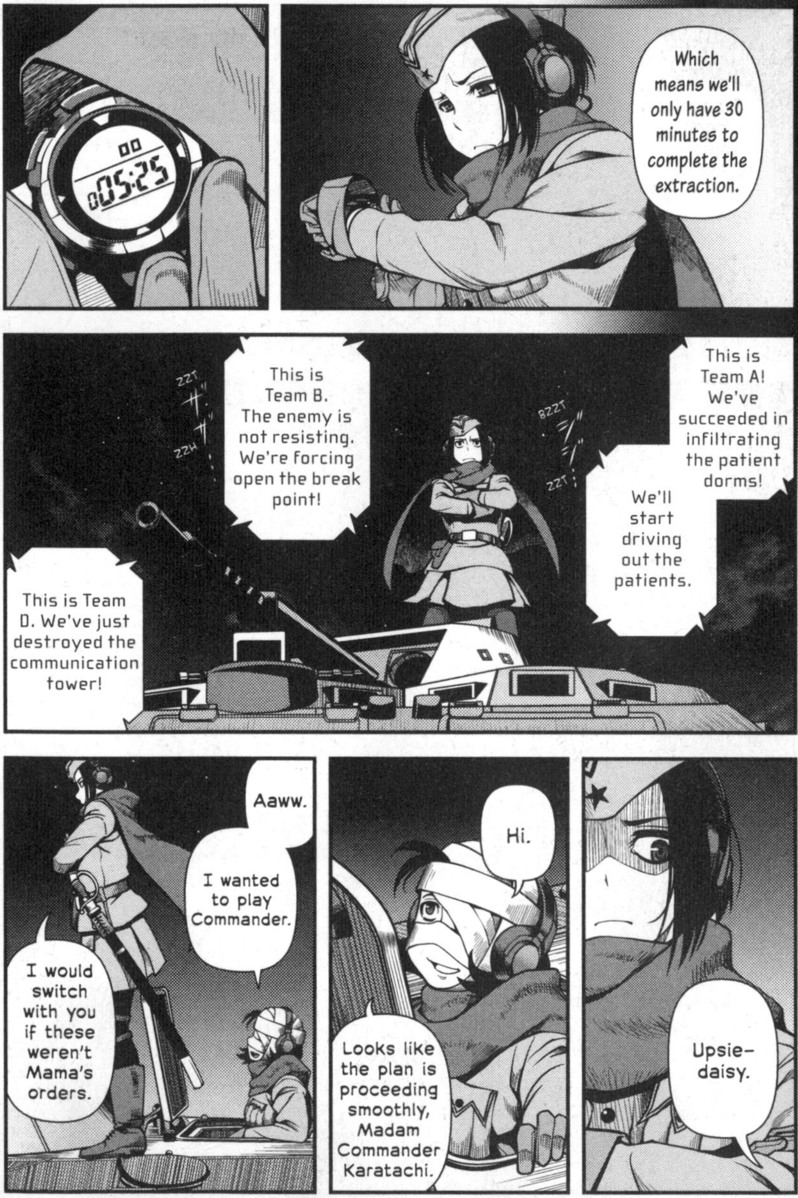
Which means we'll only have 30 minutes to complete the extraction.
00
05:25
This is Team A! We've succeeded in infiltrating the patient dorms!
BZZT
ZZT
We'll start driving out the patients.
This is Team B. The enemy is not resisting. We're forcing open the break point!
ZZT
ZZH
This is Team D. We've just destroyed the communication tower!
Upsie-daisy.
Hi.
Looks like the plan is proceeding smoothly, Madam Commander Karatachi.
Aaww.
I wanted to play Commander.
I would switch with you if these weren't Mama's orders.

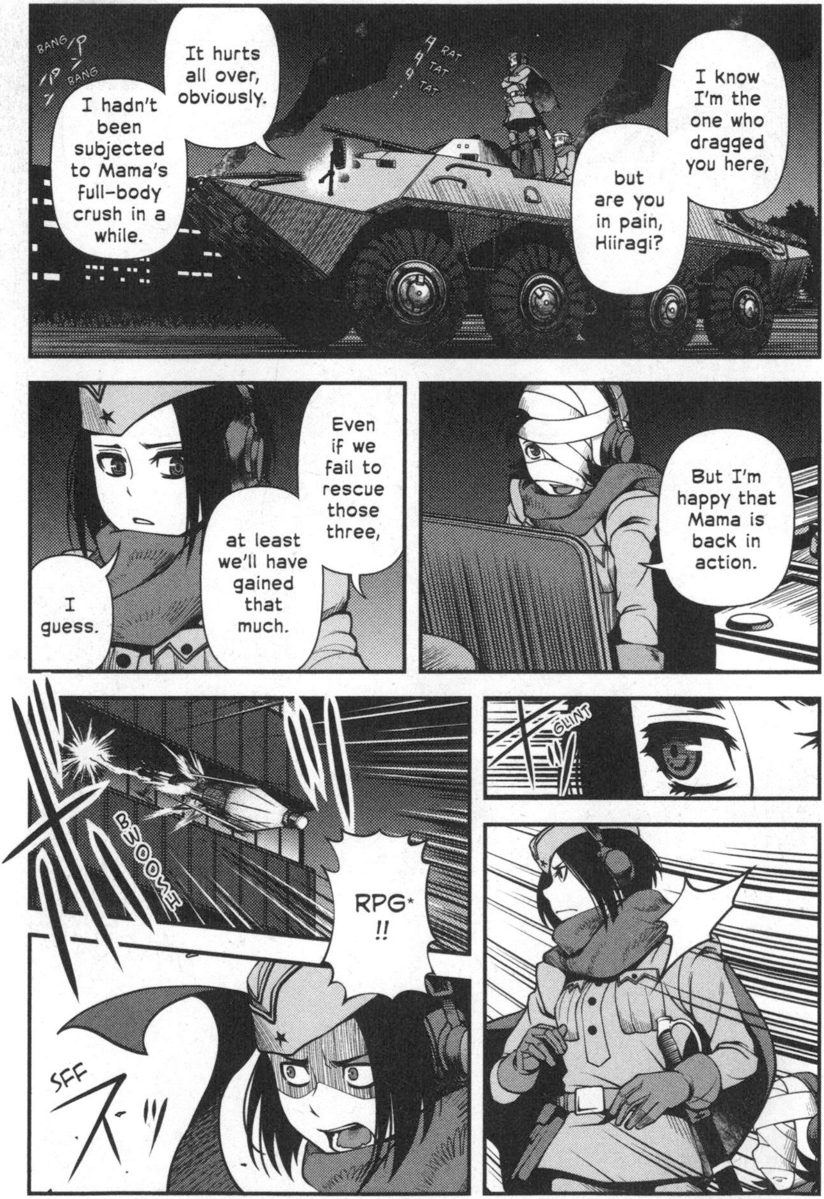
I know I'm the one who dragged you here,
but are you in pain, Hiiragi?
RAT TAT TAT
It hurts all over, obviously.
I hadn't been subjected to Mama's full-body crush in a while.
BANG BANG
But I'm happy that Mama is back in action.
Even if we fail to rescue those three,
at least we'll have gained that much.
I guess.
GLINT
BWOOM!
RPG* !!
SFF

*Ruchnoy Protivotankoviy Granatomyot (hand-held anti-tank grenade launcher)

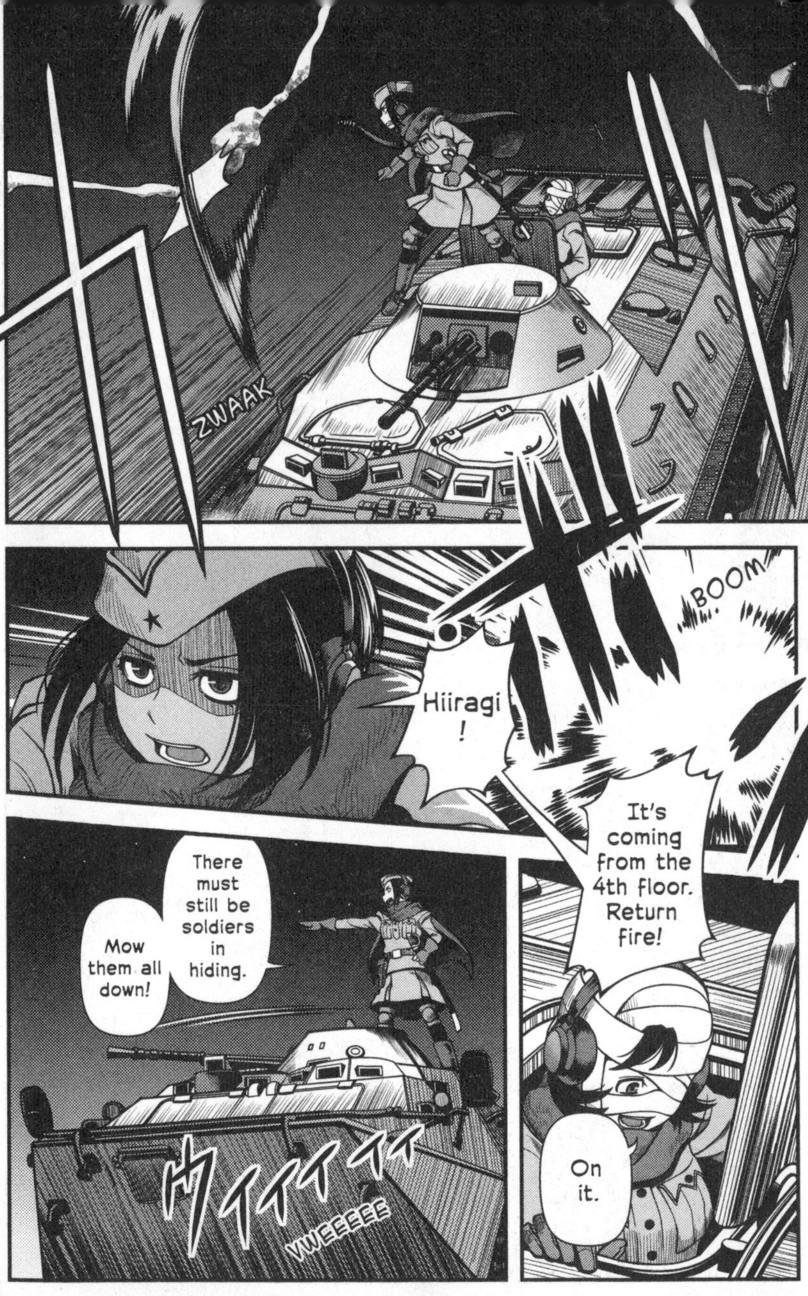
ZWAAK
BOOM
Hiiragi!
It's coming from the 4th floor. Return fire!
On it.
There must still be soldiers in hiding.
Mow them all down!
VWEEEEEE

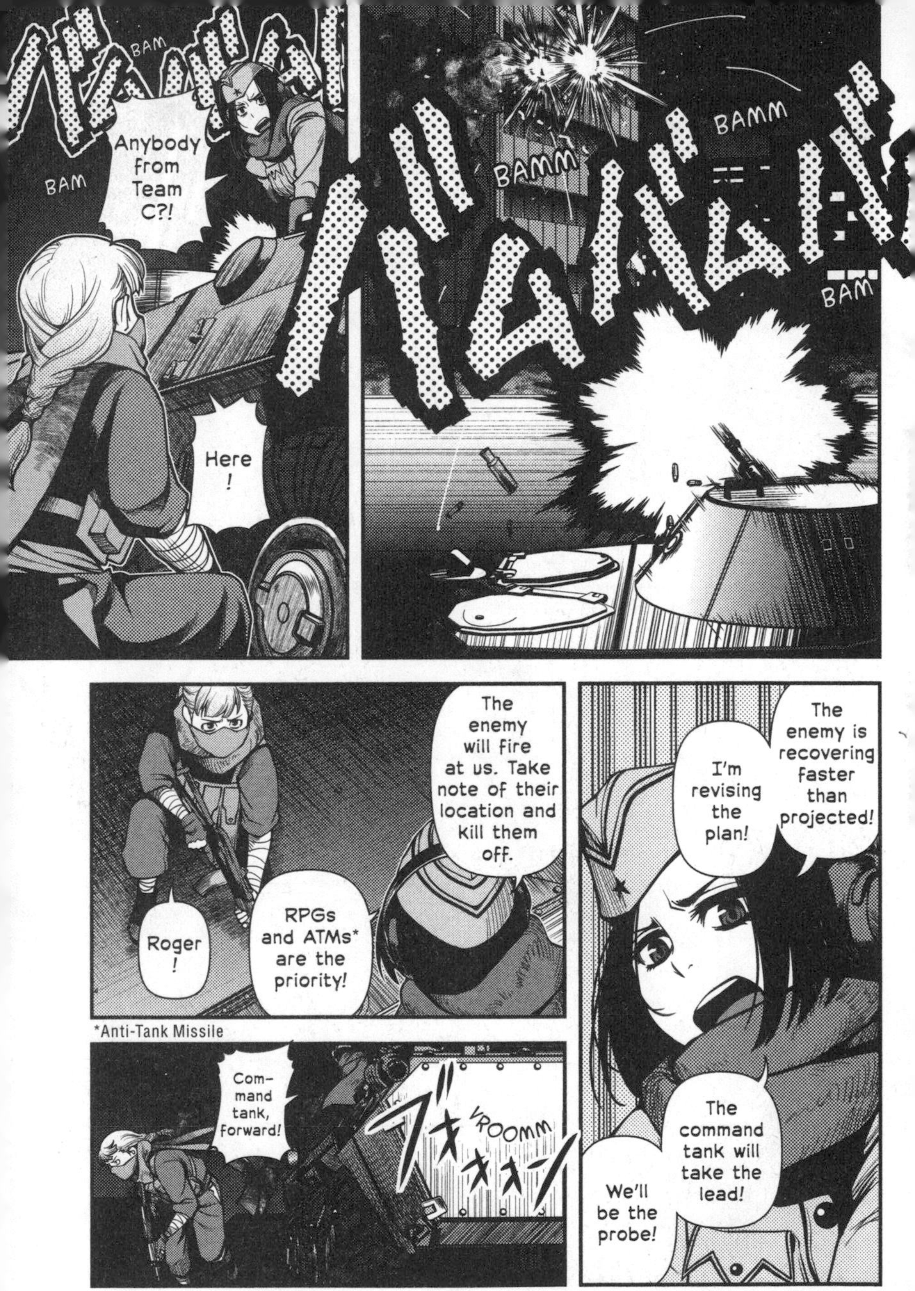
BAMM
BAMM
BAM
BAM
BAM
Anybody from Team C?!
Here!
The enemy is recovering faster than projected!
I'm revising the plan!
The command tank will take the lead!
We'll be the probe!
The enemy will fire at us. Take note of their location and kill them off.
RPGs and ATMs* are the priority!
Roger!
VROOMM
Command tank, forward!

*Anti-Tank Missile

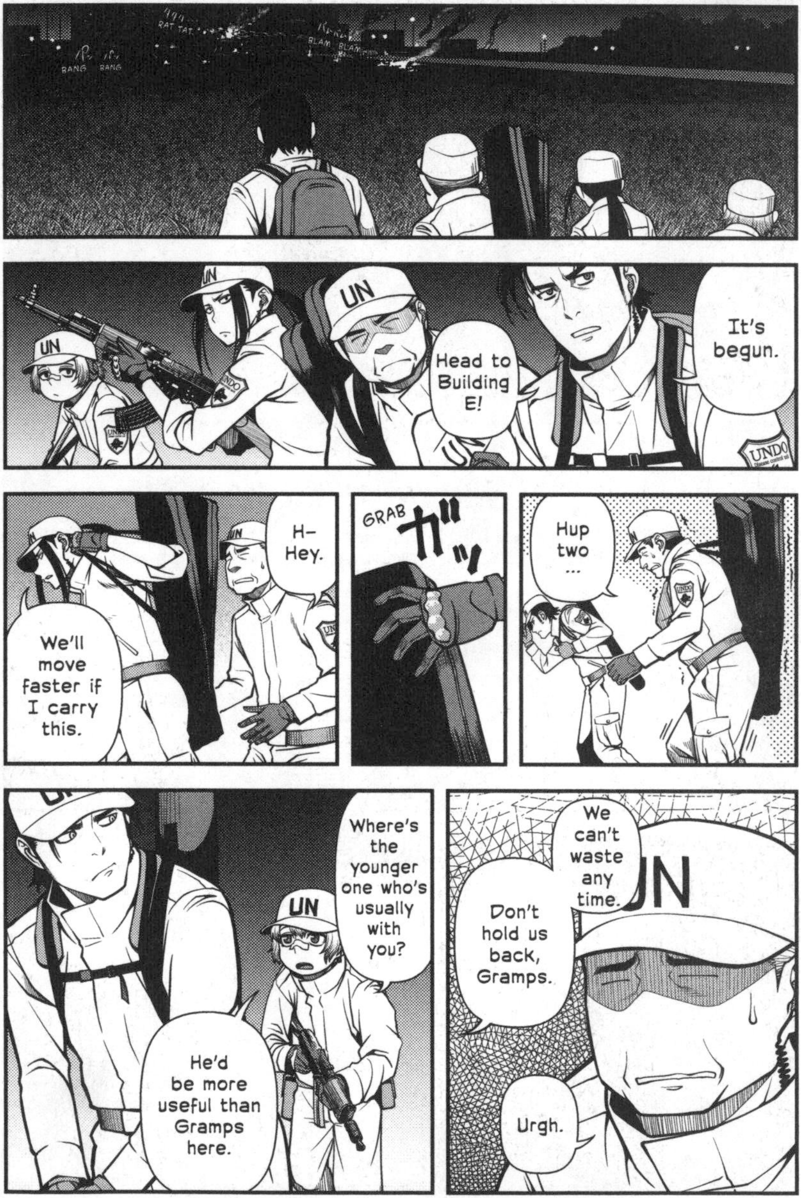
BLAM BLAM
RAT TAT
BANG BANG
It's begun.
Head to Building E!
Hup two ...
GRAB
ガッ
H- Hey.
We'll move faster if I carry this.
We can't waste any time.
Don't hold us back, Gramps.
Urgh.
Where's the younger one who's usually with you?
He'd be more useful than Gramps here.

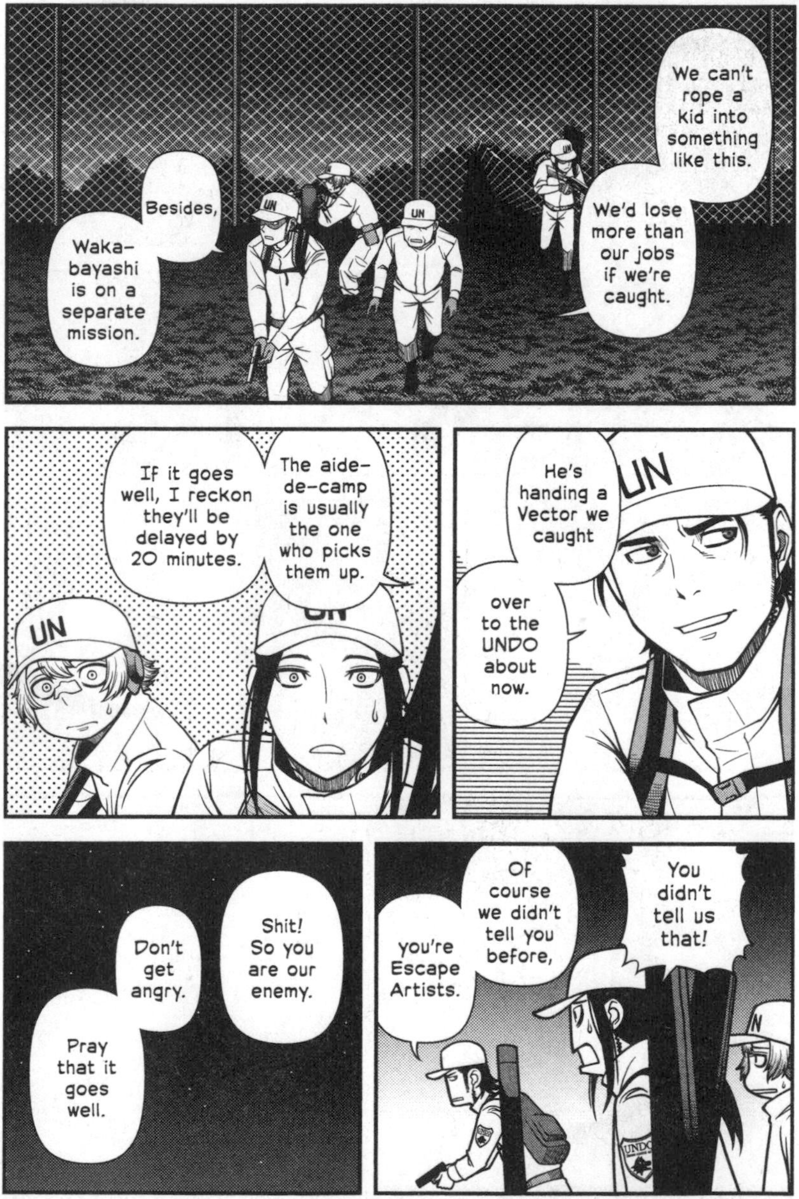
We can't rope a kid into something like this.
We'd lose more than our jobs if we're caught.
Besides,
Waka-bayashi is on a separate mission.
He's handing a Vector we caught
over to the UNDO about now.
The aide-de-camp is usually the one who picks them up.
If it goes well, I reckon they'll be delayed by 20 minutes.
You didn't tell us that!
Of course we didn't tell you before,
you're Escape Artists.
Shit! So you are our enemy.
Don't get angry.
Pray that it goes well.

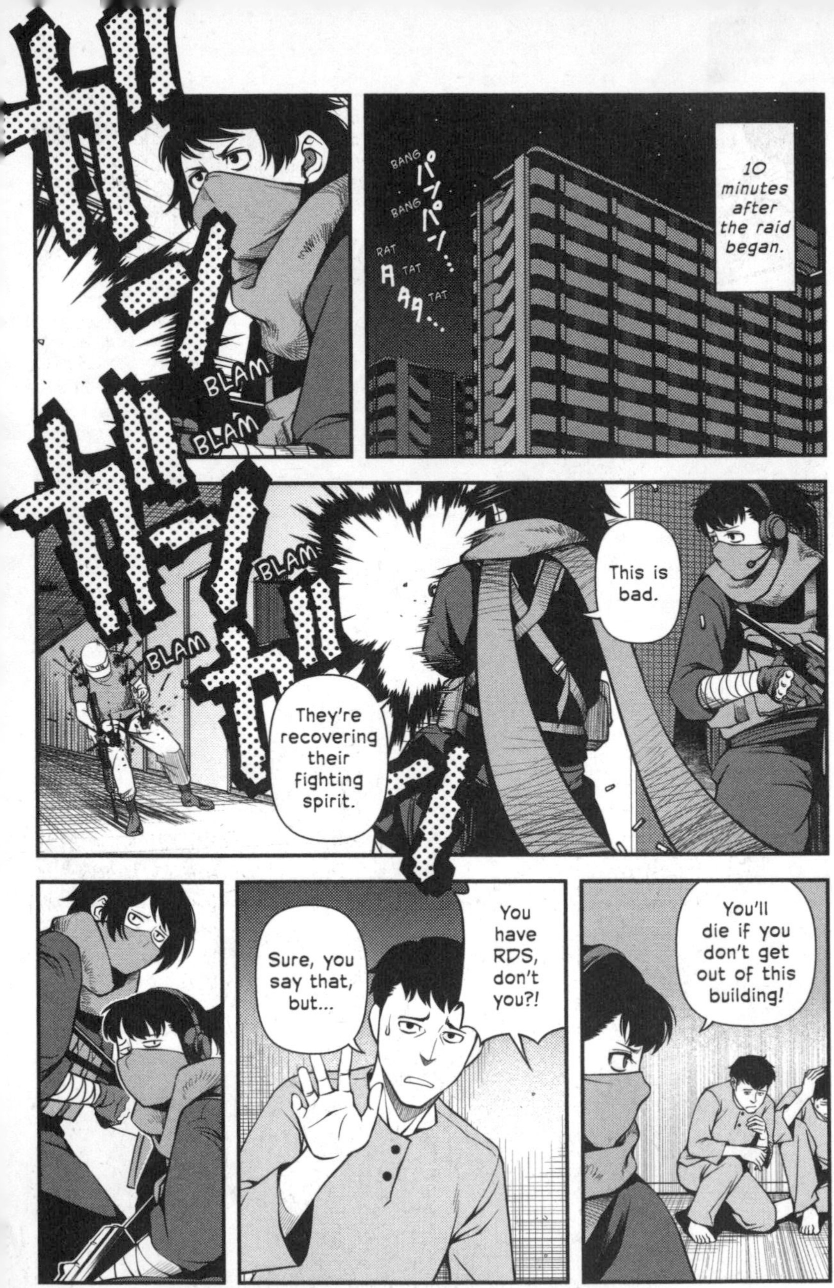
10 minutes after the raid began.
BANG
BANG
RAT TAT TAT
BLAM
BLAM
This is bad.
They're recovering their fighting spirit.
BLAM
BLAM
You'll die if you don't get out of this building!
You have RDS, don't you?!
Sure, you say that, but...

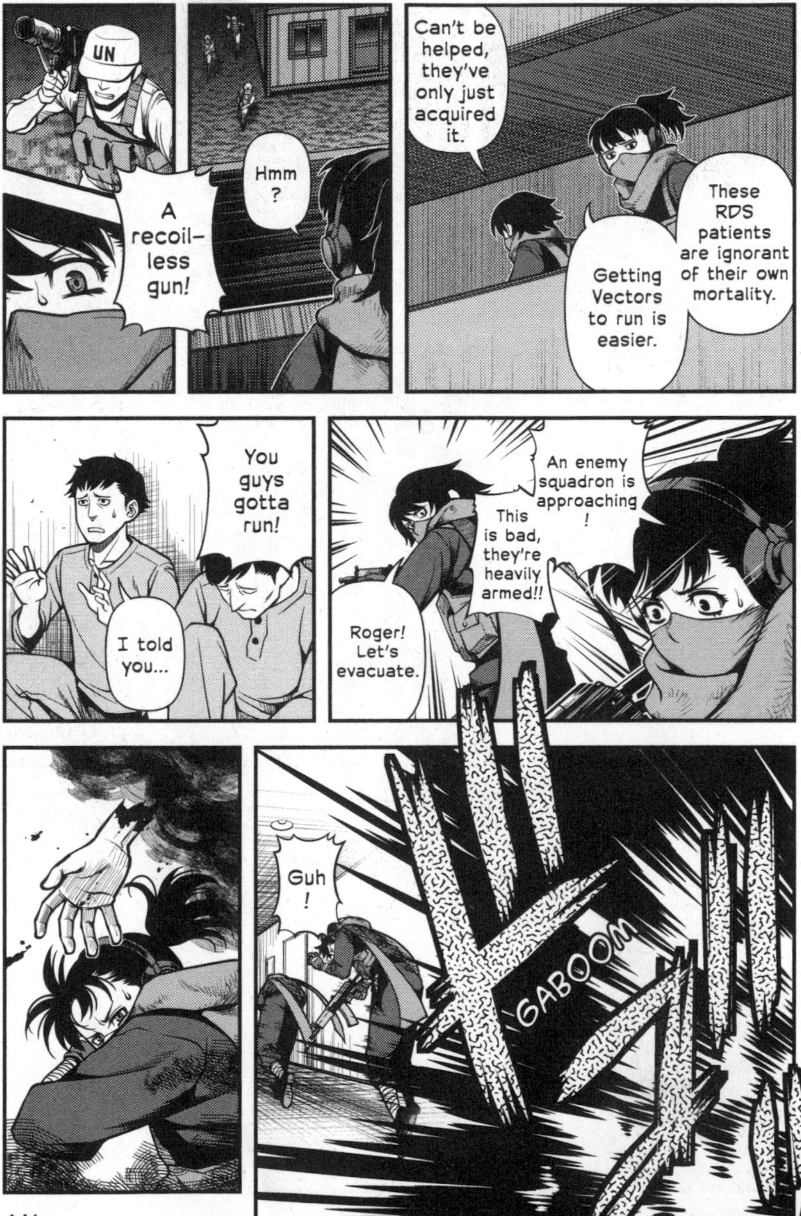
These RDS patients are ignorant of their own mortality.
Getting Vectors to run is easier.
Can't be helped, they've only just acquired it.
Hmm?
A recoil-less gun!
An enemy squadron is approaching!
This is bad, they're heavily armed!!
Roger! Let's evacuate.
You guys gotta run!
I told you...
Guh!
GABOOM

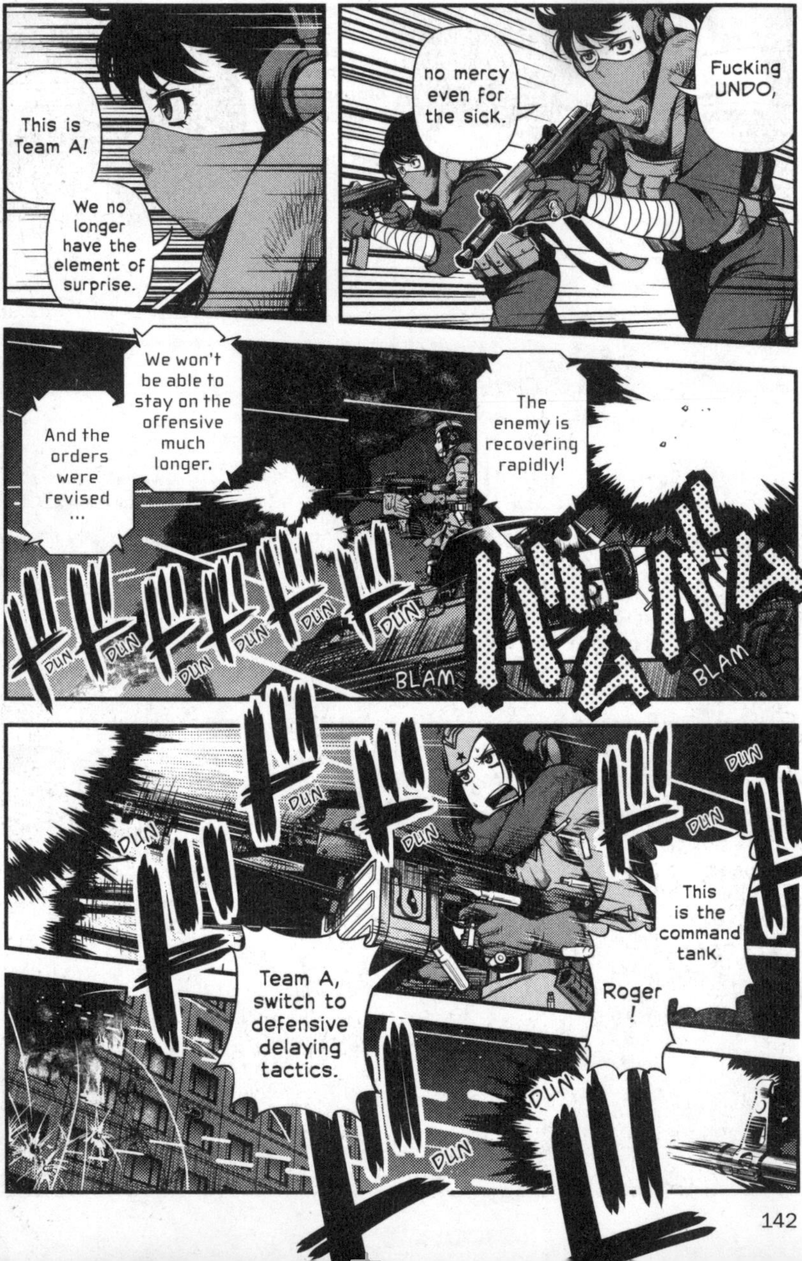
Fucking UNDO,
no mercy even for the sick.
This is Team A!
We no longer have the element of surprise.
The enemy is recovering rapidly!
We won't be able to stay on the offensive much longer.
And the orders were revised ...
BLAM
BLAM
DUN DUN DUN DUN DUN DUN
DUN DUN DUN DUN DUN
This is the command tank.
Team A, switch to defensive delaying tactics.
Roger!
DUN DUN

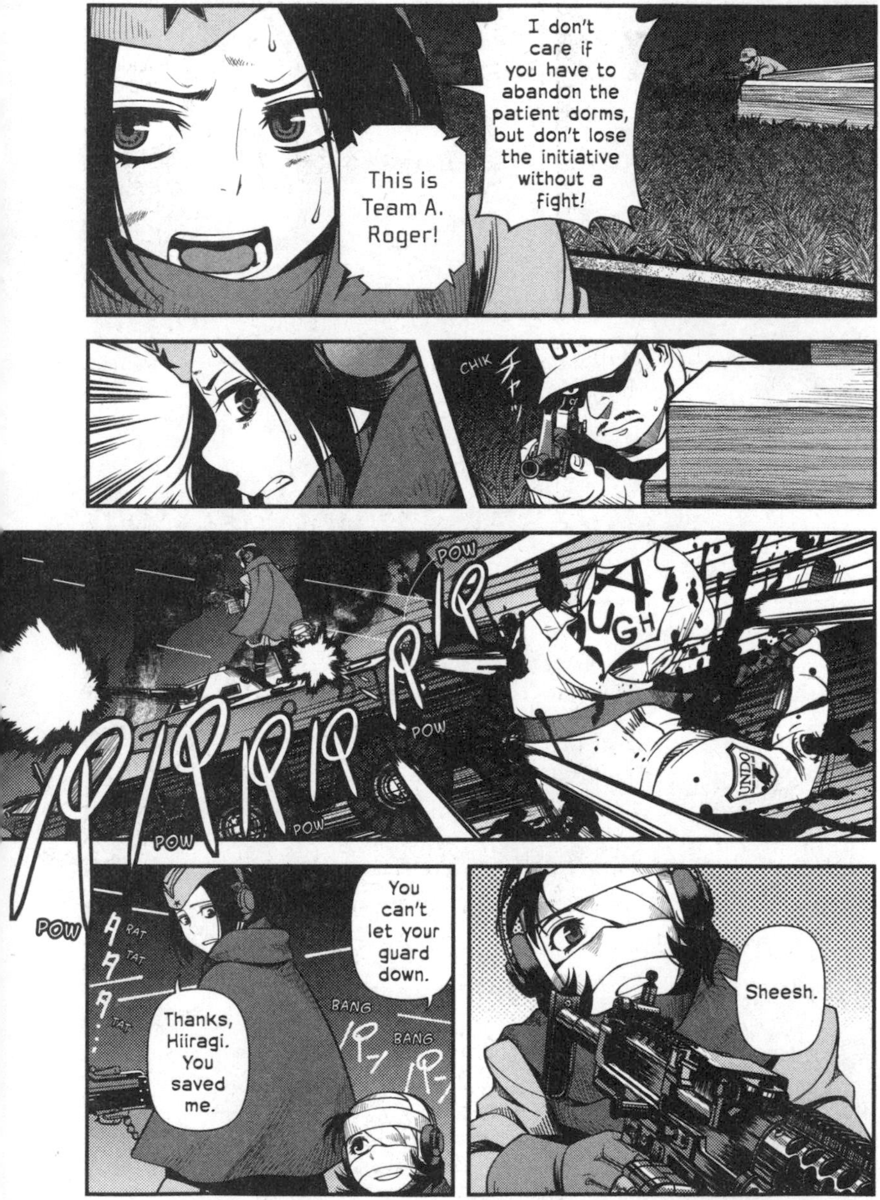
I don't care if you have to abandon the patient dorms, but don't lose the initiative without a fight!
This is Team A. Roger!
CHIK
チャッ
POW
UGH
POW
POW
POW
POW
Sheesh.
You can't let your guard down.
Thanks, Hiiragi. You saved me.
RAT
TAT
TAT
BANG
BANG

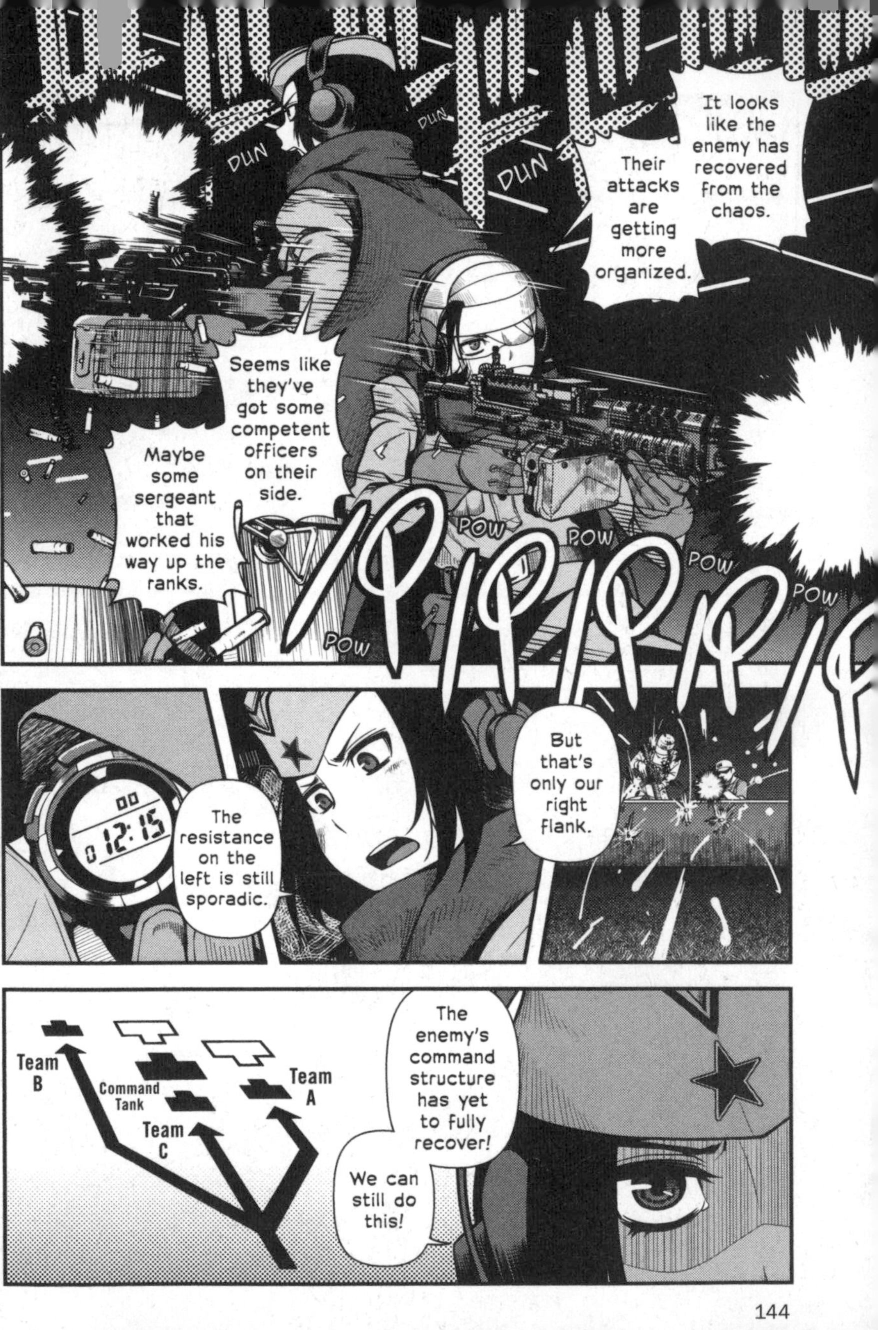
It looks like the enemy has recovered from the chaos.
Their attacks are getting more organized.
DUN
DUN
DUN
Seems like they've got some competent officers on their side.
Maybe some sergeant that worked his way up the ranks.
POW
POW
POW
POW
POW
But that's only our right flank.
The resistance on the left is still sporadic.
00
0 12:15
The enemy's command structure has yet to fully recover!
We can still do this!
Team A
Command Tank
Team C
Team B

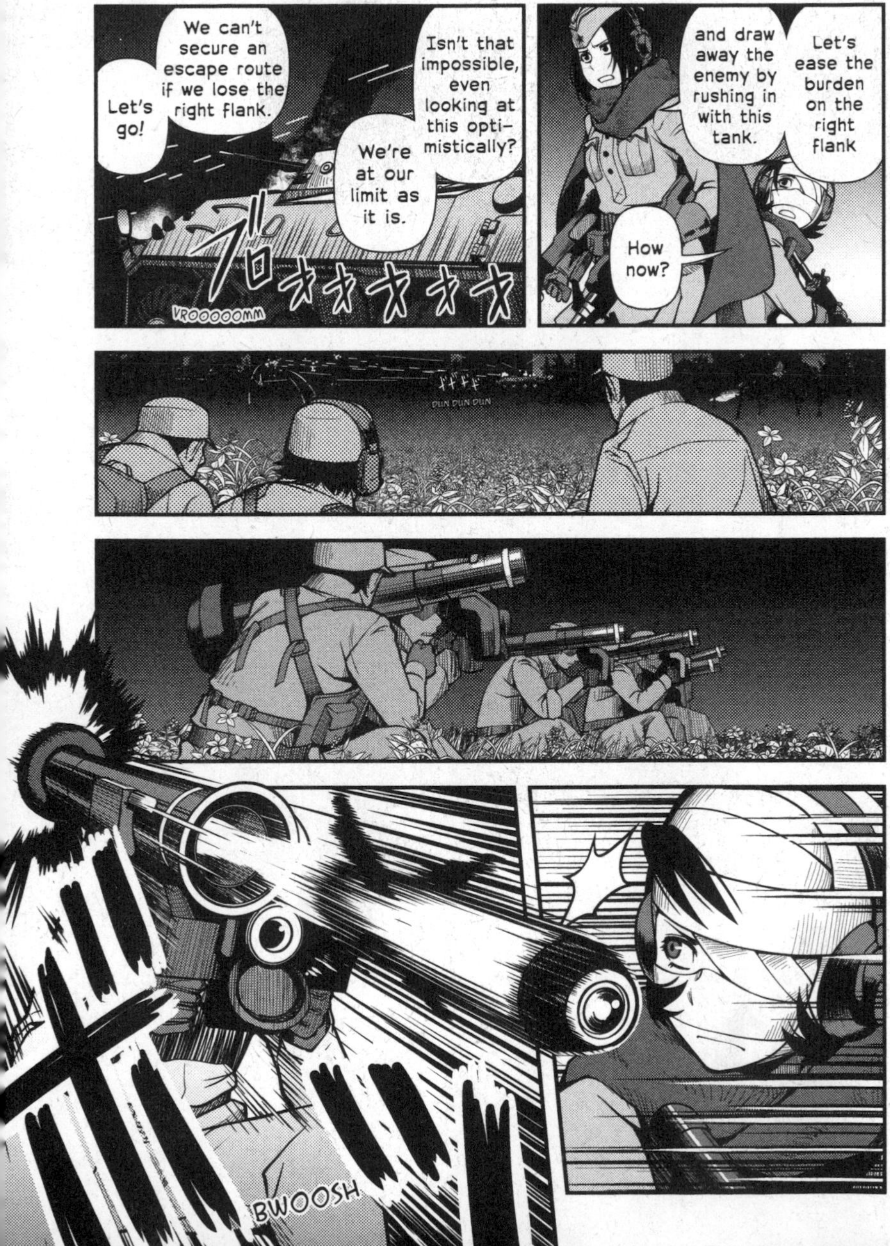
Let's ease the burden on the right flank
and draw away the enemy by rushing in with this tank.
How now?
Isn't that impossible, even looking at this opti-mistically?
We're at our limit as it is.
We can't secure an escape route if we lose the right flank.
Let's go!
VROOOOOOMM
DUN DUN DUN
BWOOSH

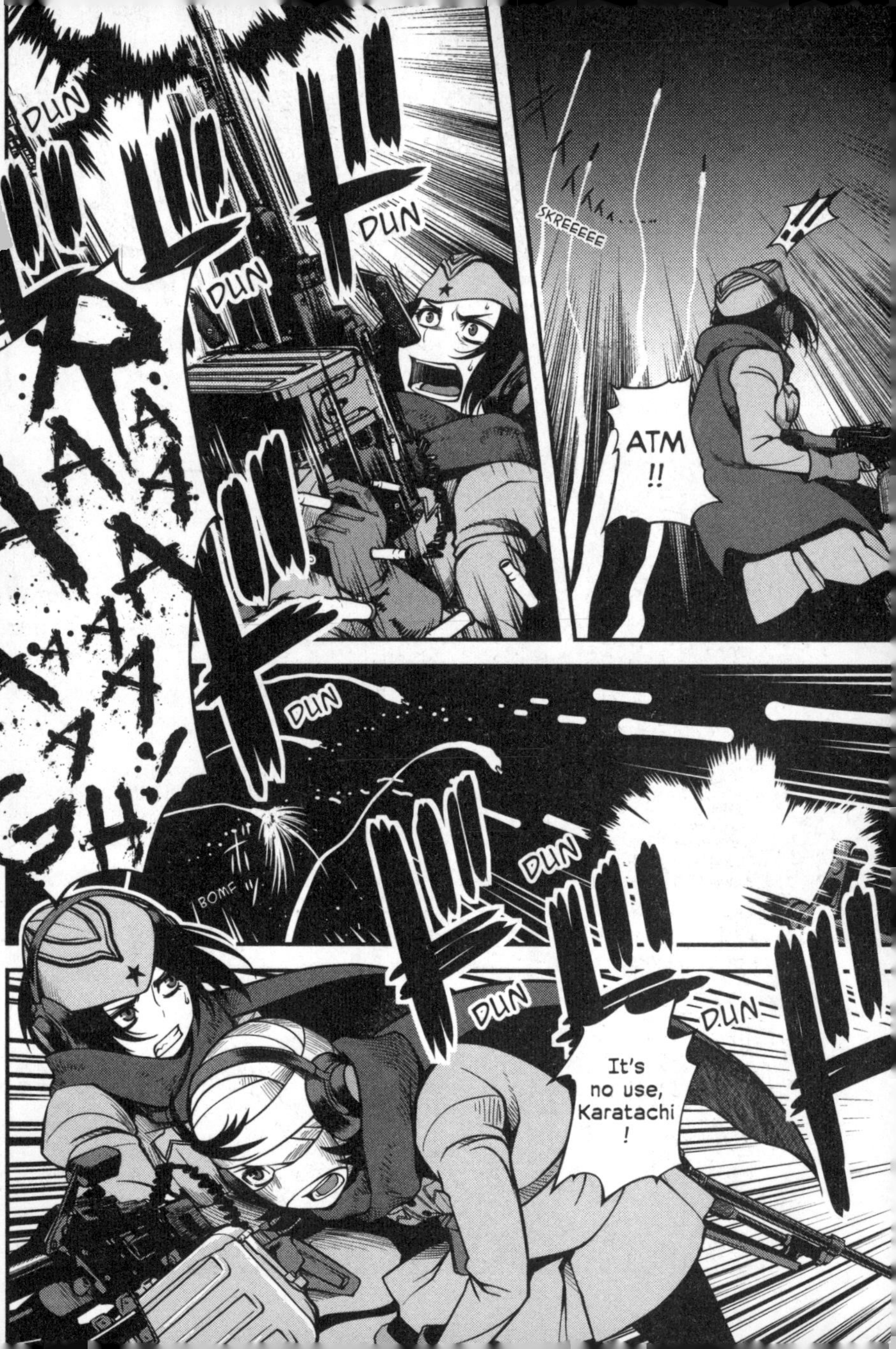
SKREEEEE
ATM !!
DUN
DUN
DUN
AAAAAAAAGH!
DUN
BOMF
DUN
DUN
DUN
It's no use, Karatachi!

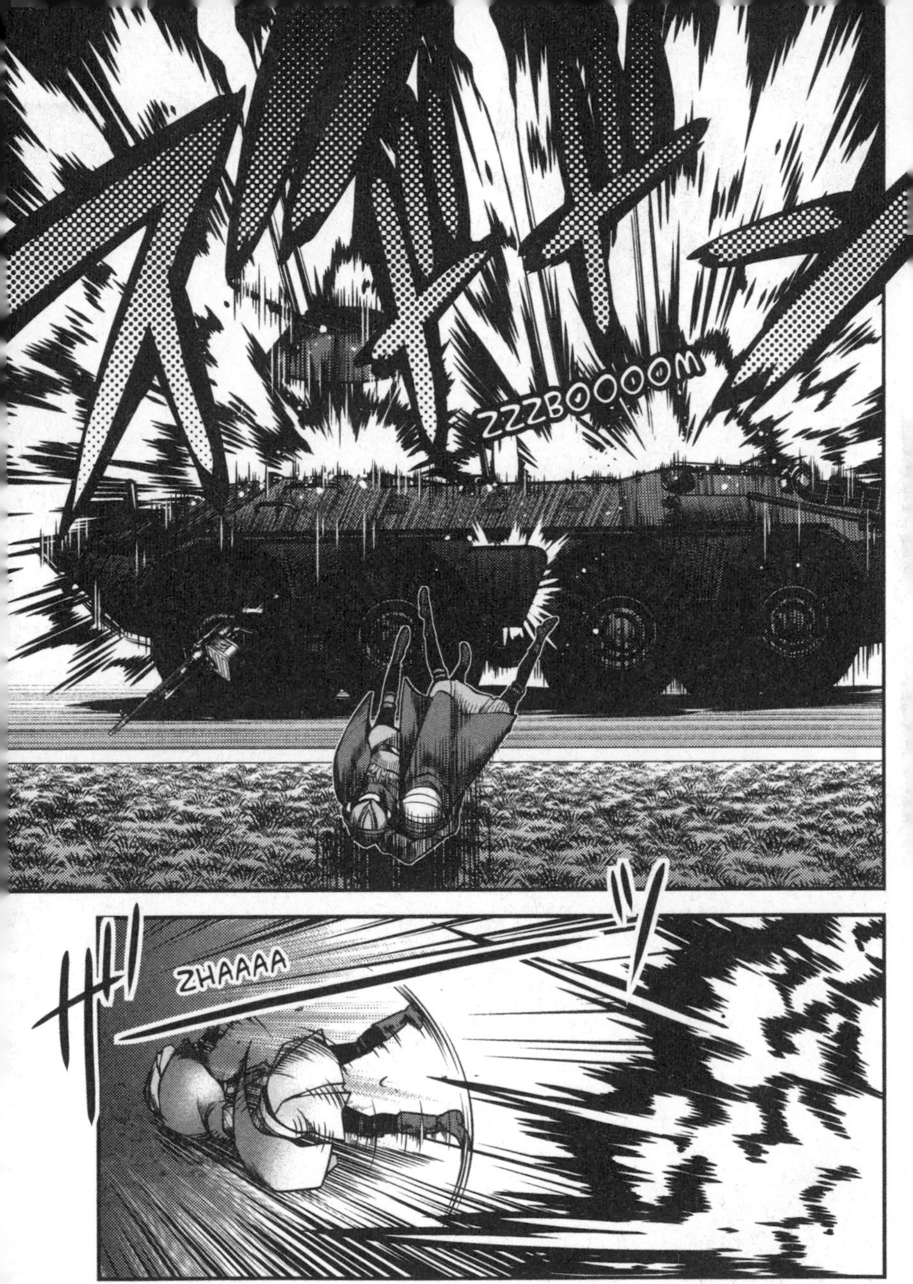
ZZZBOOOOM
ZHAAAA

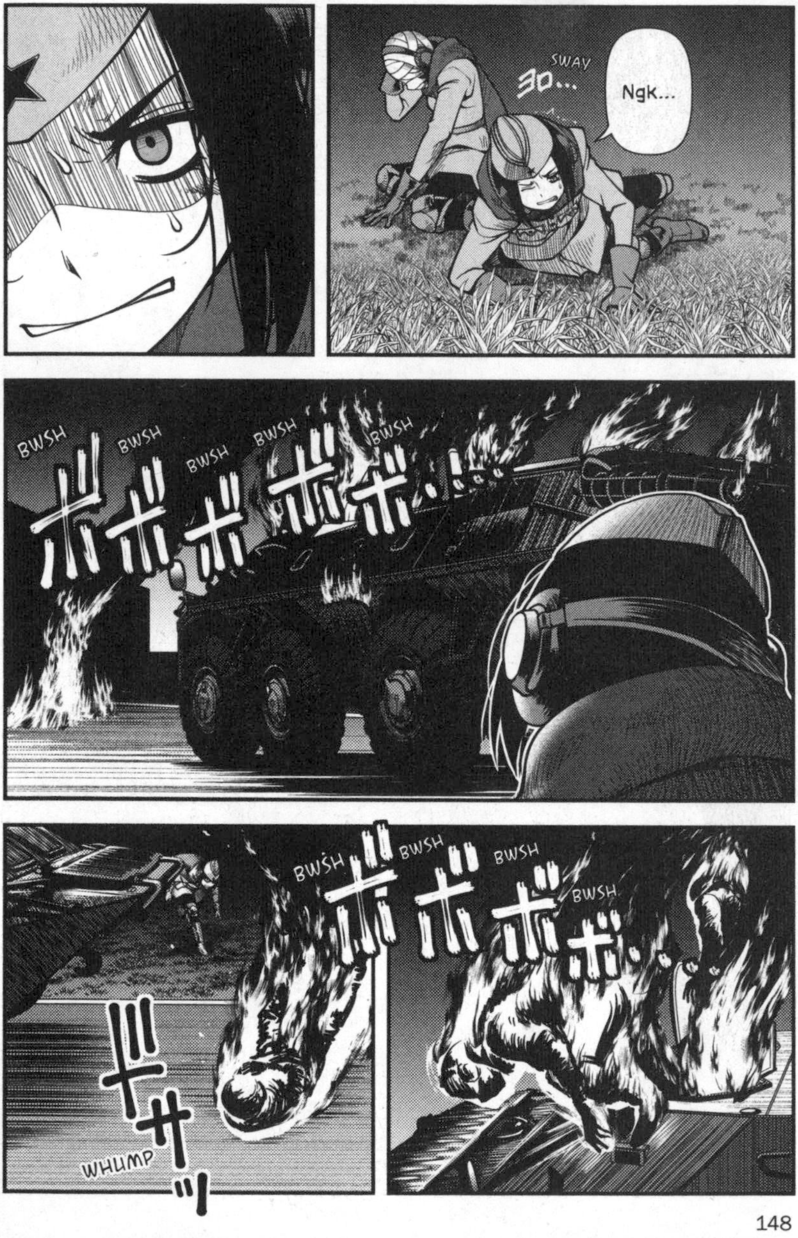
SWAY
ヨロ...
Ngk...
BWSH BWSH BWSH BWSH BWSH
ボボボボボ...
BWSH BWSH BWSH BWSH
ボボボ...
ドサッ
WHUMP

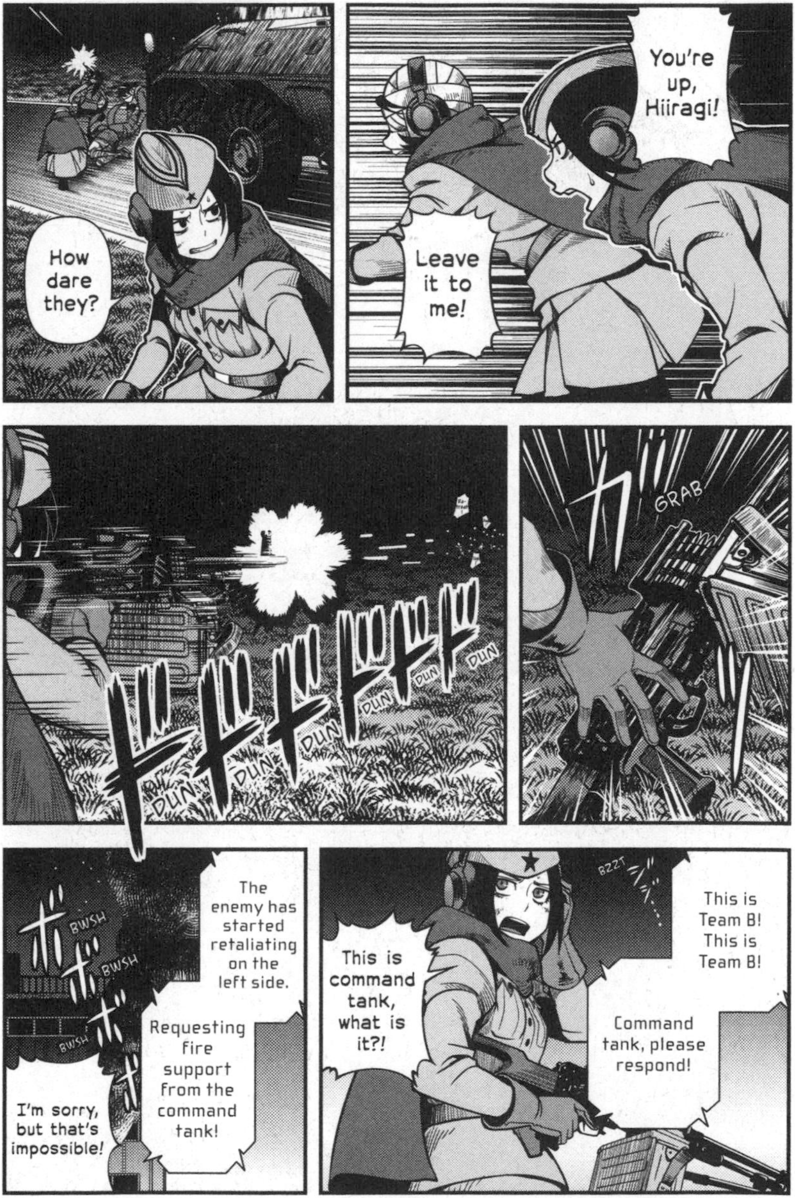

You're up, Hiiragi!
Leave it to me!
How dare they?
GRAB
DUN DUN DUN DUN DUN DUN DUN
BZZT
This is Team B! This is Team B!
Command tank, please respond!
This is command tank, what is it?!
The enemy has started retaliating on the left side.
Requesting fire support from the command tank!
BWSH
BWSH
BWSH
I'm sorry, but that's impossible!

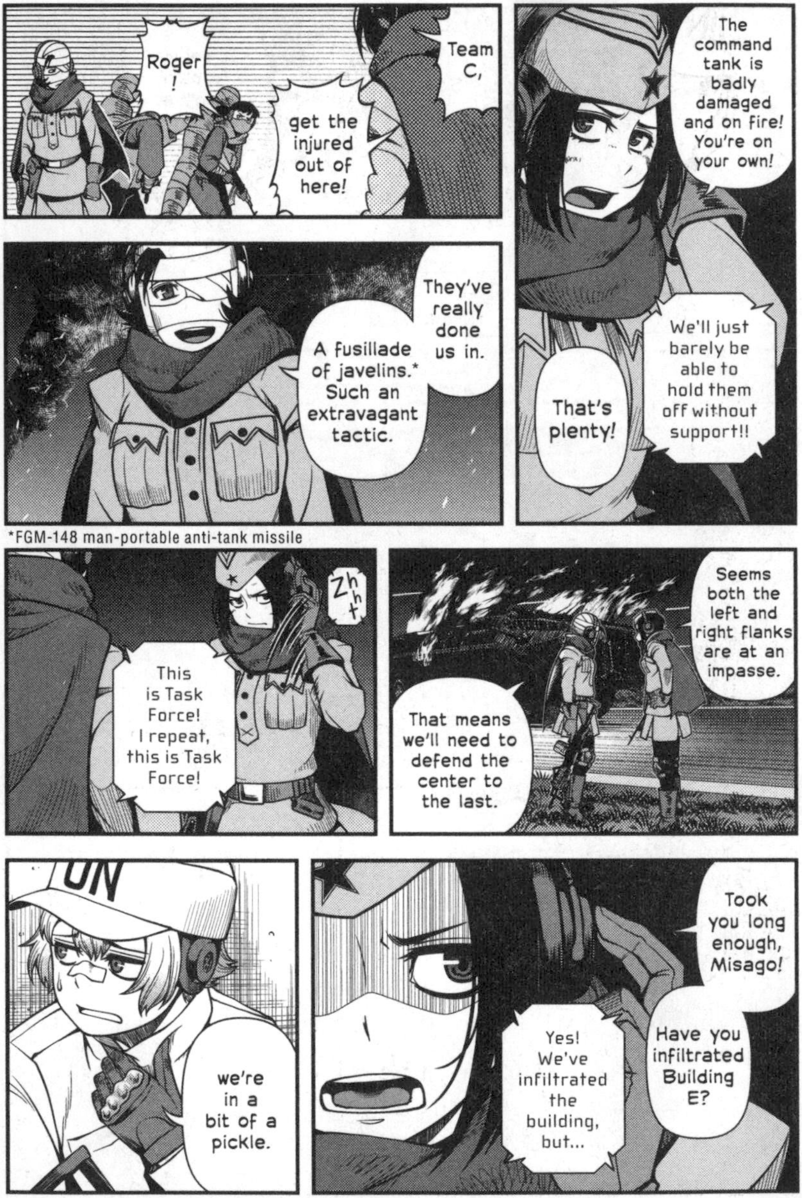
The command tank is badly damaged and on fire! You're on your own!
We'll just barely be able to hold them off without support!!
That's plenty!
Team C,
get the injured out of here!
Roger!
They've really done us in.
A fusillade of javelins.* Such an extravagant tactic.
Seems both the left and right flanks are at an impasse.
That means we'll need to defend the center to the last.
Zhht
This is Task Force! I repeat, this is Task Force!
Took you long enough, Misago!
Have you infiltrated Building E?
Yes! We've infiltrated the building, but...
we're in a bit of a pickle.

*FGM-148 man-portable anti-tank missile

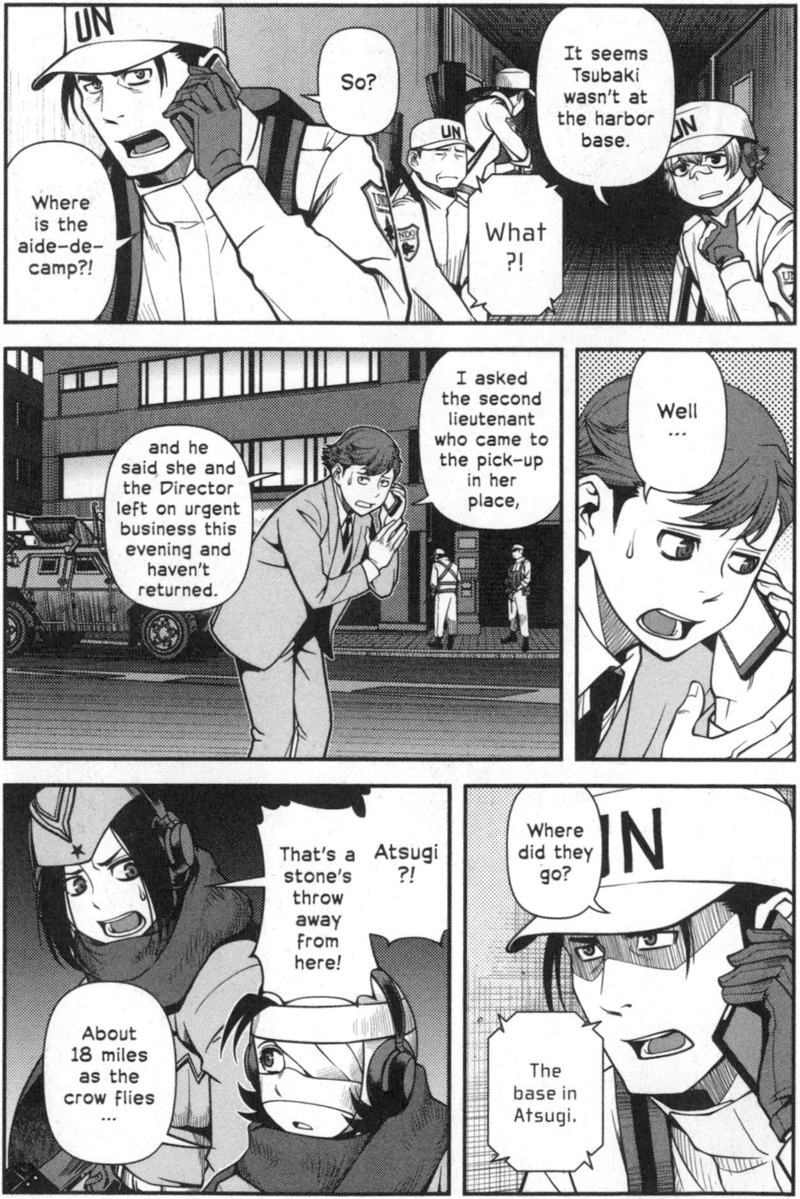
It seems Tsubaki wasn't at the harbor base.
So?
What ?!
Where is the aide-de-camp?!
Well ...
I asked the second lieutenant who came to the pick-up in her place,
and he said she and the Director left on urgent business this evening and haven't returned.
Where did they go?
The base in Atsugi.
Atsugi ?!
That's a stone's throw away from here!
About 18 miles as the crow flies ...

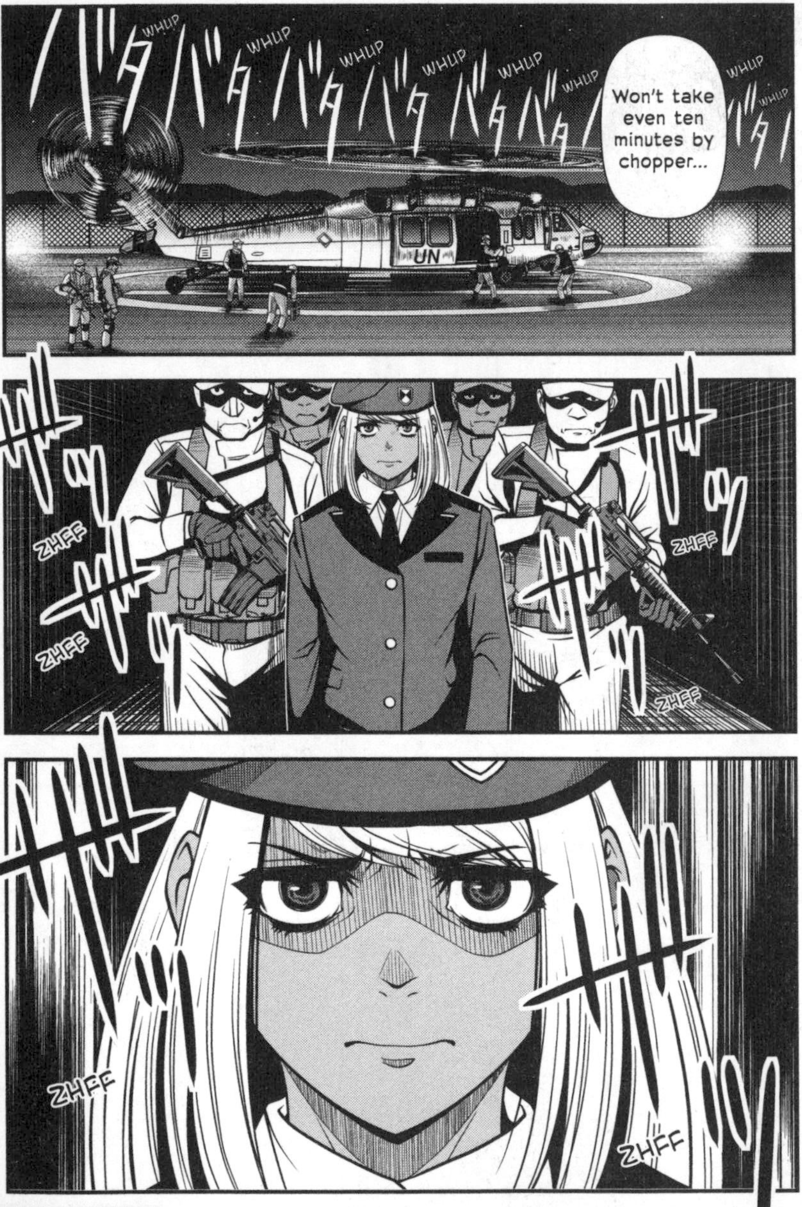
WHUP
WHUP
Won't take even ten minutes by chopper...
WHUP
WHUP
WHUP
WHUP
WHUP
WHUP
ZHFF
ZHFF
ZHFF
ZHFF
ZHFF
ZHFF

End of Chapter 32

33

Task Force

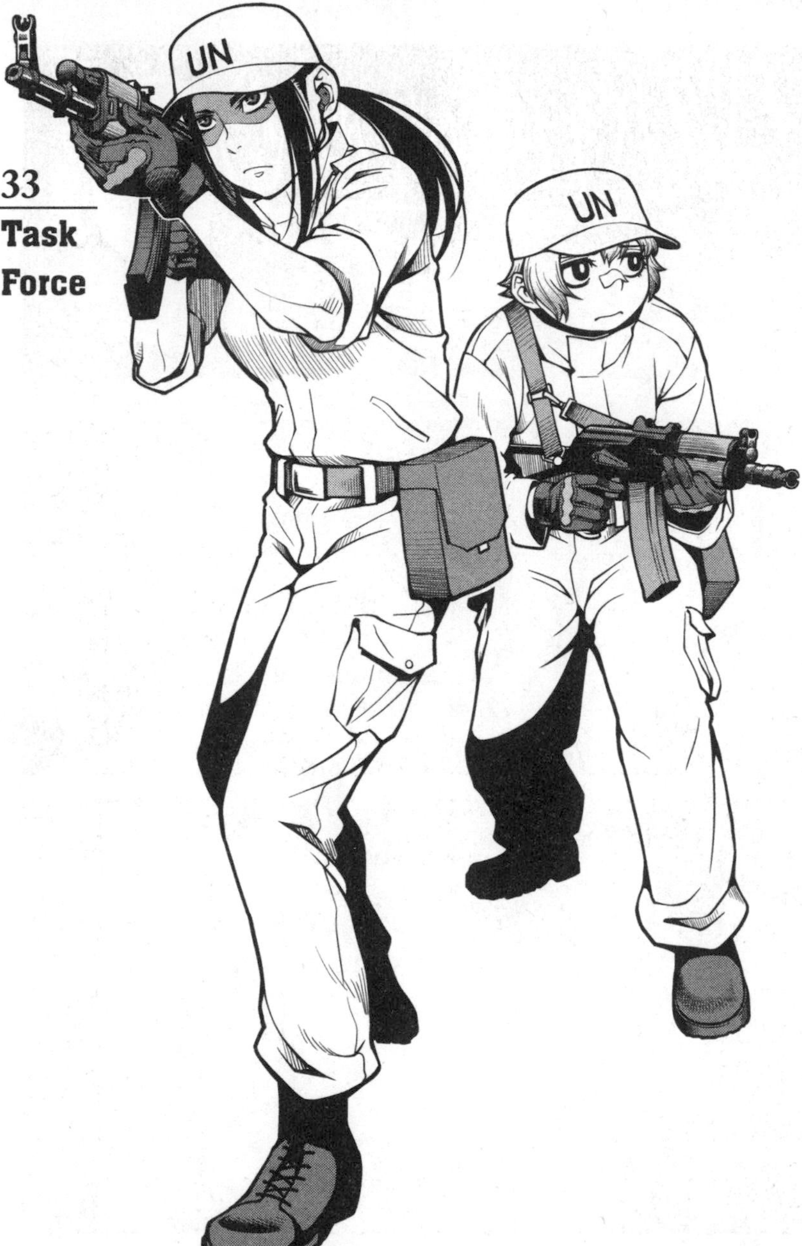
UN
UN

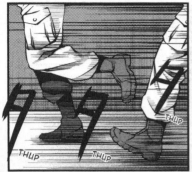

Building E cryo-prison

Task Force.

THUP THUP THUP THUP THUP THUP THUP THUP THUP

SFF

UN

HAA HAA

The stairs are clear.

GACHIK

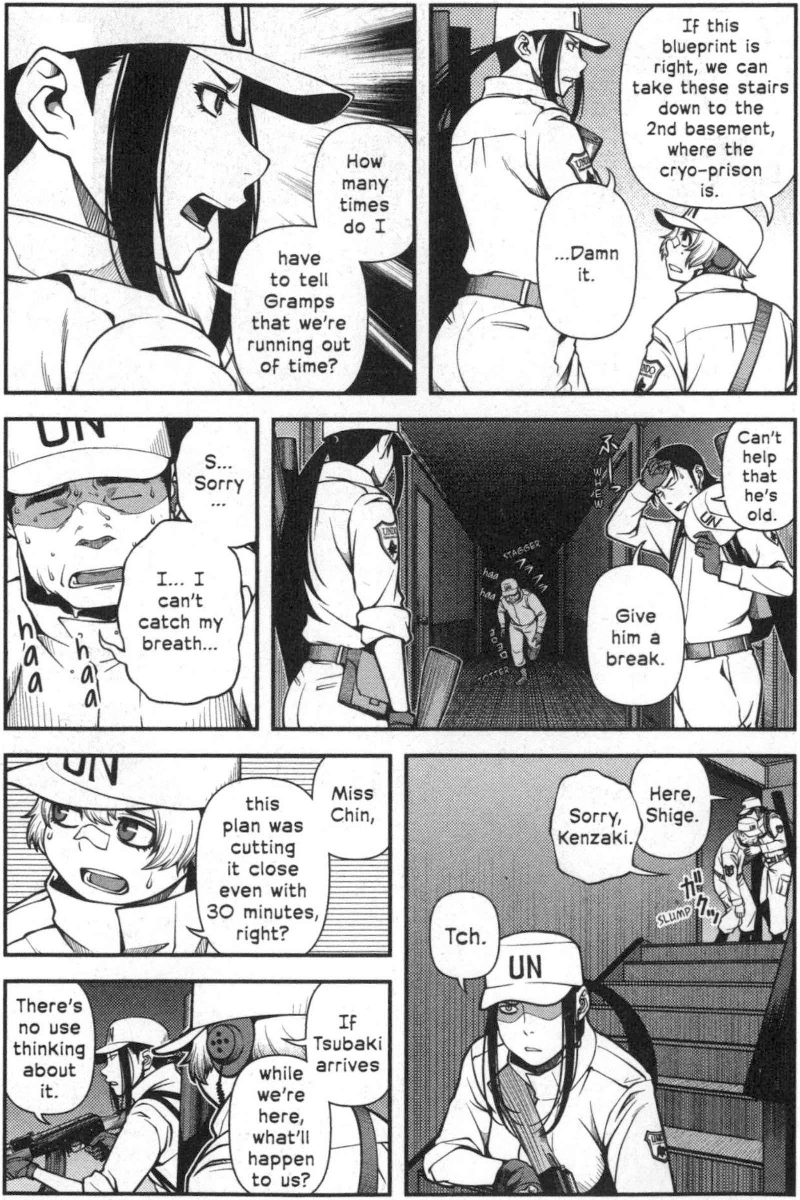
If this blueprint is right, we can take these stairs down to the 2nd basement, where the cryo-prison is.
...Damn it.
How many times do I
have to tell Gramps that we're running out of time?
Can't help that he's old.
WHEW
STAGGER
haa
haa
TOTTER
Give him a break.
S... Sorry ...
I... I can't catch my breath...
haa
haa
Here, Shige.
Sorry, Kenzaki.
SLUMP
Tch.
UN
Miss Chin,
this plan was cutting it close even with 30 minutes, right?
If Tsubaki arrives
while we're here, what'll happen to us?
There's no use thinking about it.

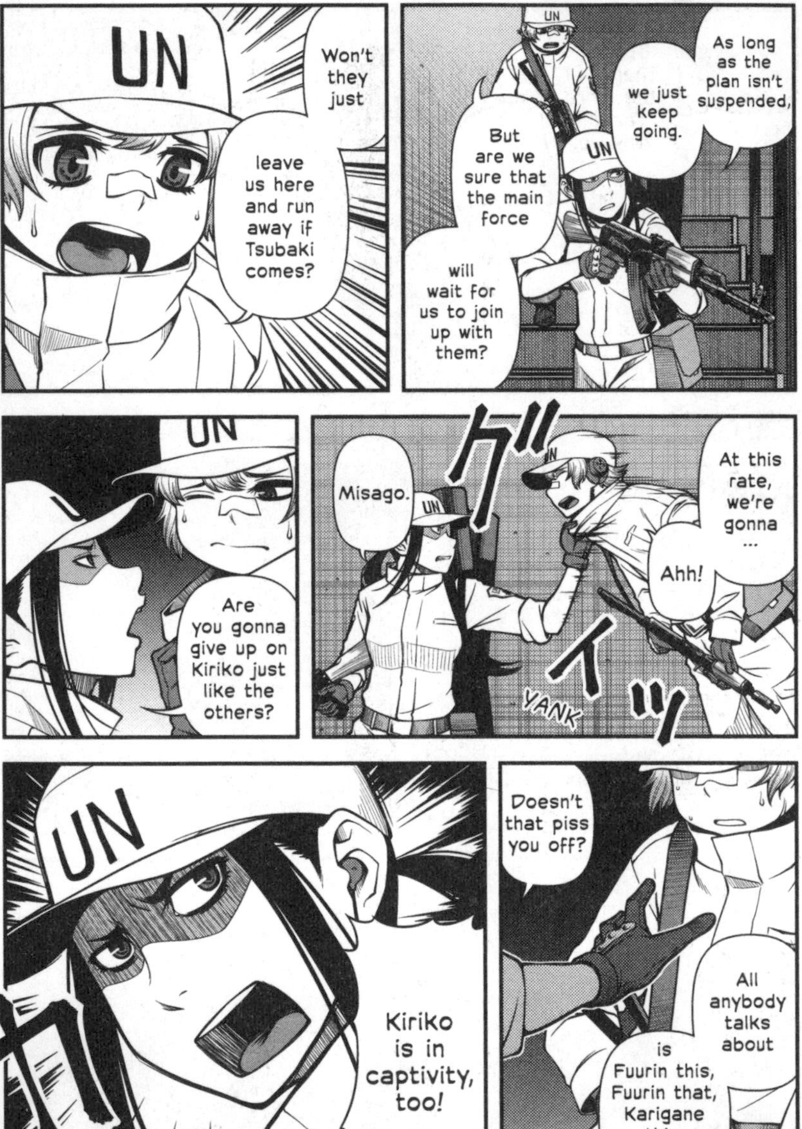
As long as the plan isn't suspended,
we just keep going.
But are we sure that the main force
will wait for us to join up with them?
Won't they just
leave us here and run away if Tsubaki comes?
At this rate, we're gonna ...
Ahh!
YANK
Misago.
Are you gonna give up on Kiriko just like the others?
Doesn't that piss you off?
All anybody talks about
is Fuurin this, Fuurin that, Karigane this, Karigane that!
Kiriko is in captivity, too!
RAGE

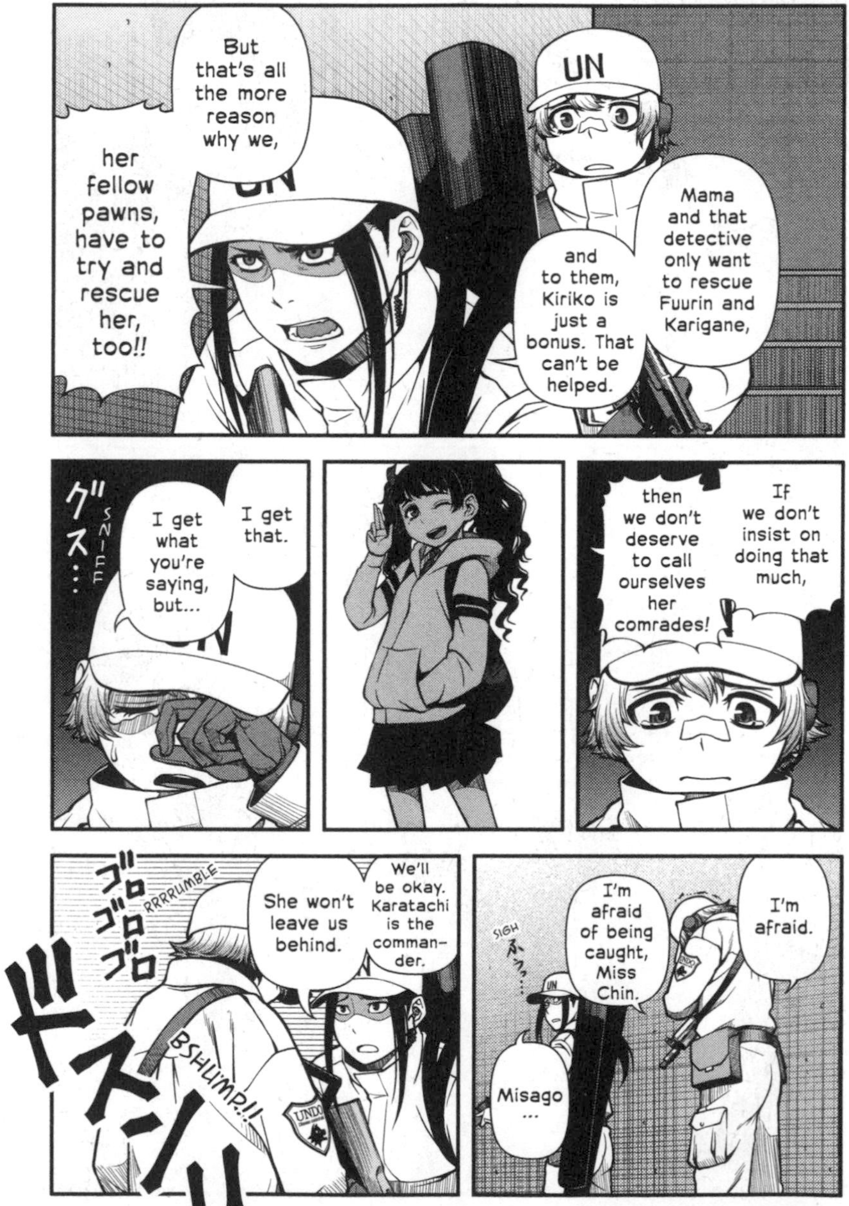
Mama and that detective only want to rescue Fuurin and Karigane,
and to them, Kiriko is just a bonus. That can't be helped.
But that's all the more reason why we,
her fellow pawns, have to try and rescue her, too!!
If we don't insist on doing that much,
then we don't deserve to call ourselves her comrades!
I get that.
I get what you're saying, but...
グス…
SNIFF
I'm afraid.
I'm afraid of being caught, Miss Chin.
SIGH
Misago ...
We'll be okay. Karatachi is the commander.
She won't leave us behind.
ゴロゴロゴロ
RRRRUMBLE
ドスン!!
BSHUMP!!

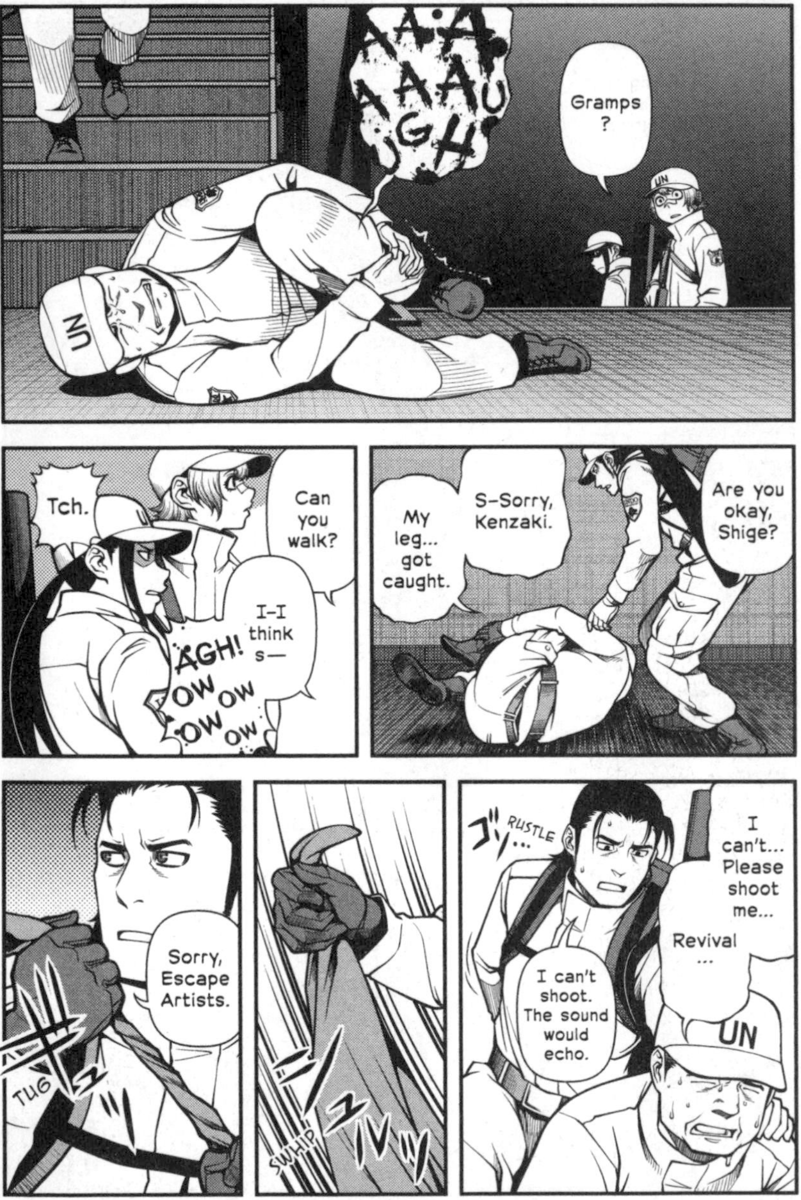
Gramps
?
AAAAAAUGH
Are you okay, Shige?
S-Sorry, Kenzaki.
My leg... got caught.
Can you walk?
Tch.
I-I think s—
AGH! OW OW OW OW
I can't... Please shoot me...
Revival ...
RUSTLE...
I can't shoot. The sound would echo.
SWHIP
Sorry, Escape Artists.
TUG

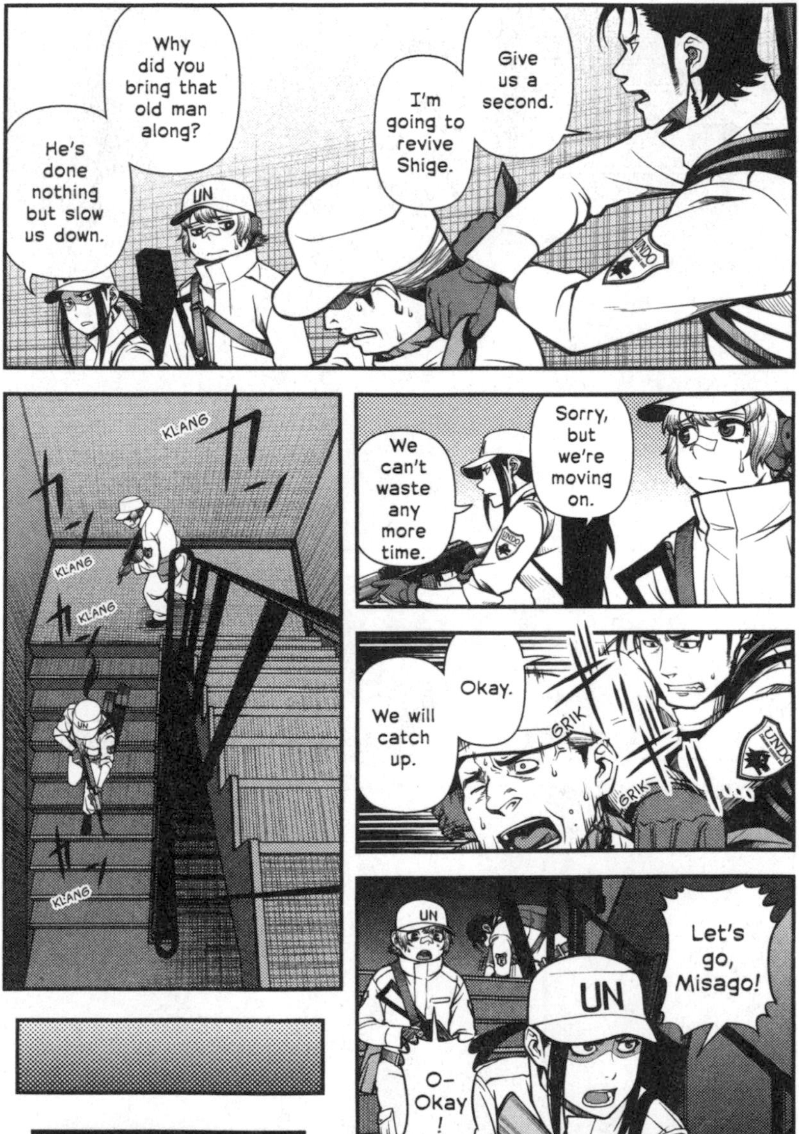
Give us a second.
I'm going to revive Shige.
Why did you bring that old man along?
He's done nothing but slow us down.
Sorry, but we're moving on.
We can't waste any more time.
Okay.
We will catch up.
GRIK
GRIK
Let's go, Misago!
O-Okay!
KLANG
KLANG
KLANG
KLANG

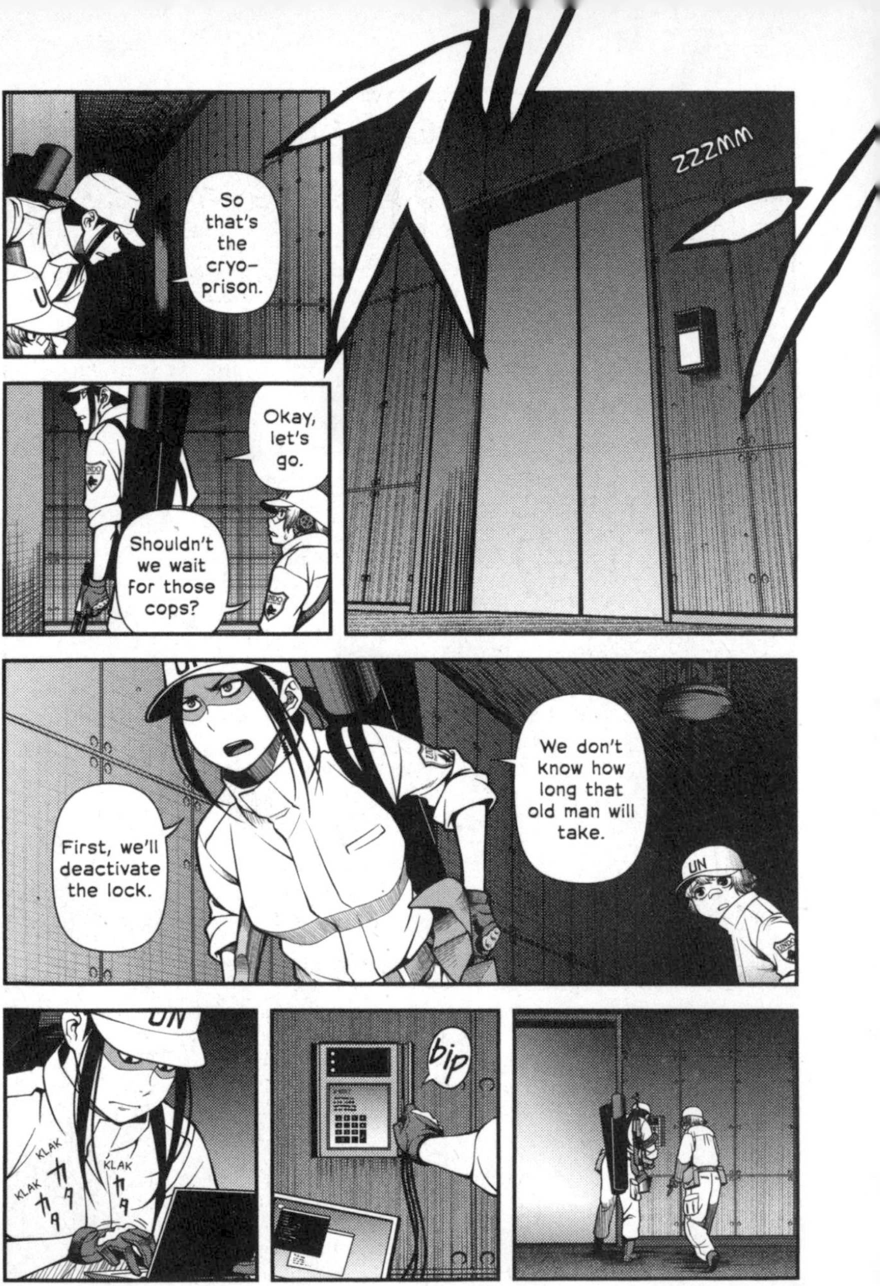
ZZZMM
So that's the cryo-prison.
Okay, let's go.
Shouldn't we wait for those cops?
We don't know how long that old man will take.
First, we'll deactivate the lock.
bip
KLAK
KLAK
KLAK

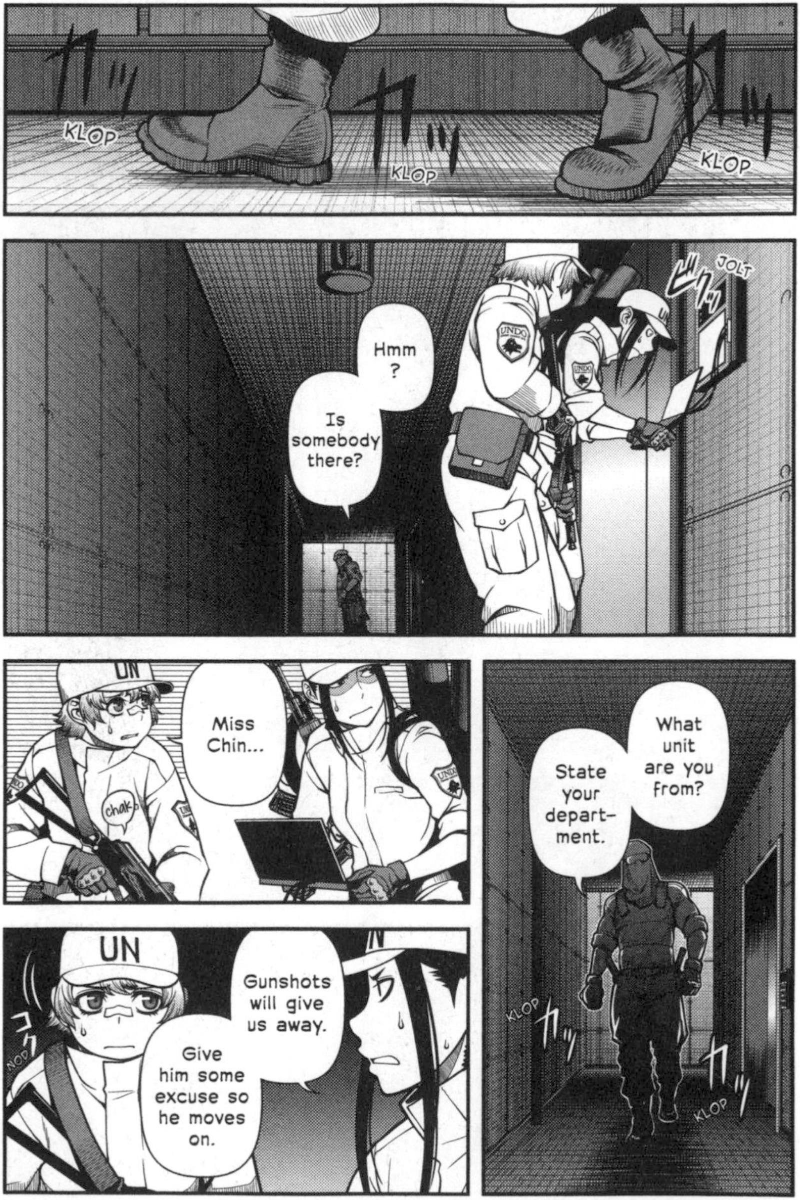
KLOP
KLOP
KLOP
JOLT
Hmm?
Is somebody there?
What unit are you from?
State your department.
KLOP
KLOP
Miss Chin...
chak
Gunshots will give us away.
Give him some excuse so he moves on.
NOD

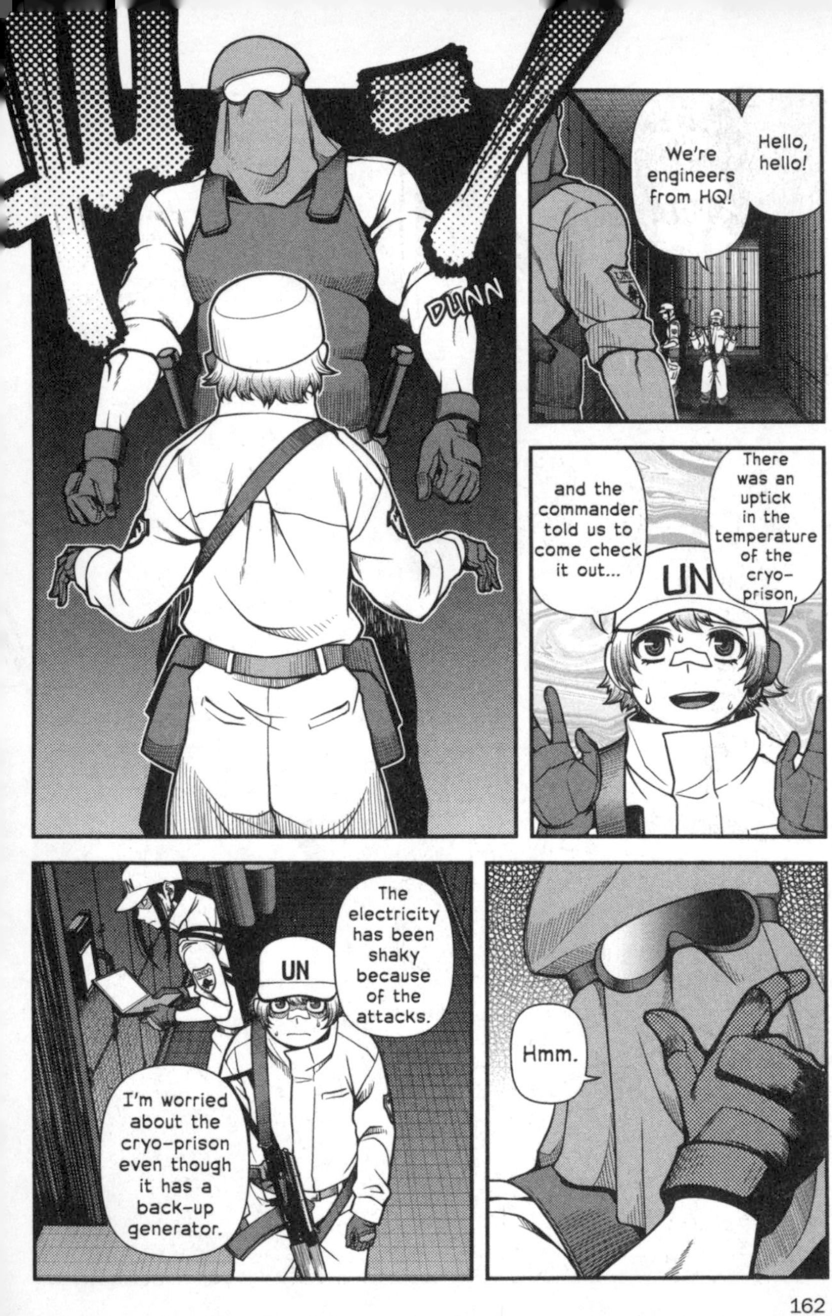
Hello, hello!
We're engineers from HQ!
There was an uptick in the temperature of the cryo-prison,
and the commander told us to come check it out...
UN
DUNN
Hmm.
The electricity has been shaky because of the attacks.
UN
I'm worried about the cryo-prison even though it has a back-up generator.

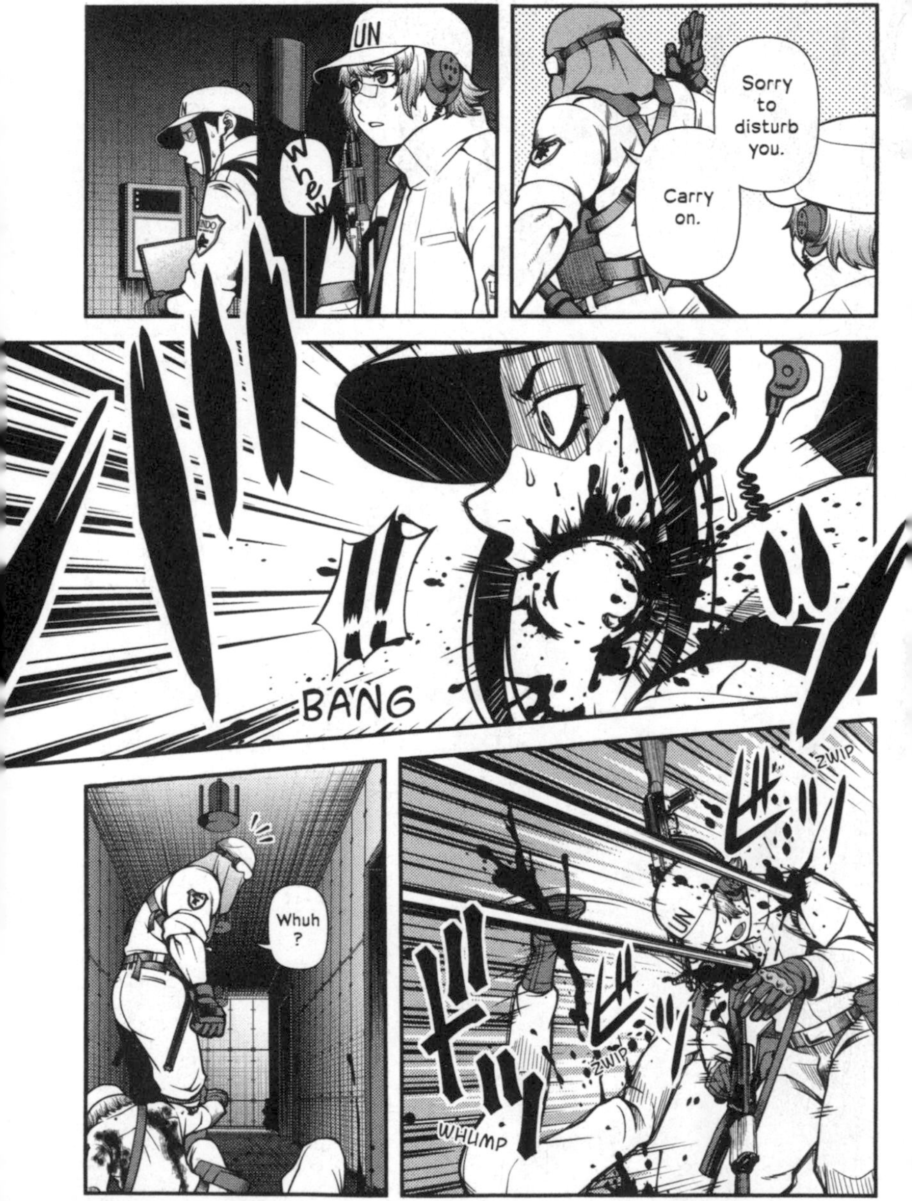
Sorry to disturb you.
Carry on.
Whew
BANG
ZWIP
ZWIP
WHUMP
Whuh?

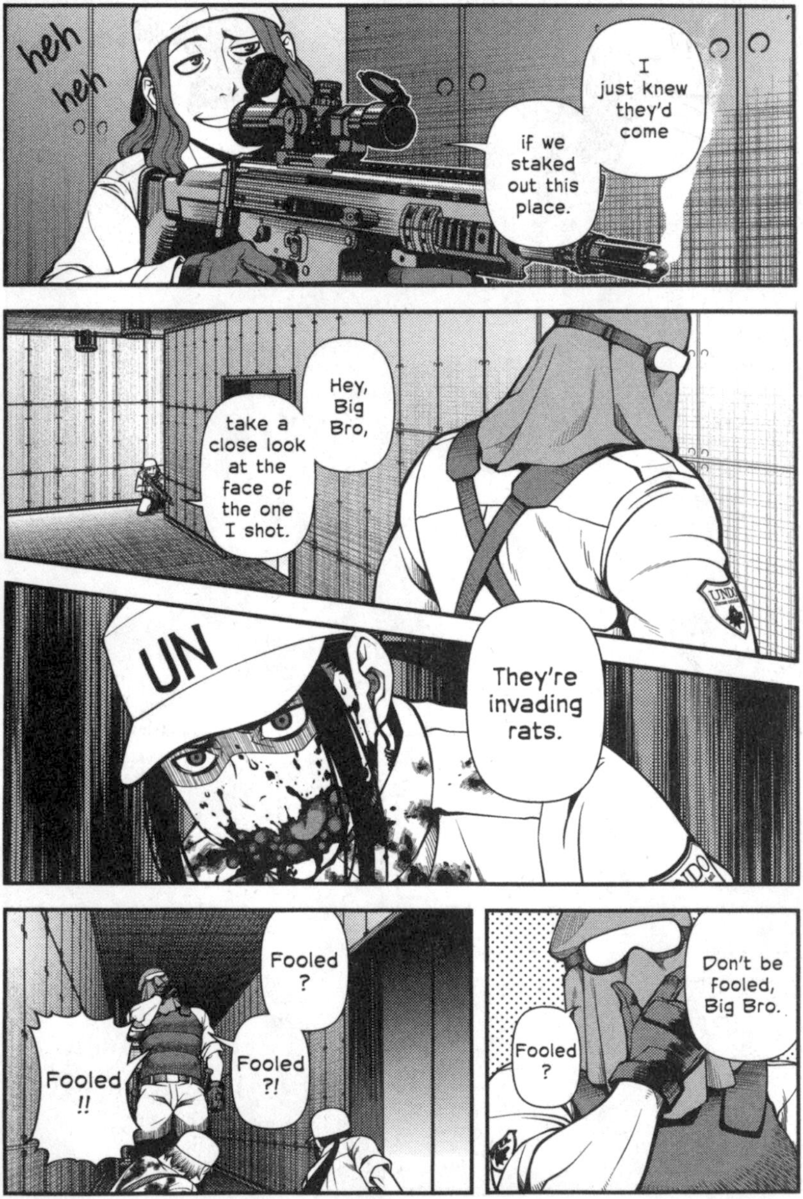
I just knew they'd come
if we staked out this place.
heh heh
Hey, Big Bro,
take a close look at the face of the one I shot.
UN
They're invading rats.
Don't be fooled, Big Bro.
Fooled ?
Fooled ?
Fooled ?!
Fooled !!

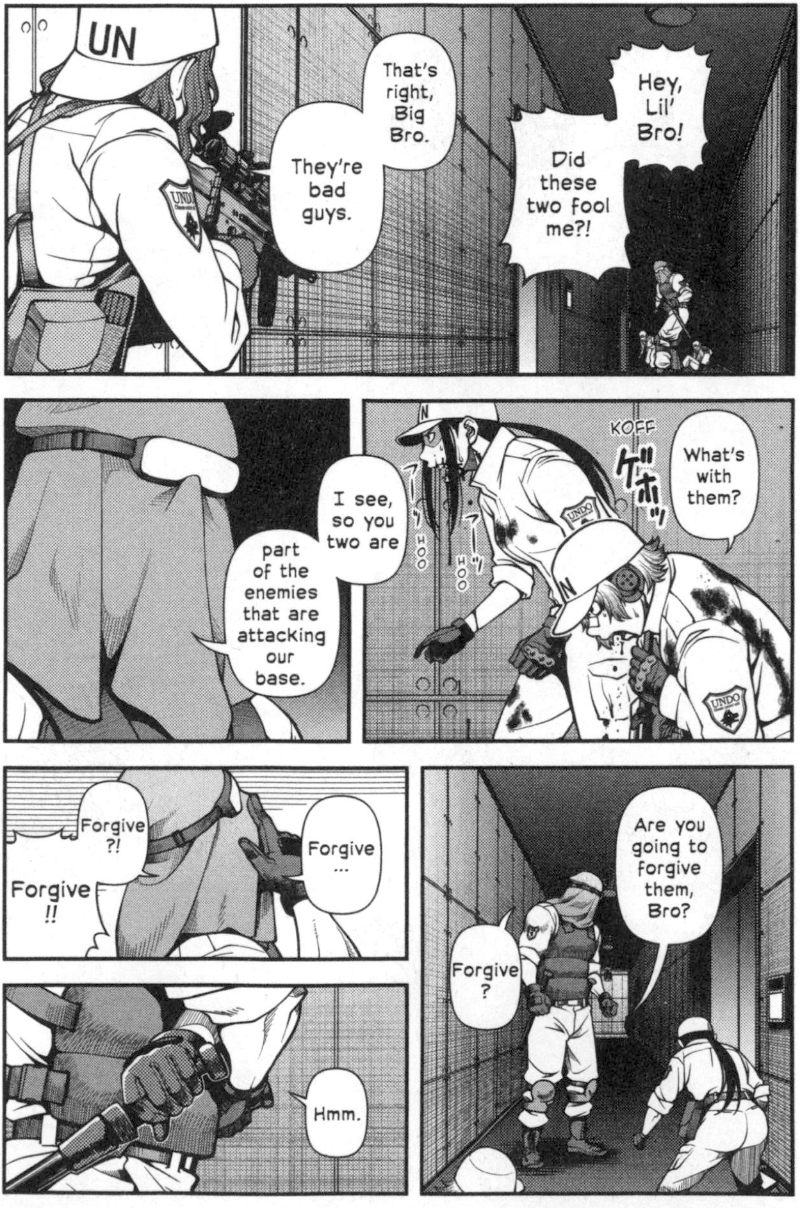
Hey, Lil' Bro! Did these two fool me?!
That's right, Big Bro. They're bad guys.
What's with them?
KOFF
HOO HOO
I see, so you two are part of the enemies that are attacking our base.
Are you going to forgive them, Bro?
Forgive ?
Forgive ...
Forgive ?!
Forgive !!
Hmm.

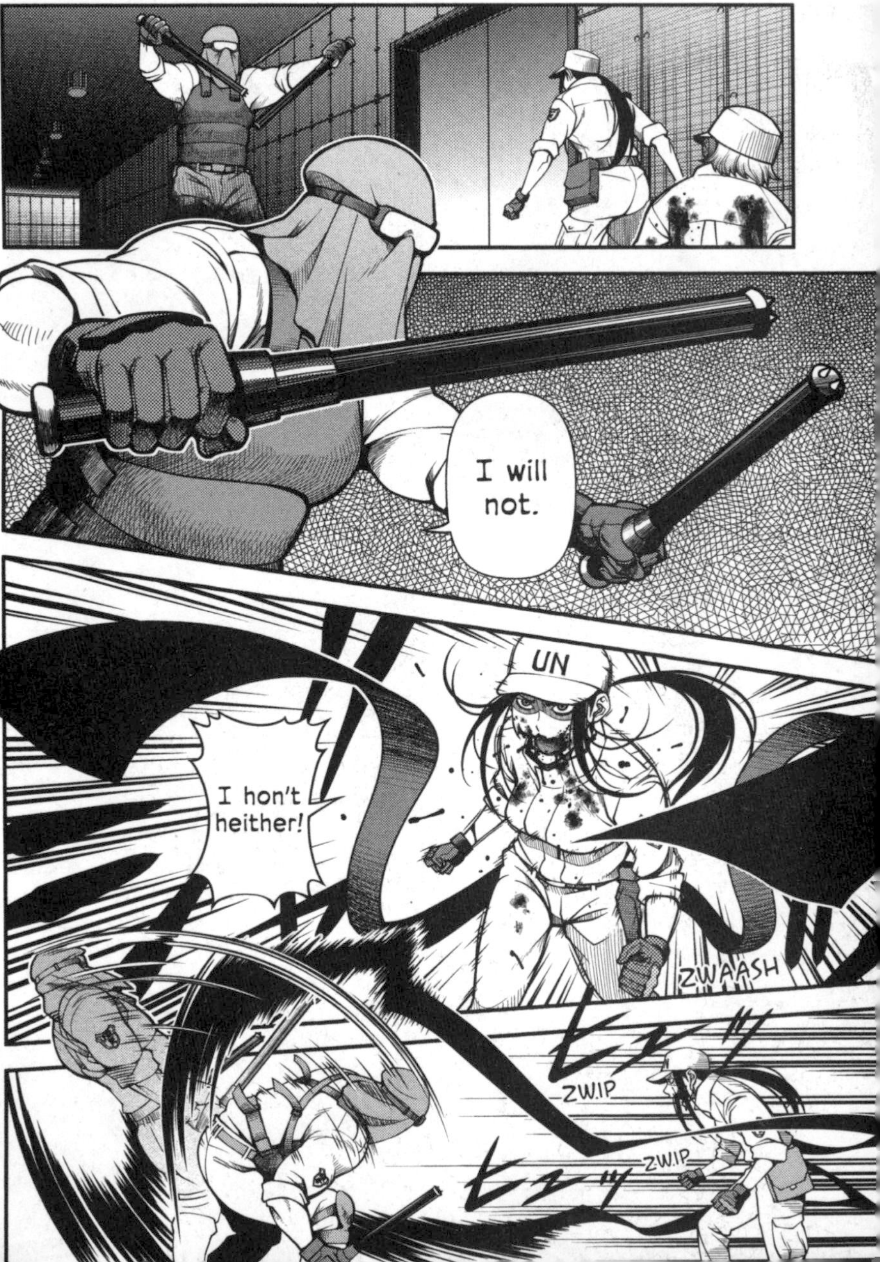
I will not.
I hon't heither!
ZWAASH
ZWIP
ZWIP

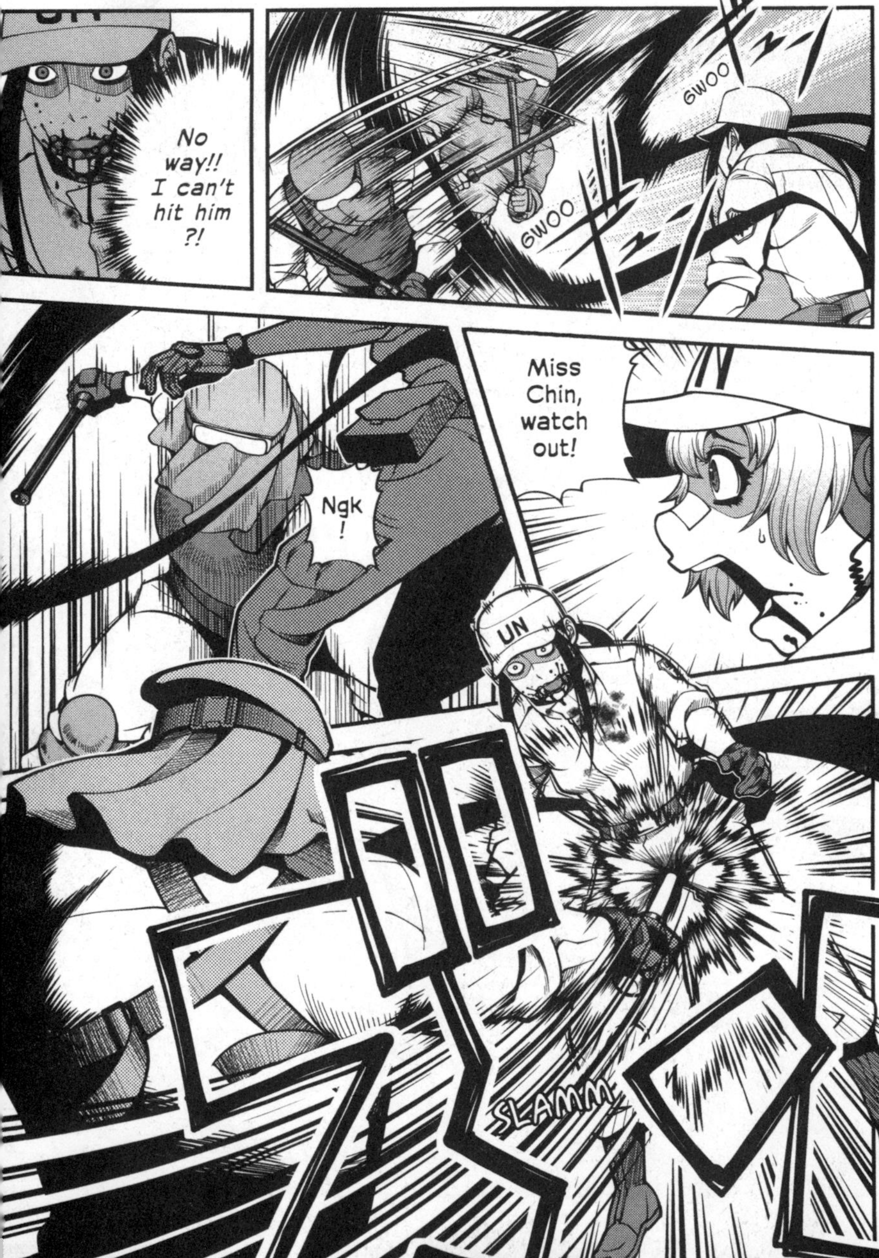
GWOO
GWOO
No way!! I can't hit him ?!
Miss Chin, watch out!
Ngk !
SLAMM

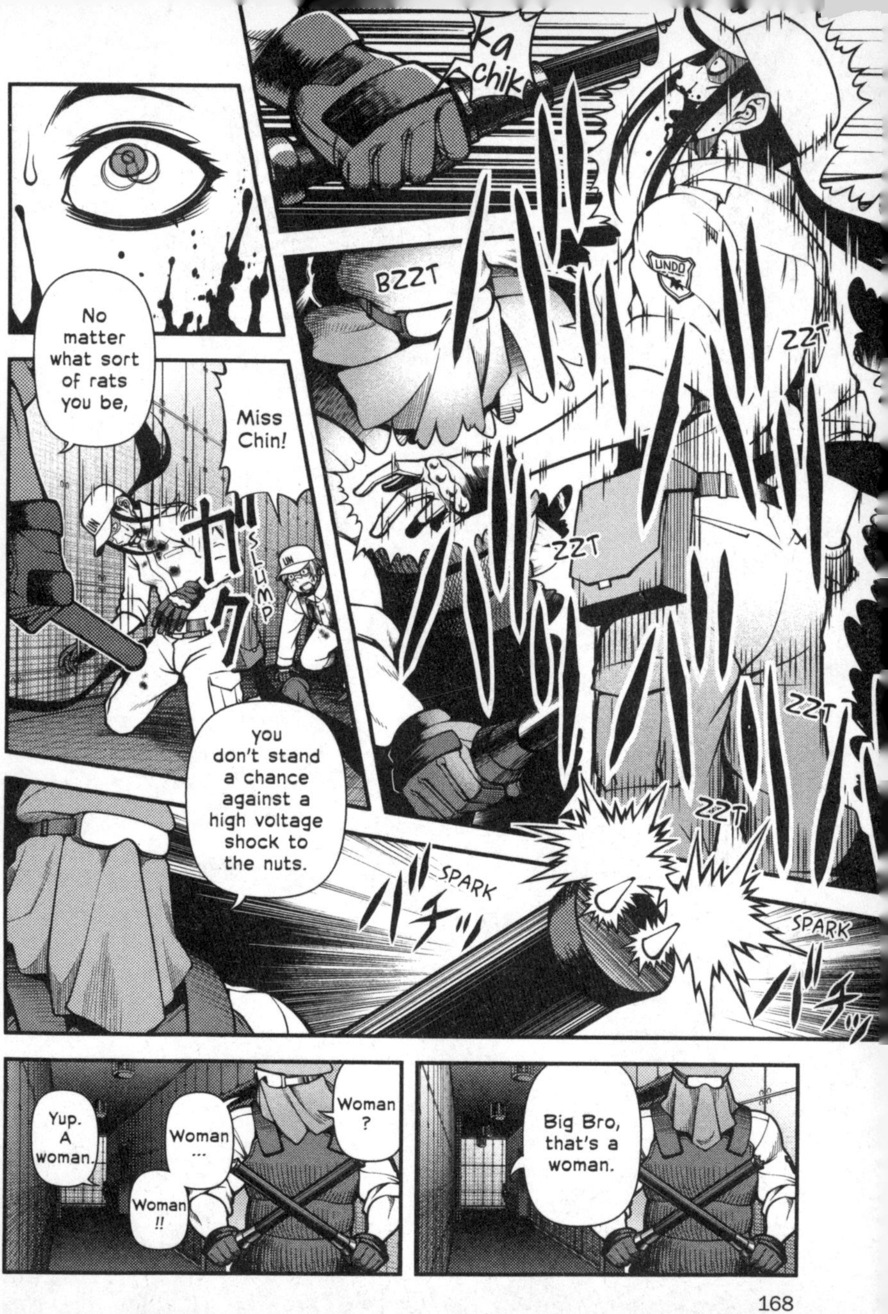
Ka chik
BZZT
ZZT
ZZT
ZZT
ZZT
No matter what sort of rats you be,
Miss Chin!
SLUMP
you don't stand a chance against a high voltage shock to the nuts.
SPARK
SPARK
Big Bro, that's a woman.
Woman ?
Woman ...
Yup. A woman.
Woman !!

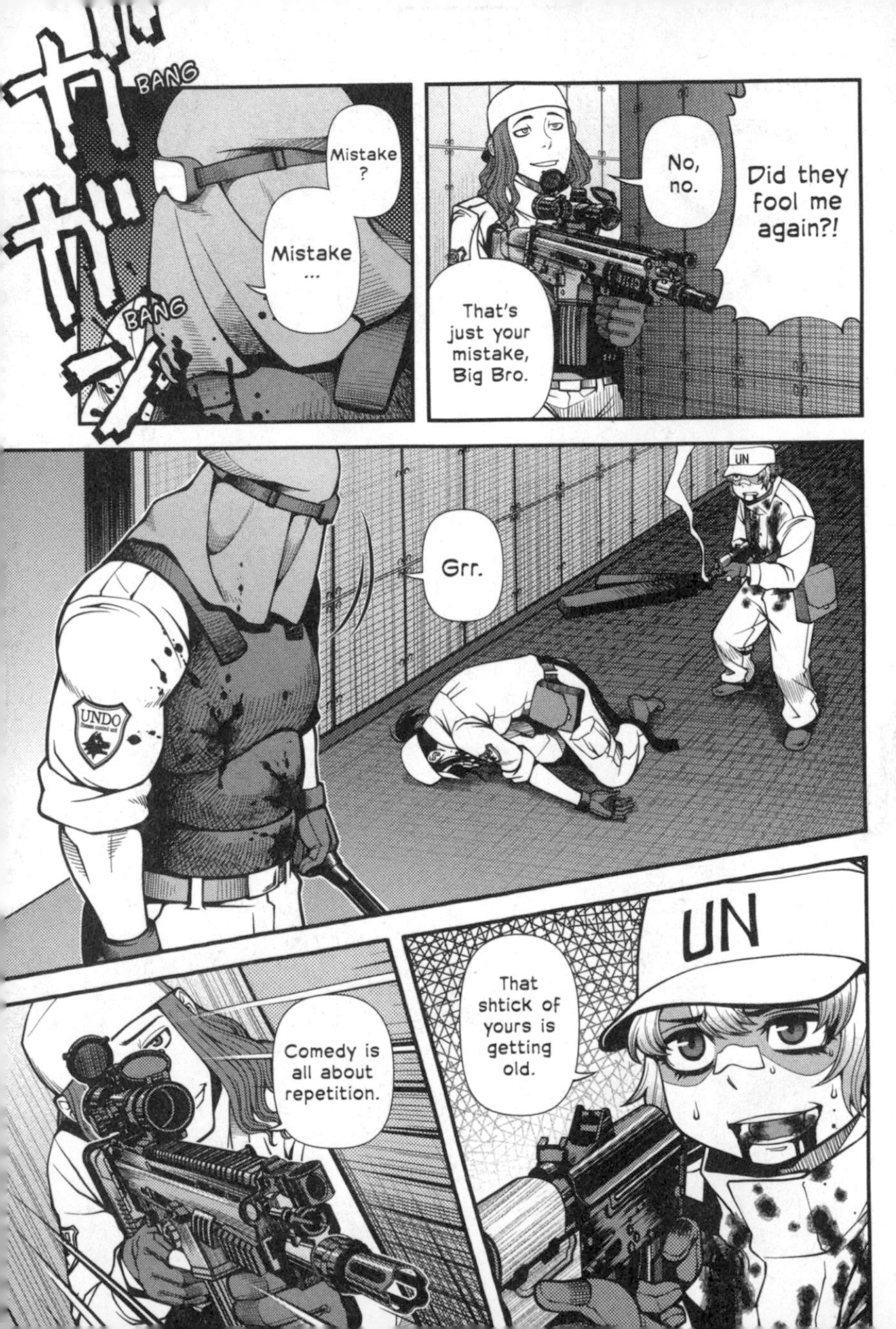
Did they fool me again?!
No, no.
That's just your mistake, Big Bro.
BANG
Mistake?
Mistake...
BANG
Grr.
UN
That shtick of yours is getting old.
Comedy is all about repetition.

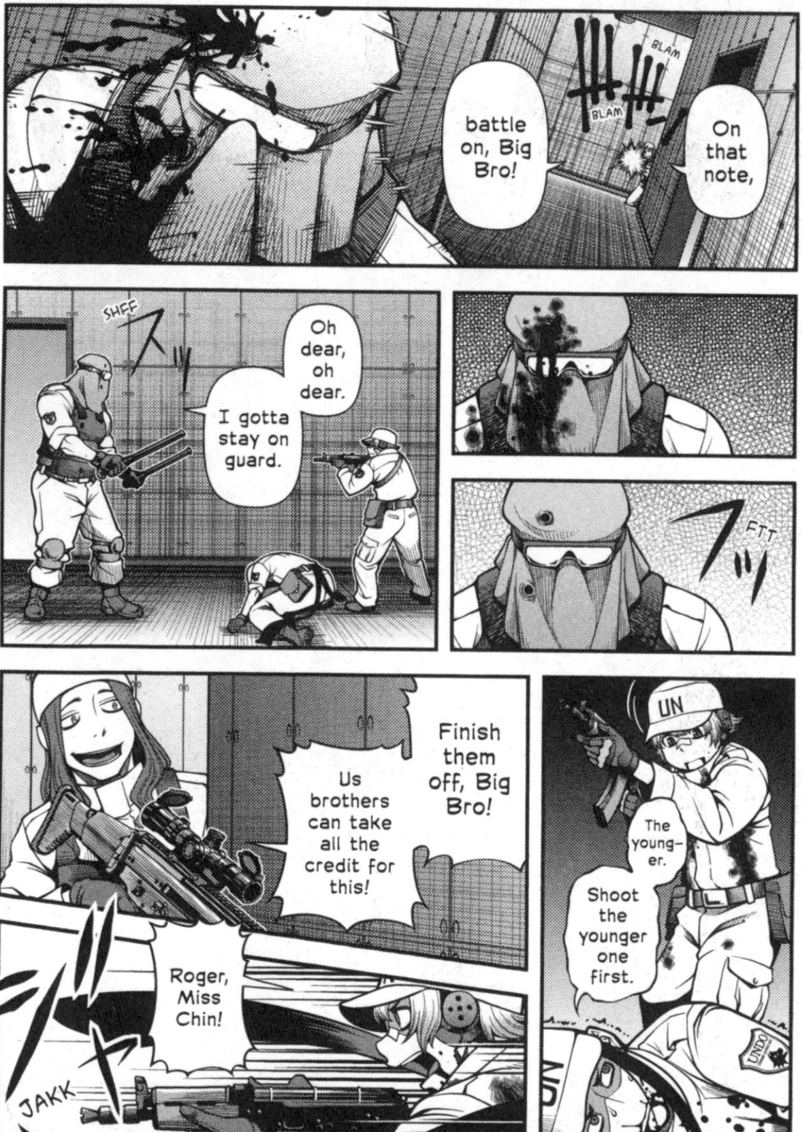
On that note,
battle on, Big Bro!
BLAM
BLAM
FTT
SHFF
Oh dear, oh dear.
I gotta stay on guard.
The younger.
Shoot the younger one first.
Finish them off, Big Bro!
Us brothers can take all the credit for this!
Roger, Miss Chin!
JAKK

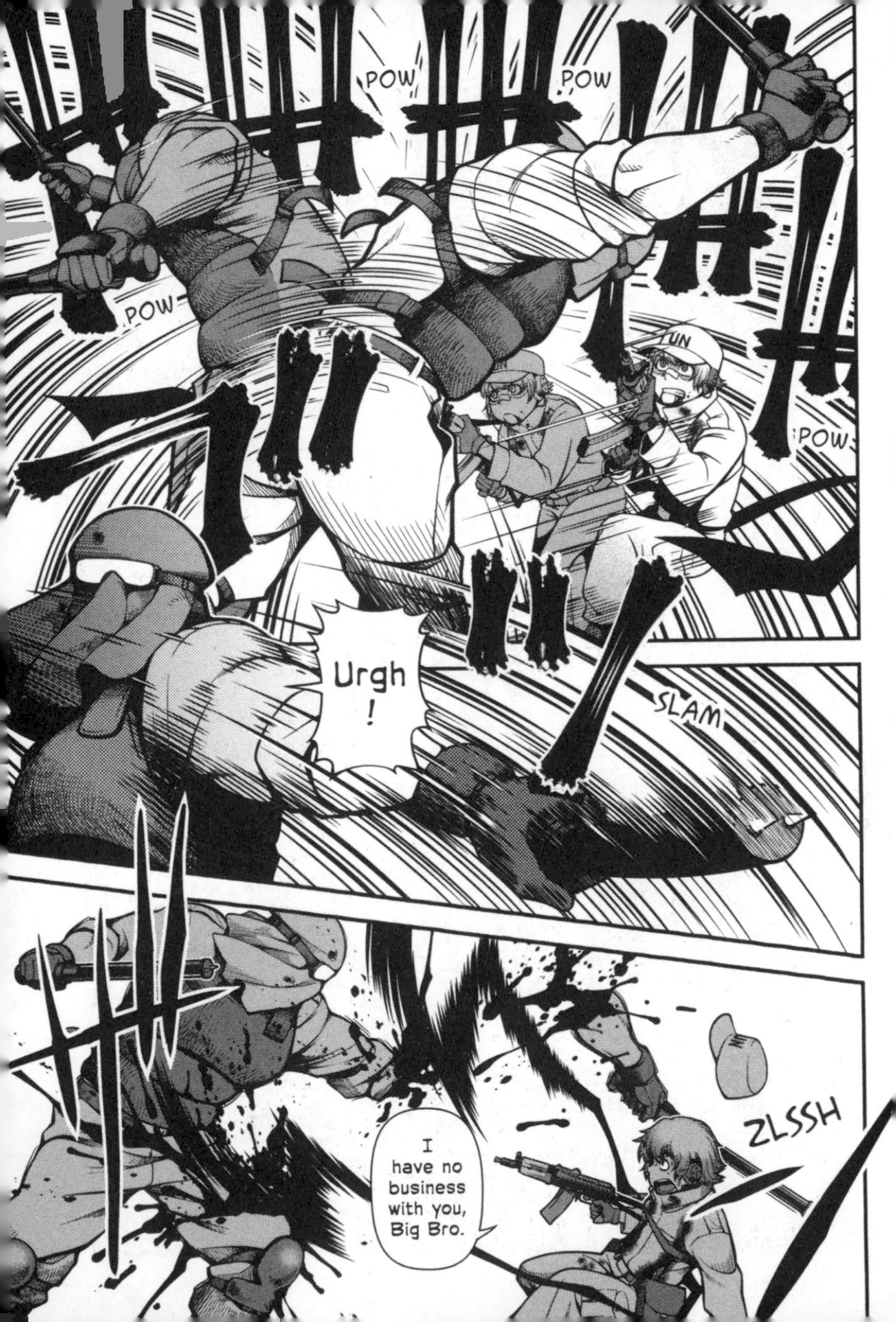
POW
POW
POW
POW
Urgh!
SLAM
ZLSSH
I have no business with you, Big Bro.

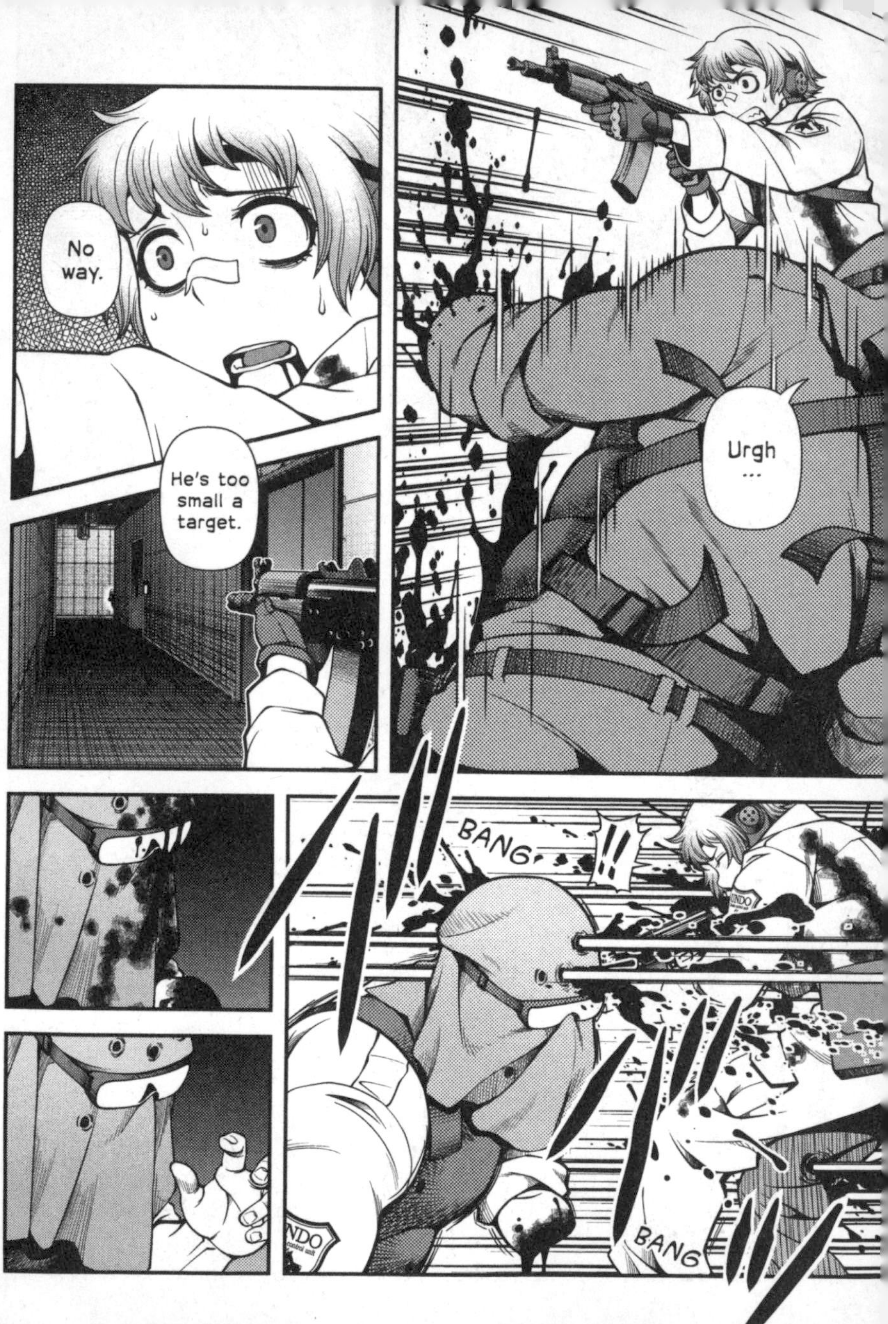
Urgh
...
No way.
He's too small a target.
BANG
!!
BANG

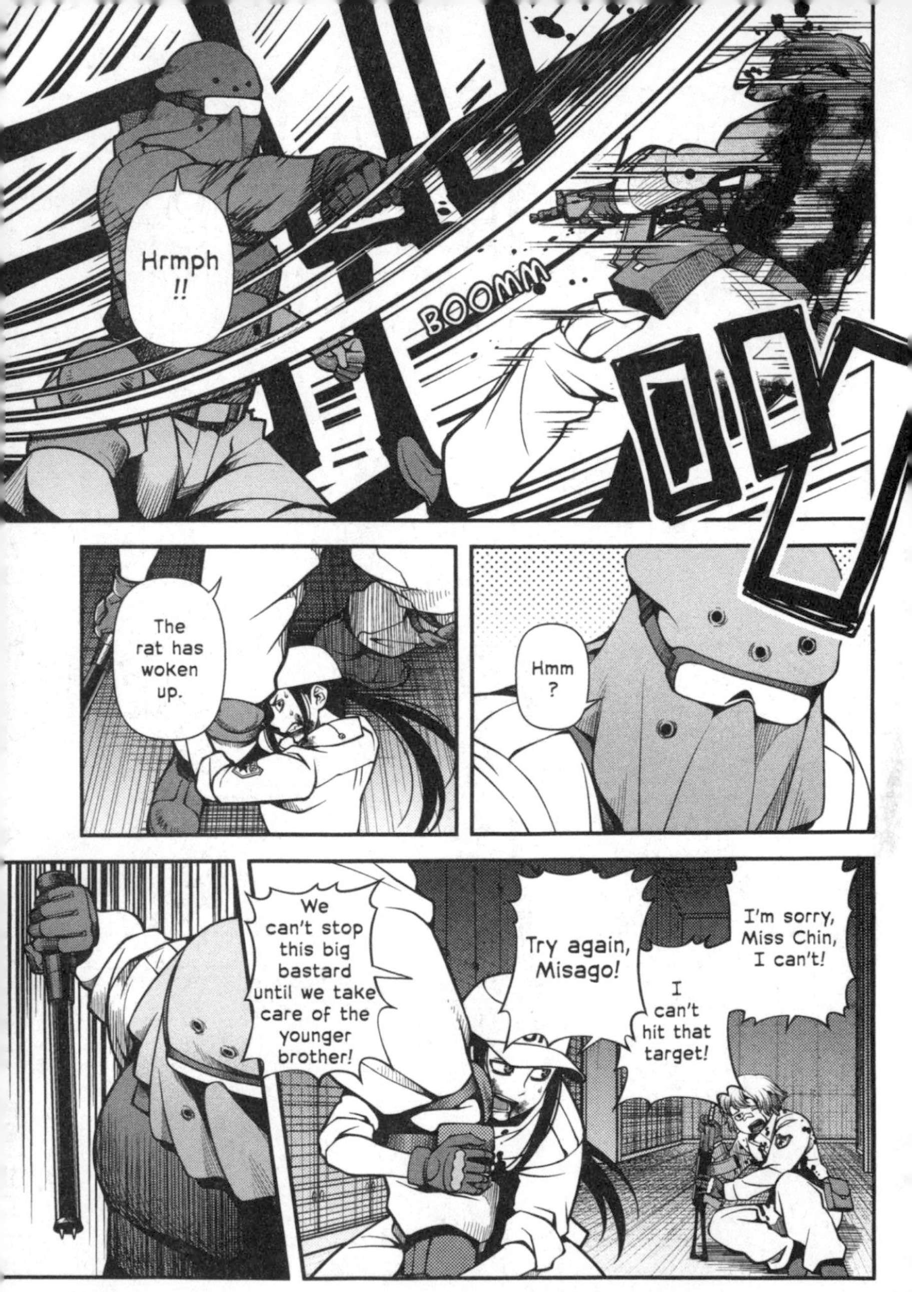
BOOMM
Hrmph !!
Hmm ?
The rat has woken up.
I'm sorry, Miss Chin, I can't!
I can't hit that target!
Try again, Misago!
We can't stop this big bastard until we take care of the younger brother!

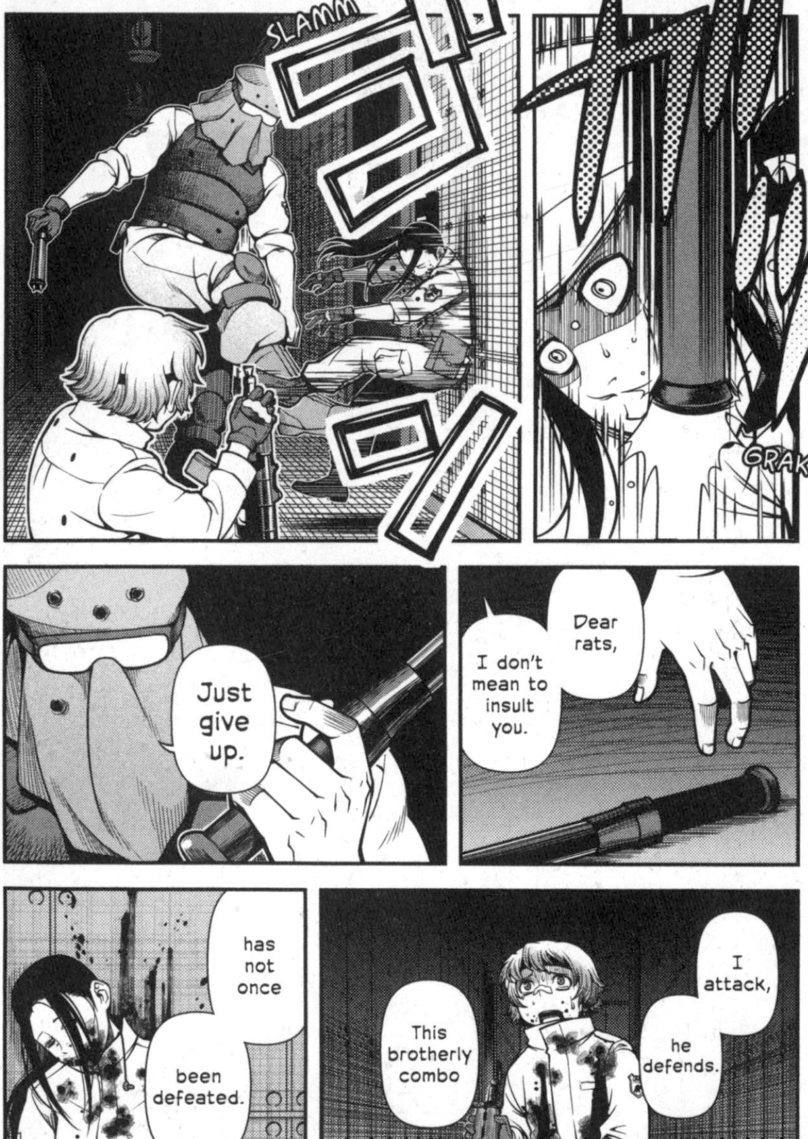
GRAK
SLAMM
Dear rats,
I don't mean to insult you.
Just give up.
I attack,
he defends.
This brotherly combo
has not once
been defeated.

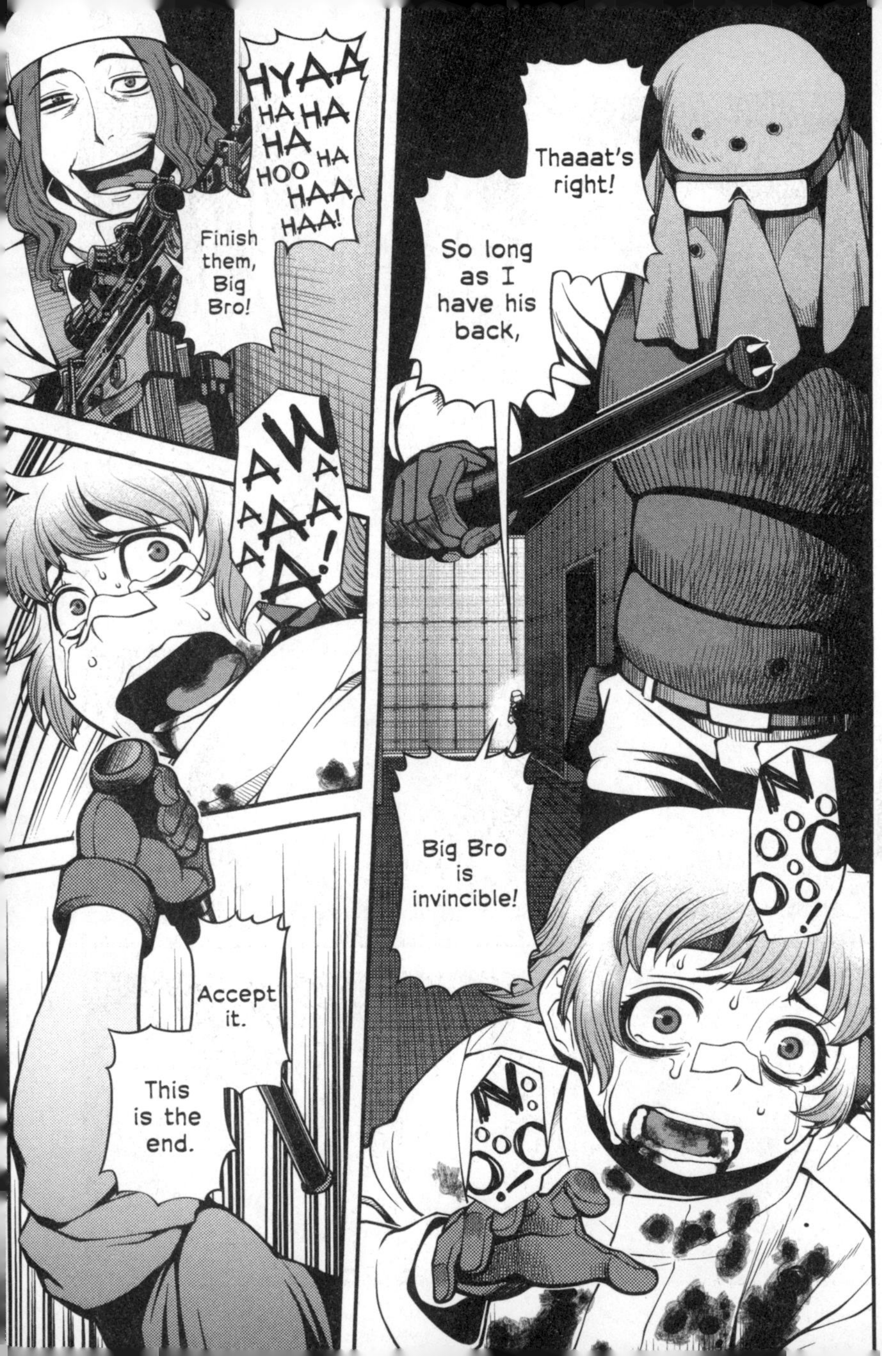

Thaaat's right!
So long as I have his back,
Big Bro is invincible!
NOOOOOOO!
NOOOOO!
HYAA HAHA HA HA HOO HA HAA HAA!
Finish them, Big Bro!
AWAAAAA!
Accept it.
This is the end.

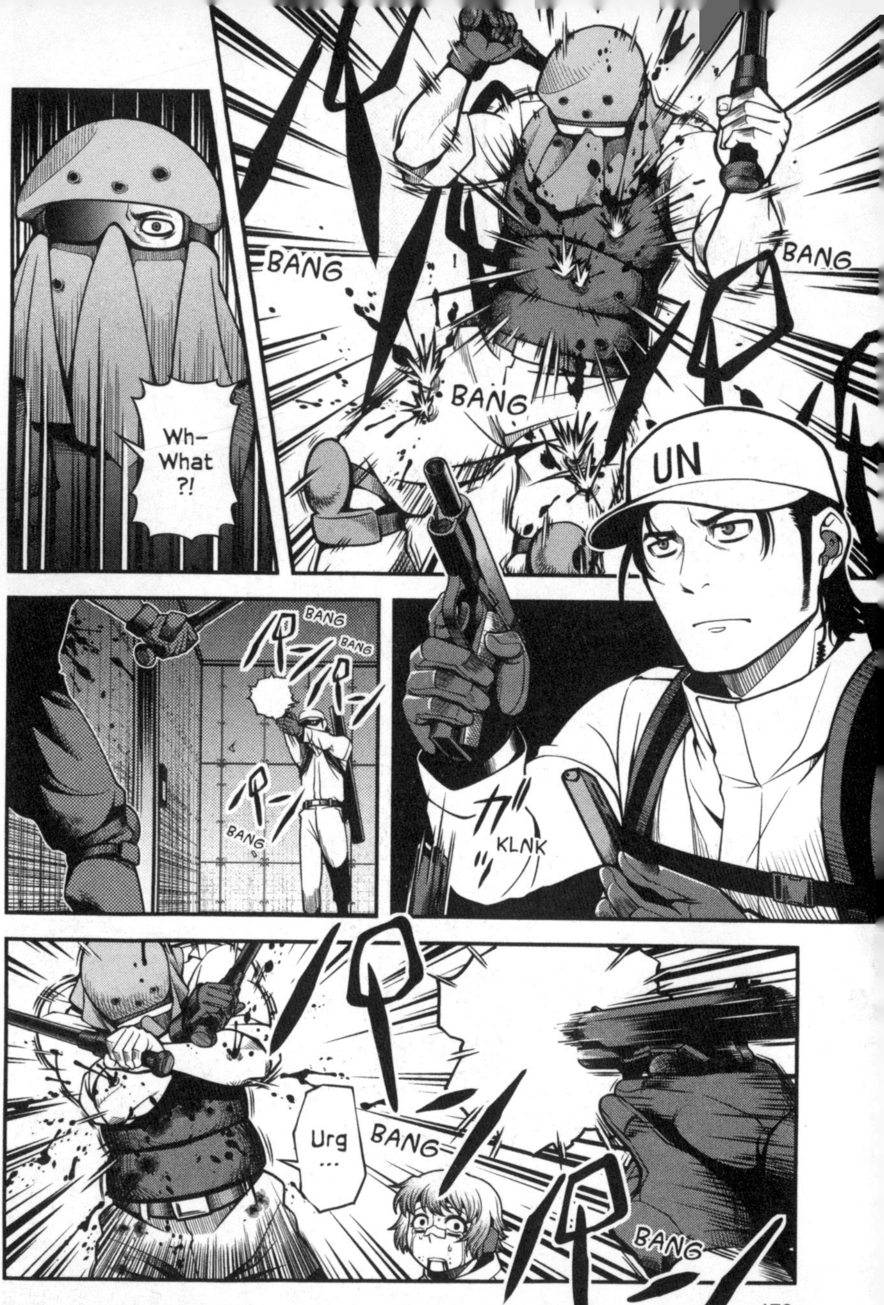
BANG
BANG
BANG
Wh- What ?!
KLNK
BANG
BANG
BANG
BANG
Urg ...
BANG

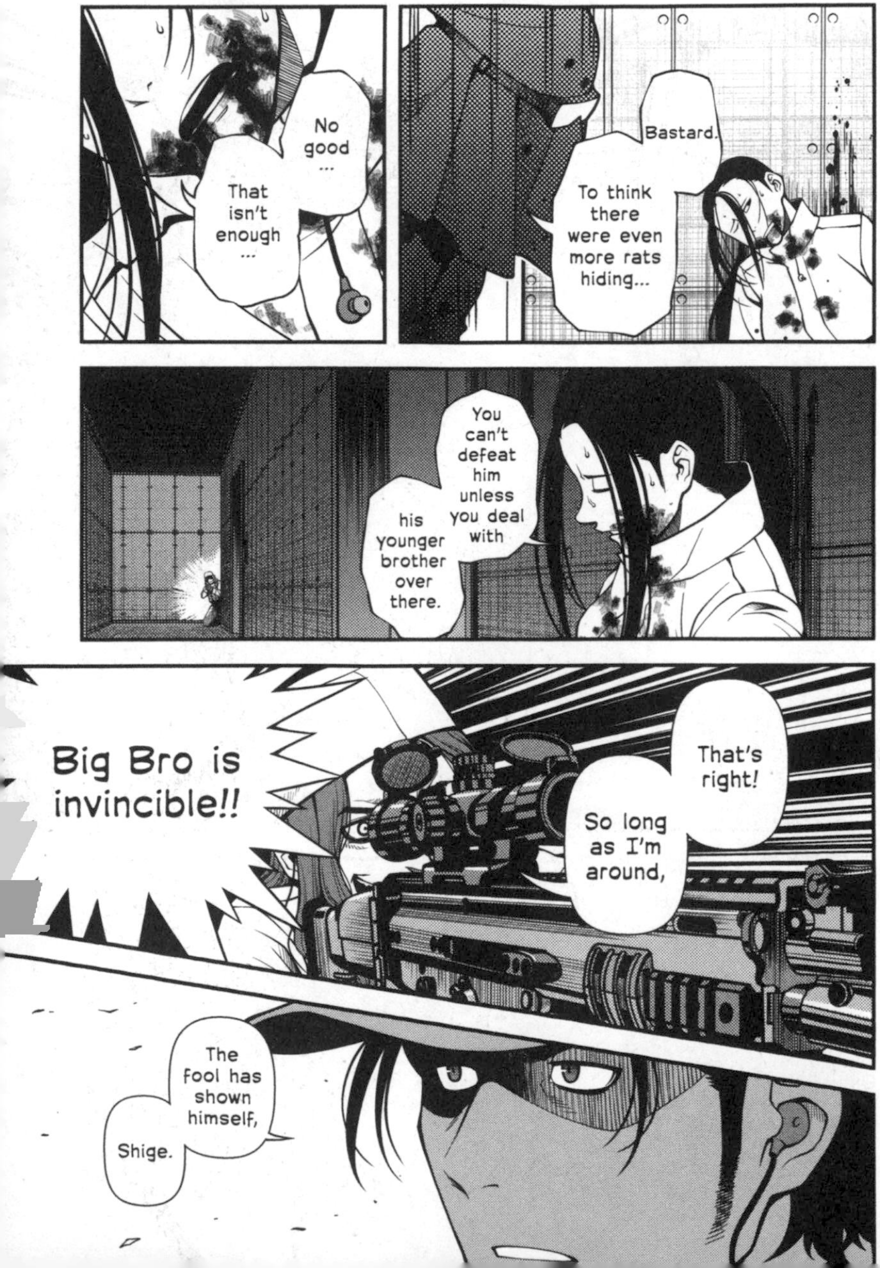

Bastard.
To think there were even more rats hiding...
No good ...
That isn't enough ...
You can't defeat him unless you deal with
his younger brother over there.
That's right!
So long as I'm around,
Big Bro is invincible!!
The fool has shown himself,
Shige.

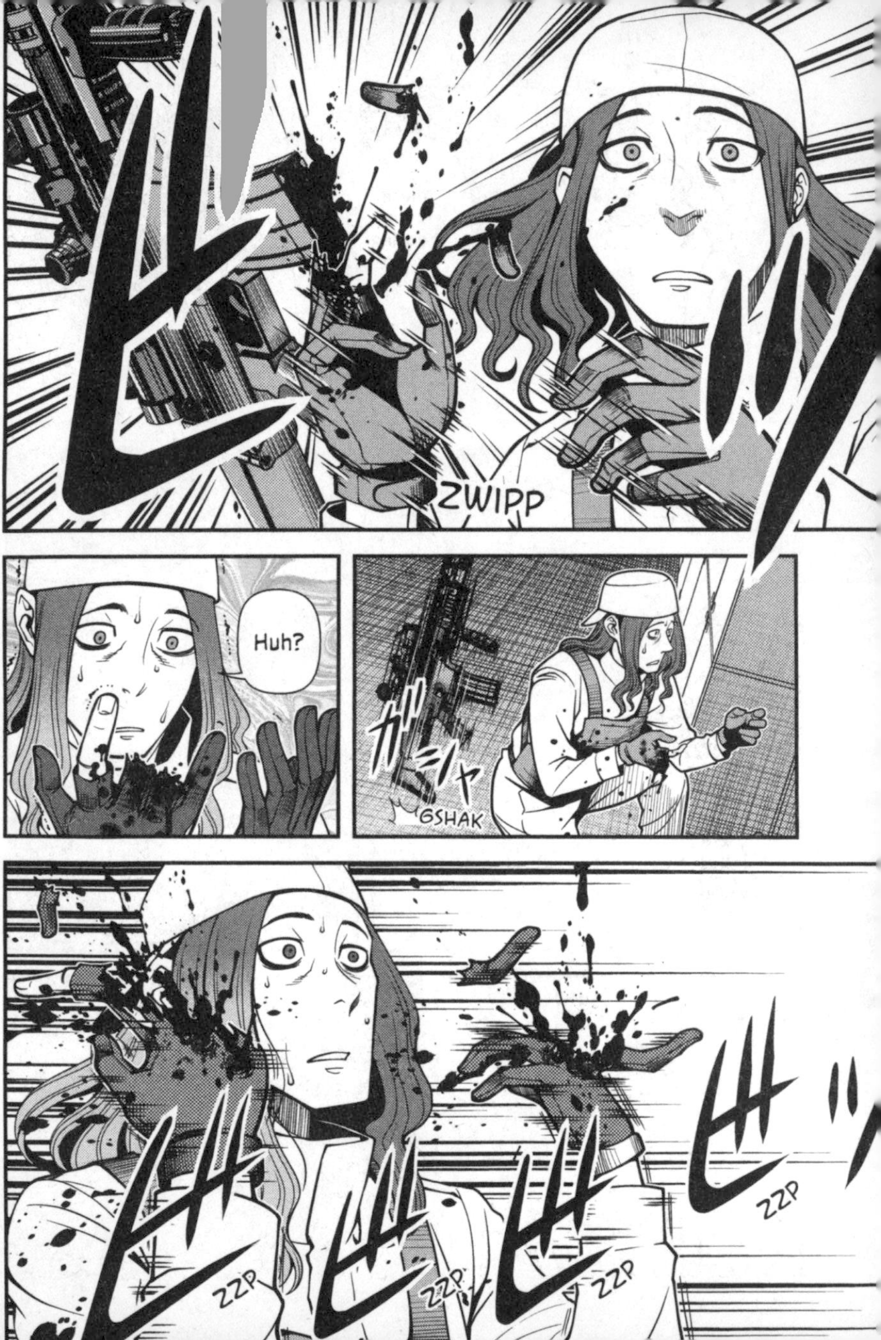

ZWIPP
GSHAK
Huh?
ZZP
ZZP
ZZP
ZZP

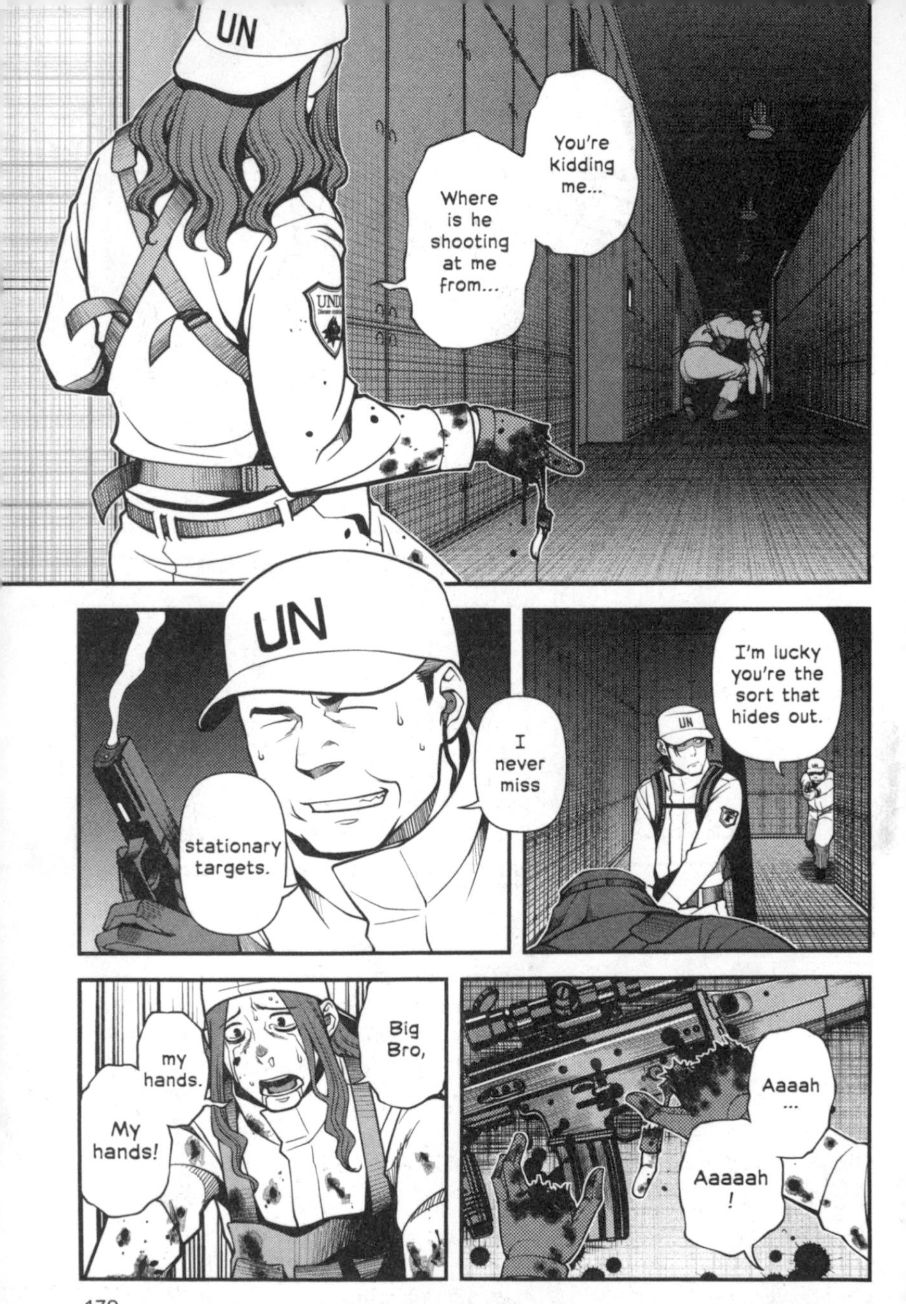
UN
You're kidding me...
Where is he shooting at me from...
UN
I'm lucky you're the sort that hides out.
UN
UN
I never miss
stationary targets.
Aaaah ...
Aaaaah !
Big Bro,
my hands.
My hands!

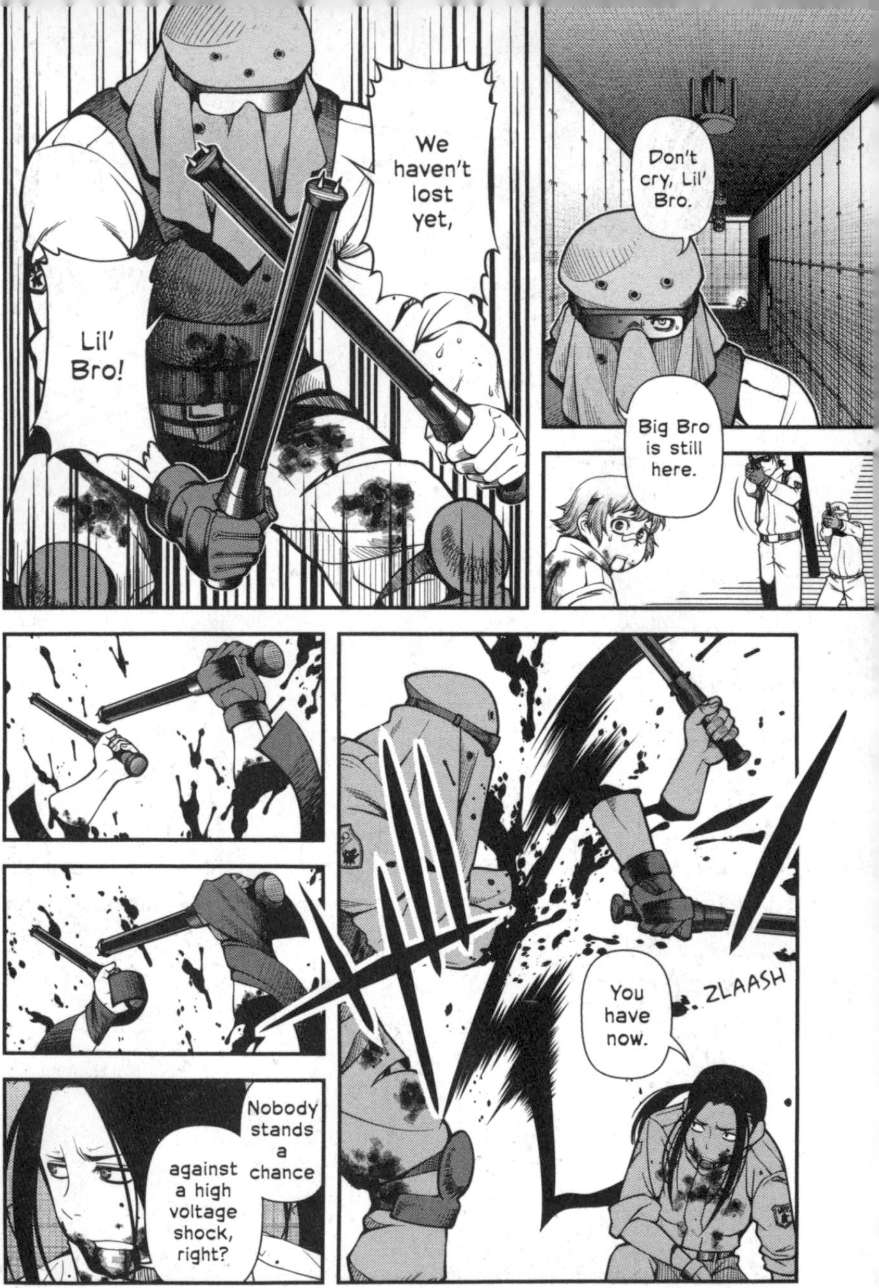
Don't cry, Lil' Bro.
Big Bro is still here.
We haven't lost yet,
Lil' Bro!
ZLAASH
You have now.
Nobody stands a chance
against a high voltage shock, right?

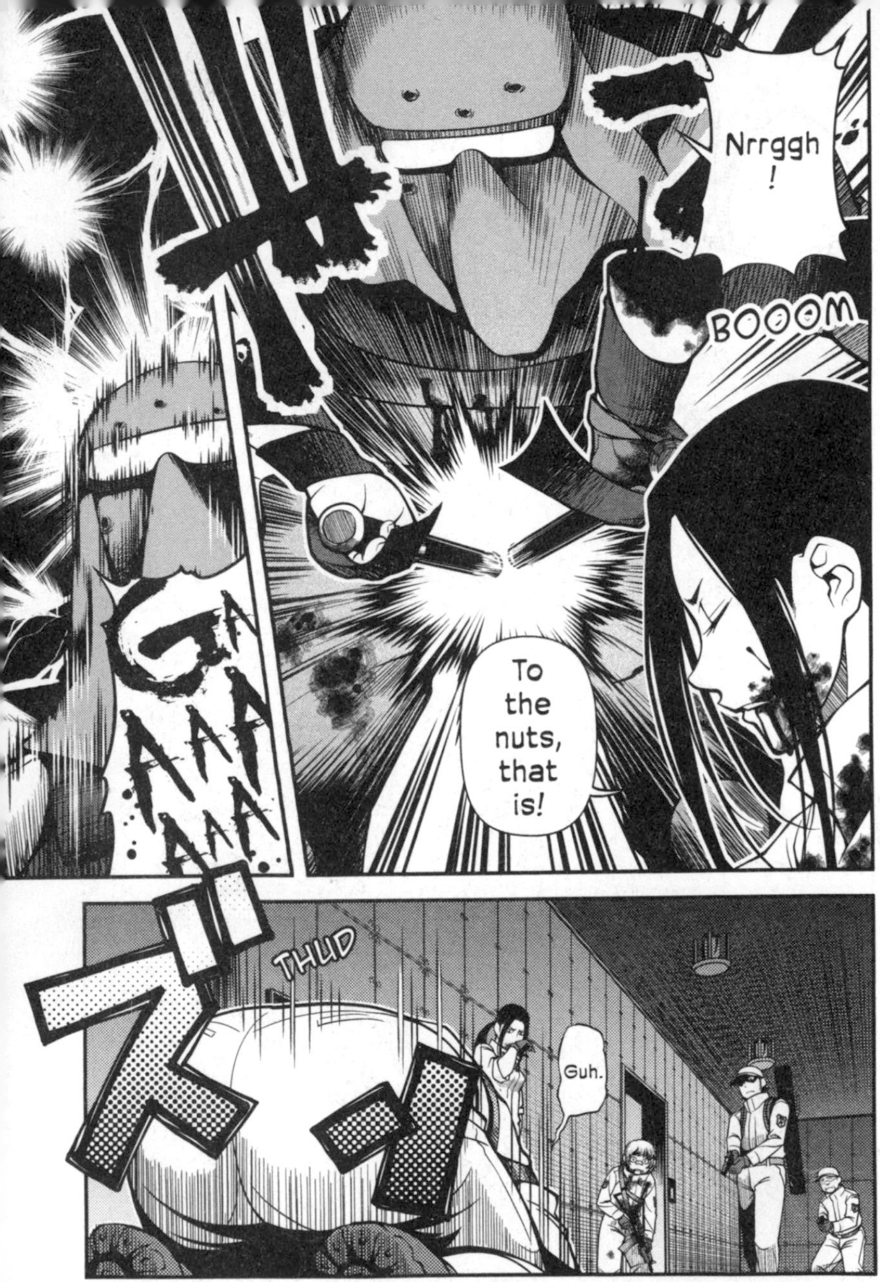
Nrrggh!
BOOOM
To the nuts, that is!
THUD
Guh.

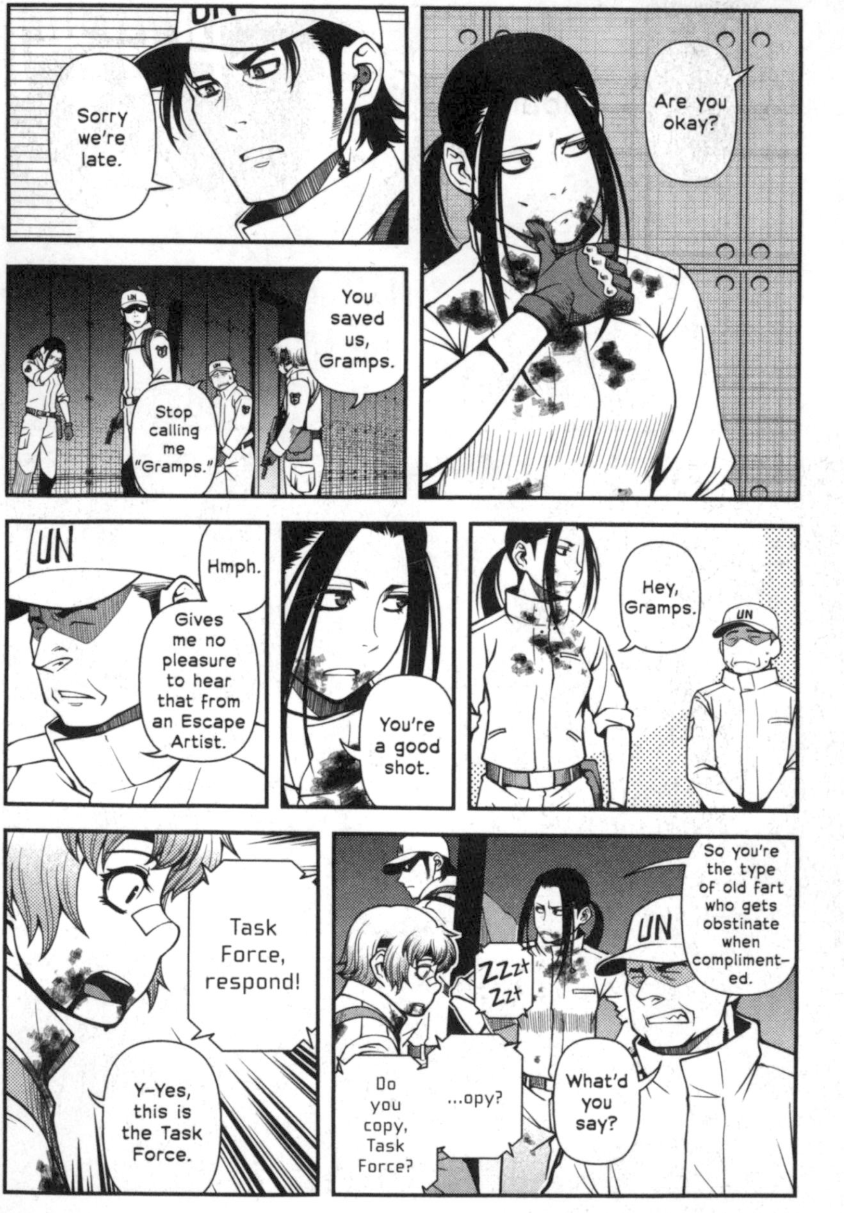
Are you okay?
Sorry we're late.
You saved us, Gramps.
Stop calling me "Gramps."
Hey, Gramps.
You're a good shot.
Hmph.
Gives me no pleasure to hear that from an Escape Artist.
So you're the type of old fart who gets obstinate when compliment-ed.
ZZzt Zzt
What'd you say?
...opy?
Do you copy, Task Force?
Task Force, respond!
Y-Yes, this is the Task Force.

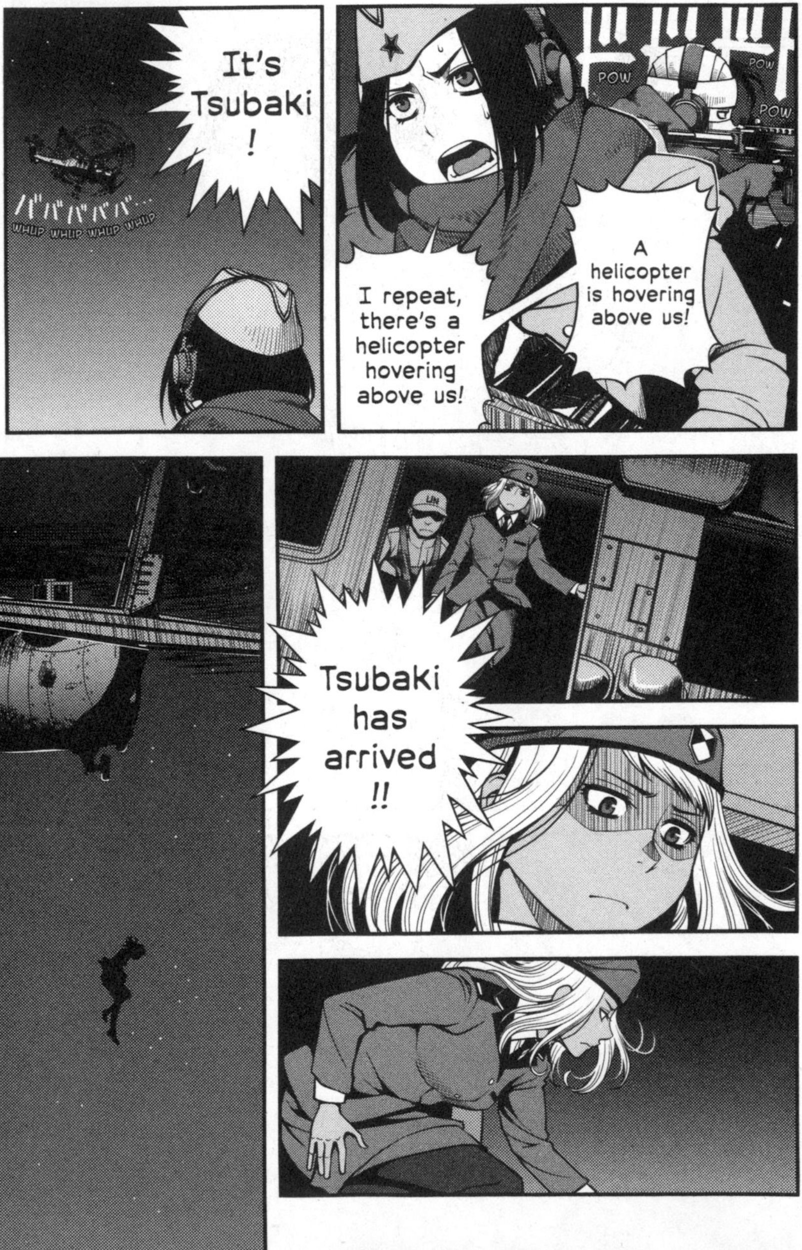
POW
POW
POW
A helicopter is hovering above us!
I repeat, there's a helicopter hovering above us!
It's Tsubaki!
バババババ…
WHUP WHUP WHUP WHUP
Tsubaki has arrived!!

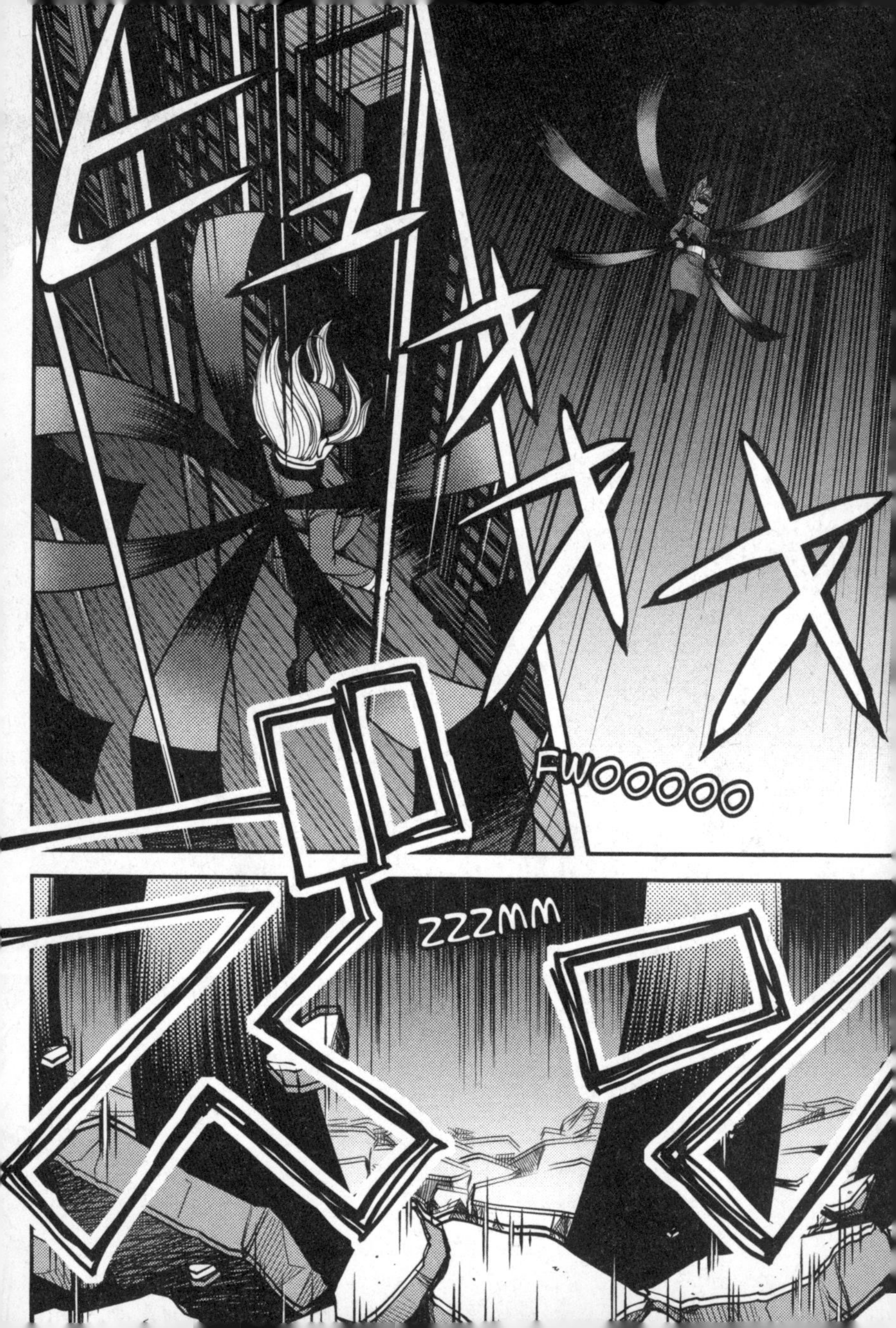
ヒュオオオ
FWOOOOOO
ZZZMM

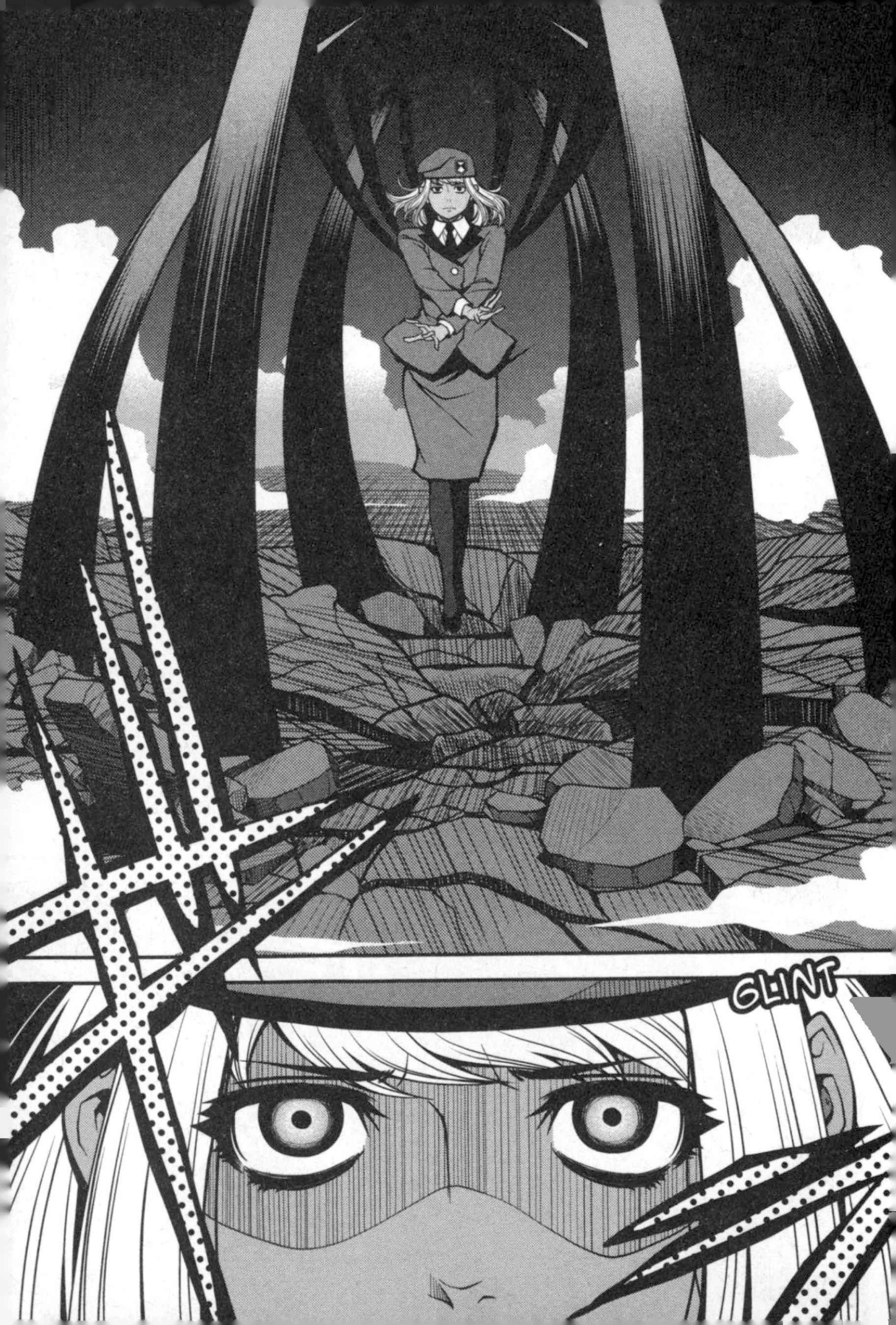
GLINT

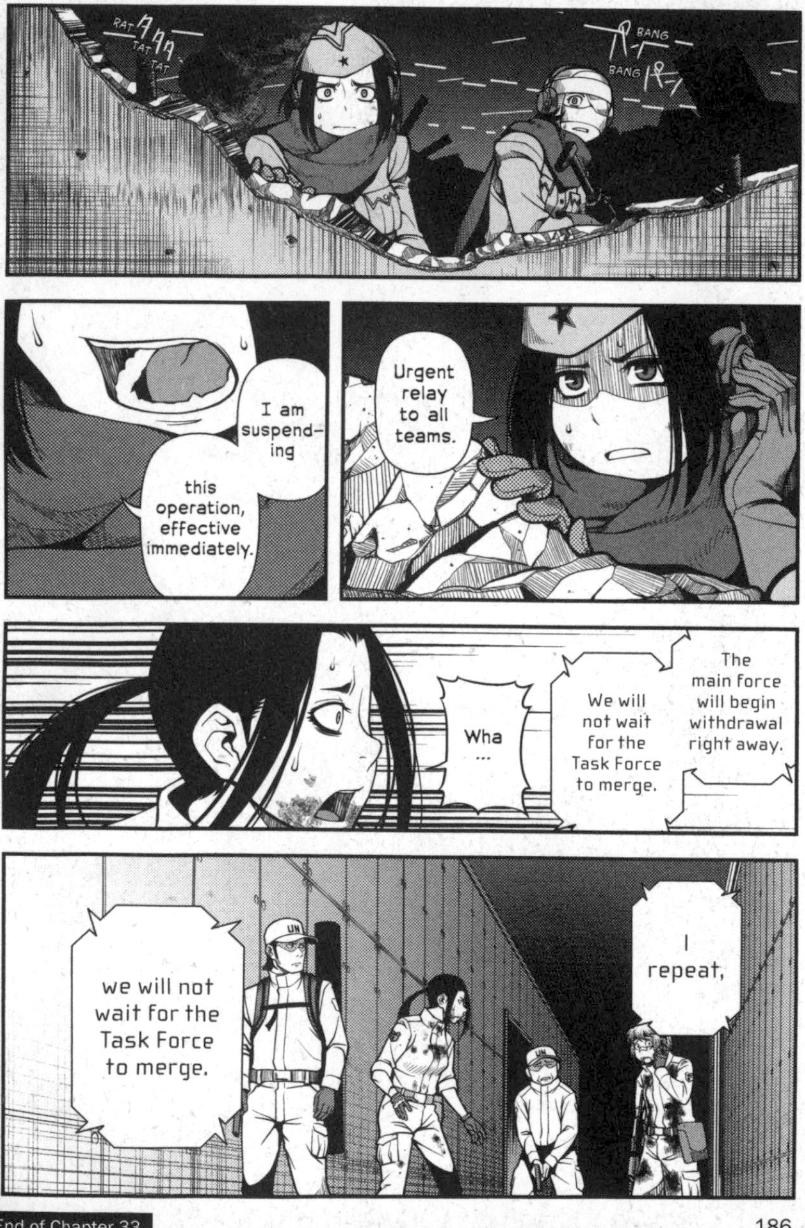
BANG
BANG
RAT TAT TAT
Urgent relay to all teams.
I am suspend-ing
this operation, effective immediately.
The main force will begin withdrawal right away.
We will not wait for the Task Force to merge.
Wha ...
I repeat,
we will not wait for the Task Force to merge.

Mobile Suit GUNDAM WING
Endless Waltz
Glory of the Losers

Story: Katsuyuki Sumizawa
Art: Tomofumi Ogasawara
Original Concept: Hajime Yatate and Yoshiyuki Tomino

One of the biggest anime properties of all time returns with the release of *Mobile Suit GUNDAM WING*. Following the actions of five fighters and their mobile suits, *GUNDAM WING* is a heavily political, dramatic action work that is centered around a war between Earth and its surrounding colonies in space.

In the year A.C. (After Colony) 195, mankind had flown its nest, the Earth, to search for new hope while living in space colonies. However, the United Earth Sphere Alliance has used its military might under the guise of "justice and peace" to seize control of some colonies, and those colonies have lost their autonomy and have been forced into silence. But the seeds of resistance have not been entirely crushed. "Operation Meteor" is about to take flight...

Volume 1 On Sale This Summer!

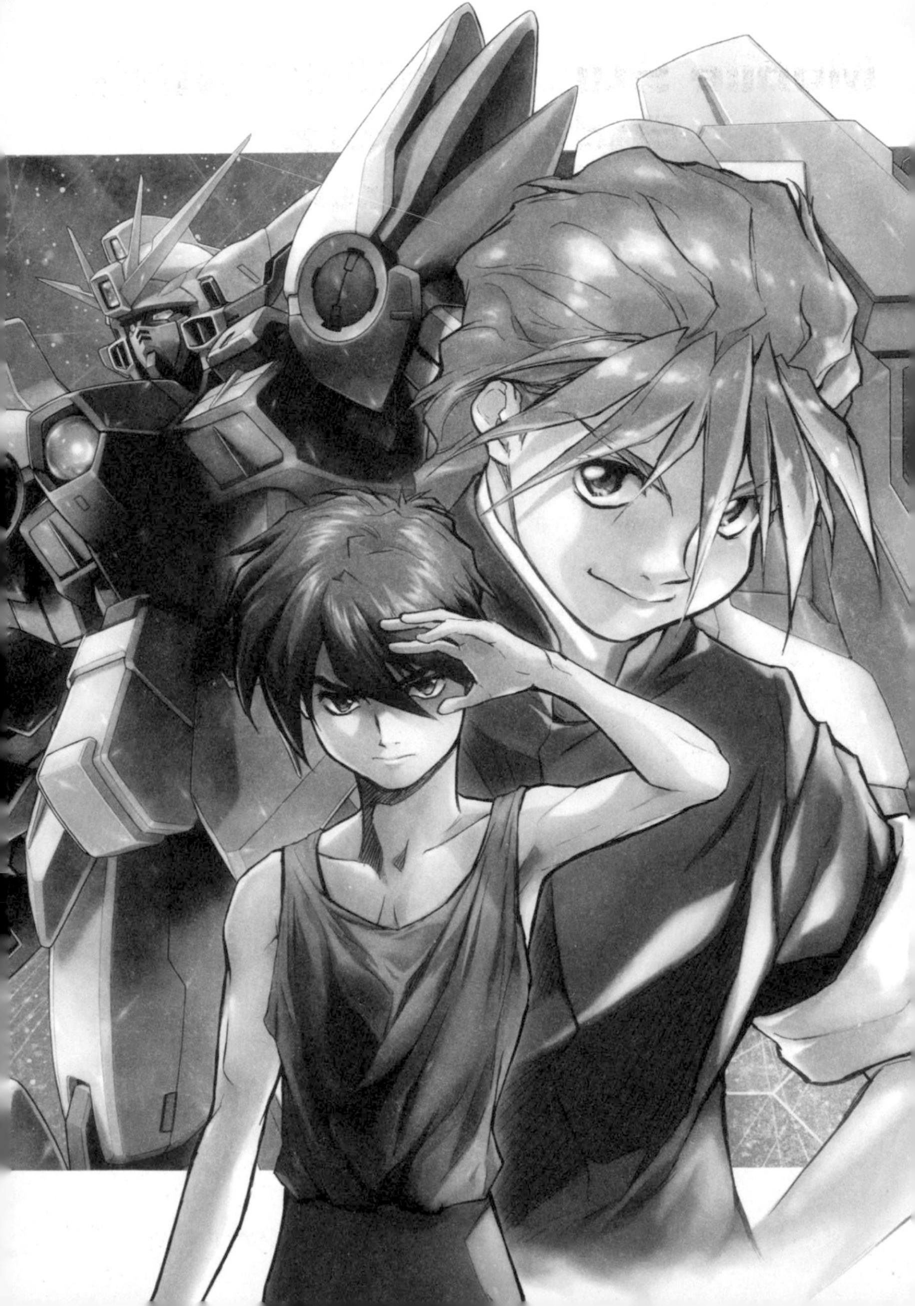

KILL ALL NINJAS

The Neo Saitama of the future is a sprawling urban landscape constantly flooded by neon light. And in its shadows lurks a vast criminal world filled with all sorts of shady characters. Among them are the deadliest force known to humanity...ninjas!

A force known as Ninja Slayer is determined to rid this world of Ninjas, and he's willing to go through heaven or hell to do so.

Volumes 1-8 On Sale Now!

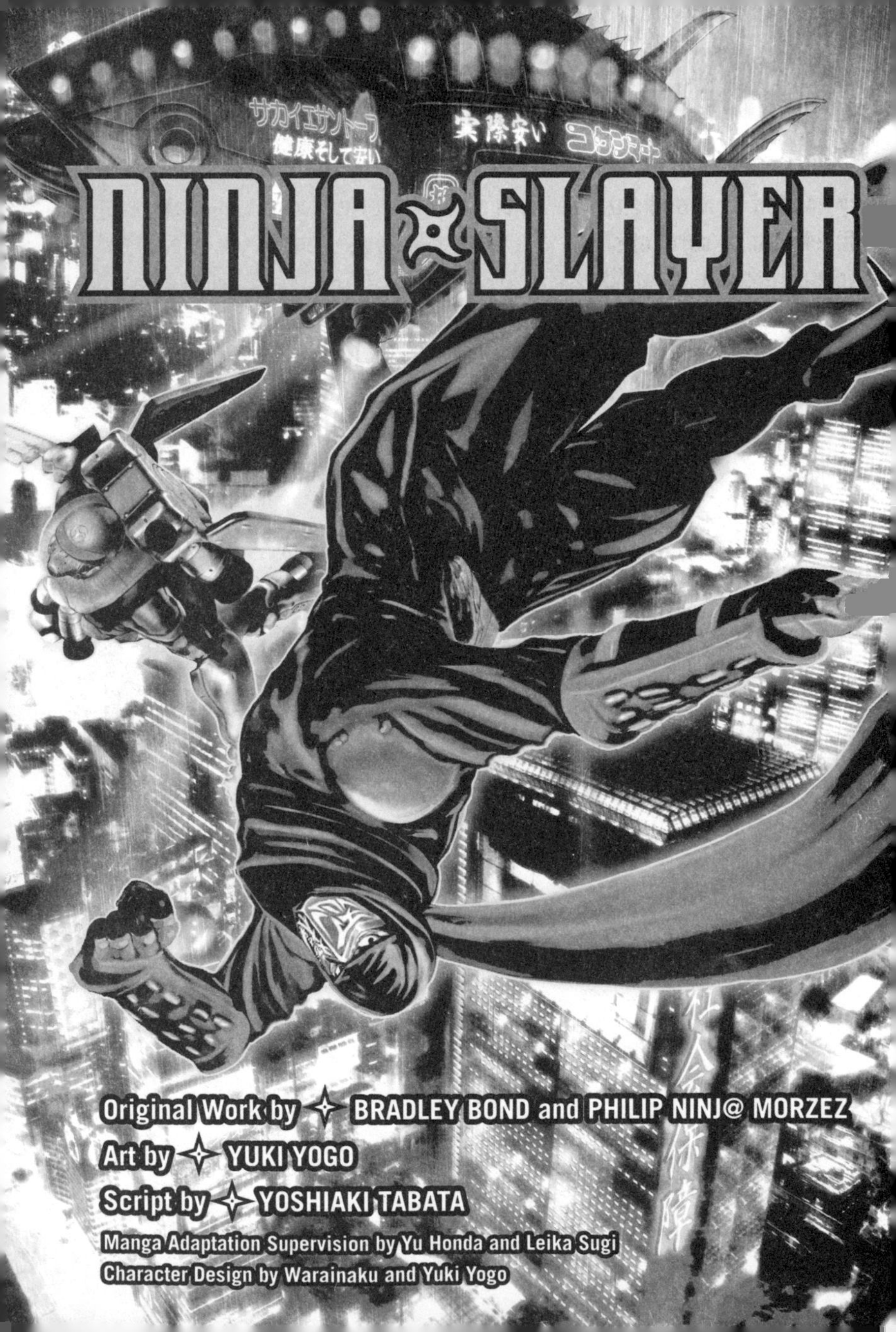
サカイエサントーフ
健康そして安い
実際安い
コケシマート

NINJA SLAYER

Original Work by BRADLEY BOND and PHILIP NINJ@ MORZEZ
Art by YUKI YOGO
Script by YOSHIAKI TABATA
Manga Adaptation Supervision by Yu Honda and Leika Sugi
Character Design by Warainaku and Yuki Yogo

Immortal Hounds 5

A Vertical Comics Edition

Translation: Yota Okutani
Production: Grace Lu
            Anthony Quintessenza

© Ryo Yasohachi 2016
First published in Japan in 2016 by KADOKAWA CORPORATION, Tokyo.
English translation rights arranged with KADOKAWA CORPORATION, Tokyo
through TUTTLE-MORI AGENCY, INC., Tokyo.

Translation provided by Vertical Comics, 2017
Published by Vertical Comics, an imprint of Vertical, Inc., New York

Originally published in Japanese as *Shinazu no Ryouken 5* by Kadokawa Corporation, 2015
Shinazu no Ryouken first serialized in *Harta*, Kadokawa Corporation, 2013-

This is a work of fiction.

ISBN: 978-1-945054-27-3

Manufactured in Canada

First Edition

Vertical, Inc.
451 Park Avenue South
7th Floor
New York, NY 10016
www.vertical-comics.com

Vertical books are distributed through Penguin-Random House Publisher Services.